England's Turning Point

Essays on 17th Century English History

England's Turning Point

Point

Essays on 17th Century
English History

Christopher Hill

BOOKMARKS

London, Chicago and Sydney

England's Turning Point – Christopher Hill
First published 1998
Bookmarks Publications Ltd, c/o 1 Bloomsbury Street, London WC1B 3QE, England
Bookmarks, PO Box 16085, Chicago, Illinois 60616, USA
Bookmarks, PO Box A338, Sydney South, NSW 2000, Australia
Copyright © Christopher Hill

ISBN 1898876 26 6

Printed by BPC Wheatons Ltd, Exeter
Cover by Sherborne Design

Bookmarks Publications Ltd is linked to an international grouping of socialist organisations:
Australia: International Socialist Organisation, PO Box A338, Sydney South, NSW 2000
Britain: Socialist Workers Party, PO Box 82, London E3 3LH
Canada: International Socialists, PO Box 339, Station E, Toronto, Ontario M6H 4E3
Cyprus: Ergatiki Demokratia, PO Box 7280, Nicosia
Czech Republic: Socialisticka Solidarita, PO Box 42, Praha 42, 140 02
Denmark: Internationale Socialister, Postboks 642, 2200 København N
France: Socialisme International, BP 189, 75926 Paris Cedex 19
Greece: Sosialistiko Ergatiko Komma, c/o Workers Solidarity, PO Box 8161, Athens 100 10
Holland: Internationale Socialisten, PO Box 92025, 1090AA Amsterdam
Ireland: Socialist Workers Party, PO Box 1648, Dublin 8
New Zealand: Socialist Workers Organisation, PO Box 8851, Auckland
Norway: Internasjonale Socialisterr, Postboks 5370, Majorstua, 0304 Oslo 3
Poland: Solidarność Socjalistyczna, PO Box 12, 01-900 Warszawa 118
South Africa: Socialist Workers Organisation, PO Box 18530, Hillbrow 2038, Johannesburg
Spain: Socialismo Internacional, Apartado 563, 08080, Barcelona
United States: International Socialist Organization, PO Box 16085, Chicago, Illinois 60616
Zimbabwe: International Socialist Organisation, PO Box 6758, Harare

Contents

Christopher Hill was educated at St Peter's College, York, and Balliol College, Oxford. From 1936 to 1938 he was assistant lecturer in Modern History at University College, Cardiff, and from 1938 to 1965 Fellow and tutor in Modern History at Balliol College. He was Master of Balliol College from 1965 to 1978, and then for two years a Visiting Professor at the Open University. He was also a Visiting Professor at Lancashire Polytechnic for several years.

Christopher Hill is the foremost historian of the English Revolution and the author of numerous books which include: *Economic Problems of the Church*; *The Century of Revolution 1603-1714*; *The English Revolution 1640*; *Society and Puritanism in Pre-Revolutionary England*; *Intellectual Origins of the English Revolution*; *Some Intellectual Consequences of the English Revolution*; *Reformation to Industrial Revolution*; *The World Turned Upside Down*; *Milton and the English Revolution*; *A Turbulent, Seditious and Factious People: John Bunyan and his Church*; *God's Englishman*; *The English Bible and the 17th Century Revolution*; *A Nation of Change and Novelty*; *The Experience of Defeat*; *Change and Continuity in 17th Century England*; *Puritanism and Revolution*; and *Liberty Against the Law*.

Foreword

The lectures, articles and reviews in this volume date from 1938 to 1994. They are arranged as far as possible in chronological order. I was unable to date one or two of them. These have been inserted arbitrarily, either where they seemed appropriate or to fill chronological gaps.

I am sometimes told that my attempt to suggest analogies between the English, French and Russian Revolutions has been disproved by recent events in Eastern Europe. This suggests that I am writing not history but politics, according to preconceived dogma, and is insulting as well as untrue. What I write about 17th century English history is derived, to the best of my ability, from 17th century evidence. Some historians disagree with me, but I don't think anyone can suggest that I invent my facts.

Indeed events in Eastern Europe suggest a further analogy that I had not anticipated. The French Revolution was defeated, and its idea suppressed by rulers of France after 1815; but its influence on the world has been immense. The English Revolution was defeated, its ideas rejected by those who believed that the restoration of monarchy and the church of England in 1660 meant that democracy and republican ideas had failed. But the ideas of the English Revolution lived on in the European Enlightenment and in dissent; they inspired the American Revolution and helped to inspire the French. Similarly the Russian Revolution has had a world impact, and though dictatorship of the soviet type has failed, the ideas of collectivism, of full employment and a right to work for all citizens and other similar ideals will survive. The victory of capitalism does not mean the end of history here, any more than the restoration of Stuarts and Bourbons meant the end of democracy, of republicanism and of religious liberty after 1660 and 1815.

Chapter 1

'The girl who took the wrong turning'

This first appeared as a review of H A L Fisher's History of Europe *in the* Modern Quarterly, Vol 1, No 3, 1938. *A new and revised edition had recently been published by Eyre and Spottiswode in three volumes, at the price of ten shillings a volume. I have restored my original title to the review (quoting Fisher himself). The editor of the* Modern Quarterly *thought my title lacked higher seriousness.*

This was, I think, my first appearance in print, apart from school and college publications. Fisher was a great man in Oxford, Warden of New College, a historian of some standing, author of the best selling History of Europe. *To my consternation, a week or so after the review was published, the Warden invited me to dine with him at high table in New College. Such an invitation was in effect a command, and I could think of no possible way of escape. I had no idea whether the Warden had read my impertinent review, but many of the Fellows of the college sitting round the dinner table had read it and enjoyed my discomfiture. Isaiah Berlin—not yet Sir Isaiah— decide that the Warden had not read it. In Oxford terms I was very junior indeed. I had just been elected Fellow and Tutor in Modern History at Balliol College, and it was apparently the Warden's agreeable habit to issue such an invitation to any newly appointed Fellow of an Oxford college who was an historian. The Warden treated me graciously, and certainly gave no sign that he knew of my scurrilous attack.*

The provocative vocabulary which I employed here (as in The English Revolution, 1640, *published in 1940) reflected the despairing anger which many of us felt at the approach of World War II, which we foresaw and were striving desperately to the best of our limited abilities to prevent. I saw the Oxford history establishment as somehow responsible. In my youthful arrogance I gave Fisher no credit for the considerable labour which must have gone into a work whose subject seems more obviously important now than it did to us then.*

> There is a strong case for the view that the type of political faith most likely to conduce to good historical writing is Whig rather than Tory or Radical. The Whigs occupied a central position... (H A L Fisher: 'The Whig Historians', *Proceedings of The British Academy, 1928,* p326).

Histories of all European civilisation by a single man are rare, and it is even rarer for them to be written by professional historians. Rarest of all is it for others in the profession to praise such a history. Yet when Dr H A L Fisher's *History of Europe* first appeared it was warmly eulogised by persons of considerable standing in the historical world, and on its publication in one volume form it was hailed by reviewers as the ideal history—cheap and popular, yet thoroughly learned and of broad sweep. It is therefore worth considering the book now that it has been republished in a new edition.

The conception of the book is clearly admirable: a continuous history of the civilisation of Europe since the Greeks, its detail increasing as the centuries proceed. In an age of uncoordinated research it is gratifying to find a historian who is not afraid to act as intermediary between specialists and the general public. And the Warden of New College is no mere historian: he has himself been a man of affairs, and the scope of his interests is apparent throughout the book. He quotes Heine on the state of Paris in 1842, and has a detailed chapter on the art of the Italian Renaissance. His story is traced right down to the present day, with a single philosophy throughout. The author, too, has clearly taken pains with his style—and how few historians do!—though the results are not perhaps to everyone's taste. (He himself occasionally feels the need for appending a translation— 'In the art of poliorcetics the Dutch had lost none of their ancient cunning. They could take cities and defend them,' p628.) The whole achievement is a tour de force, and if in what follows I draw attention to aspects of the book which seem to me inferior to its conception, this has been made necessary by uncritical overpraising in the past.

Suspicion is first roused by the material on which the book appears to be based. In his Preface, Dr Fisher says: 'I have confined myself to drawing attention at the end of each chapter to a few illustrative books, choosing by preference those which are modern and accessible in the English or French languages.' Yet in the chapters covering the period 1216-1789 more than four fifths of the books cited are over 20 years old: and on the periods where modern research has most modified traditional views—Renaissance, German Reformation, English Civil War—the proportion is even higher. One has grounds for fearing that the views put forward may prove to be those which were current 25 years ago, when the author was himself a practising historian. An examination of these views will justify the suspicion.

First, the philosophy behind the phrases, the attitude of mind in which the book is written, is, in the worst sense of the word, Whig. What I mean by Whiggism is defined in the Preface, with mock humility. 'Men wiser and more learned than I have discerned in history a plot, a rhythm, a predetermined pattern. These harmonies are concealed from me. I can see only one emergency following upon another as wave follows wave.' The only explanation, in fact, is that there is no explanation. Sir Charles Oman, who also began writing in the 19th century, recently said something similar. Yet Dr Fisher is too modest. At various stages he does offer explanations. He has, for instance, a pleasing anthropomorphic theory of the development of European history. 'With a sharp gesture of impatience Europe turned away', on page 433, 'from the vast literature of commentaries and glosses.' On page 793 the author confronts Europe with 'the facts of the industrial revolution in England', and gives us half a page of what he holds (rightly) there is strong evidence for believing Europe did not then say. But the silent goddess acted, and acted unwisely. 'Europe said nothing of the kind. So far from attending to the faint signals of the coming industrial democracy which were visible in the sky, it plunged into the wars of the French Revolution and the Empire.' Such neglect of astronomy prepares us to find the goddess on page 902 turning a deaf ear even to Alfred Lord Tennyson, for 'Europe was not ready for internationalism'. Equally now 'Europe...declines to accept the iron programme of Russian Communism' (p61). Clio herself takes the wrong turning sometimes. 'We may be disposed to think', the author writes of the English civil wars, 'that with a little more elasticity and allowance for the workings of the Puritan conscience[!]...much trouble might have been avoided. But history took the other turning' (p643). In consequence of the muse's mistake there was really quite considerable trouble. There is also a beneficent 'spirit of liberty', who is particularly active in the 19th century. 'Surviving the crimes of the French Revolution and the terror of Napoleon, *it* succeeded by the end of the end of the 19th century in founding parliamentary institutions in every important European country with the exception of Russia' (p791). Who can complain that she is now taking a well earned rest? There are other motive forces to which the cautious author commits himself. I list a few. '*The trend of the human spirit* being in the direction of despotism, the Church

13

followed where the State had led' (p170). 'The difference between East and West, between Aryan and Semite, between Jew and Gentile...is liable even yet, as in the violent paroxysm of racial hysteria which has shaken the Germans, to give rise to bursts of savage oppression' (p5). 'By an astonishing dispensation of fate the one people of genius in the annals of the world is the earliest of the European races to emerge into the full light of history' (p15). 'Suddenly the warm current of living scientific curiosity, after flowing freely for half a century, froze and was lost' (p346). (Why ?) 'A love of personal glory was a feature of the age...The days of anonymous architecture...were past' (p448-449). (Why ?) 'Not that the age which we are about to survey was barren of political ideas or happy improvements' (p792). All these explanations, the reader will find, explain absolutely nothing. They restate a fact with a phrase, and the equation cancels out to x = x: things happened because they happened. Yet the phrases are intended to mean something, surely: his denial of a pattern of events is in fact an assertion of an idealist theory of history, of the power of abstract thought to shape action. A class theory would 'underrate the rich and varied stuff of human nature, the distractions of statesmen and the waywardness of events' (p793). 'Not until the 19th century did the downtrodden peasantry of Galicia or the Balkans begin to experience any sensible change or improvement in their condition' (p430). Let no one suggest the peasants had to struggle for these reforms: they were just another 'happy improvement', as when 'the wild Greek clans took to city life' on page 14.

Yet not all events are wayward. The author adopts wholeheartedly the theory of 19th century Whig historians, that there was a 'true' principle of cabinet government laid up in the mind of God which successive generations of distracted statesmen gradually discovered. Lesser breeds could never master this principle, try as they would, and so got into the mess they are in today. 'The framers of the American constitution failed to understand the nature and function of the cabinet system. That it should have been so long missed by the politicians of the Stuart age is no matter for surprise' (p645). Its discovery was 'an accident and a happy accident'. 'After that momentous administration [Walpole's] the true principle of responsible government, that is to say of government by a cabinet responsible to a parliament which is in its turn responsible to the electorate, was established' (p703). (There is no need to draw attention to the antedating here, which will be apparent to anyone who has looked at the modern secondary sources for 18th century history.) The author also apparently believes that tucked away somewhere there is a solution to the contradictions of the capitalist system, which (if we are patient and do not distract them unduly) our statesmen may yet find. 'The problem of bringing happiness to the swiftly expanding democracy of hired town workers…was far too vast and complex to be solved quietly or by any single body of statesmen' (p792). Dr Fisher has unlimited belief in the efficacity of talk. It was 'not without significance' for the abolition of slavery that Wilberforce was known as the 'Nightingale of the House', and that Fox was the greatest parliamentary orator of his time (p1,031). And this brings its compensations in those periods of history which depress the democrat. Under the July monarchy, 'though the suffrage was limited to a narrow circle of two hundred and fifty thousand electors, the parliamentary oratory of France was never richer in volume and splendour' (p904). There you have a Whig scale of values: oppression of 99 percent of the population set off against 'a rich volume of oratory'.

For not only has Dr Fisher inherited a Whig tradition which was still current before the war; he has also himself been a liberal politician and was a member of the Coalition Cabinet during World War I. This perhaps explains his slighting treatment of 'the spirit of liberty' in describing the promise of the German Tyrol to Italy in 1915: 'Such…was the price of Italian help, and such the deviations from ideal justice to which necessity, knowing no law, constrained the democratic governments of London and Paris' (p1,132). (This seems to mean that liberals have their principles but the facts, 'knowing no law', will not always live up to them: compare the adjuration to the historian in the Preface to 'recognise in the development of human destinies the play of the contingent and the unforeseen'.) The younger Pitt—a parallel case— 'was suckled in the Whig religion of constitutional liberty,' and so, though 'under the stress of the French war he found himself obliged to postpone enlargements of the franchise', he 'never became a narrow or selfish Tory. Like Disraeli afterwards he divined the lamentable condition of the industrial poor' (p899). (Whatever his actions may suggest to the contrary, his heart was pure.) The ex cabinet minister has an unusual explanation of why the English working class 'began to experience an extension of the franchise in 1918. It owed nothing to the demands of the workers themselves, but everything to the emotions of our friends the statesmen. 'The stay-at-home landlord felt humble in the presence of his wounded gardener. The railway porter who had risked his life took on a dignity never to be obtained by the secure plutocrat. What, statesmen asked themselves, can be good enough for a population which is willing to stake its all for the country's safety?'(p1,152). Where he is not himself involved, however, the author recognises why concessions are made. 'Of all the political *inventions* [another happy accident!] of the

19th century none was *so valuable a preservation of society* as the *discovery* of a system of insurance...That revolution was so long staved off in Germany was partly due to these *valuable* measures, by which Bismarck robbed the Social Democratic Party...of a compelling and irresistible appeal to the poor' (p1,052). 'It is to the credit of Lamartine...that he refused to substitute the Red Flag for the tricolour, and in place of a dangerous military crusade contented himself for the moment with a liberal manifesto. The social revolution was kept at bay by a brave but disastrous promise of employment for all' (p909). On foreign intervention in Russia after the October Revolution the author makes an unexpectedly happy remark: 'The motive of the Allies was to keep Russia in the war against Germany by giving assistance to those elements in the Russian population who were still willing to honour *their* engagements entered into by the Tsarist government' (p1,189). That is true: the engagements entered into by the Tsarist government were on behalf of a single class, the class which afterwards called in foreign intervention. But elsewhere in dealing with the Russian Revolution the author is more the politician than the historian, concluding, 'At the cost of its civil liberties a vast population is enabled to enjoy a prison ration of the goods of life' (p1,217). Hostility was perhaps to be expected: perversion of the facts was not. To call the Cheka 'a secret police inherited from the Tsarist regime' (p1,188) is odd; to describe the Communist Party as 'organised in an hierarchy of committees or soviets' (p1,216) is more than odd—it is downright ignorant. (*The Communist Manifesto*, incidentally, is quoted only from a summary by E H Carr; it is of course much less necessary to the understanding of 'the liberal experiment' than A *Tale of Two Cities*, a recommended book.) Another purely political judgment is on page 1209. 'The Hitler revolution is a sufficient guarantee that Russian communism will not spread westward... But there may be secrets in fascism or Hitlerism which the democracies of the West will desire, without abandoning their fundamental character, to adopt.' One of these secrets 'may perhaps be the equalitarian democracy of present day Germany' (p1,205); not, however, 'the irrepressible fecundity of this wholesome and monogamous race', which has existed from the time of Tacitus (p110). After 'equalitarian democracy' it is no surprise to learn that 'the English succeeded in conquering India because they brought with them peace and deliverance from oppression' (p1,020). (Like the Italians in Abyssinia.) Following an elaborate half page explaining why 90 percent of the Indian people are still illiterate—the argument is (1) there is 'a surplus of twelve million males', and so of course (2) 'the impossibility by reason of the social customs of India of using unmarried women teachers in elementary schools' cannot be got round, (p1,021)—Dr Fisher praises the association of 'patriotic and educated Indians' in the tasks of government. Education clearly means the same thing for this ex-president of the Board of Education as for General Franco, who has found it necessary to 're-educate' some of the Basque children repatriated from England. 'That a population of 350 million should be defended [from whom?] by a force not much greater than that which is required for the protection of Belgium is proof that the rule of the British in India commends itself to the great mass of the Indian people' (p1,023). The voice is the voice of Gladstone, but the sentiments are the sentiments of Blimp. 'If the squires winced at the four shilling land tax, which was the spine of Godolphin's war finance, they paid up to the end notwithstanding. Such was the English spirit' (p684). Never let it be suggested that they got good returns on their money. Similarly it was because Canning 'was not prepared to see the most illustrious corner of Europe and the original home of its civilisation settled by a population of fellaheen and negroes' (p881) that he intervened in Greece: his classical education, not his City connections.

Those are a few instances of national bias. Now for some of class blindness. On page 652, 'Irrevocably also the civil rights of the subject were protected henceforth [after the Long Parliament] from the arbitrary interference of the Crown,' but nothing is said of the more arbitrary and more frequent interference of justices of the peace. 'England under George II must have seemed to all who were above the level of poverty to have reached a position of assured and fortunate inner peace... An air of comfort and stability pervaded the country' (p704). Many of the rich minority may have been as insensible as that, but it is outrageously obtuse to adduce Swift—Swift!—to prove that English men of letters did not 'encourage their countrymen to believe that they [were] living under a regime of intolerable indignity and injustice'. To describe the handling of the naval mutinies of 1797 as a 'commixture of firmness and good sense' (p826) is prejudiced, but to dismiss the Paris Commune in half a page and say that 'it was counted to the Government for righteousness that it...stamped without mercy' on the Communards (p999) is to write exclusively from the point of view of the possessing class. It is disingenuous to claim (p173) that it is not possible 'to discern any trace of class conscious motives' among the early Christians and give proofs drawn from the 5th century, when the religion of the poor had already been taken over by the ruling class.

Less pernicious than this perversion of the past is an amusingly smug assumption that the code of behaviour of an English gentleman be applied to all ages and countries as a moral and indeed political measuring rod. It is news for historians, for instance, that 'the beauty of Elizabeth Woodville was no compensation for the fact that her father, though the husband of a duchess, started life from the lowly grade of a knight. The Yorkist dynasty sank under the burden of the misalliance' (p473). It would be caddish to observe that it was succeeded by a dynasty whose origins were even more open to question. A cardinal objection which 'the country' had to the 'Puritan tyrants' was apparently that many of them were 'low-born and ill-bred' (p661). This was the more disappointing after the fine spirit shown during the civil war, when 'a humane and enlightened aristocracy of sportsmen, slow to anger and quick to forgive, drained war of its more malignant poisons, and robbed it of some of its barbarity' (p654)—in Ireland and elsewhere. The welcome to Botha in London as 'a good sportsman' and 'a good loser' (p1,077) was also pure sportsmanship, and must not be taken as suggesting that the English working class had been unenthusiastic about the Boer War. But only Englishmen are born sportsmen: 'The French legislator did not hunt the fox. No French Epsom or Newmarket sweetened the severity or abated the logic of his political meditations.' (That is really to be found, just as quoted, on page 887. Cf: 'The great landowning nobles of Persia won from [Alexander] the sympathy and respect which the spectacle of a gentleman and a sportsman never fails to evoke in the hearty nature of the open-air man' (p42).) In the Germany of the Thirty Years' War 'there was marauding, there was starvation, there was even cannibalism...and [*crescendo*] as is always the case in extreme and desperate calamity, moral restraints broke down and ceded to wild bursts of profligacy' (p611). In the intervals of eating one another they even sank so low as to break the seventh commandment. After Tilsit the upstart Napoleon was 'undeterred by the eloquent entreaties of Queen Marie Louise' (p848); but some members of royal houses connected with ours by marriage acquire the gentlemanly virtues. William I of Germany was 'the soul of honour' (p988); Nicholas II was 'the only perfect gentleman in a long list of Russian rulers' (p718).

This sort of nonsense cannot merely be dismissed as funny; it has a seriously distorting effect. So, too, has Dr Fisher's idealist attitude to religion. Weber and Tawney might never have written a line: the Reformation, the 'religious wars', the Thirty Years' War and even the English Civil War are treated as misguided conflicts about doctrinal niceties. The root cause of both these superficial explanations of historical action is a neglect of the economic factor. 'War, infanticide and malaria' are given on page 61 as reasons for the decline of the population of Greece in the second century

BC, as though child murder were just a bad habit Greek women had fallen into. Geography is blamed for Germany's failure to share in 17th century colonisation (p611) and not lack of economic and political organisation. Geography had an even more remarkable effect on Spanish history. 'All ways in France led to Paris. No ways in Spain led to Madrid. Iberian mountains and Iberian men are obstinate things' (p628). That is why Spain, unlike France, did not go through the stage of the new monarchy in the 17th century. But on page 850 we find an additional reason: 'A certain negligence, half pride, half indolence, had impeded the development of the forms of material prosperity...' A notable confusion of cause and effect! Geography, however, is responsible for both cause and effect; on page 937 we read: 'The parching sun, the dry, bitter, dust-laden winds seem so to work that afflictions of the soul such as communism and socialism, clericalism and syndicalism, develop in the Spanish climate in their most violent forms'. If General Franco had read that, he would have realised that the irrigation undertaken by the Popular Front Government would in itself 're-educate' the electorate from socialism without the assistance of military force, and history might have taken another turning. Geography and landscape gardening are advanced before economics to account for the Italian Renaissance. 'It is natural that the rebirth of European art and letters should have taken place in a land where the marbles of antiquity still gleamed among the cypresses and olives' (p446)—and which also happened to be the richest country in Europe. The fact is noted that the unification of Italy had the warm sympathy of the English press and was followed by an expansion of railway construction: but no connection is suggested between the two. Louis Philippe's government fell because it 'took no pains to conciliate the intellectuals' (p905). Louis Napoleon was wiser. Two reasons are given for the 'liberalisation' of his Empire—(1) the deterioration of his health, (2) a desire to realise the Napoleonic legend (p973). Crude economic considerations and the pressure of the working class are again brushed aside. Where economics is mentioned, it is the Cobdenism that was the stock-in-trade of the pre-war Liberal politician. Colbert is upbraided for a 'childish delusion' (p665), though since 'political economy had not been invented' (p436) this seems rather severe. 'The discovery that trade prospered best when freed from fiscal fetters' (p792) was one of the 'happy accidents' of the age of liberalism. But the 'civilised aspirations of free traders'— 'the policy of the cheap loaf postulated a navy which could rule the waves'—were unreasonably shattered by 'an explosion of militarist nationalism' (p902-903), and liberalism remained an 'experiment'. The author, however, is not convinced that any 'happy improvement' has yet been discovered to take its place. 'Political economy' has 'found out'

Blum (p1,235); and, ' "Economic planning" on the grand scale is never likely to be successful over a tract of time' (p767). It is particularly neat thus to dispose of the old colonial system and the five year plan in a single phrase.

The deplorable thing is that the author frequently aligns facts which scream aloud for an economic interpretation: but he shuns the 'pattern'. Chapter 1 of Book 2 on 'The New Europe' is especially instructive. Beginning, 'Mankind is slower to move than city dwellers in the western countries are always willing to allow' (p429), he proceeds very correctly to note the survival of feudalism and Catholicism, 'in certain places and on certain minds'—in the economically backward countries. 'The thinking of Europe' had been carried on by monks in the Middle Ages, and so though there were 'flashes of the human mind' there was no steady scientific development. The lay culture of the 16th century offers 'the sharpest contrast' to this. But why? Why did culture pass from one leisured class to another? Why was there this new need for technical advance? Who paid for it? And why? The political effects of the rise of the bourgeoisie are similarly missed. 'The political framework of the mediaeval Empire *had given way* before the growth of national states'—'Europeans began...*to think* in nations' (p434-435). 'The more *vigorous north* falls away from Rome' (p444). *Cui prodest?* is never asked. A consequence of this idealist misinterpretation is to give disproportionate weight to individuals— 'In the initial stages of that great movement of the human spirit...Louis Bonaparte played a decisive role' (p912); 'In a population of more than 20 million [in Spain] there were, according to the estimate of Alphonso XIII, only some 6,000 politicians' (p937). History has here taken another turning again. But these idiosyncrasies of history had been anticipated on page 414: 'Such is the way of the world. The future passes under our eyes and we do not see it.' If we do try to see it, we are forcing a predetermined pattern, to be dismissed with playful irony. Let us lead one another into the ditch.

This manner of writing history is bankrupt, and an absconding bankrupt at that. Its denial of the possibility of interpretation conceals its own bland assumption of the absoluteness of the narrow standards of the English ruling class. Its impartiality turns out to be a synonym for Liberal politics. Its concentration on the thinking of the past abstracted from its economic background alone makes possible the postulate of 'wayward events', influenced for good or ill by statesmen, inventors of genius, and members of the royal families. Anything can happen, because everything is in the last resort a flight of fancy. History is not influenced by ponderable, analysable, material factors. It is worth exposing this Whig view of history, not because it any longer holds respect in the academic world, but because it still probably informs most of the history of our schools, the history, that is to say, of all but specialist historians (witness the early newspaper reviewers of this book). It is the basis also of that maddening fatalism of present day Liberals far to the left of the Warden of New College, whose hatred of fascism will lead them to do everything but understand it. For it is clear to what conclusion this attitude towards history leads. If nothing is analysable, nothing is predictable. Events in the future will be as wayward as in the past. 'Let us hope that, contrary to all the signs, men will act reasonably in future,' is in effect the author's last word. Nothing we can do will influence history (unless we have had an education which fits us for seats in the Cabinet). In his Preface Dr Fisher affirms the fact of progress, but this is an act of faith; and anyway 'the *thoughts*[!] of men may flow into the channels which lead to disaster and barbarism'. And if distracted Whig statesmen cannot stop thoughts flowing the wrong way, they shrug their shoulders at the folly of mankind, put their liberalism into the refrigerator— 'not because I wish to disparage Freedom, for I would as soon disparage Virtue herself', (foreword to volume 3)—and in the face of another necessity knowing no law console themselves by reflecting that Hitlerism is better than Communism. They would have been happier, would have understood the world better, if the capitalist system (which their theories were invented to explain) had continued to develop. But Europe has taken another turning. The crisis has brought 'passion, prejudice and hysteria' (p1,222) and a lot of other unpleasant things which do not fit into the old rationalised scheme. The Whig would like to pass by on the other side, pretending it is not his neighbours who are affected; to bury his head in the sand so as not to be convinced of the irrationality of his own behaviour. It is our job to dig him out again.

Chapter 2

G M Trevelyan

I reviewed Trevelyan's The English Revolution, 1688-9, *in the* Spectator, *14 October 1938. My review of his* English Social History *(from Chaucer to Queen Victoria) was first published in the* Communist Review, *March 1946.*

I

From the moment of its completion the revolution of 1688 passed into legend. It was the summit of human achievement, the triumph of reason over reaction and force, the liberation of the nation. Of late sceptics have pointed out that only part of the nation benefited by the liberation, that nine tenths of the population had as little share in real government as before. Professor Trevelyan sums up judicially, and reminds us that if counter-revolution had not been defeated in 1688, 19th century democracy would have been impossible. Judicial independence of the executive and control of the latter by parliament, freedom of the press and worship (in limits)—these we owe to the men of 1688, and recent events, as Professor Trevelyan wisely observes, are increasing their value with their scarcity. He reproves Mr Bryant for not allowing sufficient weight to the real danger to the English state and parliamentary institutions from the aggression of Louis XIV and the international reaction. 1688 was an event of international importance. With all his caution, Professor Trevelyan still feels able to call 1688 'a moral revival', to be contrasted with 1678-85, when 'Whigs and Tories act like the nervous and hot-blooded factions of a South European race.'

Why was there this sudden change from bitterness to compromise? Why was the conflict so much more fierce in Scotland? Why did English Tories and the Church of England abandon their passive resistance theories? (Or rather, perhaps, why had they gone on preaching passive resistance for so long?) What did James hope to gain from throwing the mace into the Thames, dissolving the army, and appointing no commission of regency? Part of the answer is to be found in 'that last flash of the old Roundhead fervour', Monmouth's rebellion, with its threat to the settlement of 1660. Charles II had been restored not to rule as his father had done in 1640 but to consolidate the achievements of the interregnum against a social revolution from Levellers and Anabaptists. It was a compromise settlement, from which restored landlords, new landed class, and City alike gained: the old law secured the new social order. The abolition of feudal tenures had ended the division between two types of property: after 1660, as Professor Clark has pointed out, there was no real cleavage between landed and moneyed interests. The gulf was between the parliamentary class and the democratic sectaries, whom it was the object of the Clarendon Code and the Test Act to exclude from civil life. The danger to the parliamentary class from Charles II and James II's policy of 'indulgence' to Catholic and Protestant non-conformists was that it threatened to unite two excluded groups, and to use their support in local government for a royal dictatorship against the parliamentary class. At the time of Monmouth's rising, the Tories and many Whigs stood solidly by James.

Later, when James had ousted Tories from local government to put in sons of republicans, parson and squire were forced to realise that they were the king's only so long as the king was theirs. The squirearchy approved of passive resistance to constituted authority until it lost its monopoly of authority. Yet pushing James out was a tricky business: all men remembered how 1642 had led to 1649. So William brought over an army which became the rallying centre for all propertied classes once James had made his appeal to anarchy by attempting to dissolve the state. Thanks to this force and James's capitulation there was no need to risk another revolutionary army. The settlement was hastily rushed through, and as in 1649 a doubtful army was then diverted to Irish and continental wars. The City sponsored and profited by a new and expansive foreign policy. In Scotland a front bench agreement was impossible because a far stronger feudal class still survived there, not only in the Highlands. It is the measure of James's lack of support in England that he was forced into dependence on a peasant revolution in Ireland. For Ireland was the backdoor for Louis XIV, and invasion. The safety of the political victories of 1640-60 was at stake, not doctrinal niceties. Irishmen were put into James's army, papists into office, in order to carry out a specific policy of absolutism. Once all possibility of pursuing the policy was removed by bringing the state under control of the parliamentary class, relative tolerance to dissenters and even Catholics was no longer dangerous.

1688 was bloodless because of the blood shed between 1640 and 1660, and because the military invasion was skilfully timed: it was glorious for the parliamentary class because the situation was kept well under their control, and the maximum of benefit extracted with the minimum of risk. The true parallel is not 1789 but 1830. Yet the real importance of the revolution is, as Professor Trevelyan shows, that it created a machinery within which (150 years later, it is true) the class in possession could hold on to a great deal in its slow retreat, and new groups could nibble off for themselves bits of the inheritance.

II

Trevelyan's *English Social History* is in many ways a masterly work. It is written by a man who has given his whole life to the study of history, and who is yet no narrow specialist. He has published books on England in the 14th, 17th and 19th centuries; but he has also written with fine eloquence and passion of Garibaldi and the unification of Italy. He understands that the past of our country cannot be interpreted merely in terms of governments and wars, and he has a genuine feeling for simple people, peasants and town craftsmen. He writes with a loving attention to detail. He recreates the past with insight and imagination and his style is a model of freshness and clarity. For all these reasons this book has been a best seller. But something is missing: we feel this increasingly as we read towards the end. What is it?

In the 19th century chapters, we become uneasily aware that the presentation is very one-sided. Thus Professor Trevelyan thinks that Wordsworth's mind had been 'aroused and disturbed' in the days when he welcomed the French Revolution; but the poet 'completely recovered his equanimity' when he became a Tory (p466). Disraeli's famous remark that there were two nations in England, the rich and the poor, is dismissed as a misleading half-truth (p546). The cooperative movement is praised because it 'gave many working people a sense that they had "a stake in the country" '—ie, of course, an interest in maintaining the capitalist system (p542). There are also surprising omissions in this section. Chartism is not mentioned. Robert Owen figures as a factory reformer, William Morris as a Pre-Raphaelite poet: neither as pioneers of socialism. Tom Mann and the New Unionism do not appear. And though Professor Trevelyan begins by defining his subject as 'the history of a people with the politics left out' (pvii), it is more than politics when the ordinary people of a country begin to explore the possibility of running it for themselves.

This gives us a clue to what is lacking in Professor Trevelyan's outlook. He entirely fails to reveal the class basis of politics. He criticises injustice, cruelty and oppression when he meets them in the past; but he never analyses their relation to the structure of society.

He is vaguely aware that economic and social life influence politics, and indeed 'may all the time be their unacknowledged and unconscious arbiter' (p93); but he does not pursue the dangerous thought. Take his analysis of the 17th century revolution: he produces pages of evidence which show the economic forces at work, the class alignments and social consequences of the revolution (pp228-255); and then blandly concludes that 'the Cromwellian revolution was not social and economic in its causes and motives' because 'the men themselves were only half-conscious' of the economic circumstances which influenced their actions (p233). Many of those who today glibly repeat anti-Soviet anecdotes are no doubt also 'only half-conscious' that they are serving the interests of reaction: but that is very far from proving that there are no reactionary forces in England today who are trying to wreck international cooperation.

Professor Trevelyan is a philanthropist. He is sorry for the poor, sometimes indignant when their sufferings seem 'excessive'—ie when their living conditions sink below those standards and conditions which are now accepted as adequate. But he says nothing to suggest that we owe these standards, such as they are, to a century of trade union struggle. When he is faced with class conflict Professor Trevelyan tries to be fair, to see faults on both sides, to hold the balance even between right and wrong. He feels sympathy for the poor peasants who were evicted to make way for large capitalist farms in the late 17th and 18th centuries. But he consoles himself by reflecting that this was 'a natural economic process, analogous to the absorption of small businesses by large in the industrial world of our own day' (p269). And that settles it: no one will dare to criticise, still less to fight against, the 'natural processes' of present day capitalism.

This is the first great defect of the book: a smug acceptance of liberal-bourgeois standards as something absolute, with no realisation that they had to be fought for in the past and that they may be changed in the future. So he can talk about 'the Englishman's instinct to "better himself" ' (p381), as though we are all born good little bourgeois.

Allied with this defect is a profound distrust of democracy, at least of the democracy of the present and future. Professor Trevelyan would indignantly deny this, for he certainly regards himself as a democrat. But his is a democracy in blinkers: it is limited by class considerations. Throughout his book there is an agrarian romanticism, an idealisation of the small peasant proprietor and the benevolent landlord, a hatred of modern industrialism. This poses as a hatred of the tastelessness and vulgarity of capitalist machine civilisation, but it is at least in part due to his fear of the working class which industrialism has called into being. Professor Trevelyan's criticisms of modern society are purely negative: he cannot see that the ugliness and the meanness which he denounces are in great part due to the exploitation of one class by another. The rural 'way of life, unique and irreplaceable in its human and spiritual values' (p554), to which Professor Trevelyan looks back so yearningly, was also ugly, though in a different way, because also based on the exploitation of man by man. (On his own figures, nearly 20 percent of the population was receiving public relief in the late 17th century (p278); that proportion was not exceeded even in the worst days of the depression of the 1930s. We should not escape from the evils of capitalism by going backwards, even if we could). Still less has Professor Trevelyan any vision of the democracy of the future, which will be genuine because classless. He foresees only 'the gradual standardisation of human personality' (p579), and contrasts it with the 'leisure and freedom' which coupon-clipping shareholders in the Victorian age used 'for the highest purposes of a great civilisation' (p573).

'The world is not likely to see again so fine and broad a culture for many centuries to come' (p521). Professor Trevelyan wisely closes his book in 1901. What has happened since that date distresses him: he cannot understand it. How should he? He sees only the disintegration of his world, not the emergence of the new. The model workman's flat cannot inspire the same affections as the insanitary country cottage (p476). Modern education 'may have gone too far' away from teaching the humble poor to keep their place (p363). But Professor Trevelyan finds consolation in reflecting that Eddington and Jeans have 'disproved' materialism. 'But where truth can be found is a more difficult matter to determine' (p566).

A sad conclusion for a great liberal historian at the end of a long and productive life: mere negative defeated scepticism, and the naively horrified question of the frightened bourgeois: 'What would be the effect on our great cities today of abolishing the police?' (p349). Professor Trevelyan's world has had its day. It was a great day while it lasted.

Our task is to rewrite this splendid story with as much learning and artistry as the Master of Trinity, with his human sympathy but without its limitations, and with a pride which he could never know: to write it as a story which did not stop or peter out with the culmination of the triumph of the middle class, a story which so far from being finished is barely beginning. The people of England have their history too — our history. Professor Trevelyan relates this sympathetically so long as the lower orders were content to follow the bourgeoisie with proper docility. But as he approaches modern times, his book becomes a *Hamlet* without the Prince of Denmark, a social history which omits the people. He ignores the most significant events and ideas of the 19th century, those which alone give us a hope that democracy can be given a real meaning. For one whose ideals and sympathies lie with the dead and buried past this is natural; but if we wish to live we must reinterpret our past as well as make our future.

Chapter 3

Letter to the *Times Literary Supplement*

This was a letter written to the editor of the Times Literary Supplement
about a review in their issue of 21 October 1949.

Dear Sir,

In his notice of Professor J E Neale's admirable *The Elizabethan House of Commons*, your reviewer begins with a series of paragraphs which caricature every naive and conventional thing that has ever been said by Englishmen in praise of their own 'ability to muddle through', their 'absence of logic'. 'Chemically pure water is unfit for human consumption': your reviewer seems to regard that as an appropriate argument for leaving parliaments unreformed.

But an interesting and large cat is let out of the bag. Your reviewer clearly intended to praise British institutions: he writes as pityingly as every schoolboy of the attempts of lesser breeds to imitate them. But what he writes is almost identical with the Marxist critique of those institutions. To say that 'the function of national representation' has been 'in an indefinable manner to reproduce and balance the complex pattern of live forces and dominant interests' is to make verbosely and vaguely the Marxist point that parliament at all stages in English history has represented the interests of the economically dominant class. Your reviewer refers to the value of 'rotten or pocket boroughs in…the making of the nation', and to 18th century 'corruption' as 'a sign of growing freedom and independence'. But freedom and independence for whom? Clearly for those who can bribe, for those with money.

One is left with food for thought if the conclusion is that throughout history parliament has proved an extremely flexible institution, which has been moulded to suit the interests of successive ruling classes. 'That peculiar interplay of influence and independence produced [in the 18th century] a House representative of the nation. Though not of any rationally defined electorate.' The 'nation', then, is for your reviewer something distinct from the majority of the population composing it?

In many respects I think your reviewer is right in his historical analysis, though I disagree with him in preferring the representation of class interests to 'arithmetical accuracy', to (most damning phrase of all for the true Briton) 'the clever conceits of reforming logic'. But I wonder if he intended to express a narrow class view quite so clearly. To equate freedom with the power of money, the nation with the propertied classes? Perhaps he did.

Chapter 4

Two books on Stuart kings

I reviewed The Stuarts: A Study in English Kingship *by J D Kenyon in the* Spectator, *24 October 1958, and* Charles II *by Hesketh Pearson in the same periodical, 6 May 1960.*

The Stuarts: A Study in English Kingship by J D Kenyon

Dr Kenyon is an up-and-coming younger historian. His life of the second Earl of Sunderland, published earlier this year, was a most impressive and scholarly work. There was a touch of astringency in the style; but it was a good example of an efficient academic biography in the conventional manner. The present book is an essay on 17th century history written around the characters of the Stuart sovereigns. It is lavishly illustrated. It contains nearly every scabrous story told about the private lives of the Stuart monarchs: and they are many. Its structure lays it open to many criticisms. It manages to say virtually nothing about English history in the 1650s—not the least important decade in our history, even though Charles II happened to be out of the country at the time. This defect no doubt stemmed from Dr Kenyon's commission. But quite clearly the author was in a different, more light-hearted, mood than that of his earlier work. The subdued, scholarly manner is replaced by a boisterous, flamboyant style; the character sketches are shrewd, succinct and mordant; the judgements have an incisive brutality. (Charles I 'and his intimates were not so much misunderstood as completely outside the mainstream of English experience and national life.' Charles II's queen 'forfeited any faint hope of managing her husband when she fell in love with him, a solecism none of his mistresses was so careless as to commit.' James II's stupidity 'was so absolute as to be a source of strength.') Dr Kenyon obviously decided to enjoy himself: in doing so he has written an enjoyable book.

It is also something of a portent—for what it does not say rather than for what it does. The 17th century has always been a happy hunting ground for historians with interpretative theories. Were the great conflicts of that century about religion, Puritanism *versus* Popery? Were they about the constitution, absolute monarchy *versus* representative government? Or about law, prerogative *versus* common law courts? Were they the result of the violent clashing of heroic personalities, Cromwell *versus* Charles I, William III *versus* James II? Or were they perhaps the result of economic and social changes, of the rise and decline of gentry? Historians have joined battle on these issues. Though few of them agree on the significance to be attached to any one of the possible causal factors, nearly all assume that deep issues were at stake. Not so Dr Kenyon. He rejects the traditional explanations. 'Religion, then, drove no clear division between the opposing sides; but neither did secular political thought.' 'There is no greater delusion in 17th century history than that the lawyers had any contribution to make to the solution of contemporary problems.' 'Most modern commentators have taken the Stuart gentry too seriously.' 'There is no greater misconception in the mythology of Whiggism than that the revolution [of 1688] was a national movement.' Down they go like ninepins, all our pet little hobby-horses. What takes their place? This is the most significant thing about Dr Kenyon's book. He accepts nobody else's theories, but, if I interpret him aright, he has none of his own. When a 17th century character proclaims a principle Dr Kenyon brushes this aside, not in order to explain that principles are rationalisations of economic or other interests—that has been done before—but more simply, because he does not seem to think principles interesting or important.

The interest of this lies in the affiliations of Dr Kenyon's attitude. It is, surely, that of Jimmy Porter. The angry young man has appeared as historian. Many of Dr Kenyon's seniors in the profession are also angry; but their anger about other people's theories conceals (or fails to conceal) a desire to substitute their own. Dr Kenyon does not seem to want to sell us anything, apart from a little amateur psychology. (Not only James I but William III and Anne—'of course'— had homosexual tendencies: one is surprised that Dr Kenyon missed Mary II's lesbianism, the subject of at least one historical novel.) It is good that Jimmy Porter's generation has produced a spokesman in the sphere of history. So many historians have picked our pockets whilst expounding their own philosophies that there is something agreeable in Dr Kenyon's use of facts as bombs to explode the theories of others. Bombs, however, are not the best building material. To welcome the appearance of a spokesman is not to agree with what he has to communicate. Like Jimmy Porter, Dr Kenyon does not say much that is original; but he says it so vigorously and so personally that it sounds more original than it is. In this book he set out to be an entertainer; and he entertains very well.

Charles II by Hesketh Pearson

Charles II is easily the most intelligent king in English history. His epigrams often incorporate very shrewd political analysis. His ironical reaction to the factitious rejoicing at his restoration could hardly be improved on: 'It could be nobody's fault but his own that he had stayed so long abroad, when all mankind wished him so heartily at home.' When he read Rochester's epitaph:

> Here lies our sovereign lord, the King,
> Whose word no man relies on;
> Who never said a foolish thing,
> And never did a wise one,

Charles's unruffled and unanswerable retort was, 'My discourse is my own, my actions are my ministers'.' Similarly his remark to his brother James was acute as well as funny: 'I am sure no man in England will take away my life to make you King.'

But it is one thing to be a wit, another to be a great king. Mr Pearson pitches his claims a bit high when he says that at the end of his life 'Charles achieved a popularity unique among rulers'. The greatest achievements of his reign owed nothing to Charles, and it is stretching facts to say that the king's 'concern for science led to the foundation of the Royal Society'. Mr Pearson has written a sympathetic and entertaining biography of an engaging man, even though not everybody would agree that he 'personified all that was best in the English character'. But, value judgments apart, Mr Pearson's historical background is rarely adequate, despite 'the 60 odd books I have read on my subject'.

It will not do to dismiss as mad those who opposed Charles II, whether they were Scottish Presbyterians in the 1650s or 'the whole nation' at the time of the Popish Plot. When Burnet tells us that the king had a man's nose slit, this was probably 'an episcopal lie', since it does not fit Mr Pearson's conception of Charles's character. The secret Treaty of Dover, the biggest blot on the reign, was 'in reality a triumph for the English king'. Charles never allowed his mistresses to influence politics, Mr Pearson assures us, adding almost in the same breath that Barbara Palmer's 'favourites were pushed into soft jobs carrying sound emoluments, and she sometimes disposed of them to the highest bidder... She even compelled the king to make her uncle the Bishop of St Asaph. Pepys described him as "a drunken swearing rascal and a scandal to the Church".' The best thing to be said for Charles is that he was lazy. If he had been as pig-headed (or high principled) as James II or if James had possessed half his brother's cleverness, England might have suffered civil war or even a revival of absolutism. As history turned out, we can afford to be sentimentally indulgent towards the Merry Monarch's pleasant vices.

Chapter 5

Puritanism and the family in 17th century England

I cannot recall when I first gave this lecture. It was not published until 1994, when it appeared in a Japanese periodical, a special issue dedicated to honouring Professor Hideo Tamura.

Puritanism emerges as the ideology of the household economy which dominated England in the 16th, 17th and early 18th centuries. The productive units of mediaeval society had been large—the village community cultivating the open fields, the monastery with its crowds of servants, the great feudal household, often with hundreds of retainers, the craft guild organising urban production. In modern society too units of production are large—the factory, the capitalist farm worked by wage labour. But in the transitional centuries the dominant economic unit was the small household, with children, apprentices and journeymen all living and working together in a community of sorts, either farming a small agricultural holding or working for a merchant employer.

The mediaeval aristocratic household, like the royal court, was not a static community. It moved round the countryside, consuming the produce of its manors on the spot. The head of a great noble family, or the abbot of a monastery, stood aloof from the productive process. He did not even exercise his economic power directly over the producers: he worked through a hierarchy of mediators—chamberlains, stewards, bailiffs and the like. But among the middling groups of society the head of the household worked with his own hands side by side with those over whom he exercised economic control—his wife and children, his journeymen and apprentices. The community of which he was the head was described as a little state, a little church, a little school.

As cause and consequence of the expansion of production for the market, the 16th and 17th centuries saw better housing and household comforts beginning to spread downwards in society. W G Hoskins has stressed the extensive rebuilding of rural England in the 16th century. For the yeomanry, houses with two floors and separate bedrooms were replacing what had previously often been a single roomed dwelling made of mud or lathe and plaster. Chairs began to replace benches, collapsible beds and tables gave way to permanent fixtures, windows were glazed. All this made possible greater comfort and privacy, a new emphasis on the home as a social centre. Neither a mediaeval peasant hut nor an overcrowded baronial castle nor the travelling household of a great noble, nor the celibate community of a monastery or nunnery was favourable to home life: that was developed by the middling classes in town and country. The 16th century household was no longer just a place where one slept when not working, from which children escaped as soon as they were old enough. The home began to replace the church and the ale-house as a centre of social life, to which friends could be invited. As the market expanded, the home also became a centre of production, in which industrial skills were learnt by apprentices and children alike. By the 17th century the new housing was spreading slowly northwards and westwards, and down the social ladder to all but the very poorest classes.[1]

We are still talking about a minority of the population. In Sheffield in 1615, out of a population of 2207, only 260 were householders, the rest being dependants or poor[2] But this group of economically independent men—yeomen, artisans, small and middling merchants—was growing steadily. Contemporaries called them 'the industrious sort of people', to differentiate them from the privileged rentiers who did not work and the lowest classes who had no property and therefore no independence. They were 'the people' as opposed to 'the poor'.[3]

Contemporaries were aware that something new was happening, not only in England. As more and more sections of the population were

1 W G Hoskins, 'The Rebuilding of Rural England, 1570-1640', *Past and Present*, 4, (1953); A R Myers, *England in the Late Middle Ages* (Pelican edn), p224.

2 J Hunter, *Hallamshire* (1869), quoted by K V Thomas, 'Women and the Civil War Sects', *Past and Present*, 13 (1958).

3 'The Poor and the People', in my *People and Ideas in 17th Century England* (Brighton, 1986).

drawn into the economy of the market, so the stable monogamous family, the household, was becoming the norm. As 'the industrious sort' grew in numbers and self confidence, so they began to evolve an ideology of the dignity of labour, hard work in one's calling, to justify their existence and distinguish their mode of life from that of the idle rentier aristocracy, the idle footloose poor. In the early 16th century men had differentiated between 'two different ways of life and conduct in Scotland', those of the 'householding Scots' of the lowlands and those of the 'wild Scots' of the north and west. Part of the achievement of John Knox and Presbyterianism in Scotland was to enforce house-holding and monogamy, at least to outward appearance, on the whole of the lowlands.[4] Sixteenth century Englishmen regarded the Welsh as exceptionally immoral, and attributed their 'whoredoms' to the in-toxicating mountain air. But this was only the English way of looking at a society which had not yet accepted the new marriage conventions[5]: rather like a 19th century protestant missionary in Matabeleland.

In 16th century England similar distinctions were drawn. 'Not one amongst a hundred [beggars] are married', said a pamphlet of 1567.[6] John Donne demanded, 'How few of those who make beggary an occupation from their infancy were ever within church, how few of them ever chris-tened or ever married?'[7] Vagabonds, we are told, 'be generally given to horrible uncleanness, they have not particular wives, neither do they range themselves into families, but consort together as beasts'. The Gub-bings, an isolated moorland group in Devon, still in the mid-17th cen-tury lived like swine and 'multiplied without marriage', living 'exempt from all authority either ecclesiastical or civil'.[8] Norden the surveyor spoke of people bred among the woods, 'dwelling far from any church or chapel', who were 'as ignorant of God or of any civil course of life as the very savages amongst the infidels'.[9] As the parliamentarian armies ad-vanced into the north of England in the 1640s they found that 'thousands of parishes…in Cumberland, Northumberland, Westmorland, the Bish-opric (of Durham), yea and a very great part of Yorkshire' were no better

4 J Major, *History of Greater Britain* (Scottish History Soicety, 1892), p48.
5 P Williams, *The Council in the Marches of Wales under Elizabeth I* (Cardiff, 1958), p101.
6 Thomas Harman, *A Caveat for Common Cursitors* (1567), in G Salgado (ed),*Cony-Catchers and Bawdy Baskets* (Penguin, 1972), p121.
7 Donne, quoted by John Carey, '16th and 17th century Prose', in C Ricks (ed), *English Poetry and Prose 1540-1674* (Sphere Books, 1970), p401.
8 T Fuller, *History of the Worthies of England* (1840), I, p398.
9 R Younge, *The Poores Advocate* (1654), quoted in P Clark and P Slack (eds), *Crisis and Order in English Towns 1500-1700* (1972), p167; J Thirsk (ed), *The Agrarian History of England and Wales*, IV (Cambridge U P, 1967), p411; my *The World Turned Upside Down* (1972), p258.

than pagans.[10] The lower groups in the highly mobile population of Tudor and Stuart England—itinerant craftsmen, squatters on commons and in forests, unemployed looking for work, town slum dwellers, the hordes of rogues and vagabonds who so alarmed the well-to-do—none of these were 'householding Englishmen' with all that that implied.

Protestantism, and especially Puritanism, was attempting to impose on the lower classes of Britain new marriage patterns as a part of new patterns of life: to push the nuclear family downwards in society.[11] The Reformation, by reducing the authority of the priest, simultaneously elevated the authority of lay heads of households, as intermediaries between the central government and their own servants and dependants, no less than between the latter and God. Edward VI's and later injunctions laid upon parents and employers the responsibility for bringing up the youth in some virtuous study and occupation. Elizabeth I insisted that heads of households saw that their children and apprentices went to church every Sunday, under penalty of a fine of £10 per month.[12] The institution of parish registers by Thomas Cromwell in the decade of the Reformation, the bastardy laws so fiercely enforced by church courts and JPs, the new ideology of love in marriage preached by Spenser and Shakespeare no less than by the Puritan guides to godliness, are all part of the same pattern. The wife acquired a new status as the 'help meet', the junior partner in the household economy.

Parliament and the common law shared this preoccupation. They too assumed that heads of households had *political* obligations. The House of Commons in 1604 asked that all masters of households should be compelled to sign the 39 Articles— excepting those which dealt with the power of bishops and the crown over the church. Sir Edward Coke's list of articles given to high constables for presentment, probably in 1606, contains one which said 'all unlawful games, drunkenness, whoredom and incontinency in private families to be reported, as on their good government the commonwealth depends.[13] One advantage of being under the rule of a good governor of a family, the Puritan Richard Sibbes thought, was that there 'servants live in obedience to God's ordinances, and not like wild creatures, ruffians,

---

10 R Johnson, 'Eboraicus, Lux & Lex', a sermon preached to the House of Commons, 31 March, 1647, p28.
11 For the failure of Counter-Reformation Catholicism to emphasise the place of the household in the development of society, see J Bossy, 'The Counter-Reformation and the People of Catholic Europe', *Past and Present*, 47 (1970), pp 68-70.
12 My *Society and Puritanism* (1964), pp432-433; cf p451.
13 Ibid, p434.

vagabonds, Cains and the like'. Dod and Clever also distinguished firmly between 'vagabonds and runagates...filthy persons...unthrifts and...thieves' on the one hand, and a 'son that is brought up...in the family' on the other. Stephen Marshall in September 1641 urged MPs to see to it that 'your families may be little congregations of saints, with whom God may delight to dwell: not like taverns and ale-houses, houses of lewd and debauched persons'. It was not until 1644 that the obligation of sending rogues and vagabonds to church on Sundays was laid on JPs: before that they seem to have been outside the pale of the church.[14]

Puritans agreed on the religious significance of the household. 'If ever we would have the church of God to continue among us', wrote Richard Greenham, 'we must bring it into our households and nourish it in our families'. 'First reform your own families', Edmund Calamy told the House of Commons in December 1641, 'and then you will be the fitter to reform the family of God. Let the master reform his servant, the father his child, the husband his wife'. Even extreme radicals like the Anabaptists of Munster in the 1530s laid it down that disobedience to parents or to one's master in a household made one liable to the death sentence.[15]

A whole Puritan literature dating from the 16th century illustrates the rising importance of the family by emphasising in quite a new way the educational functions of the home and the duties of parents to children and servants. The preachers sharply contrasted what was expected of a well conducted small household not only with the deficiencies of vagabonds but also with the loose behaviour, on Sundays and weekdays alike, of under-employed serving men in great feudal households. Thomas Taylor sums up the point: 'Let every master of a family see to what he is called, namely to make his house a little church, to instruct every one of his family in the fear of God, to contain every one of them under holy discipline, to pray with them and for them'.[16]

So long as a personal relationship existed between employer and employee there was something to be said for this patriarchal attitude. Masters beat their servants, it is true; but then parents beat their children and expected highly deferential behaviour from them. William Gouge insisted that masters should not be 'too frequent and too furious strikers'. Mutual participation in family prayers may have

14 Ibid, pp457-458; S Marshall, *A Peace-Offering to God* (1641), pp49-50.
15 *Society and Puritanism*, pp428-431; E Calamy, *England's Looking-Glasse* (1642), p60;
   G H Williams, *The Radical Reformation* (Philadelphia, 1962), p371.
16 *Society and Puritanism*, pp441-443.

contributed to household harmony. Henry Bullinger not only pointed out the economic advantages of having godly servants: he also insisted, like Calvin, that servants must be given rest and leisure. Gouge not only emphasised the necessary subordination of servants to masters: he also declared that God was 'the Master of masters. As servants are the Lord's freemen, so masters are the Lord's servants'.[17] This Puritan stress on the responsibilities of heads of households was a relatively democratic development. Servants too had some rights and duties, no less than the privileged landed ruling class, the privileged merchant oligarchies. These rights and duties distinguished them from the dependent poor, gave them something to cling on to in a world of dissolving certainties, including social certainties. Among the many relationships which Donne said the new philosophy had called in doubt were those of 'prince, subject, father, son'.[18] The most democratic 17th century groups, Levellers and Diggers, accepted the role of heads of households: Levellers would not have extended the franchise to non-householders, those who did not pay rates, to servants and beggars (or to women), because such persons were not economically free, were too dependent on their employers to be independent persons in their own right.

Both church and state then emphasised the significance of the individual household unit. So did the private charity of rich merchants and gentlemen which Professor Jordan has studied, endowing marriage portions for virtuous spinsters, giving support to apprenticeship and education. At Halifax the great Calvinist preacher John Favour ruled from 1593 to 1623. 'He encouraged the development of the cloth industry...he subdued the roistering and the criminal with the breath of fire in his sermons'; and he collected more than sixty bequests, from far and near, for the improvement and education of his community.[19]

The period from the 15th to the 17th century saw the beginnings and rapid extension of regular schooling.[20] Children began to stay longer at school, up to three or four years, and schools ceased to exist primarily for those who aspired to join the clerical caste. Until the invention of printing and the expansion of trade and industry, the skills

17 Ibid, pp437-438.
18 John Donne, 'An Anatomie of the World' (1611), in Nonesuch (ed), *Complete Poetry and Selected Prose* , p202.
19 W K Jordan, *The Rural Charities of England, 1480-1660* (1961), pp323-326; cf Jordan, *Philanthropy in England, 1480-1660* (1958), passim.
20 P Aries, *Centuries of Childhood* (trans R Baldick, 1962), pp368-369.

required for labour could be acquired in the home, without formal instruction, and were transmitted by participation in the labour process. But now reading, writing and arithmetic became conventional necessities for all but the poorest classes. In protestant countries availability of the printed Bible in the vernacular, and the importance attached to it as the source of all wisdom and knowledge, gave a great stimulus to the spread of literacy among both sexes. Some Puritans thought education was necessary to salvation: it was certainly necessary to worldly prosperity. 'Much better they were unborn than untaught', said a pamphlet dedicated to Queen Elizabeth in 1568.[21]

Economic developments thus led to an increase in the number and economic prosperity of independent households, and to increasing self consciousness among masters of families. As the home became more important, became a centre of social and cultural life as well as of labour, so the family came to focus more on the children. Proportionately there were far more of them than today: at the end of the 17th century very nearly half the population was below the age of 20.[22] Child labour was an economic asset. In the 17th century it seems to have been normal for a large proportion of children to live away from home after the age of eight or so. Children of the gentry were sent to serve in a noble household, children of the lower classes were put out as apprentices or servants; pauper children were compulsorily apprenticed. This must have helped to reduce clashes between the generations. It was thus not quite so horrifying as some historians have thought when, after the Gunpowder Plot, the House of Commons proposed that all children of Catholic recusants should be taken away from their parents at the age of nine: the novelty lay only in the insistence that they should be educated in protestant families.[23]

This habit was transplanted to the New World. About one third of the children in Plymouth, Rhode Island, seem to have spent their adolescence outside their own families. In 1643 the parents of a five year old New England child were threatened with the stocks when he repeatedly ran away from the household to which he had been apprenticed.[24] But as the 17th century advanced, more and more children, in

21 E Tilney, A Briefe and Pleasant Discourse of the Duties of Marriage (1568), quoted by K Charlton, Education in Renaissance England (1965), p202; K R M Short, 'A Theory of Common Education in Elizabethan Puritanism', Journal of Ecclesiastical History, XXIII, p34.
22 D V Glass and D E C Eversley, Population in History (1965), p212.
23 W Notestein, The House of Commons, 1604-1610 (Yale U P, 1971), p151; cf A Macfarlane, The Family Life of Ralph Josselin (Cambridge U P, 1970), pp205-210.
24 J Demos, A Little Commonwealth: Family Life in Plymouth Colony (Oxford U P, 1970), pp73-75, 113.

old and New England alike, seem to have been staying to work at home. By l655 JPs were complaining that young men and maids fit to go out to service prefer to work at home. The restoration helped to remedy that.[25]

The 16th and 17th centuries in England were a period of great economic insecurity. The opening up of new markets, the expansion of industry, the commercialisation of agriculture, offered possibilities of prosperity to the fortunate few, but great anxiety and risk of economic catastrophe for others. To the traditional hazards of mediaeval life— plague, famine, sudden death (especially of children and of women in childbirth) were added the new vagaries of the capitalist market, with no insurance against fire or flood, no social insurance against sickness, old age, being left a widow or an orphan. Even among children born to royalty and aristocracy two out of every five died before reaching their first birthday, and at least one more before reaching maturity.[26] The death rate is not likely to have been lower among the middling and lower classes.

Since each household was in effect competing against all other households, circumstances demanded close cohesion within the family unit, where all members might be engaged in production from the age of five to eight upwards. With no effective birth control, and with heavy infant mortality, children tended to be spaced out over a long period: there might well be two year olds and twenty year olds in the same family. The gap between the generations thus seemed smaller than today; children from the age of eight or so were dressed as little adults and were in many ways treated more like adults than later. Our concept of adolescence is a relatively late idea, derived from a longer period of dependent education, ending with a wide range of job choice, leading to uncertainty, identity crises.[27] In the 16th and 17th centuries most children of all but the very rich knew early on what state of life it had pleased God to call them to. They joined the adult world of production whilst still young, automatically, with virtually no choice of alternative jobs. They never knew adolescence in the modern sense. Children were subordinated to their parents not merely because of their age but because, like servants, they lacked economic independence. In the Poll Tax returns of 1380-1 children of householders are frequently described as servants.[28]

25 A E Bland, P A Brown and R H Tawney (eds), *English Economic History: Select Documents* (1914), p360.
26 G Mattingly, *Catherine of Aragon* (1963), p109.
27 Demos, op cit, pp69, 145, 150.
28 I owe this point to Professor R H Hilton.

Deference to parents had long been expected in James I's reign. The Venetian Ambassador tells us that 'every child on first meeting his parents each day' kneels and asks their blessing, even if in the street.[29] In 1612 the son of the Bishop of Bristol, aged about 19, committed suicide rather than face a threatened flogging for losing money at tennis.[30] Lord Chief Justice Coke tied his daughter to the bedpost and whipped her until she agreed to marry the brother of the royal favourite, the Duke of Buckingham. Stern discipline was also to be found lower down the social scale. In the family workshop, the family still lived in very close contact, even if it was beginning to have separate bedrooms. Only one room was likely to be heated, even in winter; candles and rushlights were expensive. Everybody lived and worked on top of everyone else. For life to be at all tolerable it was essential that family quarrels should be reduced to a minimum. This helps to explain the heavy emphasis on powerful paternal authority, so sedulously built up by Puritan divines. Children should stand up when speaking to parents, said the handbooks, should never interrupt or laugh at them, should thank parents for reproving their faults.[31]

In early 17th century New England hard and disciplined work was not only desirable but essential to survival. 'Idle drones are intolerable in a settled commonwealth', declared Robert Cushman in 1622, 'much more in a commonwealth which is but as it were in the bud'. In 1648 idleness was made a punishable offence in Massachusetts.[32] In this environment family cohesion was even more important than in Europe. It had been a capital offence in Calvin's Geneva for a child to strike his father.[33] In Massachusetts, Connecticut and even at Plymouth, Rhode Island, the most democratic of the North American colonies, the law imposed death on any child of sixteen or more years who struck a parent, unless he could prove that he had been excessively cruelly punished. Habitual disobedience also made a child—in theory at least—liable to the death penalty. Close family cohesion was accompanied, it has been suggested, by aggressiveness towards outsiders, leading to those quarrels between neighbouring families which

29 *Calender of State Papers, Venetian, 1621-23*, p451. Some Puritans opposed the 'ceremony' of parental blessing.
30 N E McClure (ed), *The Letters of John Chamberlain* (American Philosophical Society, Memoirs, XII 1939) I, p335.
31 *Society and Puritanism*, p437; R Cawdrey, *A Godly Forme of Householde Government* (amended and augmented by John Dod and Robert Clever, 1614), Sig S 1-1v; T Cobbett, *A Fruitfull and Usefull Discourse touching the Honour due from Children to Parents and the Duty of Parents towards their Children* (1656), pp90-99.
32 *Society and Puritanism*, pp137-138.
33 Calvin, *Institutes of the Christian Religion* (trans H Beveridge, 1949), I, p345.

appear so frequent in this period.[34] In England immoderate beating was not regarded (legally) as a reason for terminating an apprenticeship. It was a hard world, in which the weakest went to the wall. In 1649 a Somerset employer was relieved of his responsibility for a girl apprentice because she had become lame 'and hath divers wounds running in her body, whereby she is unable to do service'. Nothing was said about what was to happen to her.[35]

This is the background against which we must see the universal Puritan—and not only Puritan—assumption of original sin. Children are not born innocent: they are born with an inherent tendency to Adam's sin of disobedience. Their stubbornness must be beaten down, their wills must be broken. 'He that spareth the rod hateth his sin', the Good Book said (Proverbs XIII, 24). Original sin explained not only the wickedness of children but also the existence of private property, class inequality and the state which protects both. It was a doctrine held to be essential to the stability of society. As it justified the use of coercion by the state, so original sin explained the need for parental authority, for rigid discipline, at home, school and university, over children, servants, apprentices and undergraduates. 'The young child which lieth in the cradle' is 'both wayward and full of affections; and though his body be but small, yet he hath a great heart, and is altogether inclined to evil; and the more he waxeth in reason by years, the more he groweth proud, froward, wilful, unruly and disobedient. If this sparkle be suffered to increase, it will rage over and burn down the whole house. For we are changed and become good not by birth but by education… Therefore parents must be wary and circumspect… For as the common proverb is, birch breaketh no bones'. Parents 'must correct or sharply reprove their children for saying or doing ill'.[36]

The floggings of 16th and 17th century schoolchildren and undergraduates must be seen in the context of a life full of cruel pain and suffering, with no anaesthetics, with public corporal punishment a daily sight—whipping, branding, pillorying, cutting off ears, hanging, disembowelling and quartering. But the fact that schools and colleges increased in number and importance at this time meant that teachers took over the authoritarianism of the home, the assumption that to spare the rod was to spoil the child. Undergraduates were urged to look upon their

34 Demos, op cit, pp100, 49-51, 135; E S Morgan, *The Puritan Family* (Boston, Mass, 1956), p38.
35 H Bates Harbin (ed), *Quarter Sessions Records*, III, 1646-60 (Somerset Record Soc, XXVIII, 1912), p88; cf pp265-266, 287.
36 Cawdrey, op cit, Sig R 3v, T.

tutor as though he were the head of their family: flogging at Oxford, Professor Stone claims, can be precisely dated from 1610 to 1660.[37] In the process children were equated with the lower classes. Children of all classes were as rightless as the poor,[38] and flogging continued right down to our own century to be an essential part of the education of a gentleman. Both children and wage labourers tended to be regarded as inherently sinful. Servants and children, the Puritan Samuel Clarke tells us, 'naturally have an averseness to and hatred of all that is good'. Only Anabaptists, Gouge said, 'teach that all are alike, and that there is no difference betwixt masters and servants.[39]

But we must not think of Puritans only as advocates of severe paternal authority. Parents had duties as well as rights. In this brutal world, indeed, some Puritans—radicals especially—were in favour of mitigating the harshness of paternal and pedagogical authority. Maternal love and solicitude were encouraged, starting with a strong emphasis on the desirability of breastfeeding.[40] Joan Thirsk stresses that the sort of indulgence towards children for which some preachers called would be impossible in families of the very poor.[41] Many preachers opposed flogging. The great Czech educationalist Comenius thought that beating was a confession of failure. If the pupil did not learn, the teacher was to blame. Comenius and his disciples wanted education to be a delight. They also wanted it to be universal, up to the age of eighteen. 'Not the children of the rich or of the powerful only, but of all alike, boys and girls, noble and simple, rich and poor, in all cities and towns, villages and hamlets, should be sent to school'.[42]

These ideas were especially influential among the radical Puritan revolutionaries. In the 1640s and 1650s attempts were made to realise them.

The protestant emphasis on the priesthood of all believers, on the individual conscience as the final arbiter, ultimately challenged all authority in church and state. Protestantism had always been ambivalent

37 M H Curtis, *Oxford and Cambridge in Transition* (OUP, 1959), pp35, 114; an unpublished lecture on the family by Professor Stone, from which I am grateful to him for permission to quote. He points out, however, that the 15th century statutes of Balliol College give the Master the right to inflict corporal punishment on undergraduates.

38 Aries, *Centuries of Childhood*, pp261-262.

39 *Society and Puritanism*, p460.

40 Eg Cawdrey, op cit, Sig P 4-P 4v; H Smith, *Sermons* (1631), p42; M Walzer, *The Revolution of the Saints* (Harvard U P, 1965), p192. Breastfeeding no doubt helped to keep down the birth rate among the middling and lower classes.

41 Thirsk, 'The Family', *Past and Present*, 27 (1964), p121.

42 D W Singer, 'Comenius and Confidence in the Rational Mind', in J Needham (ed), *The Teacher of Nations* (1941), p71.

about the position of the wife. In some ways the evolution of the household economy may have been deleterious to the position of women. As the independence of individual families is stressed, so women lost much of the support which the kin or the community had once been able to give them. Protestantism abolished the mediating role of the Virgin and of saints, many of whom had been women, to elevate God the Father, and this reflects an elevation of the human father. His responsibility for the economic and moral welfare of all his dependants, including wife and children, enhanced the dignity of the head of the household. 'The word Father is an epitome of the whole Gospel', declared Richard Sibbes. The patriarchs created God in their own image, and regarded their authority as no less divine than that of kings: indeed the latter was derived from the authority of the father of the family. All the manuals emphasise both the father's authority and his responsibility for the welfare, bodily and spiritual, of those under him. Milton believed it would be a contribution to domestic liberty if he could restore to the master of the family that power to put away his wife which mediaeval theologians had taken away from him.[43] In this he was no doubt a little extreme: he was much more typical when he assumed that Adam was created for God only, Eve for God in him.

Yet women too have souls. In Luther's priesthood of all believers, could or could not women be priests? Orthodox protestants denied their right to be ordained, but there was an uneasy ambiguity on the general point. Puritan preachers insisted on the wife's equality in subordination, rejected the aristocratic dual standard of sexual conduct, deprecated the wife beating for which Englishmen were notorious, and in many ways fought for respect for women.[44] The wife's role as 'helpmeet', partner in the family firm, helped them. Radical protestant sects allowed women to participate in church government, and some permitted them to preach. This very different attitude may reflect tension in the small household, where the wife really was a joint partner, with considerable financial responsibility.[45] The smaller the household, perhaps the greater the authority of the mother.[46]

Robert Browne, founder of congregationalism, insisted that the authority of the father and husband must rest on agreement and covenant,

43 *Society and Puritanism*, pp436, 449.
44 *The World Turned Upside Down*, pp248-249.
45 During this period women possessed far more 'disposable wealth and certainly far greater independence of judgement than was commonly supposed', Professor Jordan concluded. The proportion of women benefactors in London increased rapidly between 1621 and 1650 (Jordan, *Philanthropy in England*, p354; *Charities of London* (1960), p29).

a point later stressed by Gerrard Winstanley. Mrs Chidley in 1641 argued that the husband had no more right to control his wife's conscience than the magistrate had to control his. Both were to be obeyed in civil matters, but conscience must not be coerced. George Fox thought that male dominion belonged to sin, and that in the new life man and wife were equals. When he married Margaret Fell—much richer than he was—he committed himself legally not to touch her property—to the scandal of his lawyers. At the crisis of *Paradise Lost* Adam decides he would rather lose Paradise and retain Eve than continue in Paradise without her. Milton's intellect told him that this was an error, Adam having been fondly overcome by female charm; but the poetry of Adam's great cry tells us that one part at least of Milton felt that love was more important than hierarchical obedience:

> How can I live without thee, how forgo
> Thy sweet converse and love so dearly joined
> To live again in these wild woods forlorn?...
> Flesh of flesh,
> Bone of my bone thou art, and from thy state
> Mine never shall be parted, bliss or woe.

Yet not even the Levellers suggested that women should be enfranchised. They organised petitions and demonstrations of women on behalf of the general Leveller programme, but this remained an exclusively male platform, aimed at enfranchising heads of households who, the Levellers insisted, virtually represented their wives, children and servants.[47] Yet women, children and servants had souls too. The great Leveller pronouncements on the equality of man, Rainborough's 'the poorest he that is in England hath a life to live as the greatest he, and therefore...every man that is to live under a government ought first by his own consent to put himself under that government'—such statements if anything reinforced the authority of male heads of households.[48]

All these contradictions came out into the open during the English Revolution. The demand for religious toleration, for freedom from control from above, suddenly revealed a new threat from below.

---

46 Cf Mao Zedong on China in the 1920s: 'As to the authority of the husband, it has always been comparatively weak among the poor peasants, because the poor peasant women, compelled for financial reasons to take more part in manual work than women of the wealthier classes, have obtained more right to speak and more power to make decisions in family affairs' (*Selected Works*, I, 1954, pp46-47).

47 *Society and Puritanism*, pp456-457.

48 A S P Woodhouse (ed), *Puritanism and Liberty* (1992), p53.

If toleration were established, the conservative Thomas Edwards wailed, it would take away 'that power, authority which God hath given the husbands, fathers, masters'. They would 'never have peace in their families more, or ever have command of wives, children, servants'.[49] Toleration was established in the 1640s, and for 10 or 15 years children and servants might be unprecedentedly free to go to a different church from that to which the head of the household used to lead them, where a respectable university trained divine preached a respectable theology. Now wives and servants might hear—and discuss—very different theological (and political and economic) ideas, in a congregation which selected its own preacher— who might be a mechanic like the majority of his audience. Wives and servants of either sex might even preach themselves in the deplorable liberty of the revolutionary years. They might decide to go to no church at all. Edwards tells us of one servant who said 'I would have the liberty of my conscience *not* to be catechised in the principles of religion'.[50]

The radical sects of the 1640s and 1650s appealed especially to the middling and lower classes, to women, and also to 'young youths and wenches', 'the younger sort', including apprentices, who were 'most free from the forms of the former age, and from the doctrines and traditions of men'.[51] Looking back after the restoration, Clarendon attributed the decay of all authority to 'the several sects in religion, which discountenanced all forms of reverence and respect, as relics and marks of superstition. Children asked not blessing of their parents, nor did they concern themselves in the education of their children... Young women conversed without any circumspection or modesty, and frequently met at taverns and common eating-houses... Parents had no manner of authority over their children, nor children any obedience or submission to their parents. but everyone did that which was good in his own eyes'.[52] It sounds like a brief glimpse of the modern world.

Insofar as there was a teenage revolt in the 17th century, it was inspired by radical sectaries. We might also recall the part that London

49 Edwards, *Gangraena*, Part I (1646), p106.
50 *Society and Puritanism*, pp463-6.
51 *The World Turned Upside Down*, p152. For the protestant Reformation as a youth movement, see N Z Davis, 'The Reasons of Misrule: Youth Groups and Charivaris in 16th century France', *Past and Present*, 50 (1971), p74; S R Smith, 'The London Apprentices as 17th century Adolescents', ibid, 61 (1973): B Capp, 'English Youth Groups and The Pinner of Wakefield', ibid, 76 (1977).
52 Edward Hyde, Earl of Clarendon, *Continuation of the Life* (1759), II, p39. My italics.

apprentices played in the radical politics of the 1640s and early 1650s, and in the Leveller movement. Hobbes thought the grammar schools bore a great responsibility for the revolution. This subject still awaits proper investigation. What we do know about is the Quaker revolt. We think of their refusal to remove their hats in the presence of social superiors, their insistence on addressing all as 'thou', instead of reserving the word for their inferiors—we think of these as gestures of social protest, and so they were. But the protest was also made within the family. John Aubrey, looking back to the days before the revolution, tells us that 'the child perfectly loathed the sight of his parents as the slave his torturer. Gentlemen of 30 or 40 years old, fit for any employment in the commonwealth, were to stand like great mutes bare headed before their parents'.[53] The conservative Richard Leigh as late as 1675 spoke of the 'Turkish rigour' of parental authority.[54] Take the example of Thomas Ellwood, son of a landed gentleman who had supported parliament during the civil war. In his late teens the son became a Quaker, and started to address his father as 'thou', keeping his hat on whilst speaking. (The sole right to wear his hat in his own house was the symbol of the authority of the head of the family.) I quote from Ellwood's account of his father's reaction the first time this happened:

> As soon as he saw me standing with my hat on, his passion transporting him, he fell upon me with both his fists; and having by that means somewhat vented his anger, he plucked off my hat and threw it away.

Ellwood then went to a Quaker meeting without his father's permission. He was so late in returning that his father became seriously worried:

> [But] the sight of my hat upon my head made him presently forget that I was that son of his whom he had so lately lamented as lost; and his passion of grief turning into anger, he could not contain himself, but running upon me with both his hands, first violently snatched off my hat and threw it away. Then giving me some buffets on my head he said 'Sirrah. get you up to your chamber'. I forthwith went, he following me at the heels, and now and then giving me a whirret on the ear.

---

53 A Powell, *John Aubrey and his Friends* (1963), p278. Such stories add point to the dedication to Oliver Cromwell of the pamphlet *Killing No Murder* (1657), which advocated his assassination: You are 'the true father of the country, for while you live we can call nothing ours, and it is from your death that we expect our inheritances.'
54 R Leigh, *Poems, 1675* (H Macdonald (ed), Oxford, 1947), pp49-50.

His father threw away all Thomas's hats. It was January, and the consequence of the young man going out without any covering for his head was, he tells us, with some satisfaction, that he:

> took so great a cold in my head that my face and head were much swelled, and my gums had on them boils so sore that I could neither chew meat nor, without difficulty, swallow liquids... I was laid up, as a kind of prisoner, for the rest of the winter, having no means to go forth among Friends nor they liberty to come to me... But whenever I had occasion to speak to my father, though I had no hat now to offend him, yet my language did as much: for I durst not say 'You' to him, but 'Thou' or 'Thee', as the occasion required, and then would he be sure to fall on me with his fists.
>
> At one of these times, I remember, when he had beaten me in that manner, he commanded me (as he commonly did at such times), to go to my chamber, which I did, and he followed me to the bottom of the stairs. Being come thither, he gave me a parting blow, and in a very angry tone said 'Sirrah, if ever I hear you say 'thou' or 'thee' again, I'll strike your teeth down your throat'. I was greatly grieved to hear him say so. And feeling a word rise in my heart unto him, I turned again and calmly said unto him, 'Would it not be just if God should serve thee so when thou sayst 'thou' or 'thee' to him?'... After this I had a pretty time of rest and quiet from these disturbances, my father not saying anything to me, nor giving me occasion to say anything to him.

Ellwood then organised the servants in the household to resist family prayers and won. His father cut off his money, and ordered him to eat in the kitchen so as not to offend his sight. There was a complete breach when Ellwood married, not in a church.[55] The battle of the hat was a special problem for sons of gentlemen who joined the Quakers. There were not many of them, and in those families the struggle was fought once for all by the first generation.

During the revolution other radical sectaries attacked the fundamental doctrine of original sin. Gerrard Winstanley said that, so far from private property and class distinctions being due to the Fall of Man, it was the establishment of private property and the covetousness which it begot that had corrupted human innocence. Children were not born sinful: they were born innocent, and were perverted by the selfishness of propertied society. Breaking their will by harsh

---

55 S Graveson (ed), *The History of the Life of Thomas Ellwood* (1906), pp46, 51-54. First published 1714.

punishments would thus lose its point. Rather abolish private property, and we can then return to the state of innocence which prevailed before the Fall. The Ranter Abiezer Coppe announced that 'sin and transgression were finished'. Coppe carried the attack into the family itself. 'Give over thy stinking family duties', he wrote, speaking in God's name. 'Give over, or if nothing else will do it, I'll at a time when thou least of all thinkest of it make thine own child…lie with a whore before thine eyes'. Other radicals argued that family duties were 'nowhere commanded in Scripture', and so 'neglected and even disputed against them'.[56] Both Coppe and Laurence Clarkson preached a doctrine of free love. 'Till you can lie with all women as one woman', Clarkson wrote, 'and not judge it sin, you can do nothing but sin… No man could attain to perfection but this way… Sin hath its conception only in the imagination. What act soever is done by thee in light and love, is light and lovely, though it be that act called adultery… No matter what Scripture, saints and churches say, if that within thee do not condemn thee, thou shalt not be condemned.' Such passages read very like a lower class reaction against the imposition of the monogamous family on earlier, freer, customs. George Fox and other Quakers denounced Puritan preachers who 'roar up for sin in their pulpits'. Mankind could reach perfection on earth, Quakers held. For Diggers and Ranters an afterlife in heaven became irrelevant. Life on earth, here and now, was what mattered.[57]

It is important not to exaggerate: these extensions of the logic of Puritanism, though they they were more widespread than historians used to think, were mostly confined to the lower ranks of society and were suppressed in the 1650s. In 1660 the restoration of monarchy, House of Lords and bishops put children, wives and servants back in their places. Censorship was restored, rights of assembly and petitioning virtually abolished for the lower orders, together with freedom of movement. The settlement laws tried to tie both the poor and itinerant preachers to their villages. Radicals were suppressed, driven underground or into exile. Even the Quakers, the most radical sect to survive, accepted the permanence of human sinfulness, and by pacifism and withdrawal from politics, virtually opted out of the world they had proved unable to transform. The Society of Friends became a sect like others. Traherne was remarkable in continuing to believe in the innocence of children.

56 D Cawdrey and H Palmer, *Sabbatum Redivivum* (1645), p171.
57 *The World Turned Upside Down*, pp172-174, 215-216, 315-321.

The restoration thus marks a turning point in Puritanism. Many of the popular connotations of that word really apply to post-1660 non-conformity rather than to Puritanism in its heyday in the 16th and 17th centuries. When we think of the latter, we should not envisage blackcoated killjoys going about desecrating churches, breaking stained-glass windows and preventing fun, drink and sex. There were some such; but when we think of mainline Puritanism we should have in mind John Milton, with his love for music and plays; of Oliver Cromwell, with his love for music and wine; of John Bunyan, who said that a teetotaller was a man who followed his own lusts, not the spirit of God.[58] We should recall the Russian ambassador who came to London after it had been under Puritan rule for four years. Reporting back to Moscow in 1646 he singled out two features of the City for special mention—the beautiful stained glass in the churches and the merry pealing of church bells.[59] It is not quite the stereotype picture of a Puritan city. The historian of law during the revolution suggests that the 1640s and 1650s were a period of sexual freedom for ordinary people unparalleled before or for many years afterwards.[60] I am sure he is right. It was only in the years of defeat, repression and persecution after 1660, when dissenters from the Church of England were excluded from political life, from the professions and from the universities, that non-conformity became narrow, provincial, sectarian.

Households survived the restoration. But the attempt to take over and remould society by their radical spokesmen had failed. A majority of householders had decided, in Milton's despairing phrase, that 'nothing but kingship can restore trade'.[61] Henceforth restraints on the accumulation of capital by the well to do were non-existent. We move into the world of the strict settlement, the Whig oligarchy, the Bank of England, the commercial and industrial revolutions. What survived among non-conformists was the protestant ethic—hard work in the calling in which God had placed one was a duty; accumulation was incumbent on those fortunate enough to be able to manage it. Poverty was prima facie evidence of divine disapproval. The sects themselves, by organising poor relief for their members, helped to impose the labour discipline necessary for capitalist society. In 1657 the Baptist

58 Bunyan, *Works* (1860), II, p201.
59 Z I Roginsky, *London in 1645-1646* (Yaroslavl, 1960), p11. In Russian.
60 D Veall, *The Popular Movement for Law Reform, 1640-1660* (OUP, 1970), pp139-141.
61 Milton, *The Readie and Easie Way to Establish a Free Commonwealth* (April 1660), in *Complete Prose Works* (Yale U P), VII, p461.

church at Fenstanton reproved the 'sin' of parents who kept a child at home who was capable of going out to service.[62]

By the end of the 17th century the position of the household in society is beginning to change. Agricultural labourers were ceasing to live in with their employers. Apprenticeship was declining, so there were fewer living-in young persons. The household, so long the most significant productive unit in society, was being eclipsed by bigger units, by the capitalist farm, formed by large scale enclosure, the farmer often an absentee; ultimately by the factory, run by a distant impersonal boss. An increasing proportion of the working class was ceasing to be footloose, becoming tied down to its own puny households as ever new sources of capitalist employment opened up—in many areas for the first time. The metal workshops of Sheffield and the Black Country, the jewelry, gun making and toys of the Birmingham trades, shoemakers in Northamptonshire and Staffordshire, the handloom weavers of the West Riding, the hop farmers of Kent, hill and moorland farmers, poultry breeders of Buckinghamshire and Berkshire, miners in Durham—all these joined the ranks of small householders.[63] In all these areas of employment the Industrial Revolution gave new life to the small-master economy, and formed the economic and social basis for the second non-conformity, for Methodism. We are all set for a world in which conservative politicians will see advantages in workers owning their own houses.

Yet there are distinctions to be drawn between the small household in the 16th-17th centuries and in the 18th-19th centuries, just as there are distinctions between Puritanism and the second non-conformity. There was a sense in which, in the England of the earlier period—as in any backward economy today—hard work, accumulation of capital, industrial discipline, were the essential prerequisites for any increase in national wealth, irrespective of the way in which it was distributed. So long as the family farm and the family firm remained the basic units of production, there was still some real community of interests as the employer worked side by side with his apprentices, journeymen and children. But the balance of forces in England after 1660 ensured that wealth would be accumulated for the benefit of a

62 E B Underhill ed, *Records of the Churches of Christ gathered at Fenstanton, Warboys and Hexham* (Hanserd Knollys Society, 1854), p210. See also *The World Turned Upside Down*, p304 and D H Sacks, *The Widening Gate: Bristol and the Atlantic Economy, 1450-1700* (California U P, 1991), pp105-123.

63 I owe these illustrations to the kindness of Mr Raphael Samuel; see also D Levine and K Wrightson, *The Making of an Industrial Society: Whickham, 1560-1765* (OUP, 1991), pp64-73, 311-329.

relatively narrow class. After the Industrial Revolution employers still insisted on obedience and hard work as duties owed to God, that idleness was a sin; but the personal connection, the visible community of interests in the household, had been lost. The newly expanding small-master households are no longer the dominant productive units of society; there is no longer relative equality among heads of households: there is permanent subordination to the dominance of big industry, big capitalist farming.

Puritanism turned sour after political defeat, at a time when the household economy was losing its leading position in society. Henceforth nonconformity was too often merely negatively repressive, had little to say to adolescents growing up and facing new identity crises in the capitalist society which Puritanism had helped to build. Wesley, creator of the second non-conformity, was a Tory who accepted the subordinate position of the working householder. Puritanism and the second non-conformity have much in common, but the horizons are now more limited: there are no heroic vistas such as men and women had glimpsed during the revolution. Rank and file Methodists continually transcended the limited outlook of Wesley and the leaders, playing a part in the evolution of the working class movement; but they showed little of the libertarianism, the transcendence of the protestant ethic, which we have seen in Winstanley, Ranters and early Quakers. There was little rational justification for heavy paternal authority in a Victorian middle class family, but the catchword 'spare the rod and spoil the child' lived on. There is not much to be said either for schools modelled on the paternalist authoritarianism of the family or the factory; but as education for the lower classes extended to a national system, discipline by the rod extended too.

Puritanism performed a valuable historical function in the 16th and 17th centuries; in the second non-conformity it lived on to give cohesion and meaning to many lives that would otherwise have been barren and empty. Today Puritanism is in full retreat, and I should hate to say anything to delay that retreat. But as we search for ideologies to replace Puritanism, let us not forget its progressive role in an earlier, very different, society. Let us remember the radical Puritans who transcended the individualist limitations of nascent capitalism: the Comenians' demand for universal and equal educational opportunities, 200 years before that came about, even in form. Let us remember Milton and the early Quakers carrying the battle for the liberty of individual consciences into the family as well as the church and the state; Coppe and Ranters denouncing sin, the great deterrent of the defenders of propertied society, calling both monogamy and the existence of hell into question. ('There's no heaven but women, nor no hell save marriage', one of them said.)[64] Winstanley explaining that the state and property are the causes, not the consequences, of sin, and so that greed and selfishness could be overcome on earth, without waiting for heaven. All these ideas came from democratic extensions of Puritan/protestant positions. The radicals had to be suppressed before Puritanism adapted itself to life in an unequal capitalist society and turned into non-conformity.

Puritanism then has always been a two edged sword. It helped to make the world safe for capitalism, via the protestant ethic: it can become negative, repressive, killjoy. But in the past radical Puritanism, by proclaiming human equality and the rights of the individual conscience, stood for human values in a world where the competitive rat-race was beginning to dominate. It is perhaps no accident that many middle class supporters of the English working class movement in our day come from a non-conformist background. Some of the Puritan values still have relevance today.

64 *The World Turned Upside Down*, p182.

Chapter 6

The historical revolution

This review was first published in the Spectator, *6 July 1962. This was my first acquaintance with a historian for whom I have great respect.*

The Historical Revolution, 1580-1640 by F Smith Fussner

Revolutions, as Marx very nearly said, are the locomotives of historians' careers. The formula for the up and coming young scholar is simple. Find some turning point mysteriously overlooked by your elders, christen it 'the X revolution of the Nth century,' and write about it at length. After nine world-shaking days your revolution may sink back into being a slight shift of emphasis, but never mind: your reputation will have been made. It is therefore with a Tiresian weariness of spirit that one picks up yet another first book with revolution in the title. For once, however, one is agreeably disappointed. Professor Fussner has written an important book. He has drawn attention to a neglected transformation in English thought.

His thesis is that, parallel to the scientific revolution in early 17th century England, there was a revolution in historical thought and writing; and that the historical and the scientific revolutions are related, both to one another and to the economic and political revolutions which were maturing in the same period. Professor Fussner singles out five historians—Ralegh, Stow, Camden, Bacon and Selden—as the leaders of the revolution, though Sir Henry Spelman and Sir Robert Cotton's library also have big roles.

But this is much more than a study of the methods of individual historians, valuable and important as this aspect of Professor Fussner's work is. He also surveys the whole historical context which gave rise to the new ideas and methods: the uses of history for religious controversy, and the part played by Selden's great *History of Tithes* as consequence and cause of anti-clericalism; the study of Anglo-Saxon antiquities and the scientific editing of texts; the new availability of public records (for a fee, or by influence in the right quarters) and of private collections (generously put at the disposal of other scholars); the fashion for heraldry, stimulated by the search for ancestors by parvenu gentlemen; the use of antiquarian research by common lawyers and parliamentarian politicians; the civic pride of Londoners, for which Stow's *Survey of London* so magnificently catered; the expanding middle class reading market; the influence of Italian and French models, and of translations into English of the great Greek and Latin historians: all these and many more subjects fall within Professor Fussner's scope.

As political revolution drew nearer in the 17th century, so historical research became increasingly dangerous. The Society of Antiquaries withered away; Cotton's library was closed by the government from 1629 to 1631; Sir Edward Coke's manuscripts were seized whilst he lay on his deathbed. 'Whosoever, in writing a modern history, shall follow truth too near the heels,' observed Sir Walter Ralegh, 'it may haply strike out his teeth.'

It is a tribute to the breadth of Professor Fussner's canvas that no very clear cut conclusions emerge from his study, except that the revolution in historical thought and method was complete by the mid-century, and that it shared techniques and personnel with the scientific revolution, with Bacon as the obvious link between the two. Sir Henry Spelman, whose great contributions to the historical revolution were his definition of feudalism and his analysis of the price revolution, referred to the former as a 'theorem'. The historical, like the scientific revolution, involved an attack on authority and an appeal to experience; a distinction between matters of fact and value judgments; 'an idea of progress began gradually to make its way into historical thought' as into scientific. 'The historical revolution was a part of the whole revolutionary transition of the 17th century.' It had far reaching effects on the future development of English thought.

Like all good books, Professor Fussner's produces disagreement. Not all of us would see in Ralegh quite so medieval a figure as Professor Fussner does; and a single reference to 'the Machiavellian meditations of Harrington' seems inadequate recognition of the man who under the Commonwealth summed up one aspect of the historical revolution. But these minor complaints cannot detract from the delight and stimulus which this book will give. Not least intriguing are some of Professor Fussner's throw-away asides—for instance, his generous recognition of the merits of Buckle as a historian, merits too often ignored by those who have never read him. Or remarks like these:

> The expansion of the market for history cannot be understood without reference to the speculation in monastic lands, the genealogies of the gentry, and the middle class quest for culture and a measure of legal security along with new political power.

> The persistence of error in popular historical accounts [in the early 17th century] may owe more to the censorship than can ever be proved.

> The English Revolution of the 17th century did as much to create feudalism as to destroy it.

There is plenty here for all of us to ponder.

Chapter 7

Republicanism after the Restoration

This article was first published in New Left Review, *May-June 1960. A main reason for reprinting it is to be able to boast of a letter which I received from the great R H Tawney, congratulating me on 'blaspheming against the glorious Restoration of 1660'. Yes, Tawney!*

I

The deeds of the cursed and the conquered, that were wise before their time. (William Morris, *The Pilgrims of Hope*).

Three hundred years ago the first, and so far the only, English Republic came to an end, after 11 years of existence. In those years England, reduced to a state of impotence and contempt under Charles I, had suddenly become a great European power, and had initiated a policy of commercial and colonial expansion which was to last for over 250 years. Yet in May 1660, Charles II returned to England amid general acclamations, and the republican leaders were publicly hanged, disembowelled and quartered. The cynical and witty king observed that it must have been his own fault that he had been abroad so long, for he saw nobody that did not protest he had ever wished for his restoration.

There will be plenty of banalities talked this year about the suitability of monarchy to the British tradition, national character, etc, etc.

It may be worth considering why the English Republic failed, and what happened to the republican tradition after 1660.

The Commonwealth was brought into existence in 1649 by men, very few of whom were theoretical republicans. After Charles I had been defeated in the civil war, first the 'Presbyterian' majority in the Long Parliament, then the 'Independent' Grandees (who commanded the New Model Army, though they were only a minority in the House of Commons) tried to negotiate a settlement with the king. Charles, obsessed with the notion that his function was divine, and that his enemies needed him more than he needed them, played all parties off against one another and instigated a second civil war in 1648. Meanwhile, outside parliament, outside the ranks of the men of property who had hitherto taken it for granted that ruling the country was their exclusive prerogative, a republican party had grown up—the Levellers. They drew their strength from those who had been the driving force in the war against the king—the artisans and small traders of London, the sectarian congregations of the capital, the Home Counties and East Anglia, and from the rank and file of the New Model Army, especially its yeoman cavalry. The Levellers called for abolition of monarchy and House of Lords, and for a wide extension and redistribution of the franchise so as to make parliament representative of the men of small property; and for legal, social and economic reform in the interests of greater equality. In 1647 they came near to capturing control of the army through an army council containing elected representatives of the rank and file.

The fact that Charles had provoked a second civil war greatly strengthened the hands of those who wanted to bring the Man of Blood to justice. To maintain their own position, Cromwell and the 'Independent' leaders opened discussions with the Levellers, envisaging a more democratic constitution. Meanwhile the king was hurried to the block, whilst the Levellers protested that he should be tried not by a military junta but by a court truly representative of the people of England. Once their coup had succeeded the generals believed they could do without the embarrassing support of the Levellers and abandoned all talk of democratic reform. The Leveller leaders were imprisoned, and in May 1649 a revolt of regiments sympathetic to them was suppressed at Burford.

So the English Republic was set up and ruled by men who, like Cromwell, would have preferred constitutional monarchy. After the suppression of the Levellers, the Commonwealth had no popular basis. Its authority depended on the power of the army. which was rapidly purged of democratic elements. The franchise was indeed redistributed (1653), but not widened. There were no legal, social or economic reforms to protect the small men. The government's main achievements—the conquest of Ireland and Scotland, the aggressive commercial foreign policy—were opposed by the democrats. And these policies were very expensive. Together with the maintenance of a vast army for internal police purposes, they necessitated far heavier taxation than any known under the monarchy. The taxes fell in large part on the men of small property.

But the men of large property too disliked this taxation and the army's dictatorship. In order to disband the army they wished to establish a limited monarchy, whether with a Cromwell or a Stuart as sovereign was immaterial, though after Oliver's death in 1658 the inability of his son Richard to control the army drove many of his father's supporters to look to the king over the water. The generals, more and more isolated, were forced (as in 1648-9) to turn to the democratic republicans for support. The men of property refused to pay taxes. The troops were forced to live on free quarter, and so property was further endangered. In the bitterly cold winter of 1659-60 prices soared and public order trembled in the balance. Shops could not be opened safely. The law courts ceased to function, and 'where the law takes not place', a gentleman noted, 'there is no such thing as property'. Levellers reappeared in London. The rank and file of the army began to organise again, as they had done between 1647 and 1649. Arms were distributed to the radical sectaries. Quakers were appointed JPs. 'Many a time have I heard them say', wrote Richard Baxter of the 'rabble' in 1659, 'it will never be a good world while knights and gentlemen make us laws, that are chosen for fear and do but oppress us, and do not know the people's sores. It will never be well with us till we have parliaments of countrymen like ourselves that know our wants.' In that year it seemed for a moment possible that the world might indeed be turned upside down. 'All this stir of the republicans', Baxter thought, aimed 'to make the seed of the Serpent to be the sovereign rulers of the earth': for it was a theological axiom with the well to do that 'the major part are not only likely but certain to be bad.'

Baxter and his kind need not have worried much. For 1659 was not 1649. The Leveller movement had disintegrated. John Lilburne, its chief leader, died in jail in 1657, a Quaker. Other leaders had got on in the world, by land speculation or as professional officers. Others again had abandoned politics, or entered into futile conspiracy, even with royalists. Many of the disillusioned rank and file democrats had emigrated to America, and more were to follow after 1660. (Indeed democratic republican influences are easier to trace in the American colonies after 1660 than in England.) Other former Leveller supporters turned to the wilder forms of sectarianism, such as Fifth Monarchism, in the hope that Christ would himself intervene to bring about the kingdom of heaven on earth, since human political action had failed. The bogey word in 1653-1660 was 'fanatics', not Levellers: sectaries and especially Anabaptists and millenarians now led the democratic movement.

Nevertheless, contemporaries thought the alternatives were clear. A former parliamentarian, Sir George Booth, in 1659 saw 'a mean and schismatical party' threatening 'the nobility and understanding commons'. (Sir George, who helped to beat the mean party, got a peerage in 1660.) A royalist saw 'the Anabaptists and their adherents' opposed by 'those having great estates'. A Scot thought the alternative to a restoration of monarchy was the rule of armed Anabaptists, Fifth Monarchists and Quakers. The physician and biographer of General Monck put 'gentlemen of good estates' against a 'violent junto of robbers and republicans'. 'The essence of a free state', wrote a pamphleteer in 1660, was that the gentry must be 'reduced to the condition of the vulgar'. Many men, Milton thought in April of that year, were prepared to prostitute religion and liberty because they believed that 'nothing but monarchy can restore trade'. The Rev Henry Newcombe was expelled from his living by the restoration government, and his became 'the despised and cheated party'; yet when he looked back in 1662 he felt it had been worth it, since England had been saved from 'a giddy, hot headed, bloody multitude'.

So Charles II was restored not by popular clamour, as the textbooks suggest. He was restored by the men of property; by Monck, the one general who could pay his troops, in close co-operation with the City of London. The rumps that were roasted in the streets of London were paid for by rich citizens, and their money was well spent. Once monarchy was restored, former Cavaliers could help to take arms away from the 'persons of no degree and quality' whom the republicans had armed, and restore them to 'the nobility and principal gentlemen throughout the kingdom'. The writer is Clarendon, Lord Chancellor in the restoration government. 'It is the privilege...the prerogative of the common people of England', he told parliament in 1661, 'to be represented by the greatest and learnedest and wealthiest and wisest persons that can be chosen out of the nation: and the confounding the Commons of England...with the common people of England was the first ingredient into that accursed dose...a Commonwealth.' Clarendon was almost echoing what

Ireton had told the Levellers at Putney 14 years earlier: that the rank and file parliamentary soldiers had fought not for the vote, but to have the benefit of laws made by their betters in parliament. Former parliamentarians and former Cavaliers now spoke the same language against the radicals: and so did Charles II himself, who said, 'Without the safety and dignity of the monarchy, neither religion nor property can be preserved.' 'The restoration', Laski summed it up, 'was a combination of men of property in all classes against a social revolution which they vaguely felt to be threatening.'

II

So the republic collapsed, ingloriously. A white terror followed. The savage legislation of the Clarendon Code expelled opponents of the monarchy from their natural strongholds, the government of the boroughs; and forced underground the sectarian congregations which had formed the revolutionary cells of the preceding two decades. The organisation of petitions by the lower orders was prohibited. The Act of Settlement of 1662 anticipated an Italian Fascist decree which authorised the police to drive back to his native parish any person who lacked visible means of support. A rigid censorship ended the relative freedom of political discussion which had existed in the 1640s and had been regained in 1659-60. Printing, one of Charles II's Secretaries of State declared, was 'a sort of appeal to the people'. For 19 years after 1660 only government newspapers were published legally.

Nor should we underestimate the effectiveness of the deliberate propaganda of the Anglican Church, again restored to a monopoly position. 'People', King Charles the Martyr had observed, 'are governed by the pulpit more than the sword in time of peace'; and the Church of England did its best. When the rebel Duke of Monmouth claimed in 1685 to die a protestant of the Church of England, a divine said to him on the scaffold, 'My Lord, if you be of the Church of England, you must acknowledge the doctrine of non-resistance to be true.' For 25 years every parson in the kingdom had thundered against resistance to the Lord's Anointed. The widely read Anglican *The Whole Duty of Man* told the poor 'to be content with whatever entertainment thou findest here [on earth], knowing thou art upon thy journey to a place of infinite happiness, which will make an abundant amends for all the uneasiness and hardship thou canst suffer in the way.' In 1652 the Digger Gerrard Winstanley had denounced priests who 'tell the poor people that they must be content with their poverty, and that they shall have their heaven hereafter'. Why, Winstanley had asked, 'may not we have our heaven here (that is, a comfortable livelihood in the earth), and heaven hereafter too?' One sees the advantage to the rich of the restoration of ecclesiastical censorship in 1660.

We can also perhaps understand the disgust and disillusion with which many of the democrats withdrew from a political struggle in which they felt they had been betrayed. After 1660 most of the sects decided that Christ's kingdom was not of this world and had enough to do to maintain a precarious underground existence, without indulging in political activity which would have exposed them to savage government reprisals. The hitherto bellicose Quakers issued their first pacifist declaration in January 1661, after the failure of a Fifth Monarchist revolt. Even this declaration was directed against acceptance of military service for Charles II, and was part of a campaign of passive resistance. The Quakers were still politically active in the 1670s, when William Penn was election agent for the republican Algernon Sidney. Only after the aristocratic Whigs had let them down in 1681 and 1685 did the Quakers turn to emigration, a refuge which they had previously condemned. Much of the Leveller tradition of equality and democracy was inherited and handed on by the radical sects, who exhibited magnificent courage in resisting persecution under Charles II and James II. But—in England if not in Scotland—it was for the most part a passive resistance. Bunyan still takes as his symbol of the common man a man with a burden on his back. But the burden falls off only in the presence of the cross, and Christian had left even his wife and children behind when he started on his pilgrimage. Some at least of those with whom Bunyan had served in the parliamentarian armies had hoped to relieve other men of their burdens, as well as themselves: and on earth too. By the time dissent won toleration in 1689 it had ceased to be politically dangerous. Those who benefited by the Toleration Act were sober, respectable, industrious citizens, narrow, sectarian and unpolitical in their outlook. All but the most hypocritical 'occasional conformists' among them continued to be excluded from political life and from the universities by the Anglican tests. So revolutionary Puritanism sank into nonconformity.

III

Yet though the republic collapsed in 1660, it had left its mark on men's minds. Charles II might date his reign from 30 January 1649, and lawyers might speak of the years between 1649 and 1660 as 'the interregnum' . But they could not be forgotten. They had shown that government could be successfully carried on without king or House of Lords or bishops. Moreover, although the men who ruled 'the Commonwealth were not theoretical republican', the Levellers, Milton and Harrington were: and their writings had been widely disseminated and discussed. There had been far more freedom of discussion in the 1640s and 1650s, and far more real popular participation in such discussion, at least in London, than ever before and ever again until the 19th century. Republicanism by 1660 was by no means a mere academic speculation. Rude and vigorous opposition to monarchy was expressed in an unmistakably popular idiom. 'A pox on all kings', said a London lady in 1662; 'she did not give a turd for never a king in England, for she never did lie with any.' A glazier of Wapping, two years earlier, 'would run his knife into [the king] to kill him'. He would gladly spend five shillings to celebrate Charles's execution: 'he did not care if he were the hangman himself.' Yorkshire yeomen in the early 1660s said they 'lived as well when there was no king', and hoped to do so again. 'Cromwell and Ireton were as good as the king.' 'All is traitors that do fight for the king.' A Surrey man 'hoped ere long to trample in the king's and bishops' blood.' Very many similar remarks have survived, made by those ordinary people who, according to the textbooks, were delighted to see Charles II's back. A constable who had helped to hand some regicides over for execution in 1660 found that in consequence he had 'quite lost his trade among the factious people of Southwark'.

Men calling themselves Levellers were in revolt in Worcestershire in 1670, and men so called by their enemies figured frequently as bogies in political speeches and sermons. There were continuous plots—Venner's rising in London and many other conspiracies in 1661: Tonge's Plot in 1662, Yorkshire Plots in 1663 and 1665, the Pentland Rising in Scotland in 1666 (led by an old parliamentarian officer), and supporting movements in England. Some of these conspiracies were no doubt fomented by agents provocateurs, freely used at this period; and the government for its own purposes certainly made the most of the danger of revolution. But the plots witness to the existence of a great deal of discontent. In 1668-9 the royal ministers Buckingham and Shaftesbury were said to be leading the old Commonwealth faction, and the Duke of Buckingham declared himself a republican. There was an organised illegal printing press, and continuous contacts were maintained between the underground opposition to Charles II and the exiles in Holland. Between 1678 and 1681, in the excitement of the Popish Plot, the Leveller sea-green colours reappeared in the streets of London: the Whig Green Ribbon Club took its name from them. The Rye House Plot of 1683 centred on a house owned by the former Leveller Richard Rumbold, famous for his dying words on the scaffold in 1685: 'I am sure there was no man marked of God above another: for none comes into the world with a saddle on his back, neither any booted and spurred to ride him.' (The sentence was quoted, whether consciously or not, by Thomas Jefferson a few days before his death in 1826. It was in fact a Leveller commonplace.) Finally in 1685 Argyll's invasion of Scotland and Monmouth's of south western England were both accompanied by many ex-Levellers and republicans. and won wide support among the common people. Their defeat marked the end of an epoch.

Throughout the years from 1647 to 1685 the conflict continued between aristocratic and democratic republicans. We have seen how the two parted company after 1649. In 1660 even Milton, convinced republican though he was, thought it was necessary 'to well qualify and refine elections: not committing all to the noise and shouting of a rude multitude', but rather to a perpetual oligarchy: that this was the 'ready and easy way to establish a free commonwealth'. Even Marvell, toughest of republicans under Charles II, had opposed the military leaders who tried to set up a republic in 1659. He was probably right to doubt their sincerity: yet it was these divisions that made the restoration possible. It is hardly a coincidence that two of the most prominent republicans were a Duke and an Earl, Buckingham and Rochester. There is no doubt about the strength of these men's beliefs. Under Charles II Marvell wrote:

> England rejoice, thy redemption draws nigh
> Thy oppression together with kingship shall die.
> A commonwealth, a commonwealth we proclaim to the nation,
> The gods have repented the King's restoration.

Rochester asked:

> What can there be in kings divine?
> The most are wolves, goats, sheep or swine...
> Then farewell sacred majesty,
> Let's pull all brutish tyrants down:
> Where men are born and still live free.
> Here every head doth wear a crown.

> I hate all monarchs and the thrones they sit on.

From the Hector of France [Louis XlV]
to the cully of Britain [Charles ll].

Yet such men, for all their courageous convictions, had no confidence in the democratic forces. Throughout Charles II's reign, although the two wings of the republicans had to co-operate, there was
latent conflict between them. During the Popish Plot, Shaftesbury's
use of the London populace lost him much support among the propertied Whigs. Even so he drew back when Charles II called his bluff
in 1681, and the apparently united Whig party collapsed. In 1685
Monmouth's revolt was the last fling of the democratic cause, to which
the weavers and dissenters of the south western counties rallied, and
small traders like Daniel Defoe rode down from London to add their
support.

But the Whig gentry held aloof, and Monmouth was persuaded by
his few aristocratic supporters to claim the crown in the hope of establishing his non-republican respectability. Disillusion with Monmouth, who grovelled to James II in a vain attempt to save his life, and
Jeffreys' ferocious Bloody Assizes so weakened popular republicanism
that when James's folly united the propertied classes against him, the
way seemed clear for William of Orange and the aristocratic Whigs.
Yet even at the end of 1687 Gilbert Burnet noted that 'a rebellion of
which he [William] should not retain the command would certainly
establish a commonwealth'. Fortunately for them, the men of property
invited William in time, and he brought a large professional army
with him; so James could be hustled off the throne without danger of
popular revolt. When Edmund Ludlow returned from his 29 years of
exile, thinking the day of the Good Old Cause had dawned at last, he
was promptly whisked out of the country at the request of the House
of Commons. In Macaulay's words, William 'ordered the magistrates
to act with vigour against all unlawful assemblies. Nothing in the history of our revolution is more deserving of admiration and of imitation than the manner in which the two parties in the Convention
[parliament], at the very moment at which their disputes ran highest,
joined like one man to resist the dictation of the mob of the capital.'
This—written in 1848—makes the point that 'our revolution' was
opposed to and forestalled that of lower class republicans. Henceforth
monarchy was something very different from what it had been, since
now it was subordinated to the laws voted by the representatives of the
men of big property—1685 was the last revolt of the men of small
property.

IV

The men of small property: here we have the clue to their failure. As capitalism developed, more and more peasants and artisans were to lose their economic independence. This process was very slow and long drawn out; but the small proprietors were at no stage a secure foundation on which to build a revolutionary party. Even in the 17th century they may not have formed a majority of Englishmen. Even the Levellers would have excluded paupers and wage labourers from the franchise: and Gregory King's table of 1636 suggests that these may have amounted to half the population. There was sense in their exclusion, since men wholly dependent on their social superiors for livelihood could not vote freely by show of hands. (The republican Harrington's much derided schemes for voting by dropping balls into urns were intended to solve the problem of secret voting for a largely illiterate population.) Yet by refusing the vote to half of their countrymen, the Levellers placed themselves in a position different only in degree from that of the Grandee Independents. They spoke in the name of 'the people', but they meant only some of the people. When the Diggers (who called themselves True Levellers) advocated the abolition of private property in the name of the unpropertied, the Leveller leaders had sharply disavowed them. So in a sense they justified the sleight of hand by which Locke in 1690 spoke of 'the people' when he meant the men of big property. He had a big blind spot, the Leveller a little blind spot.

Yet in another sense the Levellers were right in their day and generation. The Diggers were a nine days wonder: they did not succeed in organising the unpropertied. Of those entirely dependent on wages Mr Ogg rightly says that 'neither contemporary nor modern economists can explain how they lived'. Baxter's poor husbandmen in 1691 were 'usually so poor that they cannot have time to read a chapter in the Bible or to pray in their families. They come in weary from their labour, so that they are fitter to sleep than to read or pray.' The whole circumstances of their existence made such men incapable of political understanding and therefore of any political action except merely negative rioting. It needed another century and a half of capitalist development (and of painful struggles for trade union organisation, the first evidence for which dates from the later 17th century), before the urban poor were transformed into a politically effective working class movement.

So we should see the conflict between aristocratic and democratic republicans in the 17th century as a tragedy on both sides—a tragedy not without its similarities to those which have been enacted in eastern Europe in our own days. The Levellers spoke in the name of a people who would have disavowed them. When they put forward proposals for a limited widening of the franchise, their enemies distorted this into a demand for full manhood suffrage. Given the pressure of landlords and parsons on the poor and illiterate and ignorant, it could not unreasonably be argued that manhood suffrage would lead to a restoration of the monarchy, and that any significant extension was a gamble. The aristocratic republicans despaired of the people. Yet what was their alternative? Military dictatorship, which Hugh Peter had hoped to use 'to teach peasants to understand liberty', was used by the generals to further their own ambitions. After 1660, and still more after 1688, the aristocratic republicans had no real programme, only an attitude. They felt that the flummery of monarchy was an insult to human dignity; but in society as then constituted only a minority of the population was in a position to exercise free political choice; and most of this minority wanted a king to help to keep the lower orders in their place.

The most remarkable analysis of the reasons for the failure of the 17th century popular movement was made in a letter written to Milton in 1659:

> You complain of the non-progressency of the nation, and of its retrograde motion of late, in liberty and spiritual truths. It is much to be bewailed, but yet let us pity human frailty. When those who had made deep protestations of their zeal for our liberty...being instated in power shall betray the good thing committed to them...and, by that power which we gave them to win us liberty, hold us fast in chains; what can we poor people do?... Besides whilst people are not free but straitened in accommodations for life, their spirits will be dejected and servile... There should be an improving of our native commodities, as our manufactures, our fishery, our fens, forests and commons, and our trade at sea, etc, which would give the body of the nation a comfortable subsistence.

But that was to look far ahead into the capitalist epoch. The years between the defeat of the Good Old Cause and the rise of the labour movement are the age of the 'mob'. (The word does not occur before 1688.) Between 1660 and 1688 the London populace was Whig and anti-papist; after 1688 mobs could sometimes be used by Tories and even Jacobites, because the establishment was now Whig. It is significant that the weavers of Southwark, old style craftsmen and dissenters almost to a man, opposed the church and king mobs in 1709. Outside London, in the early 18th century, the Jacobites found support from the Derbyshire miners (whose ancestors had been Levellers in 1649), and from the weavers of the Monmouth area who had not lifted a finger for William of Orange in 1688. Until the rise of true radicalism in the late 18th century, 'Tory democracy' was an uneasy and wholly negative alliance of the two defeated classes of the 17th century—the backwoods gentry and the lowest urban classes—against their bourgeois and aristocratic rulers.

So by 1685 democratic republicanism, the democracy of the small proprietors, was dead; in 1688 aristocratic republicanism, the republicanism of the men of big property, had achieved most of its aims within the framework of limited monarchy. Aristocratic republicanism lived on in the early 18th century rather as an academic speculation, a philosophical attitude, than as a political creed. The Calves Head Club celebrated the anniversary of Charles I's execution 'in scandalous and opprobrious feasting and jesting'. But it is significant that a calves head dinner on that day in 1728 (in Oxford, of all revolutionary centres!) shocked Whigs no less than Tories, since the Hanoverian king was now himself a Whig. Six years later the London Club came to an end when its members were rabbled.

Aristocratic republicanism has recently been studied by Professor Caroline Robbins in her book, *The 18th Century Commonwealthman* (though she does not herself distinguish adequately between democratic and aristocratic republicans). She shows how the torch was handed on from the 17th century republicans by men like William Molyneux, Robert Molesworth, Walter Moyle, John Trenchard, John Toland the deist, to the Founding Fathers of the American Constitution, themselves republicans without much use for democracy, and to Price and Priestley.

The most important figure in the tradition was Mrs Catherine Macaulay, who from the 1760s published her very popular *History of England* in the 17th century, which revived memories of the 17th century revolutionaries just when the Wilkesite agitation was reviving popular radicalism. Henceforth the appeal to 17th century example was common form among the radicals. Mrs Macaulay's brother, Alderman Sawbridge, was Wilkes's right hand man in the City; she herself was actively involved in radical politics in England, and intimately associated with republican leaders in America and France. In the 17th century the leading examples of successful republics—Venice, the Netherlands—had been burgher oligarchies; in the 18th century the

American and French revolutions offered models of more democratic republics. Tom Paine preached a republicanism of the common man appropriate to this new atmosphere. It made the republicanism of the aristocratic Commonwealthsmen an armchair anachronism. Paine's works were eagerly read by those plebeians to whom the aristocratic republicans had never cared or dared to appeal. The way lay forward through the Corresponding Societies of the 1790s on to Chartism and the working class movement, in which at first republicanism was widespread. The Chartist Bronterre O'Brien pronounced the working class's epitaph on the aristocratic republicanism of the 17th and 18th centuries:

> Even the establishment of our commonwealth after the death of Charles I was a mere political revolution. It gave parliamentary privilege a temporary triumph over royal prerogative. It enabled a few thousand landowners to disenthral themselves from the burdens of feudal services, and to throw upon the people at large the expenses of maintaining the government... For the millions it did nothing.

It is not the job of the present article to discuss why the republicanism of its early days was abandoned by the labour movement in England. Let us rather recall that what survived of the popular republican tradition in England in the difficult years after 1660 was handed on in discussions in coffee houses, which emerged as centres of seditious activity as the non-conformist congregations subsided into sectarian isolation and political inactivity.

Chapter 8

Plebeian irreligion in 17th century England

This paper was given at a conference and first published in Studien über die Revolution, *Akademie-Verlag, Berlin, 1969.*

I

When we compare or contrast the English Revolution of the 17th century with the French or Russian revolutions, one point which we must bear in mind is that the French revolutionaries had English experience to draw on, and the Russian revolutionaries had French experience as well. But the English Revolution had no comparable predecessors. The 16th century Revolt of the Netherlands anticipated it in some respects: but that was a revolt against alien domination, and a revolt led by Protestants against a regime trying forcibly to maintain Catholic uniformity. Both these features were lacking in England. The English Revolution in consequence lacked a revolutionary ideology: there was no Jean Jacques Rousseau or Karl Marx. There were of course many intellectual, religious and political discontents: but before 1642 they had not crystallised into the form of a revolutionary theory or even an idea that fundamental change might be required. The leaders of parliament in the early 1640s believed themselves to be the true conservatives and traditionalists. They wanted to return to the days of Good Queen Bess, if not further back.

So whereas the trinities of the later revolutions—liberty, equality, fraternity; peace, bread and land—demanded something *new*, something to be fought for and achieved *in the future*, the trinity of the English revolutionaries—religion, liberty and property—was intended to defend what already existed, or was believed to exist. Get rid of the doctrinal innovations of Laud, and the true Protestant religion would be safe: get rid of the arbitrary practices of the 11 years personal rule, and liberty and property would be safe. All the early parliamentarian theories were defensive: in place of a theory of revolution they believed that all ills were due to the king's evil councillors, to papists and Arminians in high places. Any theories which probed deeper simply looked further back. But the further back the golden age is placed, the more uncertain the evidence about it becomes: the greater the possibility of disagreement. In fact the really backward looking theory becomes forward looking, creatively revolutionary. The appeal to the good old days of the free Anglo Saxons meant something very different to Levellers and Diggers from what it had meant for Sir Edward Coke[1]; Presbyterians and Quakers drew diverse lessons from the practice of the primitive church.

So when, in the early 1640s, men found themselves unexpectedly and unwillingly facing a revolutionary situation, a situation which demanded new thinking, they were ill equipped for the task. They had to improvise. What lay to hand was the Bible, which for a century had been available in English translation, and which men had been encouraged to study as the source of all wisdom. There are dangerous doctrines in the Bible: denunciations of the rich by Old Testament prophets, suggestions of human equality in the New Testament. The Lutheran doctrine of the priesthood of all believers contains explosive possibilities, for there was no certain means of identifying visible saints. During the post-reformation century social stability had been safeguarded against the logic of Protestant Christianity by a hierarchy of church courts, by ecclesiastical control of the censorship and education, and by the doctrine of the sinfulness of the mass of mankind. In the 1640s the institutional restraints collapsed with the fall of bishops, and the attempt to build up a Presbyterian disciplinary system in their place failed almost as totally. Only sin remained. But religious toleration and the lack of an effective ecclesiastical censorship allowed wholly unorthodox groups claiming to be visible saints to propagate their subversive ideas; even the fundamental dogma of the sinfulness of the majority of men and women could be challenged. Levellers demanded a wide extension of the suffrage, re-

1   I have discussed this at length in 'The Norman Yoke', in my *Puritanism and Revolution* (1958), pp50-122.

gardless of whether 'the multitude' was godly or ungodly; Ranters and Antinomians were led by the spirit to reject many traditional moral restraints; Quakers saw a spark of the divine in all men, and rejected outward forms of social subordination in the name of Christian equality; Diggers demanded heaven for the poor on earth now. No wonder all conservatives rallied to oppose toleration.

So though at first sight there seems to be nothing comparable in the English Revolution to the dechristianisation of the French Revolution or the militant atheism of the Bolsheviks, and it would be difficult to find a 17th century Englishman who advocated atheism in intellectual terms, the difference is more apparent than real. The critique of the established church made by many of the 17th century sectaries became so radically anti-clerical as to be virtually secularist in content. Almost all the sects (Baptists, Quakers, Muggletonians, many Congregationalists) rejected the whole concept of a state church, together with the tithes which paid for its ministers, and the patronage system which ensured that its clergy were appointed by the ruling class.[2] They insisted that ministers should be elected by the congregation and paid by the voluntary contributions of its members; many of them denied the need for a separate clergy at all, and would have had a gifted layman preach on Sunday whilst labouring with his hands the other six days of the week. They advocated toleration for all Protestant sects, rejecting ecclesiastical censorship and all forms of ecclesiastical jurisdiction in favour of a congregational discipline with no coercive sanction behind it. They attached little importance to many of the traditional sacraments of the church. If a programme of this sort had succeeded it would have destroyed the national church, leaving each congregation responsible for its own affairs with only the loosest contact between congregations: the church would no longer have been able to mould opinion in a single pattern, to punish 'sin' or proscribe 'heresy'. There would have been no control over the thinking of the middle and lower classes—which, as we shall see, contained elements of materialist scepticism. When, under the Protectorate of Oliver Cromwell, steps were taken to rebuild a national church, its clergy became Public Enemy Number One for the radicals. 'As for these men called ministers in this nation', declared the Quaker Edward Burroughs, 'the way of their setting up and sending forth, and the way of

---

2   This is discussed at length in my *Economic Problems of the Church from Archbishop Whitgift to the Long Parliament* (1956); and by M James, 'The Political Importance of the Tithes Controversy in the English Revolution, 1640-60', *History XXVI* (1941), pp1-18.

their maintenance...they are the greatest and most woeful oppression in the nation... The earth is oppressed by them, the inhabitants groan under them..."[3]

It is the object of this article to consider in its historical perspective the anti-clericalism and irreligion of the lower social groups during the English Revolution.

II

We need trace plebeian anti-clericalism and irreligion no further back than the late 15th and early 16th century, though no doubt it existed much earlier. Professor A G Dickens has shown how Lollard influence survived in a popular materialist scepticism which makes one 'feel appreciably nearer to the age of Voltaire than is normal in the 16th century'.[4] A carpenter in 1491 denied transsubstantiation, baptism, confession and damnation for sin; in 1512 a Wakefield man said 'that if a calf were upon the altar I would rather worship that than the...holy sacrament... The date was past that God determined him to be in form of bread'.[5] Priests, an earlier Lollard had declared, were worse than Judas, who sold Christ for 30 pence, whilst priests sold masses for 1/2d.[6] The commons, said another, 'would never be well till they had stricken off all the priests' heads.' 'There was a saying in the country', a north Yorkshireman pleaded in 1542, 'that a man might lift up his heart and confess himself to God Almighty, and needed not to be confessed at a priest'. A shearman of Dewsbury elaborated on this point: he would not confess his offences with a woman to a priest, 'for the priest would be as ready within two or three days after to use her as he'.[7]

All the evidence about such men comes from their enemies in the church courts: many similar examples could be given from those who in the later 16th century were loosely called Anabaptists and Familists.[8] Londoners in Mary's reign referred to the consecrated bread in the sacrament as 'Jack-in-the-box'.[9] Dr Collinson has shown that in many Elizabethan parishes the minister was pushed on by his congregation

---

3   E Burroughs, *A Message to the Present Rulers of England* (1659), in *The Memorable Works of a son of Thunder and Consolation* (1672), pp515-516; cf S Fisher, *The Rusticks Alarm to the Rabbies* (1660), in *The Testimony of Truth Exalted* (1679).

4   A G Dickens, *Lollards and Protestants in the Diocese of York, 1509-1558* (1959), p13.

5   Ibid, pp9, 17.

6   I A F Thomson, *The Later Lollards* (1965), p247. The jibe was common: see A G Dickens, op cit, p18.

7   A G Dickens, op cit, pp12,48.

8   See C Burrage, *The Early Engish Dissenters*, 2 vols (1912), passim.

to reject the ceremonies and vestments of the state church.[10] For the breach with Rome and especially the radical measures of Edward VI's reign had opened up hopes of a continuing reformation which would totally overthrow the coercive machinery of the state church. The Elizabethan settlement bitterly disappointed such hopes that a Protestant church would differ from popery in the power which it allowed to bishops and clergy. The episcopal hierarchy came to be seen as the main obstacle to radical reform. Puritan attacks on this hierarchy are sometimes dismissed as propagandist exaggerations, though whenever we can check them they prove surprisingly reliable. But the most impressive evidence for the unpopularity of bishops and clergy comes not from their opponents but from the pens of their defenders. Laymen 'hate priests', Archbishop Cranmer and Thomas Becon agreed.[11] In November 1547 a royal proclamation had to be issued against 'insolence and evil demeanour towards priests, as reviling, tossing of them, taking violently their caps and tippets from them'.[12] Roger Hutchinson in Edward VI's reign denounced hatred of the clergy as an Anabaptistical opinion, but agreed that it 'doth infect many'.[13]

The opening words of Bishop Thomas Cooper's *Admonition to the People of England* (1589) speak of:

> the loathsome contempt, hatred and disdain that the most part of men in these days bear...toward the ministers of the Church of God... He who can most bitterly inveigh against bishops and preachers, that can most boldly blaze their discredits, that can most uncharitably slander their lives and doings, thinketh of himself, and is esteemed of others, as the most zealous and earnest furtherer of the Gospel... The whole state ecclesiastical...is grown into hatred and contempt, and all inferior subjects disdain in any point to be ruled by them... God hath touched our bishops and preachers with this scourge of ignominy and reproach for their slackness and negligence in their office... The people...have conceived an heathenish contempt of religion and a disdainful loathing of the ministers thereof.[14]

Other bishops confirmed this remarkable confession. 'The minis-

9   H F M Prescott, *Mary Tudor* (1952), p108.
10   P Collinson, *The Elizabethan Puritan Movement* (1967), pp92-97.
11   T Cranmer, *Miscellaneous Writings and Letters* (Parker Society, 1846), p230; T Becon, *Early Works* (Parker Soc, 1843), p255.
12   P L Hughes and J F Larkin (eds), *Tudor Royal Proclamations*, I (1485-1553) (Yale UP, 1964), p407.
13   R Hutchinson, *Works* (Parker Soc, 1842), p310.

ters of the word', wrote Archbishop Sandys, 'the messengers of Christ...are esteemed *tamquam excrementa mundi*'; 'our estimation is little, our authority is less: so that we are become contemptible in the eyes of the basest sort of people'.[15]

'If we maintain things that are established', complained the judicious Hooker, 'we have...to strive with a number of heavy prejudices deeply rooted in the hearts of men, who think that herein we serve the time and speak in favour of the present state because thereby we either hold or seek preferment'.[16] Or as the gentle Isaac Walton said of Elizabeth's reign, looking back from the revolutionary decade, 'The common people became so fanatic as to believe the bishops to be Antichrist'.[17] We recall the oatmeal maker who, on trial before the High Commission in April 1630, said that he would never take off his hat to bishops. 'But you will to Privy Councillors', he was urged. 'Then as you are Privy Councillors', quoth he, 'I put off my hat; but as you are the rags of the Beast, I put it on again'.[18] Joan Hoby of Colnbrook, Buckinghamshire, said four years later 'that she did not care a pin nor a fart for my Lord's Grace of Canterbury...and she did hope that she should live to see him hanged'.[19] (Laud was in fact executed 11 years later, but we do not know whether Joan Hoby was still alive then).

Further evidence of the unpopularity of the whole church establishment is to be found in the popular inconoclasm which broke out whenever opportunity offered: in the late 1630s and 1640s altar rails were pulled down, altars desecrated, statues on tombs destroyed. 'Is it well done of our soldiers', asked *The Souldiers Catechisme* of 1644, 'to break down crosses and images where they meet with any?' The answer was, rather shamefacedly, 'I confess that nothing ought to be done in a tumultous manner. But seeing God hath put the sword of reformation into the soldiers' hand, I think it is not amiss that they should cancel and demolish those monuments of superstition and

---

14 T Cooper, *An Admonition to the People of England* (E Arber (ed), 1895), pp9, 102-103, 139, 175; cf pp118-119, 144-145, 148, 159.

15 Quoted by L Stone, *The Crisis of the Aristocracy, 1558-1641* (1965), p406; Collinson, op cit, p147.

16 R Hooker, *Of the Laws of Ecclesiastical Polity* (Everyman edn), I, p148.

17 I Walton, *The Life of Mr Richard Hooker* (1655), in *Lives* (World's Classics), p185. Thomas Brightman in 1615 confirmed that hostility to the hierarchy 'is now favoured much of the people and multitude' (*The Revelation of St John Illustrated*, 4th ed, 1644, p139).

18 See examples quoted by F W X Fincham, 'Notes from the Ecclesiastical Court Records at Somerset House', *Transactions of the Royal Historical Society*, 4th Series, pp136-138.

19 *Lambeth MS 943*, f 721.

idolatry, especially seeing the magistrate and the minister that should have done it formerly neglected it'.[20]

In 1641 there were 900 petitions against allegedly 'scandalous' ministers, one from every ten parishes in the land. Since they came mainly from the south and east, the proportion in those areas is far higher. 'If the meanest and most vicious parishioner they had could be brought to prefer a petition to the House of Commons against his minister', Clarendon tells us, the latter 'was sure to be prosecuted as a scandalous minister'.[21] It was 'the very dregs and scum of every parish' who petitioned against 'the orthodox clergy', a royalist pamphlet of 1643 declared.[22] In 1642 we find soldiers plundering *all* ministers, royalist and parliamentarian, and there was much rabbling of the royalist clergy. In 1641, 'when the glad tidings were brought to Chelmsford that episcopacy was voted down by the House of Commons, all usual expressions of an exulting joy were used', and 'bonfires were kindled in every street'.[23] Bishop Warner tells us that 'the general opinion and carriage of the people (especially near London at that time) was such to bishops that it was not easy to pass by them without reproach, yea (often) not without danger of their persons'. This was written in 1646, to explain his retreat from Rochester at the beginning of the civil war.[24] There is a similar report from Cambridge, where the clerical Fellows of Colleges 'became so hated by the weaker sort of the deceived people that a scholar could have small security from being stoned or affronted as he walked the streets'.[25] 'So generally peevish and fanaticised were the people'—it is London this time—'that not any particular discontent or personal quarrel with any private clergyman but "These bishops, these parsons".' And the writer explains this to him horrifying state of affairs: 'episcopal government in England being indeed the king's spiritual militia, and the most powerful, as commanding the consciences of subjects'.[26]

Finally, a real tear jerker from London: 'If any of the clergy, worn out with old age and former calamities, made use of a staff to support his aged weak limbs as he walked along the streets, he was pointed at as one that through drunkenness was not able to govern his steps. If

20 *The Souldiers Catechisme* (1644), pp20-21.
21 Edward, Earl of Clarendon, *The History of the Rebellion* (1888), I, p449.
22 A Letter from *Mercurius Civicus to Mercurius Rusticus* (1643) in *Somer's Tracts* (1748-51), V, p415; cf J Nalson, *An Impartial Collection* (1682), II, p760.
23 [B Ryves], *Angliae Ruina* (1647) p26.
24 E L Warner, *The Life of John Warner, Bishop of Rochester* (1901), p33.
25 [Anon], *Querela Cantabrigiensis* (1646), p13.
26 [W Chestlin], *Persecutio Undecima* (1681), pp7, 4. First published 1648.

he looked earnestly round about him with his dim eyes to find out any place he was to go in the City, some insolent scoffer would thus reflect upon him: "that person has devoured five fat livings, and see with what prying eyes he is seeking after a sixth".[27] Such anecdotes tell us rather more than their authors intended. 'The people complain of their ministers, that they are dumb dogs, greedy dogs, which can never have enough', the Rev Edmund Calamy told the House of Commons in 1642.[28] They also complained that university educated divines tended to be members of the ruling class, 'full of all outward necessaries'.[29] Indeed, one at least of the critics of the radicals suggested that their incitement to refuse the payment of tithes 'is one of the chiefest inducements that the…sectaries have to encourage the silly people and to poison them with their other errors'.[30]

Levellers, Diggers and Fifth Monarchists all denounced tithes. 'The sheep of Christ', said Winstanley expressively, 'shall never fare well so long as the wolf or Red Dragon pays the shepherd their wages'.[31] The sects turned to 'mechanick preachers' or itinerants financed by the voluntary contributions of the faithful. 'By the end of the first revolutionary decade', Mr Maclear observed, 'a militant anti-clericalism was taken as axiomatic in the popular outlook'.[32]

One other contributory factor which I have discussed elsewhere is to be found in the scientific and mathematical ideas which in London (more than in any European city, Amsterdam perhaps excepted) led to distrust of authority and scepticism about received ideas. 'There is no opinion so prodigious and strange', wrote a Scot in 1614, 'but was either invented or supported in England.' Archdeacon Barlow in 1626 complained that artisans preferred reason and experiment before the literal words of the Bible, and contrasted 'mechanical tradesmen' who favoured the new science with 'men of learning' who disliked it.[33]

27 P Barwick, *Life of Dr John Barwick* (abridged and edited by G F Barwick, 1903), p177. Cf *Persecutio Undecima*, p6.
28 E Calamy, *Englands Looking-glasse* (1642), p59.
29 E How, *The Sufficiency of the Spirit's Teaching* (8th edn, 1792), p51, and passim. First published in the Netherlands, 1639.
30 E Pagitt, *Heresiography* (5th edn, 1654), p146.
31 G Winstanley, *A New-Yeers Gift for the Parliament and Armie* (1650), p39, in: G H Sabine, *The Works of Gerrard Winstanley* (Cornell UP, 1941), p387.
32 J F Maclear, 'Popular Anticlericalism in the Puritan Revolution', *Journal of the History of Ideas*, XVII, p452. This is a useful pioneering article. Cf the same author's 'The Making of the Lay Tradition', *Journal of Religion* XXXIII.
33 Quoted in my *Intellectual Origins of the English Revolution*, pp65-66.

III

So it is hardly surprising that the breakdown of censorship and the establishment of effective religious toleration let loose a flood of speculation that hitherto had only been muttered in secret. 'Religion is now become the common discourse and tabletalk in every tavern and alehouse', said a pamphlet of 1641.[34] In England as in Switzerland, 'the lower sort of people being bred in an ancient hatred against superiors' greedily embraced the doctrines of Anabaptism.[35] Anabaptists, William Gouge had said in 1626, 'teach that all are alike and that there is no difference betwixt masters and servants'.[36] The lower we go in the social scale, Professor Jordan believes, the more tolerance we find — and the more bitter distrust of clerical leadership.

The attempt in the 1640s to replace church courts by a Presbyterian disciplinary system, 'to bring us again into Egyptian bondage to keep up and maintain the oppression of tithes', the union of the clergy to 'promote and carry on their Scottish interest'[37]— all this led to fierce hostility against what Lilburne called 'the devil and the clergy his agents',[38] and a later pamphlet called 'the black guard of Satan'.[39] 'Without a powerful compulsive presbytery in the church', reflected the Leveller Overton in 1646, 'a compulsive mastership or aristocratical government over the people in the state could never long be maintained'.[40] 'The necks of the people of the world', thought the Rev William Dell in 1653, 'have never endured so grievous a yoke from any tyrants as from the doctrine and domination of the clergy'.[41] The demand for separation of church and state was a demand for the subordination of the clergy, for an end to their coercive authority. 'Under pretence of religion', Thomas Hobbes wrote in 1651, 'the lower sort of citizens...do challenge [liberty] to themselves'.[42]

The Ranters made this claim specifically on behalf of the poor God, 'that mighty Leveller', intended to cut down 'all men and women that were higher than the middle sort', and to raise up 'those that were

34 [Anon], *Religions Enemies* (1641) p6. Attributed to John Taylor, the Water-Poet.
35 R Blome, *The Fanatick History* (1660), p5.
36 W Gouge, *Of Domesticall Duties* (1626), pp331-332.
37 W K Jordan, *The Development of Religious Toleration in England* (1932-40), IV, pp321,330.
38 J Lilburne, *London's Liberty in Chains* (1646), p42.
39 [Anon], *Light Shining in Buckinghamshire* (1648), p13, in G H Sabine, op cit, p622.
40 R Overton, *A Remonstrance of Many Thousand Citizens* (1646), p12, in *Tracts on Liberty in the Puritan Revolution, 1638-47*, W Haller (ed) (Columbia UP, 1933), III, p362.
41 W Dell, *Several Sermons and Discourses* (1709), p638.
42 T Hobbes, *Philosophical Rudiments* (1651) in *English Works* (Sir W Molesworth (ed), 1839-45), II, p79.

lower than the middle sort'. George Foster believed God would establish equality, 'the low and poor equal with the rich'.[43] Joseph Salmon wished to expedite this process by inciting the army to destroy gentry and nobility.[44] 'Howl, howl, ye nobles', cried Abiezer Coppe; 'howl ye rich men… Bow before those poor, nasty, lousy, ragged wretches', and let them go free. For God, the real Leveller, would reduce all men to equality.[45] Gerrard Winstanley too claimed Jesus Christ as the Head Leveller.[46] Others revived the old Taborite doctrine that Christ would come as a robber to the last judgment.[47] 'Thou hast many bags of money', Coppe warned the rich man, 'and behold now I (the Lord) come as a thief in the night, with my sword drawn in my hand, and like a thief as I am I say "Deliver your purse, deliver sirrah! Deliver or I'll cut thy throat".'[48] This was not the God of the propertied class

Ideas previously contraband were now publicly proclaimed, verbally or in print. In 1644 Jane Stratton of Southwark said that Christ was a bastard. John Hart claimed to have been made by the Earl of Essex and saved by Sir William Waller.[49]

The church is a spiritual whorehouse, declared Roger Crab; priests are pimps and panders.[50] There was no such place as hell, outside a man's conscience, said Thomas Tany, Gerrard Winstanley, Ludowick Muggleton and many others. The doctrine was not new: it goes back to the Waldensians and further. Queen Elizabeth in 1584 had accused the Puritans of propagating it,[51] and Marlowe, Kyd and Ralegh had come under suspicion in 1593. But now it was being put to new uses. Priests, said Winstanley, 'lay claim to heaven after they are dead, and yet they require their heaven in this world too, and grumble mightily against the people that will not give them a large temporal maintenance. And yet they tell poor people that they must be content with their poverty, and they shall have their heaven hereafter. But why may not we have our heaven here (that is, a comfortable livelihood in the earth) and heaven hereafter too, as

43 G Foster, *The Pouring Forth of the Seventh and Last Viall* (1650), Sig A3; *The Sounding of the Last Trumpet* (1650), pp17, 42.
44 J Salmon, *A Rout, A Rout* (1649), p4.
45 A Coppe, *A Fiery Flying Roll* (1649), p7; *A Second Fiery Flying Rowle* (1649), p19.
46 G Winstanley, *A New-Yeers Gift for the Parliament and Armie*, p43, in: G H Sabine, op cit, p390.
47 G Leff, *Heresy in the Later Middle Ages* (Manchester UP, 1967), II, p691.
48 A Coppe, *A Second Fiery Flying Rowle*, p2; cf J Bunyan, *Works* (G Offor (ed), 1860), II p733.
49 J R Pitman (ed), *The Whole Works of John Lightfoot* (1823-1824), XIII, p317.
50 R Crab, *Dagons Downfall* (1657), pp4-5.
51 J E Neale, *Elizabeth I and her Parliaments, 1584-1601* (1957), p70.

well as you?' 'While men are gazing up to heaven, imagining after a happiness or fearing a hell after they are dead, their eyes are put out, that they see not what is their birthrights, and what is to be done by them here on earth while they are living... And indeed the subtle clergy do know that if they can but charm the people...to look after riches, heaven and glory when they are dead, that then they shall easily be the inheritors of the earth and have the deceived people to be their servants'.[52] The social function of religion was rarely so clearly expressed before Karl Marx: two centuries later a speaker in *Felix Holt the Radical* almost echoed Winstanley's words.[53]

Winstanley was only summing up more eloquently what many were saying. In 1646 Thomas Edwards recorded with horror the remark that 'every creature in the first estate of creation was God, and every creature is God, every creature that hath life and breath being an efflux from God and shall return unto God again, be swallowed up in him as a drop is in the ocean'.[54] This led on both to Winstanley's magnificent pantheism and to the Quaker principle of the divine in every man: but it also led a Wiltshire man in 1656 to say there was 'no God or power ruling above the planets, no Christ but the sun that shines upon us... If the Scriptures were a-making again then Tom Lampire of Melksham would make as good Scriptures as the Bible. There was neither heaven nor hell except in a man's own conscience, for if he had a good fortune and did live well, that was heaven; and if he lived poor and miserable that was hell, for then he would die like a cow or a horse'. Another man of the same village said 'God was in all things': 'whatever sins he did commit, God was the author of them all and acted them in him. He would sell all religion for a jug of beer'.[55]

In 1650 a lieutenant in Cromwell's army declared 'there is no God but what is in himself and whole creation, and that He is alike in beasts as in men'. Lieutenant Jackson also believed 'that he is as perfect now as ever he shall be'.[56] Ludowick Muggleton agreed that the devil had no real existence: he personified the spirit of unclean reason.[57] Coppe thought that 'there was no devil, that it was God that swore

52 G Winstanley, *An Appeale to all Englishmen* (1650), in G H Sabine, op cit, p409; *The Law of Freedom* (1652), p62, in: G H Sabine, op cit, p569.
53 G Eliot, *Felix Holt, the Radical* (Warwick ed), ch XXX.
54 T Edwards, *Gangraena*, Part I (1646), p21.
55 B H Cunnington (ed), *Records of the County of Wilts: being extracts from the Quarter Sessions Great Rolls of the Seventeenth Century* (Devizes, 1932), p231.
56 Quoted in C H Firth, *Cromwell's Army* (1902), p408.
57 L Muggleton, *A Transcendent Spiritual Treatise* (1711), p38. First published 1652.

in them' (the Ranters). He added that 'the Scripture to them was no more than a ballad'.[58] 'The Scripture is so plainly and directly contradictory to itself', Walwyn was reported as saying, 'that makes me believe it is not the Word of God'.[59] Jacob Bauthumley thought the Bible no better than any book by a good man: it was 'not so safe to go to the Bible to see what others have spoken and writ of the mind of God as to see what God speaks within me, and to follow the ducture and leading of it in me'.[60] Laurence Clarkson agreed that 'no matter what Scripture, saints or churches say, if that within thee do not condemn thee, thou shalt not be condemned'. To the pure all things were pure. 'What act soever is done by thee in light and love is light and lovely', though men call it adultery.[61] In this spirit he went about England preaching and seducing any pretty girl he met.[62] In December 1654 Thomas Tany (Theauro John) symbolically burnt the Bible 'because the people say it is the Word of God, and it is not'.[63] A great deal of scepticism about the Scriptures was expressed: the 1650s seem to have marked a turning point away from arguments based merely on biblical texts, which some attributed to Hobbes's influence, but to which the radical critique must have contributed. In 1657 the House of Commons 'jeered when a man cited a Scripture to confirm what he said'.[64] Winstanley explained religious experience in psychological terms.[65]

From all sides we hear complaints of atheism. In 1642 Thomas Fuller recalled that the Puritan Richard Greenham had said that atheism was a greater danger even than popery.[66] Men denied the immortality of the soul. 'Many of my acquaintance did say…"There is no God, but Nature only",' Muggleton tells us of the late 1640s.[67] George Fox was tempted to believe this.[68] Bunyan in the early 1650s met Ranters who denied the existence of God: he had doubts himself. He thought

58 *Leybourn-Popham MSS* (Historical Manuscripts Commission), p57; A Coppe, *A Fiery Flying Roll*, ch 2.
59 [Anon], *Walwins Wiles* (1649), p8, in W Haller and G Davies (eds), *The Leveller Tracts, 1647-1653* (Columbia UP, 1944), p298.
60 J Bauthumley, *The Light and Dark Sides of God* (1650), pp71-84. Bauthumley too thought God was in all creatures, beasts as well as men (p4).
61 L Clarkson, *A Single Eye* (1650), pp12, 9-10.
62 L Clarkson, *The Lost Sheep Found* (1660), passim.
63 J T Rutt (ed), *Diary of Thomas Burton* (1828), I, p cxxxvi.
64 J D Ogilvie (ed), *Diary of Sir Archibald Johnston of Warriston* (Scottish History Society), III, p71.
65 G Winstanley, *The Law of Freedom*, pp60-61, in G H Sabine, op cit, pp567-568.
66 T Fuller, *The Holy State* (1841), pp334-338.
67 L Muggleton, *The Acts of the Witnesses of the Spirit* (1764), p18; cf p62. First published 1699.
68 G Fox, *Journal* (8th edn, 1902), I, p26.

the Bible might be 'a fable and cunning story', no better than the Koran, whose recent translation into English (1649) had stimulated much speculation. Bunyan hints that he had other and worse thoughts which he dared not reproduce.[69]

Bunyan thought the early Quakers' ideas were not much better than those of the Ranters, 'only the Ranters had made them threadbare at an alehouse', whilst the Quakers covered the same ideas with 'an outward legal holiness or righteousness'.[70] The picture of the jovial Ranters blaspheming over their beer reminds us of the drunken trooper who said, 'If I should worship the sun or moon, like the Persians, or that pewter pot on the table, nobody has anything to do with it';[71] or of Captain Francis Freeman, discharged from the army in 1650, who told a cornet that he 'saw God in the table board and in the candlestick'.[72] In 1659 Richard Baxter observed that the profane multitude, the rabble, were hostile to ministers and all religion.[73]

IV

When we say that the religious ideology of the parliamentarian revolutionaries was Puritanism, therefore, we are in danger of confusing two quite distinct phenomena. There was the Puritanism of the gentry and merchants, who wanted to preserve a state church under parliamentary control, with tithes and the patronage system intact, with university trained Calvinist divines. Thus the advantages of the episcopal church in controlling opinion and maintaining social discipline could be preserved, without any danger of its becoming again an independent tool in the hands of the crown. The conservative parliamentarians (like John Pym) would originally have accepted a modified episcopacy, once the High Commission was abolished and provided the king recognised the necessity of accepting parliamentary supremacy. When Charles refused, the conservatives would have settled for a Presbyterian system as the price of a Scottish alliance, but with parliamentary control at the centre and with elders from the propertied class nominated by parliament.

Entirely different was the position of the petty bourgeois radicals of

---

69   J Bunyan, *Works*, I, pp17-18; cf p552.
70   J Bunyan, *Works*, II, pp182-183.
71   Quoted by D Masson, *Life of John Milton* (1859-80), III, p525. Note the interest in comparative religion again.
72   F Freeman, *Light Vanquishing Darkness* (1650), p3.
73   R Baxter, *The Holy Commonwealth* (1659), pp92-94, 226-229.

London, East Anglia and parts of the Home Counties, of the Quakers from the North, 'composed and made up out of the dregs of the people'.[74] Spontaneously organised in their own independent congregations, with mechanic preachers elected and paid by these congregations, they wanted not only to separate from the state church but to destroy it as an organ of government lest it attempt to reassert the traditional ideological control and disciplinary supervision. They attacked the whole idea of a university educated clergy, because it created a separate clerical caste closely linked with the ruling class. Though the motives of the separatists were religious, the objective content of their demands was secularist. They wanted to separate state and church to deprive the organs of coercion of all the supernatural sanctions which had for so many centuries surrounded them. Roger Williams, a deeply religious Baptist, expressed this secularism in a way which must have seemed little better than atheism to conservative parliamentarians. 'The church, or company of worshippers whether true or false, is...like unto a corporation, society or company of East India or Turkey merchants, or any other society or company in London; which companies may hold their courts, keep their records, hold disputations, and in matters concerning their society may dissent, divide, break into schisms and factions, sue and implead each other at the law, yea wholly break up and dissolve into pieces and nothing, and yet the peace of the City not be in the least measure impaired or disturbed; because the essence or being of the City, and so the well being and peace thereof, is essentially distinct from those particular societies; the City courts, City laws, City punishments distinct from theirs. The City was before them, and stands absolute and entire when such a corporation or society is taken down'.[75] The startlingly new proposition here lies in the comparison: it is no more the state's business what church a man joins than what trading company, if any; and disagreements about religion are no more the state's concern than rows inside a City company. This would have shocked Luther and Calvin as much as the Roman or Anglican hierarchies. In such a world there could be no certainty about the visible church, no apostolic succession, no national church exercising supervision and control over the middle and lower classes, no 'compulsive mastership or aristocratical government over the people'.

74   E Pagitt, *Heresiography* (5th edn, 1654), p136.
75   R Williams, *The Bloudy Tenent of Persecution* (Hanserd Knollys Soc, 1848), pp46-47. First published 1644.

In order to win the war, the support of the sectaries had to be enlisted. They formed the backbone of Cromwell's army, and he himself genuinely believed in the desirability of religious toleration for those with 'the root of the matter in them', ie consistent revolutionaries. He was prepared to give commissions even to Anabaptists: 'if they be willing faithfully to serve [parliament], that satisfies'.[76]

In consequence the New Model Army became a formidable fighting force and won the war for parliament. Henceforwards there was something very like a system of dual power in the country. The army, committed to a degree of religious liberty, was too powerful to be ignored; and its plebeian rank and file, and some junior officers, were susceptible to radical ideas, religious as well as political. In 1646 a trooper in Northamptonshire 'laid his hand on his sword, and said "This sword should never be laid down, nor many thousands more, whilst there was a priest left in England",'[77] In March 1649 six soldiers made a demonstration in the parish church of Walton-on-Thames, within a few miles of which the Digger colony at St. George's Hill was to be started in the following month. They symbolically burned a copy of the Bible, because 'now Christ…imparts a fuller measure of his spirit to his saints than this can afford'.[78]

Yet over the length and breadth of England the gentry and town oligarchies, the 'natural rulers', whom parliament represented and who in the last resort paid for the army, were irremoveable without a vast social upheaval for which the generals had no mind. After the defeat of the Levellers in 1649, the uneasy balance of the 1650s saw Oliver Cromwell and the leading officers groping their way back to agreement with these 'natural rulers', without whose support a permanent settlement was impossible. In the 1650s men like Lieutenant Jackson, Captain Freeman and Quakers were purged from the army; but similar influences recurred. In 1655 Richard Coppin's rejection of heaven and hell was so influential in Rochester, not only with the 'many-headed monster, the rude multitude'[79] but also with the army rank and file, that the Major-General recommended that Coppin should be exiled and the troops posted elsewhere.[80] The Cromwellian state church marked a compromise in the religious sphere: tithes and patronage survived, but there was far less

---

76 W C Abbott (ed), *Writings and Speeches of Oliver Cromwell* (Harvard UP, 1937-1947), I, pp277-278.
77 I Edwards, *Gangraena*, Part III (1646), p173.
78 [C Walker], *Anarchia Anglicana, or the History of Independency*, Part II (1649), pp152-153. The soldiers also abolished the Sabbath, tithes, ministers and magistrates.
79 W Rosewell, *The Serpents Subtilty Discovered* (1656), Sig A 3, p11.
80 *Thurloe State Papers* (1742), IV, p486.

doctrinal control or coercive discipline than in the old church, and toleration was extended to independent congregations existing alongside this church, provided their beliefs and practices were not thought to be politically subversive.

Like all compromises during a revolution, this satisfied neither side. Quakers and others disrupted church services, denounced hireling priests and agitated for the overthrow of the state church, tithes and patronage. The clergy organised themselves into 'voluntary associations' in the counties, an attempt to build up a Presbyterian disciplinary system from below. Whenever parliament was in session they lobbied for support, though this was hardly necessary.

For the one consistent fact about mid-17th century politics is that any House of Commons elected on a propertied franchise was bitterly opposed to religious toleration. In the 1640s the Long Parliament tried to impose a Presbyterian disciplinary system, and passed fierce laws against blasphemy. The army's intervention in politics frustrated the operation of these laws, and produced an era of relative freedom; but whenever parliament met it returned to the attack. In 1654 it persecuted the Unitarian John Biddle, and tried to sweep away the tolerant clauses of the Instrument of Government; in 1656 it persecuted the Quaker James Nayler and replaced the Instrument by the much harsher Petition and Advice. But 'consider', a pre-Restoration pamphlet urged, 'can you at once suppress the sectaries and keep out the king?'[81] After an interlude of army rule in 1659-60, terminating in near anarchy, the 'natural rulers' came to agree that the restoration of a state church was worth even a compromise with episcopacy. So in 1660 the army was disbanded, bishops came back with Charles II; tithes and patronage were confirmed, the censorship restored. The High Commission was not revived, so church courts lost their coercive power: but so far as the lower classes were concerned this role was taken over by JPs, who gleefully carried out the policy of repression and persecution authorised by parliamentary statute.

The old opponents of 1640 were now united against the threat from lower class dissent and infidelity, which they succeeded in driving underground. In the villages the hegemony of parson and squire was re-established. Nonconformists were driven out of national politics, and from the political life of their main centres of strength, the towns. Deserted by their leaders among the gentry, the radicals emigrated, or

---

81   A *Coffin for the Good Old Cause* (1660), in *The Posthumous Works of Mr Samuel Butler* (6th edn, 1754), p300. The attribution to Butler is almost certainly incorrect.

took to hopeless plotting, or to pacifist religion: the Quakers, Baptists and Muggletonians abandoned revolutionary political action and became harmless religious sects, who were nevertheless bitterly persecuted and so reduced to a hard core of the faithful. Once the censorship closes down again it is very difficult indeed to find much evidence of the thinking of the majority of the middle and lower classes in the towns who did not turn to the sects.

The author of The Whole Duty of Man agreed with Fuller and Baxter that 'this liberty of discourse hath propagated atheism' and made it fashionable: he believed that for every household in which prayers were held there were ten in which they were neglected.[82] In 1669 the fact that atheism had many followers in England impressed a foreign observer.[83] In the same year Edward Chamberlayne added that, 'The clergy...are accounted by many as the dross and refuse of the nation... It hath been observed, even by strangers, that the iniquity of the present times in England is such...that of all the Christian clergy of Europe...none are so little respected, beloved, obeyed or rewarded as the present...clergy of England'.[84] Six years earlier Robert Blackburne, Secretary to the Admiralty Committee, had observed to Samuel Pepys that 'the present clergy...are hated and laughed at by everybody; ...[they] will never heartily go down with the generality of the commons of England, they have been so used to liberty and freedom and they are so acquainted with the pride and debauchery of the present clergy'.[85] The royalist Samuel Butler likewise spoke of the 'general ill will and hatred they [bishops and clergy] have contracted from the people of all sorts... These officers and commanders of the Church Militant are like soldiers of fortune that are free to serve on any side that gives the best pay'.[86] But Bishop Isaac Barrow noted, no doubt equally truthfully, that the Church of England enjoys 'the favour of the almost whole nobility and gentry'.[87]

Now of course a great deal of this is the conventional exaggeration about impiety which occurs in every generation. But the references to past history make sense. In 1681 the egregious Bishop Parker testified to the continuing influence of scientific ideas upon artisans: 'plebeians

82 The Government of the Tongue, Section III, in The Works of the...Author of The Whole Duty of Man (1704).
83 [L Magalotti], Travels of Cosmo III, Grand Duke of Tuscany, through England (1821), p428.
84 E Chamberlayne, Angliae Notitia (1669), pp389, 400-401.
85 S Pepys, Diary (H B Wheatley (ed), 1946), I, pp314-315.
86 S Butler, Characters and Passages from Note-books (A R Waller (ed), 1908), p318.
87 I Barrow, Theological Works (A Napier (ed), 1859), IX, p577.

and mechanics have philosophised themselves into principles of impiety and read their lectures of atheism in the streets and highways'.[88] This fear of mechanic atheism perhaps accounts for the near panic with which so many of the early members of the Royal Society warded off the accusation that their activities must lead to atheism. The passionate intensity of their denials, and their labours to prove that science reinforced faith, are the strongest possible evidence that faith was in fact being called in question, as well as that the scientists saw the social necessity of maintaining it. Their own guilty consciences made them protest too much, as Professor Westfall sapiently observed.[89]

V

In the later 18th century, worried by the atheistic influence of the French Revolution, many godly Englishmen suddenly became aware that the mass of the urban population did not go to church. How new this was is still uncertain. In theory all Englishmen until 1640 had been compelled, under legal penalty, to attend their own parish church every Sunday. We do not know how far the very poor and vagabonds in fact attended. They were not worth fining for non-attendance, so the church courts would not bother about them. Many had no clothes in which they were fit to appear before their Maker.[90] In a closely integrated agricultural village no doubt most of the poor were compelled to attend. But Norden in 1607 tells us of forest squatters, 'given to little or no kind of labour,...dwelling far from any church or chapel', who were 'as ignorant of God or of any civil course of life as the very savages amongst the infidels'.[91]

The act of 1650, ending compulsory church attendance, must have been a great liberation. It was reversed of course in 1660, but the establishment of licensed nonconformist chapels, temporarily in 1672, permanently after 1689, together with the decline in the coercive power of the church courts, must have made church attendance virtually impossible to enforce in the towns.[92] (It was very different in villages, as Addison shows us: Sir Roger de Coverley attended church himself 'in order to count the congregation [and] see if any of his tenants are

---

88 Quoted in my *Intellectual Origins of the English Revolution*, p127.
89 R S Westfall, *Science and Religion in Seventeenth Century England* (Yale University Press, 1958), pp107-111.
90 See my *Society and Puritanism in pre-Revolutionary England* (1964), pp472-474.
91 J Norden, *The Surveyors Dialogue* (1608), p107.
92 See my *Society and Puritanism*, p343.

missing'.)[93] In many London parishes, indeed, the church could not have held all the inhabitants if they had attended; and the growing habit of renting pews helped to exclude the poor.[94] A circular sent round by laymen of the Church of England in 1681 spoke of the necessity of preaching to 'poor people...who cannot...get pews in their parish churches'. In populous parishes, they recommended, there should be at least two congregations, the parish church for the parson and the rich, and a tabernacle at which lay preachers could minister to the poor.[95] The object of the circular was to help the national church to compete with nonconformist influence over the poor; but the dissenting congregations too had to rent pews in order to raise funds to pay their unbeneficed ministers. This would help to exclude the urban poor. The main appeal of the sects, after 1660 at least, seems to have been to the urban lower middle class—artisans and small merchants. Provided the poor were docile, they had a fair chance of being ignored. It seems therefore very likely that the Industrial Revolution merely revealed a state of affairs which had long existed in the larger towns, although of course the rapid expansion in urban populations would increase the numbers of those who were able to stay away from church, and so increase the danger from the ruling class point of view. Between the crude plebeian materialism revealed by Professor Dickens in early 16th century England and the secularism of early 19th century working class radicals there may be more continuity than historians have recognised. The Methodist movement may have been the first serious attempt to convert the labouring class, now expanding so rapidly, as opposed to coercing them into a formal acceptance of outward observances of religion.

93 *The Spectator*, No 112 (9 July 1711).
94 See my *Society and Puritanism*, p484; my *Economic Problems of the Church*, pp175-182.
96 Quoted by J Waddington, *Congregational History, 1567-1700* (1874), pp615-616.

Chapter 9

Samuel Pepys

This was a review of Pepys: A Biography *by Richard Ollard and* The Diary of Samuel Pepys Vol VIII 1667 *edited by Robert Latham and William Matthews, first published in* The New Statesman, *27 September 1974.*

We know Samuel Pepys—or we think we know him—better than almost any historical character of comparable importance. Thanks to the *Diary* we are more intimate with him than with our colleagues, neighbours and friends. But we tend to allow the endearing young man of the 1660s to obscure the later Pepys who was one of England's greatest civil servants, 'the saviour of the navy', and President of the Royal Society. Normally historians can see only the public face of civil servants—the official despatches, the minutes; they are fortunate if an occasional private letter survives. The great self revealers of the past—Montaigne, Rousseau, Casanova, De Quincey —show us a carefully prepared persona. Most diarists whose diaries survive, wrote with an eye to ultimate publication. None expose themselves so nakedly as the young Pepys does.

He is not concerned to create an image of himself. He is not writing for a public, but for himself: and he knows what he is like. So there are no explanations, no justifications, only a dialogue between the different aspects of his own personality. The fascination of the *Diary* is that it does not put before us a single rounded personality but a broken bundle of mirrors. It is genuine because it is utterly inconsistent. Each of us can select his own Pepys.

My Pepys was a Puritan by upbringing, living in a world in which it had become smart to be anti-Puritan; a bourgeois son of a London tailor, living in a society in which the bourgeois virtues were despised by all except those who needed them in order to thrust their way to the top. Pepys was also, as Mr Ollard rightly claims, an artist doing a prosaic job in a sordid world; and he had chameleon-like qualities which enabled him to reflect many aspects of this contradictory society.

Throughout the *Diary* we can feel a frisson of pleasure at every daring new extravagance—a sword, a wig—and at breaches of the sabbath, drinking healths, dancing, gaming. It was against his nature to owe anything to anybody, Pepys records. He continually rebukes himself (and others) for wasting time: 'business lost and money lost, and my old habit of pleasure wakened, which I will keep down the more hereafter.' Naturally he thought it 'a very excellent, persuasive, good and moral sermon' when the Rev George Gifford 'shewed, like a wise man, that righteousness is a surer moral way of being rich than sin and villainy'.

Pepys knew that he got on in this world because, with all his capacity for enjoyment, he worked harder and more methodically than others; but he also knew that he had to make the right contacts and seize his opportunities for getting rich while the sun shone. One of the unique features of the *Diary* is that it shows us the mental contortions of a man who took bribes, who enjoyed getting rich this way, and yet who had high standards of public duty for others which were not wholly inapplicable to himself. Is it an optical illusion that he seems less venal in the period when we no longer have the devastating evidence of the *Diary*?

Since Pepys was writing for himself alone, the *Diary* reveals not only his mean and petty behaviour, his lapses from his own standards, but also his attempts to discipline himself in respect of sex, drink and playgoing, and the subterfuges which he used to outwit himself. Mr Ollard rightly points out that Pepys was by no means an emancipated advocate of sexual freedom. He disapproved heartily of breaches of conventional morality, in others and in himself. This makes his candid avowal of his own peccadilloes the more fascinating.

Pepys's bourgeois background explains his contempt for those naval officers who owed their commands to birth and favour alone ('the gentlemen that could never be brought to order, but undid all' and then blamed the civil servants). He preferred 'tarpaulins', men of lower social origin who knew their job. This exactly reproduces Oliver Cromwell's preference for 'a plain russet-coated captain' over 'what you call a gentleman, and is nothing else'. It led to what Mr Ollard argues was Pepys's greatest contribution to English history—convincing his superiors that naval wars could be won only if the officer class was professionalised. After 1677 anyone aspiring to hold a lieutenant's commission must have served for three years at sea, one year at least in the lowly rank of midshipman, and must satisfy three senior officers by 'solemn examination of his mastery of the theory and practice of navigation. Naturally these conditions were not always rigorously enforced; but the standards set were such, as Mr Ollard observes, as 'people may resist but...will never dare to rescind'. The captains, gentlemen or not, were subordinated to the bourgeois civil servants. The successes of the navy in the next century and a half vindicated Pepys. He was less successful in getting regular pay for seamen, lack of which in 1667 made many desert to the Dutch.

There are many ironies about Pepys's career. The young Samuel was a great Roundhead. On the day of Charles I's execution he said that the text for his funeral sermon should be 'the memory of the wicked shall rot'. He was an admirer of Oliver Cromwell and of the naval reforms of the Commonwealth which he surreptitiously reintroduced; yet he became so committed to his Stuart masters that after 1688 there was no place for him in the new England which reverted to the imperial and naval policies of the interregnum. In his 30th year Pepys began to learn the multiplication table. Twenty four years later, as President of the Royal Society, he gave his imprimatur to Isaac Newton's Principia. In between he praised 'mathematick Admirals' and was the moving spirit in founding (with government money) the mathematical school at Christ's Hospital as a nursery for navigators.

There are also some mysteries. Why was Pepys never knighted? Men far less distinguished, and far less well placed, achieved the honour. At any time between 1684 and 1688, at least, Pepys could surely have had it for the asking. Nor does it seem in character for him not to want a title. Another mystery is why he never remarried after his first wife's death. He lived with Mary Skinner for the last 30 years of his life, and she was socially accepted even by so priggish a man as John Evelyn. Yet in the Diary Pepys criticised in others precisely this sort of liaison. Mr Ollard's explanation—that the great granddaughter of Lord Chief Justice Coke was not the social equal of the tailor's son—is unconvincing. More relevant perhaps is that Mary's uncle was Cyriack Skinner, Milton's friend and a former president of the radical Rota Club; and that her brother had got into very hot water in 1676 for trying to publish Milton's desperately heretical De Doctrina Christiana. But these prudential arguments no longer applied after 1688. It remains a mystery.

The Latham and Matthews edition of the Diary continues its majestic course. Volume VIII covers 1667, the year in which Paradise Lost and Sprat's History of the Royal Society appeared. Pepys mentioned the latter, not the former. Mr Ollard's Pepys is an artist: simplicity and innocence are his words for Pepys's hedonism. One of the many virtues of his book is that he uses the Diary to increase our comprehension of the public servant without allowing its fascination to distort our view. The chasm which separates the private from the public persona remains to make us, in Pepys's own words, 'mightily reflect on the uncertainty of all history'.

Chapter 10

Partial historians and total history

This was first published in the Times Literary Supplement, *24 November 1972.*

The writing of history has always been a battle against the self styled expert. The history of religion was slowly and painfully taken out of the hands of theologians, constitutional history from the lawyers. But new hydra heads spring up continually. In the past the problem was to make historians of, for example, religion and law aware of the existence of economics. Today the problem is to convince econometric historians of the existence of religion and law, to persuade statisticians that some things in the past are more countable than others, and that there is not much point in counting the uncountable.

Historians of science are divided into those who stress the internal self sufficient development of scientific ideas and those who stress the effects of society on science. I once heard a distinguished historian of science argue in all seriousness that a knowledge of 17th century history could add nothing to our understanding of Sir Isaac Newton. In the narrowest mathematical sense this may be true; but the Newtonian synthesis is an ideological as well as a mathematical fact, and I find it difficult to believe that Newton's secretiveness, his silences and suppressions, his passion for alchemy and Biblical prophecy, his strange, twisted personality, cannot be better understood for an understanding of the difficult world in which he lived and was knighted. It is no doubt true that too many historians venture to write about science on the basis of less knowledge than they would think necessary before writing about theology or law, and therefore have been guilty of oversimplifications which need to be corrected. But there is no reason to suppose that science is intrinsically any more difficult for historians to understand than theology or law. Charles Webster has recently very correctly criticised those whom he calls 'restrictive' historians of science, and argued that their conclusions even about science in the narrowest sense are vitiated by their approach ('The Authorship and Significance of *Macaria*', *Past and Present* No 56). We must not allow historians of science an autonomy that has rightly been denied to theologians and lawyers, nor permit them to assume that the great thinkers of the past inhabited an ivory towered vacuum. Historians of culture suffer from the same apparently inevitable tendency to strive for autonomy. Yet culture is the product of a given society. Any attempt to treat it otherwise means succumbing to 'the illusion of the epoch', to taking at their face value things which should be evaluated in relation to a larger whole. Thus Peter Laslett described England before the Industrial Revolution as 'a one class society': 'the mass of Englishmen cannot be counted as part of England for historical purposes'; 'the minority lived for all the rest' (*The World We Have Lost*). A similar error is that of historians who assume that 17th century critics of Oxford and Cambridge were enemies of education and learning. In each case the propaganda of 17th century defenders of privilege has been swallowed whole.

The word 'culture' meets with a certain resistance in England. It is all right when used by archaeologists and restricted to material objects, or by anthropologists dealing with relatively unsophisticated societies. But on the whole historians have preferred the word 'civilisation'. 'Culture' in its wider usage has a slightly alien flavour—Germanic, Marxist, at best American. There are *Histories of Culture* by the American Preserved Smith and by the English Marxist Jack Lindsay; Arnold Toynbee, Clive Bell and Lord Clark write about civilisation and civilisations.

Some of the best cultural history in English has in fact been written by Marxists, or by Marxist influenced historians. I think of George Thomson on ancient Greece, E A Thompson on the barbarian invaders, Edward Thompson and Eric Hobsbawm on 18th and 19th century England, Joseph Needham on China, Isaac Deutscher on the Soviet Union, Ernst Meyer on English music, Frederick Antal and Eric Mercer on English art. Such unlikely characters as Sir John Hicks in England, Fernand Braudel in France and T S Kuhn in the United States have recently written approvingly of some sort of a return to Marx. The advantage that Marxist influenced historians have is that they think of history as one, take for granted that there are likely to be connections between the culture and the economics of a society however difficult it may be to analyse them. The vast rumbling Marxist generalisations at least provoke thought, even if only to contradict.

Thus Ernst Fischer: 'The epic declined with the age of chivalry, and the novel grew up with the bourgeoisie; ...'polyphonic music died together with the feudal system, and homophonic music developed together with the bourgeois age' (*The Necessity of Art*). Discuss.

Good cultural history must stimulate ideas about the society which produced the culture. When Eric Gill said, 'there was not such a thing as portrait painting before about the year 1400', or the Ogdens tell us that English landscape painting is a 17th century creation, it is clear that the explanation of these facts (assuming for the moment that they are facts) must go beyond the range of art history in its narrow technical sense. A historian of ideas like V Harris, historians of music like Ernst Meyer, G M Ruff and D A Wilson, a literary historian like A Harbage, a historian of law like W R Prest, all agree in seeing a crisis in English culture around 1615. It does not need any great expertise to relate this to a crisis in English economic and political life. But once the various crises are seen as part of a social whole, they all gain in significance. It may or may not affect our attitude to the art concerned to hear Van Dyck described as 'a conscious propagandist of absolutism', or to be told that one of Baroque's most 'unequivocal statements' in English painting was made in the inner chambers of Windsor Castle which the papist Antonio Verrio decorated for Charles II. But such considerations cannot but affect our view of the place of Van Dyck, Verrio and, indeed, Baroque in English cultural history, and help us to avoid lazy over simplifications like 'Puritan hostility to art'. The hostility of most Puritans was to art of a particular kind.

The great economic historians were great historians of culture— Adam Smith, Karl Marx, Maynard Keynes. Even a generation ago an historian in search of intellectual stimulus would turn to the pages of *Economic History Review*. Now, alas, he is likely to find its pages full of methodological controversies between statisticians who cheerfully agree that what they are arguing about will not affect our conclusions about the past. One would not need to worry about the mere technologists of economic history if some of them did not attempt cultural generalisations without adequate historical knowledge, or assume that a single key—demography, for instance—will open all doors, when they do not know enough religious and social history even to grasp how unreliable is their basic source, the parish register. Historians should be pluralists. I do not accept what I take to be G R Elton's view that political and administrative history is in some sense more significant than social history or the history of culture. *The Oxford History of England* now seems pretty old fashioned with its separate chapters on 'Education and Science', 'The Arts', 'Literature', tacked on at the end like a paper tail on to a donkey in the child's game. As in that game, those who did the tacking seem sometimes to have been blindfolded.

No one can be a universal historian these days: all that can be hoped for is modesty in each practitioner, a realisation that his specialisation gives him only a partial view; and a conscientious attempt, to the best of his ability, to look for connections and interrelations. Mastery of the techniques—anthropology, computers—is a necessary preliminary. The economic historian, the historian of science or culture, the constitutional historian, like the 19th century antiquarians, will produce raw materials which other historians can use. Modesty, judgment, imagination, a sensitivity to connections: these are what all historians need over and above the special techniques of their particular sub-disciplines, need in order to keep these techniques in their proper place. The attempt to see connections is hazardous and may lead to mistakes. But these can be corrected. Failure to look for connections leads to barrenness, myopia, blinkers.

Economic history is essential to historians of culture because culture is a class phenomenon. L B Wright was absolutely correct to isolate *Middle Class Culture in Elizabethan England*—the culture of the Protestant ethic, of the dignity of labour, of love in marriage, plain prose and accurate portraiture—as distinct from the court culture of aristocratic honour, of virtuoso amateurism, of property marriage and a dual sexual ethic, 'witty' prose and flattering portraiture. The culture of Van Dyck, Rubens and the court of Louis XIV was very different from the culture of Rembrandt, Bunyan and Milton. Keith Thomas has recently used anthropological techniques to reveal the sub-culture of magic and superstition which existed below both the courtly culture and the middle class culture. His *Religion and the Decline of Magic* is perhaps the most important contribution to our understanding of English cultural history, and indeed English history *tout court*, published in the past generation.

All history should be cultural history, and the best history is. The most significant contribution to the history of religion in England made during the past decade came in a book called *The Agrarian History of England and Wales, 1500-1640*. Here Joan Thirsk and Alan Everitt distinguish between the culture of the champagne agricultural areas and the culture of the forest and pasture areas: the former stable, docile, controlled, orthodox, the latter mobile, more open, freer, more heretical. Already Professor Everitt is using this as a key to open many doors in the later history of nonconformity. Conversely one of the most important recent insights into social, political and economic history comes from Patrick Collinson's *The Elizabethan Puritan Movement*, which demonstrates that in the 1570s and 1580s a section of the gentry and peerage in alliance with town oligarchies was trying to subordinate the church to its control. This not only throws light on the social basis of Puritanism, it also illuminates the political history of the next century during which this control was fought for, in various guises, and finally won.

Admirable history of English culture in the 16th and 17th centuries has been written over the past decade by historians of the Warburg Institute. Pride of place must be given to Frances Yates's stimulating books—*Giordano Bruno and the Hermetic Tradition*, *The Art of Memory*, and *Theatre of the World*, to mention only the most recent. She manages superbly to unite cultural history with total history, to relate her most daringly exotic speculations to the real world in which Bruno, Shakespeare and Robert Fludd lived, to link magic, mathematics and machines, to associate Protestant iconoclasm with the evolution of a new philosophic method. Not every historian would accept all that she says, but this is because she bubbles over with ideas which are apt to run away in all directions; but even her errors, if errors they are, are more fertile than most people's truths. D P Walker's *The Decline of Hell* similarly deals with intellectual history in a way that is not separated from total history but an integral part of it. Dr Yates's serious treatment of Hermeticism has been developed by P M Rattansi and Charles Webster—who show how this magical ideology of the craftsmen contributed significantly to the scientific revolution.

P W Thomas's study of *Sir John Birkenhead, 1617-79*, suggests that royalist classicism emerged in the defeat and fear of the decade after the Civil War. It was the defence mechanism of an insecure elite, their retort to the challenging world of democracy and social insubordination. We may compare the relationship of French classicism to the anxieties and insecurities of the Fronde. There are analogies in other areas of English culture. The Restoration brought back bishops and aimed at restoring traditional certainties against the 'enthusiasm' of mechanic preachers and the 'atheism' of mechanic philosophers. The propagandists of the Royal Society, some of them a little tarred with the brush of radicalism, took up with gusto the attack on enthusiasm and atheism. Our most religious king, Charles II, was well advised to become patron of the Royal Society as well as head of the Church of England, and to tie both closely to the social hierarchy. It may have been no better for science than it was for religion, but it certainly helped to conserve the newly established order.

In a similar sphere the work of a literary critic like Lionel Trilling gains enormously in depth from his ability to put 'literary' questions in a cultural-historical perspective. 'Our investigation of sincerity', he says in his recent *Sincerity and Authenticity*, 'has no sooner begun than it has led to public and even political considerations.' Just because Professor Trilling is intelligently aware of what contemporary historians are up to, he can raise questions of profound interest to those who are not literary specialists—such as the implications of the fact that the word 'villain' (on the stage) evolves from the world 'villein' at a time of great social mobility, or that the writing of narrative history has become old fashioned simultaneously with the writing of narrative novels.

So I do not think the dearth of formal histories of culture in English is something about which we need worry too much. It is more important that we should not have too narrowly specialised a conception of cultural history, any more than of economic history. Lawrence Stone's majestic *The Crisis of the Aristocracy, 1558-1641*, shows how the best history includes the history of culture: what he has to say about sculpture or about aristocratic patronage of the arts is convincing because he understands the economics of the society. A L Rowse, for all his irritating idiosyncrasies, is another historian who sees culture as an integral part of total history, and writes the better about it because he is a total historian. The history of education, to take another example, is being rewritten with the aid of wills by W R Jordan, of statistics by Professor Stone, and with an awareness of the changing social background by Joan Simon and Kenneth Charlton. Since the history of culture exists as a fact, it is perhaps just as well that there are no professors, no departments, no empires, to isolate an autonomous 'cultural history' from the rest of history.

Chapter 11

The rights of man in the English Revolution

This has not been previously published. It is most likely to be a conference paper and is dated 1975.

The English revolutions of 1640 and 1688, unlike the American and French revolutions, produced no grandiose legislative pronouncements on the subject of the rights of man: least of all in rigorously practical documents like the Bill of Rights of 1689. But the idea that there are rights common to all men can be seen emerging in the revolutionary decades of the 1640s and 1650s. Traditionally rights were thought of as something belonging to communitites—to churches, universities, towns, or to a few powerful and wealthy individuals. In this sense rights were privileges, from which the non-privileged were excluded. The idea that ordinary people might have rights arose slowly with modern concepts of individualism, which appear at roughly the same time in renaissance humanism, in Protestant theology and in legal theory. In considering the origin of natural rights theories historians have tended to look only at the most famous thinkers, Hobbes and Locke. Important though they both are, even Hobbes was anticipated by some of the radicals of the revolutionary epoch; and Locke's ideas were not published for another generation. I shall concentrate on the humbler plebeian radicals of the earlier period. The doctrine of the rights of man was reached by two routes—via the liberties of Englishmen and via Christian liberty.

The claim that Englishmen (or some Englishmen) have certain historical rights as Englishmen is paralleled in the historical mythology of many countries. In England its most familiar form was to say that before 1066 the Anglo-Saxons had been a free people, but their rights were encroached on by the Norman conquerors. Englishmen had fought back and extorted concessions over the centuries, such as Magna Carta and the Petition of Right. The advantage of the myth of the Norman yoke lay in its imprecision: since no one knew exactly what was meant by 'the old English constitution', almost anything could be put into it.[1] For most members of the 'political nation' in pre-1640 England, however, the liberties of Englishmen meant primarily a right to property, and to freedom from arbitrary arrest. Both rights were held to be protected by the common law, 'the birthright, the most ancient and best inheritance of Englishmen', as Sir Edward Coke called it; and by parliament, which claimed that it alone had the right to tax the men of property whom it represented. In 1628, at a critical moment in constitutional history, the House of Lords asked Charles I to declare that 'according to the most ancient customs and laws of this land, every free subject of this realm has a fundamental property in his goods, and a fundamental liberty of his person'.[2]

The words 'free subject' suggest that these liberties were not common to all Englishmen: they were almost by definition privileges, rights which went with the possession of property. Yet the general terms in which they were claimed—the liberties of Englishmen, the birthright of Englishmen, fundamental liberties—led to unforseen consequences when during the 1640s the lower classes were drawn into political action. They were urged to fight for the ancient liberties of Englishmen: and they soon began to demand these liberties for themselves. In 1641 Sir Simonds D'Ewes, no radical, said that 'the poorest man ought to have a voice' in elections to parliament, that this was 'the birthright of the subjects of England'.[3] Six years later, after parliament's victory in the Civil War, the Council of the victorious army (which included elected representatives of the rank and file and junior officers as well as the generals) debated at Putney the future constitution of England. In these debates the Leveller John Wildman claimed that 'every person in England hath as clear a right to elect his representative [to parliament] as the greatest person in England'. More melodramatically, Captain Awdeley added, 'I would die in any place in England in asserting that it is the right of every freeborn man to

1   See my *Puritanism and Revolution* (Panther ed, 1965), pp58-125.
2   *Lords' Journals*, III, p769.
3   W Notestein (ed), *The Journal of Sir Simonds D'Ewes* (Yale UP, 1923), p43; cf p431. Several MPs spoke against D'Ewes's claim.

elect'.[4] But who are freeborn?

In the previous year another Leveller, Richard Overton, had dismissed the House of Lords on the grounds that it derived its authority from the Norman conquerors. Levellers like him came to argue that Magna Carta itself was 'but a beggarly thing, containing many marks of intolerable bondage'; 'a mess of pottage', the Leveller William Walwyn called it. 'Our very laws', said Wildman at Putney, 'were made by our conquerors'.[5] So much for Coke's deification of the common law!

The Levellers not only produced their own version of history, very different from that of their social superiors; ultimately they came to abandon the appeal to the historical rights of Englishmen altogether. 'Whatever our forefathers were', declared Overton, 'or whatever they did or suffered or were enforced to yield unto, we are the men of the present age, and ought to be absolutely free from all kinds of exorbitances, molestations or arbitrary power.' To the traditional common law deference to precedent, Overton retorted by quoting the words to parliament: 'Reason hath no precedent, for reason is the foundation of all just precedents'.[6] So liberty ceased to be a class privilege attached to property, and became the right of all Englishmen, rich or poor; then of all men, in England or elsewhere. (Wildman's use of the phrase 'every person' in the passage just quoted could be taken to imply the inclusion of persons of both sexes; but this is no reason to suppose that Wildman had any such intention.) Yet this new line of thought was far more explosive than the traditional claim to the liberties of Englishmen: for the liberties to which all men had a right were even less possible to define historically than the liberties of Englishmen.

Overton did not explicitly extend these rights to the people of other nations. But another Leveller, Walwyn, said that the Irish people had the same rights as Englishmen—at a time when Cromwell's armies were depriving the Irish of those rights.[7] Gerrard Winstanley the Digger wrote pamphlets 'for and in the behalf of the poor oppressed people of England and the whole world'.[8] The anonymous author of *Tyranipocrit* (1649), in addition to objecting to English merchants 'robbing of the poor Indians of that which God and nature hath given

4   A S P Woodhouse (ed), *Puritanism and Liberty* (1938), pp66, 81; cf pp53, 61-62.
5   A S P Woodhouse (ed), op cit, p65; D M Wolfe (ed), *Leveller Manifestoe of the Puritan Revolution* (New York, 1944), p124; W Haller (ed), *Tracts on Liberty in the Puritan Revolution* (Columbia UP, 1933), III, p314.
6   D M Wolfe (ed), op cit, p158.
7   W Haller and G Davies (eds), *The Leveller Tracts, 1647-1653* (Columbia UP, 1944), p310; cf my *Puritanism and Revolution*, p144.
8   G H Sabine (ed), *The Works of Gerrard Winstanley* (Cornell UP, 1944), p277.

them', also spoke up for the Irish.[9] James Harrington in 1656 proposed that the English Revolution should be exported: 'If thy brother cries to thee in affliction, wilt thou not hear him?' Oceana (his name for revolutionary England) was 'not made for herself only, but given as a magistrate of God to mankind, for the vindication of common right and the law of nature'.[10] Such passages have caused Harrington to be denounced as a prophet of British imperialism: we may compare Cromwell's manifesto justifying his declaration of war on Spain in 1655 as vengeance for 'the blood...of the poor Indians, which...has been so unjustly, so cruelly, and so often shed by the hands of the Spaniards: since God has made of one blood all nations of men for to dwell on all the face of the earth'.[11] One wonders how these noble principles applied to the English conquest of Ireland.

However broadly they generalised, the Levellers were normally thinking of men who lived in England. It was of them that Overton wrote in 1646, 'By natural birth all men are equally and alike born to like property, liberty and freedom.' 'We are delivered of God by the hand of nature into this world, everyone with a natural innate freedom and property.' Hence it follows that the only just government is founded on a grant from such individuals.[12] The Leveller 'Agreement of the People', the document debated at Putney in 1647, aimed at laying down the terms on which alone these free men could transfer their rights to society. The 1649 version of the Agreement claimed a vote in the 'choice of [representatives] according to natural right' for all men who were not servants or beggars or royalists. This right applied to local government as well as to parliament. Other 'native rights' in the 'Agreement of the People' were liberty of conscience, immunity from conscription, the right not to incriminate oneself, the right to own property and to trade freely, together with equality before the law—this last perhaps more far reaching than appears immediately. No government might pass retrospective legislation.[13]

At Putney the Levellers and their opponent Commissary-General Henry Ireton, Cromwell's son in law and mentor, agreed that all men

9   G Orwell and R Reynolds (eds), *British Pamphleteers*, I (1948), pp90-91, 105.
10   J Harrington, *Works* (1737), p194.
11   J Milton, *Complete Prose Works* (Yale UP), II, pp335-336.
12   R Overton, *An Arrow against all Tyrants* (1646), pp3-4. The first sentence especially shocked the Presbyterian Thomas Edwards, who quoted it in his *Gangraena* as an example of the pernicious errors which circulated in revolutionary England (op cit, Part III, p16c).
13   O Lutaud, 'L'Accord du Peuple', *Annales*, mai-juin 1962, pp501-516. 'The Agreement of the People' was translated into French in 1651 and offered by the ex-Leveller Edward Sexby to the Ormee of Bordeaux as the basis of a republican constitution for France (see my *Puritanism and Revolution*, p139).

had a right to life, and hence to sustenance. The Leveller representatives, spokesmen for the men of small property, argued also in favour
of a natural right to property. Ireton denied this. He imposed on himself the role of defender of 'the persons in whom all land lies and those
in corporations in whom all trading lies'—the gentry and merchants
who regarded themselves as the 'natural rulers' of the country. Ireton
feared lest a natural right to property might herald an attack on the
property of the rich—and he turned out to be quite right. 'Constitution founds property', he argued on Hobbist lines.[14]

'Instead of legal rights and the laws and customs of this nation,'
wrote the indignant heresy hunter Thomas Edwards, 'the sectaries...plead for natural rights and liberties, such as men have from
Adam by birth, and in many of their pamphlets they still speak of
being governed by right reason'.[15] The second approach to a theory of
natural rights was via Christian liberty. The Protestant doctrine of
the priesthood of all believers virtually set the believer above the law
and morality. The state, the product of sin, was not really required
for the elect: so in effect Luther proclaimed the kingship of all believers too. But Luther and his more orthodox followers believed that
the state and its laws were needed because the majority of men were
sinful; the state and the law were therefore accepted on prudential
grounds by the elect. 'If you take away the law,' John Pym declared in
1641, 'all things will fall into a confusion, every man will become a
law to himself, which in the depraved condition of human nature
must produce many great enormities.' He was speaking at the trial of
the Earl of Strafford, arguing that Strafford had failed to observe the
restraints which the law placed on the executive.[16]

This view seemed obvious common sense to the bourgeoisie of
Geneva, Amsterdam, La Rochelle, London. It was never so self evident to the lower classes. German peasants and Dutch Anabaptists in
the 16th century made claims for a much wider liberty. Similar claims
were repeated during the English Revolution. John Milton started
from the doctrine of Christian liberty, and always believed that the
elect should follow their consciences if ever they came into conflict
with the law. But he held that 'all men since Adam' were 'born free'.
In *Areopagitica* (1644) he argued that censorship was an insult to the
common people in general—not only to the godly among them.

14   A S P Woodhouse (ed), op cit, p69; cf pp52-58.
15   T Edwards, *Gangraena*, Part III, p9.
16   J Rushworth, *The Trial of Strafford* (1680), p662.

'Nature made us all equal', he added in 1645, 'equal co-heirs by common right'. In 1649 he defended regicide on the ground that 'all men naturally were born free': governments are 'deputies and commissioners' of the people. Power cannot be taken from the people 'without a violation of their natural birthright'. To think otherwise 'were a kind of treason against the dignity of mankind'. 'Who knows not that there is a mutual bond of amity and brotherhood between man and man over all the world, neither is it the English sea that can sever us from that duty and relation'.[17]

During the revolution Milton abandoned Calvinism for Arminianism, and many of the radicals followed the same path. Puritan preachers at the beginning of the Civil War had called on the common people to fight for Christ against Antichrist; but it had never occurred to them that any save the godly minority of themselves and their friends should rule after Antichrist had been overthrown. From the early 1640s however we hear of sectaries preaching that all men shall be saved, that we may reach perfection on earth and be absolved from the law. 'Sin and transgression is finished', proclaimed the Ranter Abiezer Coppe.[18]

Antinomians like the Ranters rejected many social restraints and conventions whose necessity had hitherto been assumed, at least in any literature which got past the censor and into print. Even Milton believed that the elect were freed 'from the rule of the law and of men',[19] though he normally expected them to obey the moral law. But in the 1640s the censorship collapsed, church courts broke down: quite different views could now be propagated, both verbally and in print. What Professor Raphael calls, a little austerely, 'the right to seduce another man's wife',[20] was claimed by many Ranters. 'For one man to be tied to one woman', they were reported as saying, 'or one woman to one man, is a fruit of the curse. But now we are freed from the curse, therefore it is our liberty to make use of whom we please.' Lawrence Clarkson worked out a sexual ethic which started from the assumption that until one had enacted a so called sin as no sin, one could not attain to perfection.[21] And similarly with property: all men had equal rights to all things.

With the Ranters this was not a well thought out theory of human

17 J Milton, *Complete Prose Works*, I, p624; II, pp551, 661; III, pp198-204.
18 A Coppe, *A Fiery Flying Roll*, Part I (1649), p7.
19 J Milton, *Complete Prose Works*, VI, p537.
20 D D Raphael, 'Human Rights, Old and New', in *Political Theory and the Rights of Man* (Raphael (ed), 1967), p103.
21 J Holland, *The Smoke of the Bottomless Piit* (1650), p3; my *The World Turned Upside Down* (1972), pp172-174. Holland, though a hostile critic of the Ranters, seems fairly reliable. for confirmation see C H Firth, *Cromwell's Army* (1902), p408.

rights, though they stressed the equality of all men. But Gerrard Winstanley the Digger went much further and made better sense of the communist ideas floating about among the radicals. The Diggers' aim, he told General Fairfax in 1649, was 'not to remove the Norman Yoke only' and restore Saxon freedom. 'No, that is not it', but to restore 'the pure law of righteousness before the Fall', by restoring community of property as against the competitive greed which private property had introduced, and which constituted the true Fall of Man.[22] Winstanley also went one better than the Ranters by proclaiming that in his reformed commonwealth 'every man and woman shall have the free liberty to marry whom they love, if they can obtain the love and liking of that party whom they would marry. And neither birth nor portion shall hinder the match, for we are all of one family, mankind.' This right, he believed, could only be fully enjoyed in a communist community, where marriage presented no economic problems, since each newly married couple could set themselves up from the communal storehouse.[23]

There were thus ambiguities in the liberties of Englishmen, for some Englishmen were freer than others. There were likewise ambiguities in the concept of Christian liberty, for some were elect and some were unregenerate. This is shown in both spheres by ambiguous demands on behalf of 'the people'. A Presbyterian like William Soughton could insist in 1604 that elders should be elected by the people: this was 'a birthright of the people of England'. Yet he assumed that the election would not be made by the basest of the people: whatever the electoral forms, de facto the better sort would be chosen.[24] Similarly when parliamentarian politicians spoke of the rights of the people, they expected these rights to be exercised by the better sort, for parliament represented the people, and parliament was clearly not elected by the many headed monster. Colonel Rich at Putney and the Harringtonian Captain Baynes in the parliament of 1659 contrasted 'the poor' with 'the people'.[25]

The Levellers never wholly escaped from these ambiguities. Maximilian Petty in the Putney Debates explained that servants and apprentices should not be given the vote because they were 'included

22 G H Sabine, op cit, p292; cf p259.
23 Ibid, p599.
24 W Stoughton, *An Assertion for true and Christian Church-Policie* (1604), pp193-195, 246-247.
25 A S P Woodhouse (ed), op cit, pp63-64; J T Rutt (ed), *The Parliamentary Diary of Thomas Burton* (1828), III, pp147-148.

in their masters'. Yet other Levellers made generalising remarks about 'the people' which certainly sound as though they were intended to apply to all the people, and were so understood by Ireton at Putney. Historians still disagree about how to interpret the evidence. The Levellers in fact never worked out a coherent philosophical basis for their political ideas. Professor Macpherson, describing the Levellers as the first political theorists to assert a natural right to property for which the individual owes nothing to society, has analysed Overton's attempt to turn all human rights into property rights, since 'everyone as he is himself, so he hath a self property, else he could not be himself'.[26] To this self property 'all the children of man have an equal title by birth, none to be deprived thereof'. All governments are limited by this natural right of all men.[27] It is the ideology of an independent craftsman or husbandman, and perhaps helps to explain why some Levellers would have refused the vote to paupers and wage labourers, since these had lost their economic independence, their self property.

What must have been a familiar query for the medieval peasant was picked up in the famous verse of 1381:

When Adam delved and Eve span,
Who was then the gentleman?

The question acquired religious overtones among radical Protestants in the 16th century. Robert Crowley in 1549 declared, 'We are all one man's children and have (by nature) like right to the riches and treasures of this world, whereof our natural father Adam was made lord and king... The whole earth therefore (by birthright) belongeth to the children of men. They are all inheritors thereof indifferently by nature'.[28] Drawing on these traditions, Overton claimed in 1647 by the 'law of nature and reason' that no man 'should be deprived of an human subsistence'.[29] This became even more ominous in *The Humble Petition of Many Thousands of Young Men and Apprentices of London*, who in March 1647 argued that 'although the meanest members of this great commonwealth', yet they had nevertheless 'by birth a right of subsistence here'.[30] A pamphlet produced in December 1648 entitled *Light Shining in Buckinghamshire* was by a group

26   A S P Woodhouse (ed), op cit, p83; C B Macpherson, *The Political Theory of Possessive Individualism* (OUP, 1962), pp137-142, 158.
27   D M Wolfe, op cit, p178.
28   J M Cowper (ed), *Select Works of Robert Crowley* (Early English Text Society, 1872), pp163-164.
29   D M Wolfe, op cit, p182.

calling themselves Levellers but in fact probably close to the Diggers (whose name for themselves was 'True Levellers'). This pamphlet argued that 'man was privileged with being lord over other inferior creatures, but not over his own kind; for all men being alike privileged by birth, so all men were to enjoy the creatures alike... No man was to lord or command over his own kind, neither to enclose the creatures to his own use, to the impoverishing of his neighbours.' It quoted *Genesis* I 26-31 and *Genesis* IX 1-18.[31]

Winstanley took up Lilburne's claim that 'the poorest that lives hath as true a right to give a vote...as the richest and greatest'.[32] This the Digger pamphleteer extended to 'the poorest man hath as true a title and just right to the land as the richest man'. 'A man had better to have had no body than to have no food for it'.[33] So the natural right to maintenance on which the Leveller and Ireton had agreed at Putney was pushed to conclusions which neither side in that debate would have relished. In 1649 the True Levellers set up an agrarian commune at St George's Hill, just outside London, and called on all the poor to join in collective cultivation of the earth. Common and waste lands everywhere, and all lands confiscated from king, church and royalists, were 'commonwealth's land...not anyone's but everyone's birthright'. The landless poor therefore had a right to cultivate these lands for their own sustenance.[34] It is the authentic voice of those squatters on commons and wastes who provided wage labour for England's earliest development. For Winstanley the rights of man included access to the means of livelihood. 'True freedom lies where a man receives his nourishment and that is in the use of the earth.' 'All laws that are not grounded upon equity and reason, not giving a universal freedom to all, ought...to be cut off with the King's head'.[35]

The Leveller leaders rejected communism.[36] They were, however, unable to reply convincingly to Ireton's case that the arguments for a natural right to the vote could be used to establish a natural right to property for everyone. The Leveller spokesmen hedged and were divided because, in the interests of the small proprietors from whom

---

30 Quoted by D W Petegorsky, *Left-Wing Democracy in the English Civil War* (1940), p89.
31 Op cit, in *Works of Winstanley* (G H Sabine (ed), Cornell U P 1941), pp611-612.
32 J Lilburne, *The Charters of London* (1646), p4.
33 G H Sabine (ed), op cit, pp321, 520.
34 Ibid, pp560-580.
35 Ibid, pp519-288.
36 Some of their followers held views closer to the Diggers: see *The World Turned Upside Down*, pp91-99 and references there cited; R Howell and D E Brewster, 'Reconsidering the Levellers: the evidence of The Moderate', *Past and Present*, No 46, p75.

they derived most of their support, they wanted to retain a right to property as one of the fundamental rights of man. Only Winstanley could be firmly consistent, because he accepted Ireton's point but drew the opposite conclusion, that private property should be abolished in the interests of equal and universal natural rights. Whereas Ireton had said, 'Liberty cannot be provided for in a general sense if property be preserved', Winstanley asserted, 'There cannot be a universal liberty till this universal community be established'.[37]

Thomas Hobbes, like the Ranters, thought men had a natural right to all things; but for Hobbes this right could be exercised only in the state of nature which was also (because of this natural right) a state of war. Hobbist men entered the state of civilisation only by means of a contract in which they specifically abandoned their natural rights. Winstanley believed that if natural rights were limited to what was necessary for the maintenance of life—quoting Paul's adjuration to be content with food and raiment—this need not give rise to the fierce competitiveness which was the justification for the Hobbist state (and which recalls Calvinist fallen man). Winstanley agreed that so long as private property existed it made some such state necessary—'the government of highwaymen'. But that seemed to him an additional argument for abolishing private property.[38]

So it is a divided inheritance. The Levellers arrived at a theory of the rights of man which included a natural right to private property. Almost immediately the True Levellers transformed this into its opposite, into a natural rights theory of communism. Both Levellers and Diggers were defeated and suppressed in the 1650s: it is difficult to know how far their ideas survived them. After the restoration of 1660 only proponents of middle class liberties could get their views into print. Arguments which appealed to the solid bourgeoisie now carried more weight than the flourishes of Leveller or Digger ideologues. In 1645, for instance, it had been claimed that 'to bar any freeborn subject from the exercise of his invention and industry to convert this universal native commodity to his best advantage at home or abroad, is to deprive him of part of his birthright.' Under Charles II this was extended by the highly respectable Sir Josiah Child to a natural right of all men to do 'what they think fit with their own estates".[39] William Penn the Quaker, who thought liberty of conscience was 'the natural right of all men', nevertheless defended

37   A S P Woodhouse (ed), op cit, p73; G H Sabine (ed), op cit, p199.
38   See *The World Turned Upside Down*, pp313-319.

religious toleration on the ground that persecution was an unjust invasion of the natural right to property.[40]

But the theoretical objections to natural right theories which Ireton and others had raised proved more difficult to overcome. Hobbes's attempted solution in *Leviathan* was not entirely satisfactory because, though it guaranteed property against 'anarchy', it did not guarantee it against the sovereign: and after 1660 the danger to property from the lower classes seemed less than the danger from the restored monarchy. Also Hobbes's stress on the complete natural equality of man was hardly acceptable after the radical revolution had been defeated.

For Locke the right to life, and so to the means of subsistence, was limited by the prior right of property. Locke pushed this back into the state of nature—where 'the people' already had servants; and Locke also established a right of infinite accumulation of property which made the rights of lesser property owners far from equal with those of the rich.[41] Publication of his theories coincided with the revolution of 1688, which guaranteed the effective sovereignty of the monied and landed classes through parliament, so ending any threat to property from the poor or the executive.

That is why neither in the 1640s nor after 1688 were there any ringing legislative pronouncements on the rights of man such as later revolutions were to produce. When the Long Parliament met in 1640, men's thinking was still confined to categories like 'the liberties of Englishmen' and 'Christian liberty'. When the Convention Parliament met in 1689, experience had taught that theories of the rights of man could open up dangerous possibilities of egalitarianism and even communism. One point on which Whigs and Tories were agreed in 1688-89 was the total undesirability of any revival of radical or democratic ideas. Better to reassert the historical liberties guaranteed by the English constitution, itself now safely dominated by the men of property through their representatives in parliament. There was sound social sense in the traditional English empiricism and distrust of theory of the men of 1688.

One wry consolation that the Englishman can draw from the failure of his revolution to produce any legislative charter of the Rights

39 [Anon], *A Discourse Consisting of Motives for the Enlargement and Freedome of Trade* (1645), p3; *Somer's Tracts*, X, p622, both quoted in J A W Gunn, *Politics and the Public Interest in the Seventeenth Century* (1969), pp234, 241.

40 W Sewel, *History of the Quakers* (1722), p617; J A W Gunn, op cit, pp178, 241. In 1644 Roger Williams had defended men's freedom to assemble and worship as they chose by analogy with their freedom to join trading companies (Roger Williams, *The Bloudy Tenent of Persecution* (Hanserd Knollys Soc, 1848), p46).

41 C B Macpherson, op cit, ch V.

of Man is that there was consequently no humiliating failure to live up to grandiose professions once the revolutionaries had obtained power. Neither Oliver Cromwell nor John Milton, for instance, ever claimed religious toleration as a universal natural right: they claimed it for God's children, for those 'with the root of the matter in them', excluding by definition papists and atheists. Cromwell seems genuinely to have done his best to live up to this limited ideal. But the radicals who never achieved power—Levellers, Ranters and Diggers—demanded many of the rights of man which were to be proclaimed with greater ceremony by American and French revolutionaries. Winstanley even anticipated rights which were to be claimed 140 years later by Babeuf and later still by Russian revolutionaries.

Chapter 12

Hudibras

This review of Samuel Butler's Hudibras (*edited by John Wilders*) *was first published in* Essays in Criticism, *IX, January 1969, No 1*

Hudibras is more quoted than read. This edition helps us to see why. Butler had a magnificent gift of phrase, and no power of construction whatsoever. He used to jot down a few lines of verse as they occurred to him, and later incorporate them in a new canto of *Hudibras* or some other poem: many of these fragments he never published. The brief prose *Characters* show him at his best, and the passages from notebooks printed by A R Waller contain a series of isolated and thought provoking epigrams. There are long tracts of *Hudibras* which are of the greatest tedium, not even of historical interest: and these increase in the Third Part, published in 1677, long after the sensational success of Parts I and II in 1662-3. One suspects that by this time the link passages had got more and more perfunctory. But the epigrams are superb:

> He could raise Scruples dark and nice,
> And after solve 'em in a trice:
> As if Divinity had catch'd
> The Itch, of purpose to be scratch'd. (p6)

> Tis a *dark-Lanthorn* of the Spirit,
> Which none see by but those that bear it. (p16)

> Honour is, like a Widow, won
> With brisk attempt and putting on;
> With entring manfully, and urging
> Not slow approaches, like a Virgin. (p27)

> As *gifted Brethren* preaching by
> A *Carnal Hour-Glass*, do imply

Illumination can convey
Into them what they have to say,
But not how much...' (p90)

All those—and there are many more—come from the First Part.

The animus and wit of the first two parts were directed against Presbyterians and sectaries impartially, and against the common people—women as well as men—who during the revolutionary decades had been impudent enough to intervene in matters of church and state which should have been left to their betters. By 1677 Butler's political emphasis had shifted. He received no royal pension until 1678, when he was 65 years old—too late and even then irregularly paid. The famous lines on the old royalists could be read as a reminder:

For Loyalty is still the same,
Whether it win or lose the Game:
True as a Dyal to the Sun,
Although it be not shin'd upon. (p239)

The reference to 'some under door-keepers Friends Friend' (p228) suggests the same disillusion.[1] So does:

Money, th'only Pow'r
That all Mankind falls down before;
Money, that like the Swords of Kings,
Is the last reason of all things. (p269)

The parliamentarians are no longer his only target. Fragments published posthumously see faults on both sides:

What else does History use to tell us,
But tales of subjects being rebellious,
The vain perfidiousness of lords,
And fatal breach of princes' words?

What makes all subjects' discontent
Against a prince's government,
And princes take as great offence
At subjects' disobedience,
That neither th'other can abide,
But too much reason on each side?

---

1. Cf 'A Court Beggar' in *Characters and Passages from Notebooks* (1908), pp38-39. The ingratitude of the Restoration government to royalists recurs at pp3-4, 384, 390, 458.

Authority is a disease and cure,
Which men can neither want nor well endure.
(*Miscellaneous Thoughts*)

In *Hudibras* the Vicar of Bray comes in for comment:

What makes all Doctrines Plain and Clear?
About two Hundred Pounds a Year.
And that which was prov'd true before,
Prove false again? Two Hundred more. (p225)[2]

Criticism of secular Vicars of Bray, which anticipates Dryden's *Achitophel*, seems to extend to all politicians:

So politick, as if one eye
Upon the other were a Spy;...
H'had seen three Governments Run down,
And had a hand in ev'ry one.

Our State-Artificer foresaw,
Which way the World began to draw:
For as *Old Sinners* have all Poynts
O'th' Compass in their Bones and Joynts,...
So guilty Sinners in a State
Can by their Crimes prognosticate
And in their Consciences feel Pain,
Some days before a Show'r of Rain'. (p245)[3]

Honour, whether social or military, is the object of sneers:

Heralds stickle, who got who,
So many hundred years ago. (p292)

Timely Running's no mean part
Of conduct, in the Martial Art.
By which some glorious Feats atchieve,
As Citizens, by breaking, thrive...
That spares the expence of time, and pains,
And dangerous beating out of Brains. (p286)[4]

One of the valuable features of Mr Wilder's skilfully annotated and

2. Cf *Characters*, p95.
3. Ibid, pp1-15.
4. Cf. 'A Degenerate Noble', ibid, pp34-35, and the remarks on gunpowder as a social leveller on p468.

definitive edition is its analysis of the different attitudes of Hudibras and Ralpho. The Knight is a Presbyterian landowner, his Squire a Baptist tailor. Hudibras has been trained in useless university scholasticism: Ralpho is a mechanic preacher, relying on the inner light and decrying university education. The Knight is an Aristotelian, who tells the time by algebra; Ralpho is a neo-Platonist and Behmenist, as so many of the radical sectaries were. In his elucidation of these complicated facets of radical opinion Mr Wilders is most useful, though he might with advantage have drawn here on the work of Dr P M Rattansi, who has established the contacts between sectarianism and the scientific underworld of 'Mechanick Virtuosi' (p200). Butler was not as capricious as Mr Wilder suggests in making Ralpho at once a Baptist and Hermetic philosopher, or Sidrophel 'both an experimental scientist and a journeyman astrologer'.[5]

Butler's attitude towards science is, however, curiously ambivalent throughout his writings. His mockery of the Royal Society is notorious, yet he was extremely accurately informed about its goings on. He took the side of the Moderns against the Ancients, and approved of the experimental method.[6] Sidrophel is an astronomer learned in:

> *Mathematicks,*
> *Opticks, Philosophy, and Staticks* (p158)

and he uses a microscope; but he makes a living as a 'cunning man', a white witch who pretends to recover lost property and heal diseases. Ralpho defends astrology because of its political usefulness to the parliamentarians:

> Do not our great Reformers use
> This Sidrophel to foreboad News?
> To write of Victories next year,
> And *Castles* taken yet in th'Air?

Has he not:

> Made *Mars* and *Saturn* for the *Cause*,
> The *Moon* for fundamental *Laws*?

5 Butler spelt this out at some length in his character of a 'Hermetic Philosopher' (*Characters*, pp97-108).
6 *Characters*, pp461, 320.

The *Ram*, and *Bull*, and *Goat* declare
Against the Book of *Common Pray'r*? (p157)

Hudibras is the great English anti-poem. It is mock epic, by implication a criticism of heroic poetry. Its imagery, among other things, parodies the metaphysical conceit:

The sun had long since in the Lap
Of *Thetis*, taken out his *Nap*,
And like a *Lobster* boyl'd, the *Morn*
From *black* to *red* began to turn. (p128)[7]

Not that the rhymed couplet fared any better:

For, one for *Sense*, and one for *Rhime*,
I think's sufficient at one time. (p101)

Butler criticises romantic love by contrasting it with the property marriage which so often went with it:

Tis true, no Lover has that Pow'r,
T'enforce a desperate Amour,
As he that has two *Strings* t'his *Bow*
And burns for *Love*, and *Money* too. (p191)

Their Fortunes! the perpetual aims
Of all their Extasies, and Flames. (p216)

Who would:

Be under Vows to *hang* and *dy*
Loves Sacrifice, and all a *lie*? (p124)

Butler was writing in the Restoration era, when the idealists on both sides in the civil war had been ditched by the practical politicians: it was natural for him to look for material interests concealed under hypocritical phrases. Property, he suggested, was theft. '*Courts of Justice*, for the most part, commit greater Crimes than they punish.' 'The solemn Professions of Religion, Justice and Liberty are but Pretences to conceale Ambition, Rapine, and usefull Cheate'.[8] Butler was especially suspicious of ideology: its good intentions could do incalculable harm:

---

7. Cf. the harsh words about Benlowes and his like in *Characters*, pp47-57. Peter le Motteux cribbed Butler's lobster for his translation of *Pantagruel's Voyage* (1694), Book V, ch 8. There is nothing corresponding to it in Rabelais's original.
8. *Characters*, pp292, 298, 389; cf pp74-75. Butler's own legal expertise adds point to these remarks.

As if Religion were intended
For nothing else but to be mended. (p7)

Opinion governs all mankind…
And nothing's so perverse in nature
As a profound opinionator.

A teacher's doctrine, and his proof,
Is all his province, and enough;
But is no more concern'd in use,
Than shoemakers to wear all shoes.
                    (*Miscellaneous Thoughts*)

Butler regarded himself as the spokesman of the man whom the shoe pinched. Religious fanaticism, science that was all theory and no practice, romantic professions which concealed sordid reality, whether in love or war or politics: these were his enemies:

Was no dispute afoot between
The *Catterwauling Bretheren*?
No subtle Question rais'd among
Those *out-o'-their-wits* and those i'th'wrong? (p49)

Ideology was self indulgence, and led merely to self indulgent quarrels:

As Pedants out of School-boys breeches
Do claw and curry their own Itches. (p119)

Like many later clever men whose ideals had turned sour, Butler proclaimed, a little prematurely, the end of ideology for everyone else too.

Chapter 13

The court and the country

This was a review of Perez Zagorin, The Court and the Country: The Beginning of the English Revolution, *first published in the* Nation *on 8 June 1970.*

Somewhere about the 1860s a great historian, Samuel Rawson Gardiner, invented the concept of 'the Puritan Revolution'. The 17th century English Revolution, according to Gardiner, had been about religious and constitutional issues: it was not a class struggle. This interpretation dominated the English speaking world for two generations until the publication of R H Tawney's *Religion and the Rise of Capitalism* (1926) and the English translation of Weber's *The Protestant Ethic and The Spirit of Capitalism* (1930), each in its very different ways suggesting connections between Puritanism and the needs of nascent capitalism. The idea derived ultimately from Marx, and in the 1930s even the most insular of British and American historians became aware of the work of Continental historians operating in the same tradition.

By 1941 Professor Tawney seemed to have established a new orthodoxy, a sociological interpretation of the English Revolution. Even when his views were attacked, no one proposed to revert to 'the Puritan Revolution'. All participants in the controversy which followed discussed the origins of the revolution primarily in economic and social terms. Professor Trevor-Roper saw the civil war as a battle between Court and Country, Ins and Outs, and thought the declining gentry were the driving force on the parliamentary side. A bout of sharp infighting revealed that both schools were better at shooting down their opponents' models than at producing a satisfactory alternative. Statistics were lacking on both sides. Since then a lot of detailed research has been done, and the time is ripe for a new synthesis. I turned eagerly to Professor Zagorin's book in the hope that he had produced it.

Zagorin's proclaimed object is 'to penetrate the specific factors, political, social and religious, that engendered the revolt against Charles I.' Narrative, he claims, is subordinate to this aim. So far as I am concerned, however, the narrative parts of this book are much the most stimulating. In the best tradition of S R Gardiner and C V Wedgwood, the generalisations are implied in the way the story is told; and Zagorin has many new and interesting facts to relate on the way.

His description of nonconformity in the church before Laud's advent to power, and of the disastrous results of Laud's innovations, is excellent. So is the account of the undercover links and activities of the opposition in the 1630s, and the account of 'the citizen element' with its careful recognition that 'the political stand of the urban segment of the society was, in fact, by no means uniform.' Zagorin rightly distinguishes between ruling oligarchies, which needed government protection and the mass of rank and file citizens who came to resent government policies. This adds force to his account of the coup d'état in London in December 1641, by which the parliamentarians snatched control of the city from the royalist ruling clique. Zagorin has read widely in the sources and has an eye—again like Gardiner and Miss Wedgwood—for the telling quotation.

But he is less successful at saying anything new about the causes of the revolution. Like Gardiner, he denies that the civil war was a class conflict, emphasising constitutional and religious issues—like Gardiner he leaves us with no very clear idea why the two sides lined up as they did in 1642. He uses Trevor-Roper's concept of a conflict between Court and Country in discussing the years before 1640; but he shows (as others have done before him) that this model cannot explain the division between parliamentarians and Cavaliers in 1642. It is helpful to have this clearly stated; but we are left wondering what the use of the model is.

Trevor-Roper's version purported to provide a sociological explanation of the origins of the civil war. It had the drawback that it did not fit the facts. Zagorin's model fits them better, but offers no sociological explanation. 'The Court', so far from being a sociological or even geographical category, turns out to be a state of mind. For 'the Country', as Zagorin honestly reveals, 'received support from many who held offices'; and 'not all attached to the Court were deeply or unalterably committed to it.' Nor is this a matter of a few individuals or of 'the intermediate ranks of the royal service' only: peers and privy councillors 'abetted' or even 'belonged to' the Country. 'The weaker faction in Court did strive always to pull down the stronger by a parliament,' the Duke of Newcastle reminded Charles II.

'The Country' is no more capable of precision. It covers dismissed courtiers, potential courtiers who, for reasons of political, religious or other conviction, withdrew from, or refused to take their natural place at the Court; and it covers the vast mass of backwoods gentry, most of whom were to be royalists in the civil war. 'The Country' means nothing more precise to Professor Zagorin than it did to Gardiner a century ago. Is it any more useful than rejected 'economic abstractions' like 'rising gentry', 'declining gentry' or 'progressive landlords'?

Professor Zagorin tells us that 'the conflict between the Court and the Country was...not rooted in social or economic contradictions. Fundamentally, it expressed a political opposition among the governing and wealthy members of the society.' But, in what appears to be a dubious oversimplification, Zagorin claims that this political opposition 'produced no original political doctrine'.

To use the Court/Country antithesis, given the slightly pejorative flavour of 'courtier' and the more favourable patriotic overtones of 'Country' is of course to repeat the political mythology of the parliamentarians. This is harmless provided we know what we are doing, and how much ignorance the words conceal. My prejudices, like those of Professor Zagorin, lead me to presume that contemporaries understood their society better than 20th century historians imposing their own sociological patterns. I admire his use of literary evidence to elucidate what contemporaries thought. But we must exercise discretion here. To make distinctions 'because the society itself did so,' is the beginning but surely not the end of wisdom. 'The society' often fails to notice what is happening, wishes to pretend it is not happening or to stop it happening.

However, the one point at which Professor Zagorin vehemently rejects contemporary evidence is illuminating. The Earl of Clarendon 'was guilty of gross misrepresentation' for 'conveying the impression that the parliamentarians' resistance was an outbreak of social insubordination.' The warmth of the language—Professor Zagorin is normally equable and urbane—arouses our interest. What had Clarendon done? He had supplied the evidence which wicked Marxist historians (like myself) have used in suggesting that class divisions underlay the civil war.

'The civil war *in its beginning* was no revolt of the inferior orders,' writes Professor Zagorin (my italics), and the parliamentarian leaders wished for no such outcome: a remark which could be made equally well of the beginnings of the American, French and Russian Revolutions. Professor Zagorin's indignation reminds one of Sir Charles Firth's complaint that Clarendon's *History* 'has the fundamental defect that it is a history of a religious revolution in which the religious element is omitted.' A historian who knows in advance that the English Revolution was about religion, or was not about class, naturally feels let down by Clarendon. This solid, impeccably conservative participant in the revolution, so well informed, so centrally placed, so judicious, cannot be laughed off so easily as Baxter, Dugdale, Hobbes, May, Warwick, Winstanley and a host of others whom Professor Zagorin does not bother to refute or even rebuke.

I should perhaps have begun this review by declaring an interest. Professor Zagorin complains of historians, including myself, who use the French Revolution as a model with which to compare and contrast the English Revolution though he recognises them both as 'great revolutions...fittingly linked.' He states, and I agree, that it is wrong to believe that 'a single morphological structure exists to which the explanation of events of a certain kind must necessarily conform.' But he sometimes seems himself to use the Russian Revolution as a yardstick. Otherwise why insist on 'the conscious, unremitting will to transform fundamentally the condition of humanity' as a necessary part of the concept of revolution?

Professor Zagorin easily shows that there was no such will among those who made the English Revolution of 1640-1. They did not even use the word 'revolution' in exactly our sense. 'Is it not therefore apparent,' he asks, 'that a revolution initiated by men who had no thought of what we have come to understand by "revolution" and, moreover, no awareness of being revolutionaries, must present, in significant respects, another character than the type of revolutionary change predominant in aftertimes?' This consideration, however, surely applies to the originators of the American, French and indeed February Revolutions—even though all these had earlier experiences to draw on. Here too men 'groped blindly toward the new, instead of boldly embracing it'; and 'set forth on a revolutionary path whose consequences [they] were far from perceiving.'

We must not confuse words with things. Men can perform actions without knowing the names by which later generations will describe them. 'It is', Professor Zagorin rightly says, 'a universal characteristic of revolutions that their course can neither be predicted nor controlled.' Before 1640 the adherents of the Country opposition 'were unconsciously shaping a different conception of the polity—one that gave the power of decision over policy to parliament, rather than the king.' 'Revolution is never a sudden birth': Professor Zagorin shows how inexorably events drove the Long Parliament's leaders along a revolutionary path which they had not chosen. Much of the analysis, *mutatis mutandis*, could be transferred to 1789 or early 1917. There were, moreover, sound political and social reasons for the refusal of ruling class Englishmen in the later 17th and 18th centuries to look back with any pleasure to the events of 1640-60: 1688 seemed to them a much more desirable sort of 'revolution' because it had been accompanied by a minimum of social disorder.

If in this review points of criticism predominate, this will no doubt be ascribed to odium theologicum on my part. I would myself attribute it to disappointment that a historian who dismisses his predecessors with such promising brusqueness (Elton, 'wrong'; Curtis and Walzer, 'anachronistic'; Laslett, 'confusing') has not himself squared the circle. We would all like someone to 'penetrate the specific factors...that engendered the revolt against Charles I and determined its character and progress.' But this book, full though it is of admirable details, does not realise its more ambitious claims.

Chapter 14

The Fifth Monarchy Men

This was a review of B S Capp, The Fifth Monarchy Men: A Study in 17th Century English Millenarianism, *first published in the* Cambridge Review, *20 October 1972.*

In the past three years there has been a rush of books on millenarianism in 17th century England—Professor J F Wilson's *Pulpit in Parliament*, Dr W M Lamont's *Godly Rule*, the collection of articles edited by Mr Peter Toon, *Puritans, the Millenium and the Future of Israel*, Dr J A De Jong's *As the Waters Cover the Sea*. Taken in conjunction with Mr K V Thomas's trail-blazing *Religion and the Decline of Magic*, these works all encourage historians to take seriously the wilder and apparently more irrational 17th century radicals. We can no longer dismiss them as 'the lunatic fringe'.

Dating the end of the world was a serious scholarly problem, which occupied the best theologians, historians and mathematicians from Melanchthon to Sir Isaac Newton. Given the assumption that the Bible was the source of all wisdom and knowledge, it was reasonable to suppose that the prophetical books contained the answer to the problem. The issue attained scholarly respectability in post-Reformation Protestant countries, as a consequence of the doctrine that the pope was Antichrist. For the overthrow of Antichrist was one of the signs of the last times, and from the middle of the 16th century the downfall of the papacy seemed a real possibility. In Britain, on the defensive against the Roman Catholic world, interest in the mysteries of Daniel and Revelation developed rather late. But with the victories of the Protestant Netherlands and England in the 1590s, the union of England and Scotland in 1603, the ending of the Spanish threat to France and Ireland, serious research began to appear—Napier's *Plaine Discovery of the whole Revelation* in 1593, Brightman's *Apocalypsis Apocalypseos* in 1609.

The great crisis of the Thirty Years War appeared to many continental theorists like Alsted to be the final showdown between Christ and Antichrist. This interpretation was spread in England, as far as the Laudian censorship would allow, by continental refugees like Samuel Hartlib and native scholars like Joseph Mede and John Archer. The four monarchies of Babylon, Persia, Greece and Rome correspond to the four beasts in Daniel; after the destruction of the last (Roman) beast the kingdom would be given to the saints in the Fifth Monarchy. Timetables differed, but there seemed to be a consensus that the prophecies pointed to exciting things happening at latest in the 1650s, the downfall of Antichristian Rome coming not later than 1666.

With the outbreak of the English Revolution in the 1640s, the press was set free from censorship. Summaries and translations of the seminal work of Napier, Brightman, Alsted, Mede and Archer poured from the press, some with official parliamentary approval. They helped tremendously to bolster morale, and to encourage hopes that the millennium might be very near. Here we must recall another tradition. Before the Reformation the view that the pope was Antichrist had been held by many heretical sects, including the Lollards in England. But for Lollards, as for most mediaeval heretics, this was only part of a more comprehensive theory which rejected the whole hierarchy of the church, its bishops, courts, laws and ceremonies, as Antichristian. After the Reformation the Church of England selectively took over the identification of the pope with Antichrist, but preserved the episcopal and judicial hierarchy of the church, together with many of its ceremonies. The notion that all these were Antichristian passed on to the more radical sects, Anabaptists, Familists, Brownists.

The major Protestant propagandist work of Elizabeth's reign, Foxe's *Acts and Monuments*, claimed Lollards as predecessors of the Church of England, and depicted all history as a battle between the forces of Christ and the forces of Antichrist, with support for the former coming mainly from the lower classes in society. Now it was precisely these classes to whom the identification of the whole state church with Antichrist appealed; and it was also the lower classes on whom the parliamentarian preachers had to call for support at the beginning of the civil war. So there was every encouragement for the popular heresy to emerge and spread in the heady atmosphere of the 1640s. The censorship had broken down; the repressive machinery of the state church no longer functioned; hitherto proscribed sects could worship and discuss in public, their sermons could be reported, their writings printed.

Many even among the propertied classes became increasingly disillusioned with bishops under the Laudian regime; the idea that bishops as well as the pope might be Antichristian had ceased to be merely a lower class heresy. There were no doubt many like the Rev Robert Maton, on whom Dr Capp quotes Anthony Wood: he 'was always in his heart a millenary, which he never discovered in public till the rebellion broke out' (p31). Taken in conjunction with the widespread expectation of cosmic events in the 1650s, the English Civil War came easily to be seen as the beginning of the last battle between right and wrong: the royalists were labelled the Antichristian party.

So for Milton in 1641 and for thousands of others Christ's kingdom was 'shortly expected'. 'Tis prophecied in the Revelation, that the Whore of Babylon shall be destroyed with fire and sword', parliamentarian soldiers told a horrified royalist divine in 1644; 'and what do you know, but this is the time of her ruin, and that we are the men that must help to pull her down?' Victory in the civil war seemed to such men divine confirmation of the righteousness of their cause. Everywhere there was intense excitement, deep speculation, enthusiastic hope. Without appreciating this atmosphere we cannot fully understand the spiritual elan of Oliver Cromwell, the dedicated service of Milton, the optimistic political theory of Levellers and Diggers, the searching speculations of Seekers and Ranters, the anarchic individualism of the Quaker inner light.

Seen against this background, the Fifth Monarchy Men cease to be unique religious maniacs, and become merely one variant of a general spiritual exaltation and hope. Dr Capp calculates that of 112 clergymen who were supporters of parliament and who published at least three new works between 1640 and 1653, no less than 78, or over two thirds, can be identified as millenarians. They include Presbyterians as well as Independents and Baptists (pp38-39, 46-49). The specific Fifth Monarchy movement of the 1650s emerged from this milieu 'as a reaction to fading, not rising, expectations' (p58). Its violence and extreme activism perhaps relate to earlier disappointments and frustrations. Jesus Christ had to intervene personally to bring about his kingdom on earth, because so many parties in turn had tried and failed to establish it in England.

The almost hysterical urgency of the Fifth Monarchists differentiates them sharply from other millenarians, but the main body of their thought was by no means unique. The specific reforms for which they called were often those which Levellers had demanded and which Quakers were to demand. Fifth Monarchists opposed tithes, servile tenures and primogeniture (pp147, 174). Many of them refused 'hat-honour' and used 'thou' to social superiors (pp143-144). They shared the general radical hostility to the universities as places for training a separate clerical caste (pp116, 188-189). They favoured law reform in the interests of small proprietors (Chapter 7, passim). Placing the Fifth Monarchy Men thus in context, Dr Capp is able to study them coolly and dispassionately, without condescension, as one of many radical groupings thrown up by the English Revolution. He has made an excellent job of it; his book will replace Louise Fargo Brown's *Baptists and Fifth Monarchy Men* as the standard work.

As early as 1642 a pamphleteer claimed that 'millenaries are most frequent with us; men that look for a temporal kingdom, that must begin presently and last a thousand years... To promote that kingdom of Christ, they teach that all the ungodly must be killed, that the wicked have no property in their estates... This doctrine filleth the simple people with a furious and unnatural zeal' (p43). Dr Capp indeed suggests that 'many of the ordinary laymen who were attracted to millenarianism may have been drawn primarily by the wish to humiliate their superiors and oppressors' (p39). Christopher Feake taught that there was in monarchy 'an enmity against Christ', a view which was repeated by many other Fifth Monarchists (pp52-53, 89, 208). It almost certainly helped to create an atmosphere in the army which made it impossible for Cromwell to accept the crown when parliament offered it to him in 1657. Feake included aristocracy too among Christ's enemies, and many Fifth Monarchists attacked 'the old, bloody, popish, wicked gentry' as a class, the 'profane swaggering gentry' and 'corrupt naughty nobles'. In the millennium, Feake taught, there would be 'no difference betwixt high and low, the greatest and the poorest beggar' (pp142-143).

To whom then did Fifth Monarchism appeal? One of the most valuable aspects of Dr Capp's book is his sociological analysis of the 233 known Fifth Monarchists. This list naturally includes all the gentry (20), ministers (34) and other professional men (14) who adhered to the movement. Of the remaining 165, only 21 were engaged in agriculture. It was 'an essentially urban movement', with London always dominant. It was strong in the clothing areas of East Anglia and Devon: 55 of the 165 worked in the clothing or leather industries, though none of them were big capitalists. Fifth Monarchism appealed to 'the very bottom strata of society (except paupers), the labourers and servants, that is apprentices and journeymen'—to lower and more specifically urban social groups than the Quakers. Dr Capp even suggests that 'the Fifth Monarchists seem to have been the only movement to appeal to these groups, treat them as equals and include them within their projected franchise'—though this is surely to forget Diggers and Ranters (pp76-86).

In fact, as Dr Capp argues elsewhere, 'their programme seems to have been one attractive to the small producers, sharing the aspirations of mercantilist society. Usury was accepted tacitly. The relief of debtors [which Fifth Monarchists advocated] meant also the security of creditors, and the reprieve of the thief meant the return of the value of the goods stolen. Humanitarianism coincided with the better protection of property' (p166). Although they suffered routine accusations of advocating communism, this was certainly incorrect (p146). Fifth Monarchists parted company with the Levellers especially in their rejection of any proposals to extend the parliamentary franchise. They had no more use for democracy than for monarchy: almost alone among the revolutionary groups they called openly for a dictatorship of the godly (pp63, 91-92, 144-145, 173, 178). They wanted to use political power 'to enforce godly discipline on the masses'. They, alone among the radical groups, really were 'Puritan' killjoys (pp140-141, 164).

Dr Capp uses the connection of Fifth Monarchists with the clothing industry to explain one otherwise odd feature of their policy. Like many radicals, though in rather more bellicose terms, Fifth Monarchists envisaged the forcible export of their revolution. John Canne and many others expected that the Lord would 'eminently appear...overthrowing the thrones of kingdoms everywhere in Europe' (p53). 'John Rogers demanded "how durst our Army to be still, now the work is to do abroad? Are there no Protestants in France and Germany even now under persecution?" Venner's men called for an invasion of France, Spain, Germany and Rome. Llwyd, Feake, Rogers, Tillinghast and Trapnel all promised that the saints' army would overthrow the Turks and the pope and his helpers, especially the Habsburgs and the French' (p151).

Yet Fifth Monarchists were among the most enthusiastic supporters of the Long Parliament's war against the Protestant Dutch Republic. This they rationalised by arguing that the Dutch tolerated Armenians, that they allied with Spain, that they were covetous and ungrateful in refusing England's proffered offensive alliance. A beachhead in the Netherlands would facilitate an invasion of Europe and the conquest of Rome. But more mundane economic considerations were also involved. Thanks to the war, 'the Dutch were cut off from their Spanish source of raw wool, and the English gained a monopoly of the sale of finished cloth to Spain. Moreover the English could hope to end and even usurp the virtual monopoly of trade in the Baltic (a major vent for cloth) which the Dutch had acquired since 1650... The war was accordingly popular with the cloth workers, and the sects in which they were well represented' (pp152-153). 'The Dutch must be destroyed', argued John Rogers, 'and we shall have an heaven upon earth' (p154). Similarly Fifth Monarchists condemned Cromwell's attack on the arch-Catholic power of Spain. 'Since the war involved abandoning to the Dutch the Spanish sources of raw wool, and the market for finished cloth, it seems likely that the real or potential economic effects of the war on the cloth workers were also a decisive consideration' (p154). In the millennium, Venner's manifesto of 1661 explained, 'There would be a complete ban on the export of unwrought leather, of fuller's earth, used in the cleansing of cloth, and of other raw materials' (p149).

The Fifth Monarchists were a nine year wonder. Appearing after the defeat of Levellers and Diggers, we may suspect that their popularity owed more to vehement denunciations of the ungodly rich, and to the presence in their programme of many traditional radical demands, than to their specific eschatology. The two Fifth Monarchist revolts organized by Thomas Venner were very small scale affairs, though in 1661 some 50 Fifth Monarchists terrorised the whole of London. After 1660, beset by informers, stoolpigeons and agents provocateurs, the movement rapidly disintegrated. Yet in 1665 an arrested Fifth Monarchist was rescued by the London populace. In 1671, when a cow broke into Palace Yard, Westminster, the cry went up that 'the Fifth Monarchy Men were up and come to cut the throats of the lawyers'. The jurors who acquitted Shaftesbury in 1681 were said to be nearly all Fifth Monarchy Men, and in 1684 the funeral of one of their leaders attracted 5,000 mourners (pp205, 209-211, 220-222).

There are many incidental delights in Dr Capp's book. The beast which made the lawyers scuttle from the Westminster courts was not an unusual sight in the capital: a Fifth Monarchist cow-keeper of London, executed in 1661, left 15 cows (p260). It is nice to know that the church-wardens of the parish of Amwell Magna, Hertfordshire, thought it worth reporting in Charles II's reign that 'several of the inhabitants come constantly to church' (p195). But Dr Capp's main achievement is to place the Fifth Monarchy movement firmly in its historical context, to analyse its membership and policies as carefully and thoroughly as the evidence permits. It is a very valuable service to historical scholarship.

Chapter 15

Two appreciations of R H Tawney

The first of these appreciations was a review of R H Tawney and His Times: Socialism as Fellowship *by Ross Terrill, first published in the* Balliol College Annual Record 1974. *The second was first published in* History Today, *Vol 30, December 1980.*

I

Tawney was, it might be argued, the greatest Balliol man of his century. As much as any single individual, he created the Workers' Educational Association as a serious educational force. His classes in Lancashire and North Staffordshire before World War I became legendary. He was President of the WEA from 1928 to 1943. In 1919 he was a member of the Royal Commission on the Coal Mines, of which Beatrice Webb said he was 'the great success'. His cross-examination gave the coal owners such a rough ride that the *Saturday Review* thought it 'a national outrage' that Tawney should hold a fellowship at Balliol. Through *The Acquisitive Society* (1921) and *Equality* (1931) he did more to influence socialist thinking of the inter-war period than anyone I can think of—including Shaw, the Webbs, G D H Cole and Harold Laski. From 1920 Tawney taught history at the London School of Economics: its golden age ended with his retirement in 1949.

As a historian I would place Tawney among the top two or three who have written in English during this century. *The Agrarian Problem in the 16th Century* remains a classic. Despite his aphorism, 'What historians need is not more documents but stronger boots', Tawney's own editions of economic documents are still in use. The controversies started by his *Religion and the Rise of Capitalism* (1926) and by his two essays of 1941—'The Rise of the Gentry' and 'Harrington's Interpretation of his Age'—these controversies still reverberate. *Business and Politics under James I* (1958), Tawney's study of Lionel Cranfield, is a soberer work, but also essential reading for any student of 'Tawney's century', 1540-1640. His *Land and Labour in China* (1932) is a remarkable tour de force; and for 50 years he kept up a constant flow of pamphlets and articles on history, on politics, on education. Mr Terrill's bibliography lists 427 titles, plus 145 reviews.

But for those of us who had the good fortune to know him, Tawney's greatness cannot be separated from his personality—an enormous scruffy bear of a man with deep and democratic human sympathies, a profound contempt for mere worldly success and an impish delight in provoking the smug and the self important. Mr Terrill quotes the conversation which Tawney attributes to William Temple:

Take a chair, Mr Jones.
Mr Montague-Jones, if you please.
Indeed? Take two chairs. Mr Montague-Jones (p126).

For my generation of historians Tawney's work was enormously stimulating, with its broad sociological sweep, its liberating escape from academic pedantry, its alignment with the common man and its exquisitely cadenced ironical style. His matted, allusive prose sounded as if it had been written with meticulous care and labour: but he could speak in the same rich plum cake style without a note. Tawney succeeded, more than anyone of his generation, in writing history which was popular without being vulgar. He saw history as a whole, believed that it mattered, and thought it too important a subject to be left to professional historians. He didn't think it morally wrong to make generalisations which—even if he subsequently had to modify or abandon them—were provocative of new thought. And how successful he was at provoking! For all his scholarship, I suspect he never differentiated in his own mind between his passion for historical truth and his passion to leave the world a better place than he had found it. Above all Tawney was a man—prodigal with his gifts (much of what he wrote is still unpublished), utterly unselfseeking. In Rousseau's phrase, he might be deceived but could not be corrupted.

Oxford gave him a second class degree, and he always seemed something of an outsider in the academic world: the establishment never succeeded in taming him. 'No dog ties a tin can to his own tail,' was his retort to the offer of a peerage. His most creative teaching period was with the WEA in Lancashire and the Potteries before World War I. I shall never forget, some time in the mid-1950s, holding forth to a WEA Summer

School in Balliol on 'Recent Interpretations of the English Civil War', and being told afterwards by an old North Staffordshire miner, 'I heard all that in Tawney's class 40 years ago!' Tawney was par excellence the historian of the common man.

Mr Terrill is a Lecturer in Government and Research Fellow in East Asian Studies at Harvard. His book is a labour of love, a determined effort to recreate Tawney's personality, to make sense of his political philosophy, and to estimate the reciprocal relationship between Tawney's ideas and the epoch in which he lived. Mr Terrill depicts Tawney as the greatest English democratic socialist, hostile alike to the economic tyranny of capitalism and to political tyranny whether of the left or of the right. He was suspicious of any power, whether economic or political: economic power was apt, he thought, also to give political power. He believed that power was based on people's acceptance of it and so was impatient with determinist theories, whether Marxist or of the 'you-can't-change-human-nature' species.

Tawney owed much to Balliol and the liberal tradition of T H Green. Even more important was the experience of World War I, which taught him that a sense of common purpose could facilitate social change on a scale impossible in time of peace. Mr Terrill emphasises Tawney's moral approach to political problems. Capitalism inculcated 'not only arrogance in the successful but an unworthy subservience in the stragglers'. 60 years ago Tawney had this to say about education:

> It is not enough that a few working class boys and girls should be admitted to universities, and that a great many more will be admitted in the future... Perhaps our educationalists have not hitherto allowed sufficiently for the surprising fact that there is no inconsiderable number of men and women whose incentive to education is not material success but spiritual energy, and who seek it, not in order that they may become something else, but because they are what they are. The oversight is not unnatural. The attitude is not one that is common in the ordinary seminaries of youth.

Mr Terrill sees Tawney's socialism as more relevant to the 1970s than to the decades between 1930 and his death in 1962. In the 1930s Tawney's refusal (unlike Laski, Strachey, the Webbs) to accept the then fashionable approval of the USSR isolated him from the liveliest socialist minds; yet his profound belief in the potential capacities of ordinary people saved him from the revulsion of an Orwell. In the late 1940s and 1950s, Tawney refused to accept the then fashionable Cold War stance and confidence in bureaucratic collectivism, or to agree that economic growth is all that we need to produce a good society. He was once more out of what appeared to be the mainstream (Strachey again, Crosland). 'The social problem is a problem not of *quantities* but of *proportions,*' he told himself in 1912; 'not of the *amount* of wealth but of the *moral justice* of your social system.' Today, when 'the end of ideology' has ended, Tawney's fundamentally moral approach, his 'socialism with a human face', appeals to a younger generation disillusioned alike by Stalinism and by Labour governments. An educationalist who was sceptical of intelligence tests 45 years ago is very relevant today.

All this is plausible and sensible. Why then do I find Mr Terrill's competent and thoroughly well intentioned book a little unsatisfactory? He aims to make Tawney comprehensible to American students of the 1970s. He translates Tawney's ideas into a semi-sociological, semi-political-science jargon which I sometimes find more difficult to understand than Tawney's own rich prose. In this idiom even Tawney's ideas sound woolly. Mr Terrill rebukes Tawney for 'remaining British to the bootstraps', for thinking England important, for underestimating the greatness of America (pp92, 233-234). I am perhaps too easily prepared to regard this as a venial sin. Tawney is blamed too for writing with upper class urbanity, wit and irony. His 'biblical and classical allusions, snippets from Shakespeare, Milton, Burns and Tennyson...must inevitably seem too narrow and complacent to the alienated utopians who have fallen heir to the socialist tradition. Stylistically he seems too adorned with the enemy's clothes, too familiar with the enemy's mode of life' (p234). I am irritated, unreasonably, by little mistakes, like putting Robert Crowley in the wrong century, or inventing a miners' secretary called Jack Horner who unites some of the characteristics of Arthur Horner, John Horner and little Jack who sat in the corner. It is a Balliol pedantry to worry about the spelling 'Dervoiguilla' (pp26, 317, 355). 'Amalakite' may well be the printer's fault, as the erratum slip tells us 'Jack Horner' is.

There is a real cultural problem behind my carping. Mr Terrill is irritated by Tawney's echoes of the Bible. 'His prose drips with biblical allusions, and a new generation may boggle at these phrases' (p346). The Bible is, however, more than a religious work. It is part of the English cultural tradition—Shakespeare, Milton and all those others from whom Tawney quotes snippets. Tawney's phrase about putting 'a hook into the jaw of these leviathans' is not a reference to his interest in the unfortunately aristocratic sport of fly fishing (as Mr Terrill appears to think—p83). It recalls Hobbes as well as the Book of Job. When Tawney writes 'an erring colleague is not an Amalekite to be smitten hip and thigh' he is not making a theological allusion. He wants us to see Professor Trevor-Roper as a barbarian killer from a primitive stage of Middle Eastern history.

Above all Mr Terrill seems to me to miss one crucial aspect of Tawney—his irreverence, his undergraduate desire to shock and provoke, sometimes almost irresponsibly when he thought his victim was being irresponsibly smug. Mr Terrill has flead Tawney's rump and pared his claws, made him far too reasonable, sensible, moderate. He might have done better to talk to more of Tawney's pupils (especially his WEA pupils) and to fewer of his colleagues. I suspect that Tawney showed most of his creative self to those whom he thought he could help.

Take his reply to a question about 'the sufferings of the peasantry in the 16th century'. 'The sufferings of the peasantry in the 16th century', Tawney boomed out, 'are due to the invention of printing.' It was a heightened and telling if rather cryptic lesson in the importance of source criticism, and in the danger of repeating cliches. 'Bourgeois revolution?' he replied to another question, about the English Civil War this time. 'Of course it was a bourgeois revolution. The trouble is the bourgeoisie were on both sides.' Mr Terrill wisely did not quote the remark attributed to Tawney in the winter of 1939-40. 'If the Communists had some machine guns,' he is alleged to have said, 'I would join them tomorrow.' It was not a serious political analysis: Tawney would certainly not have been in favour of a Communist military putsch, even had it been on the cards. The remark (if he ever made it) was a cry of protest, at the depth of the phoney war, against the hypocrisy of those who were more anxious to fight Communism than to fight the Nazis.

Tawney was not solemn and judicious, he was passionate and impulsive, and he hated the phrase-mongering which covered up lack of thought. He never suffered stuffed shirts gladly. 'Those who say that what they desire is a change of heart usually mean that they object strongly to a change of anything else.' During a debate in the WEA, when someone said, 'God made the middle classes no less than the working class,' Tawney demurely asked, 'Are you sure?' He did me a great deal of good by one unkind phrase which was repeated to me. 'I don't mind Hill being a Marxist, but I do wish he wouldn't sing the doxology at the end of every piece he writes.' That got right under my skin because it showed me that to him I looked exactly like what I was reacting against. I have tried ever since to keep the doxological element in my writing under control.

Tawney anecdotes are endless, and they nearly all turn on a concern for realities as against shams, for truth as against self advertisement, for ordinary people as against the self important. I was present on the famous occasion when an ambitious young scholar aggressively heckled Tawney. 'Why hadn't Professor Tawney said anything about X?' 'Why had he neglected Y?' 'And Z?' Tawney replied courteously the first two or three times, but as the cross-examination proceeded he heaved a deep sigh and replied, 'Ignorance, my dear sir, sheer ignorance.' You might regard that as a snobbish literary allusion, or a snub to a keen young scholar; in context it seemed to me a self deprecating cry to the rest of the audience: 'Do I have to go on being baited by this young cub? Please help me to get back to the subject.' We did.

Yet these nuances are based on my fallible and no doubt biased recollections. There are here deep issues affecting the nature of history and biography. I have been very unfair to what is in many ways an estimable book, and in no sense a bad book. Mr Terrill is a conscientious historian who has read his documents carefully (except the Bible). He is very well disposed to Tawney, tries to interpret him sympathetically. And yet he seems to me, who knew Tawney only slightly, to miss the essence, the 'feel' of that great man, to flatten his contours.

Mr Terrill did not have the advantage of knowing Tawney, and he comes from a different culture. But when I (or anyone else) write about 17th century England (for instance) I know none of the characters, and the culture is as different from that of 20th century England as Tawney's England was from the USA of Mr Terrill. Is the task of the historian impossible, in so far as he aspires to recreate a different civilisation? Must the mere fact of translating it into another idiom—which is necessary if it is to be understood at all—destroy the original? Is Tawney so dead that historians can only recreate him after their own image? Must any historical reconstruction based only on written evidence inevitably fall short? Or was I too involved, and are my views therefore suspect? I would have said of Tawney, banally, that he would live on in the minds of men. But what will live? A few dry bones? These are the uneasy questions with which I put down Mr Terrill's book. They may explain, if not excuse, the carping nature of this review.

II

R H Tawney, the centenary of whose birth we celebrate this year, was one of the greatest historians writing in English—some would say the greatest—of our time. Tout and Namier were superb professional historians, but Tawney fired the imagination of my generation. His output was relatively small, but almost all of it stimulated profitable discussion.

He became an academic fairly late in life, and his historical writing was almost a by-product of his other activities. From 1909 his main commitment was to the Workers' Educational Association, and his first great book, *The Agrarian Problem in 16th Century England* (1912), related closely to his work as a tutor in North Staffordshire. It opened up a new subject with great erudition and even greater human sympathy; its conclusions are still discussed nearly 70 years later, though not all them are now accepted. *Religion and the Rise of Capitalism* (1926), perhaps his most famous book, popularised Weber's thesis that Protestant doctrines contributed to the emergence of capitalist society. Tawney set the connections in a more precise historical context, and emphasised that they were two way: Protestantism was a response to social needs, though it also played its part in the development of capitalism. This book too is still relevant to modern discussions. It is written in Tawney's most gorgeous style—witty, epigrammatic, packed with allusions. When I first read it I thought its perfection was due to very careful elaboration. I was astonished to find that Tawney lectured without a note in the same rich and pregnant plum cake style.

A long essay on 'The Assessment of Wages in England by the Justices of the Peace' (1913-14) escaped the notice of many historians because it was published in a German periodical and was not reprinted until 1979; but it is relevant to present day discussion of parish elites and of the role of the Poor Law and wage assessment in maintaining social subordination. The long introduction to Tawney's edition of Sir Thomas Wilson's *Discourse on Usury* (1925) is still the classic study of the significance of money lending in early English capitalist society.

More controversial were two essays published in 1941, 'The Rise of the Gentry' and 'Harrington's Interpretation of his Age'. Both derived from the Ford Lectures which Tawney delivered in Oxford in 1936 but never published. Some of Tawney's statistics in 'The Rise of the Gentry' were severely and effectively criticised by John Copper and H R Trevor-Roper in the 1950s. But Tawney's case did not rest merely on statistics: he showed that the concept of a rise of the gentry was shared by some of the best early 17th century thinkers, from Ralegh to Harrington. This aspect of his argument has to be ignored by those who reject his case. Finally, *Business and Politics under James I* (1958), another fragment of the Ford Lectures, is a more conventional monograph. Excellent of its kind, it is not the work by which he will be most remembered.

Tawney remained devoted to the WEA, among his multifarious activities. When I talked to a WEA summer school in the 1950s on 'Recent Interpretations of the English Civil War', a North Staffordshire miner asked, 'Why do you call it recent interpretations? I heard all that in Tawney's WEA class 40 years ago.' I am sure he was right. Tawney was a staunch egalitarian democrat, whose brilliant *The Acquisitive Society* (1921) and *Equality* (1931) were very influential and will remain worth reading so long as our society is unequal and acquisitive. When Tawney was offered a peerage he indignantly refused: 'No dog ties a tin can to his own tail,' he declared in the process of lecturing the Labour prime minister on equality.

'What historians need is not more documents but stronger boots,' was one of Tawney's famous epigrams. The school of economic historians, of which W G Hoskins and Joan Thirsk are the most outstanding, might have taken that as their motto. Some historians today reject Tawney's history with surprising violence. This is partly ideological, partly the natural reaction of one generation against its predecessor. But the violence betrays consciousness of the underlying strength of Tawney's attitudes, which are easier to criticise in detail than in general, easier to proscribe than to refute. Tawney's broad historical vision embraced economics and religion, literature and political theory: nothing human could be alien. The past was not just dead facts, but full of meaning for us in our society, facing our own problems. His writings will remain a stimulus to anyone who shares Tawney's generous historical imagination. Above all, the brilliance of the writing will not go away.

Chapter 16

Isaac Newton and his society

This was a review of two books, A portrait of Isaac Newton *by Frank Manuel and* Philosopher at War: The Quarrel between Newton and Leibniz *by Rupert Hall, first published in the* London Review of Books, *17 September 1980.*

There are at least three possible portraits of Isaac Newton. Traditional internalist historians of science depict him as an aloof scholar, remote from the world, solving in his Cambridge ivory tower problems which derived logically from the state of contemporary mathematical knowledge. A second approach, which originated with the Soviet scientist Hessen, relates the problems which Newton studied, together with other scientists of his day, to the economic needs of rising capitalist society, or draws attention to the continued influence of his Puritan background on his mode of thought. This school finds it easier than the first to explain the later Newton, the dictatorial Master of the Mint and President of the Royal Society, and to take account of his continual obsession with alchemy, Biblical chronology and the end of the world—grave embarrassments for the purist 'internalists'. The latter do not like to be reminded that Newton said he first turned to trigonometry and geometry in order to understand a book on astrology. A third approach is psychological, seeking the key to Newton's achievement in his personality.

Far and away the best psychohistorian of Newton is Frank Manuel. His *Portrait* was first published in the USA in 1968, and is here reproduced without alteration: even a howler on page 112 stands uncorrected. Manuel has published two other more specialised books on Newton, but this is his best all-round study. Manuel briskly dismisses 'such antediluvian notions as the absolute autonomy of science', and sometimes his criticisms of more austere Newtonists like Whiteside and the Halls are sharp. He emphasises Newton's childhood—the under-sized posthumous son of a Lincolnshire yeoman, whose mother (a gentleman's daughter) remarried when he was three and left him in the care of his grandmother. On the death of his stepfather, when Newton was 11, they were reunited. Until her death in 1679, when Isaac was 36, his mother remained almost the only human being who was close to him. Newton's annus mirabilis, 1665-1666, in which he discovered the calculus, the nature of white light and the theory of gravity, was spent at her house; the apple fell in her garden.

Manuel's theory, put forward with judicious tentativeness, is that Isaac's early separation from his mother left a wound that never healed. This accounts for his withdrawn personality, his secrecy and evasiveness, his insistence on absolute loyalty in his dependants and his rejection of them when they fell short by his exacting standards. Newton's fierce hatreds of rivals are associated with childish desires to murder the stepfather who had robbed him of his mother. No earthly father figure could replace the father he had never known. Newton, born on Christmas Day, regarded himself as in some special sense the favoured son of a Father in heaven who was all powerful and all demanding.

Manuel thus need posit no break between the Cambridge recluse reluctant to publish his astonishing discoveries and the later Whig hero. Newton first came into political prominence when he led the opposition to James II's attempt to intrude a Benedictine monk into Cambridge without his taking the statutory oath of loyalty to the Established Church. Newton refused to take Anglican orders, but Popery for him had always been absolute evil: in 1714, he tried to get an Act of Parliament passed declaring that Rome was a false church. Under William III, Newton became first Warden and then Master of the Mint, offices which had hitherto been virtual sinecures. Newton turned them to important uses, including the establishment of the gold standard, which, Manuel wrily notes, 'lasted just about as long as his universal system'. At the Mint, Newton enjoyed powers which, in Manuel's view, enabled his aggressive feelings to be rationalised into ruthless and unforgiving persecution of coiners, clippers, forgers and other sinners.

As its president for the last 24 years of his life, Newton saw to it that the Royal Society 'was represented on any governmental body which might remotely be involved with a scientific question', presaging 'a new form of scientific organisation and control'. 'Even if allowances are made for the general truculence of scientists and learned men', observes

Manuel, Newton 'remains one of the more ferocious practitioners of the art of scientific controversy'. Yet he was always able to persuade himself that his rivals had sinned against the truth and Newton's unique revelation. When Leibniz claimed to have invented the calculus before him, Newton used his now dominant position in the Royal Society to mount a campaign in which he never appeared publicly but which he masterminded. 'The violence, acerbity and uncontrolled passion of Newton's attacks, albeit directed into socially approved channels, are almost always out of proportion with the warranted facts and character of the situations.' This is true of his historical no less than of his scientific controversies.

Manuel sees the outstanding characteristic of Newton's God, his absolute power, as related to Isaac's own deprivation and search for an all powerful Taskmaster. Other elements in Newton's intellectual life fit into this picture. His denial of the divinity of Christ enhances the glory of the Father by diminishing the significance of that other Son born on 25 December. Rejection of the Trinity, even after 1689, was punishable by death and would certainly entail loss of office: this increased Newton's obsessive secretiveness and his sense of a special private relation to the Father. Newton's wholly serious experimental alchemical studies, which continued throughout his working life, seem to be an attempt to solve the crucial problems in chemistry as he had solved their equivalents in physics and astronomy. In anyone else, this would appear insane ambition: but if Newton was God's special interpreter it was his duty to reveal all that he could. He did not share our hindsight knowledge that alchemy had no more secrets to reveal. The millions of words which Newton devoted to biblical chronology, and to the interpretation of biblical prophecies dating the end of the world, are again explained by his position as interpreter of the divine mysteries. 'Newton was pursuing the same fundamental purpose with kindred methods in whatever sphere he laboured.'

Such a summary does no sort of justice to the careful scholarship, the learning, judgment, wit and literary sophistication with which Manuel builds up his case. But it may suggest reasons for thinking this much the most stimulating book on Newton and his science which we have. Manuel makes it abundantly clear that he is not 'explaining' Newton's genius, but only the outward forms in which this genius was expressed. Work published since 1968, notably that of Margaret Jacob, amplifies some of Manuel's conclusions and reinforces my feeling—with which Manuel would not disagree—that many of Newton's peculiarities can be explained in sociological terms, or in terms of his religious inheritance and of the demands of post-Restoration England for order, authority, law.

'In all these youthful scribblings', Manuel writes of an early notebook:

> there is an astonishing absence of positive feeling. The word love never appears, and expressions of gladness and desire are rare. A liking for roast meat is the only strong sensuous passion. Almost all the statements are negations, admonitions, prohibitions. The climate of life is hostile and punitive. Competitiveness, orderliness, self control, gravity—these are Puritan values that became part of his being.

There can be no doubt that Newton's unusual personality contributed a great deal to his way of life and perhaps to his scientific assumptions. Manuel has brought this before us with a brilliance and a human warmth rare in historical writing.

Manuel is far from being a vulgar debunker. Newton's historical research, he shows, was concerned among other things with establishing the tolerance and latitudinarianism of the primitive church: for Newton, as for Milton, persecution of heretics was a historical evil of Catholicism. Newton urged an inventor to destroy an artillery model 'on the grounds that it would soon become known to the enemy and that it tended to the annihilation rather than the preservation of mankind'—a logic that has still not been mastered.

Manuel concludes:

> In the latter part of the 20th century the faces of Newton and of his science have lost their pure luminousness. The polarities of his nature are paralleled in the ambiguous nature of science itself… The overwhelming question remains whether Newton's science, which gave him great power and little wisdom, can in some other incarnation bestow that wisdom upon his fellow men… A closed scientific system like Newton's, which was consonant with his personality, must in some measure have affected the evolution of western science by excluding alternatives… When Europe adopted Newtonianism as its intellectual model, something of his character penetrated to the very marrow of the system.

Rupert Hall's is a more conventional but very useful study of 'the quarrel between Newton and Leibniz'. It arises from the author's labours as editor of Newton's correspondence during the last 18 years of his life. Here are none of Manuel's overtones: Hall lays little emphasis on Newton's personality, none on his vision of himself as defender of God's truth. Nor does he see Newton as the aggressor in his controversy with Leibniz. The whole unfortunate affair was the product of misunderstandings as the protagonists were egged on by their malicious epigones. This is all much more in keeping with the dignity of science. Wherever possible, Hall gives Sir Isaac the benefit of the doubt, returning verdicts of 'not proven' where Manuel categorically proclaims him guilty of manipulating puppets behind the scenes.

Hall regards 'psychological complexities' as 'indeed fascinating': but consideration of them is 'unprofitable'—they 'must remain purely speculative'. His only mention of Manuel is to dismiss as 'empty speculation' the view that Fatio de Duillier aroused in Newton, 'as Frank Manuel has maintained, a powerful homosexual passion'. (I cannot find any suggestion as crudely precise as that in Manuel's discussion of Newton's 'friendship' with Fatio, which concludes that 'the nature of their intimacy remains obscure.')

Hall starts from the fact that 'Newton's claim to priority in discovering the calculus, as against Leibniz's, is perfectly justified by the ample remaining documents.' Leibniz had by the 1690s established himself as 'the doyen of mathematicians on the Continent'; his calculus was used all over Europe. But Newton, a compulsive hoarder, retained enough documentary evidence to establish his priority nearly half a century after the event—in private if not in print. But this was not enough. Newton convinced himself, and tried hard to convince others, that Leibniz was an incompetent mathematician who had requited Newton's kind help by stealing his discovery.

Here some such hypothesis as Manuel's appears necessary. Hall lucidly argues that simultaneous discovery is a frequent phenomenon in the history of science, and says, without explanation, that the 17th century 'was the moment when European intellectual development toward freedom and maturity offered the highest opportunity for creativity'. There were perhaps social reasons for convergence in the discovery of the calculus. Although he does not account for the titanic nature of Newton's wrath, Hall makes some interesting points: for instance, that it was Wallis who first pushed Newton on against Leibniz, on nationalist grounds. 'You are not so kind to your reputation (and that of your country) as you might be.' 'Nearly all the mathematicians of this time, nearly all the ardent Newtonians, were Scots...a fact that no doubt provides ground for comment on the characteristics of education in the English and Scottish universities.' Hall is especially interesting on a point which Manuel did not take up: Leibniz's 'deep (and unchanging) philosophical criticism' of Newton. 'It pleases some to return to occult qualities or scholastic faculties, but because these have become unrespectable they call them *forces*.' Leibniz feared lest Newton's theory would revive the philosophy of Robert Fludd, against whom Mersenne and Gassendi had first defended the mechanical philosophy.

Hall leaves open the questions 'whether one views the Newtonian point of view as consistent with a then normal Christian view of God's purpose or (with Leibniz) as merely naive; whether one regards Leibniz's mechanical philosophy as marking a necessary independence of secular thought from theology or rather as a step toward excluding God from the universe altogether.' Certainly there were other contemporaries besides Leibniz who did not think Newton's the 'normal' Christian view, and many today would agree with Manuel in regretting that the victory of his 'closed scientific system' excluded 'the looser models of a Hooke or a Leibniz'.

Chapter 17

'A thraldom abjured and detested'

This was first published as an article in the Guardian *on 27 July 1981.*

The English Republic was established in several stages. In January 1649 Charles I was tried, condemned and executed as 'a tyrant, traitor, murderer and public enemy'. In March 1649 monarchy and the House of Lords were abolished. Two months later England was declared to be a free Commonwealth. The republic lasted, with vicissitudes, until Charles I's son was restored as Charles II in May 1660.

The republic was established in this piecemeal, almost shamefaced way because most of those who established it were not republicans by conviction. Kings were still hedged about by divinity, and regicide was profoundly shocking to the sort of propertied Englishmen who sat in parliament. They created the republic because they could think of no other solution to their immediate political problems

In the civil war of 1642-6, Charles I had been defeated so decisively that restoration of the old style semi-absolutist monarchy was impossible. Yet the king, even when a prisoner, refused to accept defeat or compromise, and rejected numerous attempts to settle for a constitutional monarchy of the type which ultimately emerged after 1660. Meanwhile indignation was growing in London and among the rank and file of the army which had defeated him. They were apparently not so superstitiously attached to monarchy.

As early as 1643 a royalist reported that the lower classes in Chelmsford were saying that 'kings are the burdens and plagues of those people over which they govern.' By 1645 the army rank and file, we are told, 'took the king for a tyrant and an enemy...they were never more to trust him.' In order to win the war, parliamentarian preachers and propagandists had called on ordinary people for support against the king, and had received it. After the fighting was over, such people began to demand the good society that had been promised them—as they were to do again in 1918 and 1945.

Their views were expressed by a democratic group known as the Levellers, which had grown strong in London and the army in the aftermath of the war. By 1646 the Levellers were declaring that 'the continual oppressors of the nation have been kings,' and demanding that 'the intolerable inconvenience of having a kingly government' should be ended.

Levellers and their army supporters argued that the traditional constitution had broken down—hence the civil war—and that a new one must be created. In creating it, natural right rather than historical precedent should be followed, safeguarding the interests of the common people as well as the traditional rights of the gentry. 'The poorest that lives', wrote the Leveller leader John Lilburne in 1646, 'hath as true a right...as the richest and greatest' to choose their legislators.

'God made men and the devil made kings,' said a Leveller in 1649. Only rich men 'cry for a king,' said another, so that 'the poor should not claim his right.' A republic was associated in such men's minds with political, legal, economic and social reforms which would put the middling and lower classes on an equality with those who had hitherto been their betters. Gerrard Winstanley, the True Leveller, argued that the enemy was 'kingly power', not the person of the king. 'The laws of kings', he said, 'have always been made against such actions as the common people were most inclinable to.' It was 'those oppressing...laws whereof he enslaved us that we groaned under.'

The army generals and the propertied classes whom parliament represented believed that democracy would endanger their property. They saw no objection to a monarchy, provided the king became dependent on them. But this is just what Charles refused to accept. After he had forced a second bloody civil war on the people, the patience of the army snapped, and they demanded that 'the Man of Blood' be brought to trial. For fear of worse happening, the generals purged parliament, set up a court which tried and condemned the king; the rump of the parliament proclaimed a republic. The generals had stolen the Levellers' clothes, had given them a republic without any of the democratic, legal or economic reforms which they had expected would accompany it.

In 1646 Cardinal Mazarin, effectively prime minister of France, had warned his sovereign that a republic in England would be 'an evil without comparison for France'. A republic would be more efficient since taxation would be far easier to collect if voted by popular consent. Mazarin proved right. The English Republic was far more powerful than the monarchy had ever been, and enjoyed unprecedented successes in foreign and economic policy.

They set England on the road to becoming the greatest world empire and the country of the first Industrial Revolution. One of the most unpleasant of these achievements was the brutal subjugation of Ireland—a crime whose consequences are with us to this day, but a policy which was new only in the ruthless effectiveness with which it was carried out. The only voices raised in protest were those of democratic republicans.

One of the earliest actions of the new republic in 1649 was to appoint John Milton their public relations man, with the task of defending the new Commonwealth before the public opinion of Europe. It is perhaps the only case in history when a great poet became spokesman for a revolutionary republic.

Milton had already asserted the right of peoples to call their rulers to account. 'No man who knows aught can be so stupid to deny that all men naturally were born free,' he asserted contemptuously, at a time when royalists in England and elsewhere were denying just that. Kings are 'deputies and commissioners' of the people. 'Freeborn men' have a right 'to be governed as seems to them best.' 'A king exists for the people, not the people for the king.' To suppose anything else 'were a kind of treason against the dignity of mankind.' Milton told a hostile world that the achievement of the English in freeing 'the state from grevious tyranny' were 'the most heroic and exemplary…since the foundation of the world'—a large claim which appears to put the English Revolution above the life and death of Christ.

Milton agreed with Mazarin that a republic was cheaper and more efficient than monarchy. Charles I's 'lusts and pleasures…his domestic extravagance wasted huge sums of money…all stolen from the state'.

Monarchy was socially divisive because of its maintenance of class divisions, as well as costly. Milton returned to the point in 1660 when he saw men ready 'to creep back…to their once abjured and detested thraldom of kingship'.

Milton found it hard to believe 'that any nation styling themselves free can suffer any man to plead hereditary right over them.' Faced by 'this noxious humour of returning to bondage', Milton nailed his colours to the mast, blasting monarchy in general and Charles II in particular. He ran a serious risk of being hanged, disembowelled and quartered for his pains. Monarchy was restored a month after his pamphlet was published, and many of his friends and colleagues suffered the horrible death of a traitor. Milton's name was on the execution list for some time: we do not know how he escaped. But he survived to write *Paradise Lost*. In this epic, written under a strict censorship, with Milton himself a marked man, his chances of preaching republicanism were small. But he managed to suggest that the parsimonious ant, 'joined in her popular tribes/Of commonalty was a pattern of just equality perhaps/Hereafter.' He hinted that among the Hebrews monarchy was established by a rebel, Nimrod:

> Who not content
> With fair equality, fraternal state
> Will arrogate dominion undeserved
> Over his brethren

Milton's Bible-trained readers would not need telling that Nimrod was a bad man.

Milton's republicanism was high minded but elitist. Only in his last despairing pamphlets published just before the Restoration did he advocate reforms supported by more democratic republicans: free schools in every city and town, more land for smaller men, as well as the abolition of tithes, whose forcible collection led to 'the seizing of pots and pans from the poor'.

The democratic republican tradition survived in the words of a Leveller who was finally caught and executed in 1685: 'None comes into the world with a saddle on his back neither any booted and spurred to ride him.' That proclamation of human equality was quoted by 18th century English republicans, and by Thomas Jefferson, one of the founding fathers of the American Republic.

Republican memories then survive. In the 18th century Catherine Macaulay wrote a republican history of the 17th century English Revolution. Men quoted Andrew Marvell (if it was Marvell), who made Britannia say:

> Too long in vain I've tried
> The Stuart from the tyrant to divide.
> Tyrants like leprous kings for public weal
> Must be immured.

In another poem they promised that England's:

> Oppression together with kingship shall die
> A commonwealth, a commonwealth we proclaim to the nation.

They quoted Rochester (if it was Rochester):

Then farewell sacred majesty,
Let's put all brutal tyrants down.
When men are born and still live free
Here every head doth wear a crown.
I hate all monarchs and the thrones they sit on,
From the Hector of France [Louis XIV] to the cully of Britain [Charles II].

The names of the great republican writers of the 17th century were not forgotten: Algernon Sydney, Marchmont Nedham, Edmund Ludlow. Oliver Goldsmith praised the Levellers. American and French revolutionaries quoted the example of the English Republic. And Wordsworth thought:

Milton, thou shouldst be living at this hour.
England hath need of thee.

Chapter 18

Lawrence Stone

The review of The Past and the Present *was first published in* New Republic, *30 September 1981 and the review of* Road to Divorce: England, 1530-1987 *was first published in* Social History, *Vol 16, No 3, October 1991.*

I

Lawrence Stone is one of the most distinguished historians of the English speaking world. His work *The Crisis of the Aristocracy*, on 16th and 17th century England, is a classic; so is his slimmer volume *The Causes of the English Revolution*, a collection of essays on the educational revolution of 1540-1640 in England. His massive study on domestic life in early modern England, *The Family, Sex and Marriage*, opened up a vast subject in a provocative manner; and there are many more books and articles. Lawrence Stone seems to have boundless energy. His books appear in rapid succession; some of them are very long. They abound with fertile ideas (and some less fertile ones) and they are all written with gusto that communicates itself to the reader.

The present volume is a collection of articles and reviews published over the past 20 years. They exhibit all of Lawrence Stone's strengths and some of his weaknesses. The book begins with three historiographical essays which show the wide range of his reading, his concern with history as a subject. In 'History and the Social Sciences in the 20th Century' he assesses new developments in the last generation—the influence of sociology, anthropology, psychology, demography, the computer, conscious use of theoretical models—and tries to sort out what is of permanent value from what is fashion and fad. Stone is no cloistered academic, defensive about his discipline. He has been second to none in his readiness to try out new methods. This makes some of his trenchant warnings the more significant.

'The computer is a machine in the elementary use of which most professional research historians should be trained—a six week course is ample for the purpose—but it is one which should only be employed as the choice of last resort.' 'This immensely powerful but very obtuse machine' has its own distorting effects on material presented to it: its use is enormously time consuming and it 'precludes that feedback process by which the historian normally thinks, thanks to which hunches are tested by data, and the data in turn generate new hunches.' Stone has some devastating criticisms of the techniques and results of some fashionable cliometricians. 'Intemperate and injudicious use of quantification' is not a 'solution to all problems'. This is especially true when dealing with periods before the 20th century, when much of the most important evidence is not quantifiable and what is quantifiable is of minor significance. 'A modest proposal for improving slightly the honesty of our profession would be to pass a self denying ordinance against the publication of any book or article based on historical evidence before the 20th century which prints percentages to even one decimal point, much less two.'

An essay on prosopography (the method of collective biography) assesses the virtues and dangers of the Namier method. Stone rightly points out that this method is more successful when applied to epochs of political stability than to those of revolutionary change, and when analysing ruling elites:

> At all times and in all places, the lower one goes in the social scale, the poorer becomes the documentation... The only elements of the lower classes about whom something can be done in anything more than a highly impressionistic way are persecuted minorities, since police reports and legal records often supply much of the necessary information... The odd result is that the only groups of poor and humble about whom we can sometimes find out a good deal are minority groups, which are by definition exceptional since they are in revolt against the *mores* and beliefs of the majority.

I am suspicious of that conclusion, since it assumes that groups that reject the beliefs of their society must be minorities, that the majority accept the mores and beliefs of their rulers. This sometimes may be true; but it was not in Montaillou, and we have only to look around the world today to find societies of which it is almost certainly untrue. Did Athanasian Christianity overcome 'heresy' in the third and fourth centuries because it represented the views of a majority of the population? Did Protestantism triumph in England because a majority wanted it to?

Many of Lawrence Stone's generalisations derive from his personal experience. England, France and the USA, he says, are the countries in which significant history is written today. They are also the countries whose languages he knows best. Modern historical writing starts with the foundation of Annales in 1929; so, I imagine, did Lawrence Stone's historical awareness. The journal *Past and Present* 'began a sudden upward trajectory of popular success in 1960'. Lawrence Stone joined its editorial board in 1958. The important shift in historians' awareness of the social sciences occurred in the 1960s and 1970s: Lawrence Stone left England for America in 1963. All our generalisations are no doubt related to our personal experiences, but Stone's are perhaps a shade less Olympian than they might appear.

Lawrence Stone's wide curiosity, his enthusiastic if critical appreciation of what is novel, and his courteous and tolerant if trenchant statement of his disagreements make him an admirable reviewer. He has a gift for summing up epigrammatically what most of us would say in several laborious pages. What could be better than these two sentences from his essay on the Reformation?

> Anti-clericalism has long been recognised as one of the principal forces behind the Reformation, but only recently has it been appreciated that this feeling is the product less of a change for the worse in the character of the priesthood than of a change for the better in the demands of the laity.

And:

> The development of movable type some centuries before the development of an efficient police force gravely weakened the power of the state to control ideas within its own borders (once police powers increased, of course, the balance shifted back again, and today there is overwhelming ideological power in the hands of the state).

Such remarks justify the last three words in Lawrence Stone's title: history is not just about the dead past, it is an aid to understanding the present. After saying that, within a generation of the Reformation, ideology had 'ceased to be analysable in terms of class or group feelings, and had become a mere matter of geography', he goes on to compare 'the 20th century, the second era in which Western civilisation has been split ideologically down the middle', to the disadvantage of both halves. Or take this statement on the relative importance of magic and religion in 16th century England:

> The average Elizabethan was probably less worried about the prospect of torment in hell in the next world than he was about his current

sufferings in this world—sickness, poverty, robbery or cuckoldry. These were matters about which the parson could do little, except to ascribe them to the sinfulness of the victim or the inscrutable providence of God. They were, on the other hand, precisely the things that the black witch was thought able to cause, and the white witch to be able to cure.

His present-oriented approach stands Lawrence Stone in good stead when he criticises less sensitive historians. Discussing—and praising—G R Elton's account of England under the rule of Thomas Cromwell, Stone concludes:

> The story of repression has to be told, not only from the point of view of the policeman, as Dr Elton tells it, but also from that of the victims, as Professor Cobb has tried to tell it... What really happened to the English in the 1530s—indeed, what really happens to any people at any time—cannot be discovered merely by examining the correspondence of the leading minister.

It is a just criticism, a credit to Lawrence Stone's head as well as to his heart.

Lawrence Stone rightly rebukes English historians 'capable of taking a cool and dispassionate view of Karl Marx', who 'are driven to frenzies of hatred by the writings of that mild Christian socialist, R H Tawney'. It is the more surprising that Stone himself, normally so free from conventional prejudices, should never have taken the trouble to find out the difference between Marxism and economic determinism.

Occasionally the epigram runs away with him. 'Reliance on the Bible is perhaps even less liberating intellectually than reliance on Aristotle' sounds all right until we read in the next sentence: 'Over the greater part of Europe (except for the Calvinist areas) the higher education bubble burst in the middle years of the 17th century.' It was honest—and scholarly—to insert the words in parentheses, but weren't the Calvinist areas also the Bible reading areas?

I part company from Lawrence Stone when he depends most heavily on social scientists, demographers, and psychologists to interpret the sex lives of our ancestors. He writes that:

> The experiences of the average child were so damaging that I believe that a large number of adults, at any rate of the gentry class in the period with which I am most familiar, namely, the 16th and 17th centuries, were emotionally stunted and found it extremely difficult to establish warm personal relationships with other people.

How can we be sure that a generalisation of this sort is true? How can we measure stuntedness and compare it across the centuries? We may know about a few individuals, but is it safe or even sane to generalise from them to a whole society? 'The rise of family love, both between parents and children and between spouses or lovers', Stone thinks, is to be dated not from the late part of the 18th century (as Philippe Aries suggests) but from the early part. Again I find the apparent precision totally unconvincing. No definition of love would convince me that it did not exist in the age of Chaucer and Shakespeare. Historians surely have confused sentimental expression of feelings of love with the emotion itself. They may be talking about literary styles or an extension of the reading public rather than about the realities of family life.

But these are large matters, and I should hate to end on a note of disagreement when I am with Lawrence Stone 90 percent of the way. Especially admirable are his zest, his turbulent moral energy, his insatiable curiosity, his encouragement of new ideas and new techniques, his love of stirring things up. He seriously, actively, and tirelessly works to improve the study of history. Because history is for the present as well as about the past, it must be written to be read. Few historians who write in English can maintain such a continuously lively, engaged style. An ounce of Stone being usefully wrong is worth a ton of Dryasdust telling us what we already know, or a thousand computer printouts giving the right answers to the wrong questions.

II

Lawrence Stone always writes long books, but they are never boring. This one is written with his usual clarity and vigour. He leaves us in no doubt about where he stands in the controversial matters about which he chooses to write. He opens up big themes with forthright confidence. When he disagrees with an established orthodoxy he says so. Demographic statistics can establish changes in the average age at which men and women married, but they 'tell us little about what was in the minds of people when they delayed marriage, or went through a clandestine marriage, or conceived a child out of wedlock, or broke up a marriage'(pp8-9). Statistics about human behaviour raise questions: they do not solve them.

England's position on divorce was historically anomalous. In nearly all Protestant countries (including Scotland) reform of divorce law was part of the Reformation liberation from the Catholic church. Under Edward VI an attempt was made to make divorce available as in other Protestant countries, but this was thwarted by Edward's death and the succession of the Catholic Mary. Attempts to revive it under Elizabeth were defeated by bishops and lay conservatives. The proposals were reprinted during the English Revolution and in 1643 Milton dramatically argued that divorce should be granted for incompatibility leading to irremediable breakdown of marriage—the principle which was adopted only 326 years later (pp302-303, 406-407).

Fifteenth century Lollards had opposed church marriage, and from the introduction of parish registers in the 1530s to Hardwicke's Marriage Act of 1753 there was a long and imperfectly recorded history of attempts to enforce monogamous church marriage on a population which had its own traditional but different marriage customs.

Marriage was concerned with property. Until the present century the possibility of divorce was open only to those with money. 'The propertyless poor, who comprised perhaps the bottom third of the population' did not suffer the restrictions imposed by parents' concern with marriage as a property transaction (p62). Gerrard Winstanley in the 17th century, Daniel Defoe and Jonas Hanway in the 18th, insisted that the poor could marry for love far more easily than their social betters.

What exactly we mean by marriage is a difficult question in England between the 16th and 18th centuries. The church's canon law differed from common law. Some pious demographers assume that church marriage was the accepted norm, but this is highly doubtful. Stone rightly accepts that before 1753 'there were large numbers of persons who were quite uncertain whether they were properly married', and probably did not care. Marriage by verbal agreement, accompanied by the exchange of gifts, sometimes without parents' consent, even without witnesses, was valid at canon law. Stone suggests that contract marriage flourished especially after the breakdown of ecclesiastical authority in the 1640s and 1650s, and the establishment of civil marriage in 1653 (Chapter 3). The practice is certainly far older.

Clandestine marriage, without banns or licence, performed by a venal parson, not necessarily in a church, was also popular: it was cheaper than church marriage, and much less public. Poor couples used it to avoid opposition from parish officials worried about the production of children likely to be a burden on the poor rate. By the 18th century at least one in five, perhaps one in three, of the population were marrying by licence outside their own parish. Fees for a 'Fleet marriage' were only about one third of those charged for a regular church service. In the 1740s 6,600 marriages a year were conducted clandestinely in the Fleet prison, out of an English total of 47,000. This must include the majority of Londoners as well as a significant proportion from the home counties. 'By the early 18th century the church had covertly come to live on the illegal profits from the clandestine marriage trade' (pp115, 120, Chapter 4 passim). The frequency of rural clandestine marriages in the late 17th and early 18th centuries, Stone observes sardonically, 'wreaks havoc upon the data available to modern demographers' (p104).

Hardwicke's Marriage Act put an end to contract and clandestine marriages, though Gretna Green offered facilities for runaway matches because Scotland still accepted contract and clandestine marriages as binding (pp128, 135, 358). But the act did nothing to stop 'stable cohabitation', informal marriage with no church ceremony at all, which was accepted by many local communities (pp64-66). We have no idea of the extent of this practice: Stone might perhaps have emphasised more that it was almost certainly widespread.

If marriage for love was easier for the poor than for the rich, so was de facto divorce—at least for men. A husband could simply desert his wife and disappear—to sea, to the army, to the anonymity of London. Deserted wives in Norwich in the 1580s amounted to one tenth of women on poor relief. In the 18th century around 6 percent of women on poor relief in south east England were abandoned wives. A man moving to a new area would have little difficulty in establishing a new marriage, whether informal, clandestine or bigamous. But again numbers are impossible even to guess. Stone concludes that desertions were almost certainly far more numerous than wife sales, a conventionally accepted popular form of divorce (pp142, 145-148).

For the propertied classes 'irremediable marital breakdowns' were dealt with by private separation deeds. These date from the revolutionary 1650s, when church courts had been abolished. They amounted to 'a form of quasi-legal semi-divorce' (pp149-150, 182). Later in the 17th century 'Whig ideology helped to instigate parliamentary divorce for wifely adultery in cases in which the patrilineal descent of property was endangered.' Property was what mattered—'not justice, equity, the need to follow the sayings of Christ, or a desire to bring England into line with other Protestant countries like Scotland' (p312).

Lawyers turned divorce by act of parliament into 'a convenient collusive agreement between a rich husband and his wife for a divorce by mutual consent in order to remarry'. This 'escape hatch exclusively confined to a handful of wealthy males' was 'clearly indefensible on grounds of theology, morality or logic'; but it lasted until 1857. But then the middling sort, who had won the vote in 1832, got cheaper divorce. There followed a 25-fold increase in the annual rate of divorce (pp346, 354-356; cf p186). Propertied legislators, bishops and judges all expressed horror at the prospect of making divorce available to the lower classes (much as the church does in Spain today). 'Equal justice to the poor', said Bishop Wilberforce in 1856, 'would be purchased at the price of unlimited pollution.' Despite changes in 1923, 'the cost and complexity of legislation...remained substantially unchanged' until 1937. Only in 1969 was the principle enunciated by Milton in 1643 finally accepted (pp365-366, 371, 375, 406-407). It is difficult to explain this attitude rationally, since many of the most respectable of the working classes were living in de facto marriages unsanctified by the church.

Stone traces 'a very slow and hesitant redefinition of male honour', again dating from the mid-17th century. In 1653 a father sued the seducer of his daughter (his property) for compensation for 'loss of her services'. A gentleman would traditionally avenge himself on the seducer of his wife by a duel or some other form of violence. But as capitalist society developed, a wronged husband came to prefer monetary compensation for trespass on his property in the body of his wife (pp83, 237, 296). Simultaneously Milton, Samuel Butler and others were ridiculing the traditional military virtues of honour: and epic was on the way out.

Stone's book appeared too late for him to take account of Susan Steve's important *Married Women's Separate Property in England, 1660-1833* (Harvard University Press, 1990). She is less sympathetic to lawyers than Stone, showing with much detail how they could always help male clients with money to wriggle round the law. Wives, who could not sue their husbands, remained inevitably at an enormous disadvantage. Most were ignorant of their husbands' finances (p197). In separation cases wives were not allowed to testify against their husbands, whose property they were. They had to sit silently in court, listening to lies told by their bribed servant (p289). Stone cites the shocked disapproval of the law lords in 1663 when a wife claimed the enforcement of a premarital contract 'that she shall not be subject' to her husband. That must date from the brave days of the English Revolution; but now it was declared 'void and contrary to the law of God and Nature, and public honesty' (p17). When some 18th century judges tried to reduce immorality by imposing punitive damages on the guilty (male) third party, this had the unintended consequence of increasing collusion between husband and lover (pp284-285, 291-292). In the 19th century 'the key agent of change' in divorce laws was not the judges but public opinion, enforced by juries, who found the practice of husbands profiting from their wives' adultery repugnant to romantic ideas of wedded love (p206).

Lawrence Stone's book is very solidly based on hitherto unused evidence from the archives of ecclesiastical courts. In addition, he has drawn on contemporary legal handbooks, novels and pamphlets, and unpublished correspondence. He promises us two further volumes of selected case studies. It is unlikely that his book has said the last word about the road to divorce. But it raises a multitude of issues, clearly, trenchantly and provocatively, which can now be discussed. And it is a pleasure to read.

Chapter 19

Religion and democracy in the Puritan Revolution

This was first published in Democracy: A Journal of Political Renewal and Radical Change, *April 1982*.

In the English Revolution fully articulated theories of political democracy were put forward by an organised political party—the Levellers—probably for the first time. In what used to be called 'the Puritan Revolution' all politics were expressed in religious terms. Oliver Cromwell sought guidance from the Lord in every political crisis; Charles I thought it was his religious duty to die rather than give up his royal prerogative; wild Quakers disrupted services of the state church wearing nothing but loincloths. Whether religious arguments were used to support or attack constituted authority, all thought that they were defending the true Christian religion—Charles I and his bishops, Oliver Cromwell and the Puritans, the extreme radical sects.

It is too facile to say that the 17th century was a more religious age than our own, which is the resort of some lazy historians. More relevant is that in the 17th century church and state were indissolubly linked. All English men and women were members of the Church of England whether they liked it or not. All had to attend their own parish church every Sunday, under penalty of fine. There they might have to sit through sermons preached by a parson in whose selection they had had no say, and whose theology or personality they might detest. It was also an offence to attend a church outside one's own parish, even though the preaching there might be more congenial.

The 17th century church had a monopoly of opinion forming, and performed functions that today have passed to other media. Church courts punished men and women for a wide variety of 'sins' which would not be regarded as crimes today, such as extra-marital sex, working on saints' days, failure to pay tithes (the 10 percent income tax which everyone was supposed to pay in order to maintain their parish priest). Church courts put men and women on oath and asked questions designed to make them incriminate their friends and neighbours; sentences such as public penance or excommunication were imposed, which could mean the severing of all social, business, and legal relations with one's fellows. The church controlled education and censorship.

We live in a society in which the church is separated from the state, and consumers' choice has replaced religious monopoly: religion has become a one day a week affair; one can choose to have no religion at all. But in the 17th century religion and politics were inevitably closely linked. The parson was probably the best educated man in the parish (apart possibly from the squire, who no doubt appointed him). He was trained to interpret the sacred text of the Bible, which was believed to contain all truth. To reject the state church was an act of political insubordination. Before 1640 religious sects were underground cells: many who could not accept the church emigrated (if they could afford to) to the Netherlands or America.

Control of the pulpit was a matter of political power, and was recognised as such. Charles I said that 'the dependency of the church upon the crown is the *chiefest* support of regal authority' (my italics): 'People are governed by the pulpit rather than by the sword in time of peace.' The clergy read from the pulpit government handouts, and were often instructed on the position they were to take (or the silence they were to observe) on delicate political matters. They were described as 'the king's spiritual militia'. Just as today the first action of a revolutionary group would be to seize control of the broadcasting system, in the 17th century its most important action was to take control of the church.

Before 1640 the church was a prop of the social order. 'No bishop, no king, no nobility' said James I—accurately enough, for the monarchy and the House of Lords were abolished precisely three years after the abolition of episcopacy in 1646. The patronage system ensured that almost all the clergy were conservative in outlook: they were appointed by local gentlemen, or by the king, or by bishops and other ecclesiastical bodies (deans and chapters, Oxford and Cambridge colleges). If a clergyman had received a higher education, it would have been at Oxford or Cambridge, where ecclesiastical control tried to ensure that he acquired no dangerous ideas. Episcopacy was defended on social grounds: 'parity' (equality) in the church, men argued, might lead to parity in the state. The poet Edmund Waller in 1641 resisted popular attacks on the bishops because episcopacy was a 'counterscarp or outwork'; 'if this assault of the people' overcame it, they might turn next to the rents and properties of landlords.

Mainline Puritans did not want parity. They wanted to change the government of the state church, to eliminate bishops (too closely dependent on the crown), and establish far more lay control over the church—by gentlemen and merchant oligarchies in the parishes, at the centre by parliament—the representative body elected by the men of property.

We should not think of 17th century Puritans as gloomy killjoys. We should think rather of Oliver Cromwell, who said that religious intolerance was as bad as keeping all wine out of the country lest men should be drunk; of Milton, a great lover of music who urged parliament to establish a national theatre; of John Bunyan, who said that a teetotaller walked not after the spirit of God but after his own lusts. Mr Veall, the latest historian of law reform in 17th century England, believes that the 1640s and 1650s were decades of greater sexual freedom for ordinary people than any before or for a long time afterwards. When a Russian ambassador came to London in 1645, after the city had been under Puritan domination for four years, the two things which most caught his attention were the stained glass in church windows and the merry pealing of church bells. Some 20th century historians could have told him that 'Puritans' had broken all such windows in churches and cut down the church bells. It was only after the defeat of the 'Puritan Revolution', after 1660, that dissenters were excluded from national and local political life and from the universities and so inevitably became inturned, provincial, sectarian, and 'Puritan'.

Puritanism then was mainly a political movement with a revolutionary ideology, though its ideas were expressed in religious idiom. Ever since Henry VIII's reformation had declared England's independence of Rome, Protestantism and English patriotism had been closely linked. Puritans were the most anti-Catholic and therefore the most vociferously patriotic of all Protestants. John Foxe's *Book of Martyrs* taught Englishmen to see the whole of history as a conflict between good and evil, Christ and Antichrist, with God's Englishmen on the side of Christ. More: Foxe emphasised that it was the humbler English people, yeomen and artisans, who had been the staunchest supporters of God's cause and the main victims of persecution in the reign of the Catholic Mary. Cromwell drew on this tradition in 1645 when he reported to the Speaker of the House of Commons on the victory of Naseby, the decisive battle of the civil war. As he surveyed his troops before the fight, he said, he knew they were a 'company of poor, ignorant men'; but he had 'assurance of victory, because God would by things that are not bring to nought the things that are... And God did it.' Cromwell helped God a good deal, but such confidence that one was cooperating with divine purposes had a tremendous effect on morale. Islam and Marxism have given their adherents a similar confidence that history was on their side; it helps to make sense of a confusing world.

But such lines of thought proved to be dangerous. God could speak to the consciences of the lower classes as well as to their betters. For at least two and a half centuries before the revolution of 1640 there had been underground heretical movements in England, whose adherents were at various times called Lollards, Anabaptists, Familists. When the government of Charles I and the bishops broke down in 1640, the ideas of these sectaries could suddenly be freely expressed, both verbally and in print. Church courts and the censorship no longer operated. There was a fantastic outburst of discussion. What we call 'religious toleration' meant that ordinary people no longer had to go to their parish church every Sunday. Instead, many of them formed their own discussion groups, meeting every Sunday not to listen to an upper class parson but to talk themselves about what they were interested in, under the chairmanship of a so called 'mechanic preacher', someone who worked with his hands six days a week and took the chair at one of these discussion groups on the seventh. Women took part in congregational discussions and government; some women preached. No wonder the conservative Thomas Edwards thought religious toleration the worst of evils. But John Milton in *Areopagitica* hailed it ecstatically, with a genuine belief that uninhibited discussion would lead to the emergence of agreed truths.

The number of books and pamphlets collected by George Thomason rose from 22 in 1640 to 1,966 two years later; and he tried to collect them all. The number of newspapers rose from zero in 1640 to 722 in 1645. A printing press was a small, cheap, and mobile piece of equipment; it was not yet monopolised by the rich. So for a few intoxicating years anything could be discussed, and most things were. A fierce anti-clericalism proclaimed the equality of laymen with priests.

A millenarian political enthusiasm was abroad. Milton believed that Christ was the 'shortly expected King', whose coming would 'end all earthly tyrannies'. All Protestants had long known that the pope was Antichrist; now men identified Charles I and his supporters as agents of Antichrist. A royalist parson was shocked when he talked to parliamentarian prisoners who applied the ideas of Foxe's *Book of Martyrs* to current politics. 'What do you know', they asked him, 'but this is the day of his [the Antichrist's] ruin, and we are the men that must help to pull him down?' The clergyman explained in vain that Antichrist was in Rome, and that pulling him down was a job for kings, not for the common people. On the contrary, was the reply: Antichrist is here in England, and the Book of Revelation says the common people, the multitude, shall pull him down.

For centuries the person of the king, the Lord's anointed, had been sacrosanct. Yet in the 1640s parliamentarian preachers and propagandists were inciting ordinary people to fight against him, and to pay taxes and endure the hardships of civil war. By what right? If the king and his advisers were agents of Antichrist, it was a religious duty to resist them. Another line of argument was that even if the king were sovereign by legal and historical right, parliament represented the people of England, and in the last resort the whole people was greater than any single man, even the king.

But this argument backfired. The royalist Sir Robert Filmer had great fun pointing out that parliament represented not the people but perhaps one in ten of the adult males. Therefore, he argued, parliament could not be superior to the king. But when in 1645-6 the Leveller party began to be organised in London, they gave a different twist to the argument. True, parliament did not represent the people of England. But it could be made to represent them—by extending the vote to all men, by enfranchising towns at present unrepresented in the House of Commons. Then the cause of parliament would be justified— even more so if monarchy and the House of Lords were abolished and the Commons became the sole legislative assembly, responsible to 'their masters, the people who chose them'.

So the arguments of the parliamentary leaders were turned back against them. This became serious when military stalemate led to the Self Denying Ordinance of 1645 and the foundation of the New Model Army. The effect of the Self Denying Ordinance was to remove all peers from the commands in the parliamentary army which they had assumed as a right. The New Model Army, 'in which there is not one lord', as a Leveller proudly boasted, was drawn largely from the Army of the Eastern Association which Cromwell had built up on the principles of complete religious toleration, liberty of discussion, and the career open to the talents. Within a year the New Model had finally defeated the royalists and captured the king. When parliament proposed that this army should disband without even having its wages paid, it mutinied and took the unprecedented step of electing 'Agitators', representatives of the rank and file, to an army council. The generals, perplexed and disapproving, but determined to preserve the unity of the army, tagged along behind even when, on the Agitators' orders, Cornet Joyce forcibly removed Charles I from the custody of parliamentary commissioners. In the summer of 1647, again under pressure from the lower ranks, the army moved on London and, in effect, seized political power.

In the famous Putney Debates of October–November 1647 we see the army council, composed of generals, representatives of junior officers, and Agitators, discussing what to do with power. The generals advocated a constitution very like that which was to be established after 1688, with the king subordinated to parliament. The Agitators, supported by some officers, put forward the Leveller draft constitution, the 'Agreement of the People', which would have established a republic with a single chamber elected by manhood suffrage, or at least with a widely extended electorate. In the debates we can trace a curious amalgam of religious and secular motifs. When the debate got stuck, Cromwell would call for a prayer meeting. The Levellers argued that men had a natural right to the vote, and were badly rattled when General Ireton pointed out that by the same logic the poor might claim a natural right to equality of property. The Levellers represented mainly small proprietors, and had no wish to encourage communist ideas. But they could produce no more satisfactory reply than that the Bible said 'Thou shalt not steal', and thus sanctified property. But ultimately the Levellers were happier with fully secular arguments. John Wildman thought 'it was not easily determinable what is sin by the light of nature.'

Gerrard Winstanley, leader of the much smaller group of 'Diggers' or 'True Levellers', received a divine message in a trance which told him to set up a communist community by cultivating the waste land near Cobham in Surrey. But in the pamphlets he wrote to defend his ideas, he too verged on secularism. His allegorical use of the Bible almost destroyed the historical significance of the text. The incarnation, the resurrection, the second coming, the last judgement, were all treated as occurring within the hearts and consciences of believers. Christ and the devil were not to be found above the skies or below the earth but 'within a man, fighting against each other'. Of the biblical stories, Winstanley wrote 'whether there were such outward things or no, it matters not much.'

Winstanley tells us that he used the word 'Reason' instead of the word God, by which he had been held in darkness. For him the second coming was not a descent of Christ from heaven but 'the rising up of Christ in sons and daughters', the spreading of reason among all mankind. Reason ('or universal love') will 'make mankind to be all of one heart and one mind', and will lead to agreement to establish a co-operative society. Heaven will be found here in this world, not in the afterlife, and 'salvation, which is liberty and peace', will be won through community political action.

The orthodox had always stressed that since the fall of Adam the mass of mankind was incurably sinful. The Calvinist theology accepted by Puritans and most other clergymen of the Church of England assumed that the elect were a tiny minority, perhaps 0.1 percent of the world's population thought the New England divine Thomas Shepard. The English Fifth Monarchist John Spittlehouse more generously put it at 25 percent. Bunyan wavered between 5 percent and 0.02 percent. It was therefore logical for Richard Baxter to write that 'to plead for a democracy is to plead that the sovereignty may be put into the hands of the rebels' against God. (The illogicality of the tacit assumption that it is the godly minority who now rule escaped such propagandists for the status quo.)

The doctrine of the sinfulness of the majority of men and women naturally appealed to an elite: it was less acceptable to the many when they had the opportunity to think about and discuss it. William Perkins and a host of early 17th century divines bewailed the ignorance of the common people who 'look to be saved by their good serving of God and by their good deeds.' They were, Perkins added, 'enemies of Christ'. English Anabaptists in the mid-16th century had rejected original sin, and thought that 'as when there was no sin, all things were common, so they ought now to be'. The social conclusions were not always so directly drawn, but when the censorship broke down in the 1640s large numbers of people began to challenge the doctrine of predestination. The Leveller Richard Overton insisted that Christ died for all. The Leveller William Walwyn hoped that all men might be saved. The third of the Leveller leaders, John Lilburne, virtually ignored the Fall. Sin lost its power as the great deterrent.

If men 'believe sin, death and the curse to be abolished, they are abolished' declared Richard Towne in 1644, the year *Areopagitica* was published. Abiezer Coppe and Laurence Clarkson used this doctrine to justify the practice of free love, thus confirming the worst anticipations of conservatives. Winstanley and Richard Coppin were the first to proclaim in print, in 1648-1649, that all mankind would be saved. Teachers of absolute predestination were defenders of inequality, declared the anonymous author of *Tyranipocrit Discovered* (1649): 'He that teacheth a partial God loveth partiality.' All men had the grace to be saved if they only looked to God within themselves. Popular ideas were summed up in the Quaker doctrine of the inner light in all men and women, which transformed the Protestant 'priesthood of all believers' from an oligarchical to a democratic doctrine. The gentry accepted original sin, declared Samuel Fisher in 1653, but ordinary people rejected it. After he had become a Quaker, Fisher argued in a large and scholarly tome that the contradictions and inconsistencies of the Bible made it impossible to accept it as the inspired word of God: it was a book to be judged and criticised like any other. Some went further still. 'Many thousands in these three nations,' wrote John Reeve in 1656, 'count the Scriptures mere inventions of wise men, to keep the simple in awe under their rulers.'

Faced with such dangerous ideological tendencies, former parliamentarians and former royalists closed ranks, and in 1660 king, bishops, and sin were restored. Radical ideas were driven underground in a return to what some historians call 'normality', by which I think they mean the restoration of censorship. The ideas did not of course disappear, though we get only chance references to them in the censored press. The possibility of a sinless society had been a dream of the heady 1640s, but the Quakers survived to bear witness to the divine spark in all men and women. The later 17th century saw a progressive decline in belief in hell and magic, whether black or religious. Less than a century after the English Revolution so unoriginal a thinker as Bolingbroke refused to impute predestination to damnation 'to the all-perfect being'. 'Reason...in the breast of every Christian that can appeal to her tribunal' was against it.

Chapter 20

Words and things

This was first published in History Today, No 33, 1983.

Seventeenth century Baconians used to insist that things were more important than words. Provided we know exactly what things our words indicate, I think they were right. Twentieth century historians sometimes forget that things had to exist before words could describe them. In his book, *17th Century Britain 1603-1714*, John Morrill, for instance, recently argued against 'applying to individuals in the past' criteria unknown to them: we must 'be more sensitive to contemporary vocabulary and conceptualisation'. There was no 17th century word 'to conjoin "mere" gentlemen and yeomen, or yeomen and urban master craftsmen': in describing 17th century society we should not use tools of analysis evolved later.

I think Dr Morrill is wrong in saying contemporaries had no phrase to link yeomen and master craftsmen: 'the middling sort' was in frequent use. And in the vocabulary of Harrington, Locke and other political thinkers the word 'people' is used to describe those of the unprivileged who were neither servants nor paupers. This usage is so different from our own that we really need a phrase to translate 'the people' when we meet it in this sense in the 17th century. I see no objection to using a later term of analysis like 'class' even if contemporaries did not use it: provided we define clearly what we mean. Apples fell from trees before Newton discovered the laws of gravity; people died of tuberculosis before the disease was named; revolutions happened before there was a word for them.

It was indeed during the 17th century that the word 'revolution' changed from meaning 'a completed circular motion'. It acquired its modern significance because of the experience of the English Revolution. Men did not invent a word—'revolution', 'gravity', 'tuberculosis' —and then say, 'Let's have one'. They observed the thing and then named it. How could it possibly have happened otherwise? So I disagree with Professor John Bossy (in a recent article in *Past and Present*) when he says we must always 'use the word as it was used by those we are writing about'. He instances the words 'state', 'property', and 'society'. 'The objection that those we write about must have had the thing though they did not have the word is surely an invitation to misdescription.'

The danger of misdescription seems to me far greater if we can use words only as contemporaries used them. If we use the phrase 'the county community' as 17th century English gentlemen did, we shall exclude all but the gentry from that community, thus falling for what Marx called 'the illusion of the epoch'. Before we know where we are we shall be talking with Mr Laslett in *The World We Have Lost* of a one class society. To exclude the poor and servants from 'the people' when discussing political theory of the electorate offers similar prospects of ambiguity. And we shall have to speak of 'the English innovation' instead of the English Revolution.

There were states and revolutions before the words acquired their modern sense. We need to be aware of changes of meaning, and we need to define; but that applies the other way too. The words 'parliament', 'monarchy', 'professor', and 'backside' were used in 17th century England, but the things they refer to were not the same as in our usage.

There are reasons for blackballing some of these words. It might be nicer if there were no 'classes' or 'revolutions' at all. The danger of importing such prejudices into history seems to me at least as great as the danger from using modern terms of sociological analysis. If the latter are misapplied, this can be pointed out; but the first prohibition precludes certain types of explanation. One historian made his intention very clear by stating 'we cannot usefully indulge in grand generalisations about the causes of the Civil War' since men did not think 'of the consequences of their actions'. It is like arguing that a car crash has no causes because neither drivers nor passengers intended it. Nobody wanted revolution in England in 1640; few wanted one in France in 1789 or Russia in 1917. But they happened. Professor Hexter long ago tried, with some success, to abolish the words 'middle class', 'bourgeoisie'. When a pupil of his contributed to his *Festschrift* a nice article on 'The Elizabethan Bourgeois Hero-Tale' she had to explain that 'even if there was no large middle class...there were bourgeois hero-tales in Elizabethan England'. The thing, alas, remained obstinately there. Tearing words out of the dictionary does not obliterate things from history. But dictionaries can help us to define.

Chapter 21

Revolution and rebellion

This was a review of Revolution and Rebellion: State and Society in England in the 17th and 18th Centuries *by J C D Clark, and was first published in* The Journal of Ecclesiastical History, *Vol 3, No 3, July 1987.*

This is an unusual book in that it openly proclaims its political bias. Most of us are either unaware that our political prepossessions influence our historical judgements or we try to overcome them. Mr Clark runs his colours up. He quotes with approval a remark about 'the electoral shock of 1979' which ended the intellectual torpor of Fabianism and Keynesianism (p20). His enemies are a mixed bag of 'Whiggish and socialist histories' written by liberal and socialist historians. Feiling and Trevelyan are Old Hat historians of the 18th century, but Trevelyan is differentiated by the fact that he 'unthinkingly absorbed Marxist ideas' (pp144, 163). The ideas are wisely unspecified.

Among more recent historians 'whose minds were formed in the matrix of interwar Marxism', belonging to 'the Marxist Old Guard' (pp2, 9), Mr Clark includes Trevor-Roper and Stone, Hexter and myself. Not all of us will be happy with the company in which Mr Clark puts them, or with the Marxist label. Some (unnamed) are guilty of 'a character-twisting hatred of orthodox religion' (p30) . The advantage of lumping us all together is that the less defensible words of any can be quoted to belabour all (eg p37). The maverick Lawrence Stone is cited most frequently as though he spoke for us all. Mr Clark makes quite an issue of 'the generation effect'. His final knockdown argument is to print the dates of birth of Hexter, Trevor-Roper, Stone, myself and seven other bêtes noires, between whom and himself Mr Clark finds 'a gulf opening up' (pp2, 170).

Mr Clark is a clever man, who writes wittily and often perceptively.

He rightly tells us that we should not speak of the English Revolution to the exclusion of Scotland and Ireland (p66). He sees the silliness of some of the excesses of 'revisionist' historians over their new toy of 'patronage structures' (p155). He is critical of 'localist' historians, whose conclusions he wishes to use but whose extremer arguments he finds unconvincing. Their approach was in part 'an historiographical echo of the value nexus of the Social Democratic Party' (pp56-57). If Mr Clark were to study the work of Ann Hughes, Clive Holmes, David Underdown and Anthony Fletcher he would find localism meshed successfully with 'the political world of Westminster' (p66) in a way that will not support his theories. His work has all the qualities of a good undergraduate essay. Arguments are swiftly clinched by epigrams. He uses secondary sources highly selectively but skilfully to make his case.

What is it all about? Mr Clark thinks that historians are too specialised, too confined to a given chronological field (p1). Admirable, and he wishes to remedy this by comparing early 17th with early 18th century English history (p7). An interesting idea. But specialisation is not only a matter of chronology; it also relates to subject matter. Mr Clark is a ' high political' historian; history is about the goings on of kings, courts and parliaments. His argument is that the king was important in early 18th century politics; that there were parties in early 18th century England as, he thinks, Old Guard historians believe there were in early 17th century England. Therefore—a large jump from an insecure taking-off ground—nothing significant happened in between.

Mr Clark does not like revolutions. There was no 17th century English Revolution and no Industrial Revolution either: only a 'reified category' (pp39, 66). 'A proper study of the intricacy and uncertainty of human affairs' will 'show the values and *intentions* [my italics] of past men, seen at close quarters, as often quite different from anything which could be fitted into a teleological explanation of English liberties' (p18). By such arguments Mr Clark claims to have rendered 'untenable the teleological rearrangement of the English past into an account of the inevitable unfolding of Whig gradualism or of revolutionary change' (p164). 'The whole experience of England's ancien regime was thus made to seem a temporary aberration from trends naturally successful before 1640 and after 1832' (p7). 'Naturally' is tendentious; but the question raised is a good one. Why was there an apparent time lag between 1660 and 1832?

'The danger', Mr Clark warns, 'is to infer from the currency of a word or phrase at a particular moment that it was then invested with its later meaning' (p135). He repeatedly risks this danger himself. If we press the analogies between the reigns of James I and George I we may mistake words for things. 'The House of Commons under the Georges was far more susceptible to manipulation than it had ever been under Charles I' (p75). But then under Charles I parliament and monarchy had been very different institutions. As William III had to be told, the question was not whether a man favoured monarchy or not, but which monarch he favoured. The Hanoverians sat on the throne because they accepted the preponderance of institutions and social forces which had proved too strong for Charles I and James II, as Anthony Fletcher's *Reform in the Provinces* admirably demonstrates: and because the Navigation Act, a big navy and the Bank of England were there, whilst Star Chamber, High Commission and feudal tenures were not. George I was, at most, what Harrington called 'a prince in a commonwealth', not a king in Charles I's sense. 'The constant agonisings over monarchy', Mr Clark himself says, 'had concerned not so much its power as an institution as the uses to which that power was put' (p80). Precisely.

After 1688 the state was stronger, and that meant a stronger parliament and a stronger executive (p76). Mr Clark asks, 'If Charles I had had a standing army comparable to the early Hanoverians, would he have lost his throne?' The answer is that George I's army was strong because it was paid for, and therefore ultimately controlled, by parliament and the monied interest; it performed functions acceptable to those interests. It was *not* attempting to establish its independent power against them. In 1604-1629 MPs did not want 'to shackle the power of the Crown as such' (p83). But they did not want to pay heavy taxes for policies which were not theirs. 'The refusal', says Mr Clark 'was political': it had no deep causes. But the refusal was repeated in 1610, the 1620s, 1640-1641; the 'inherent, objective, structural' objection was overcome only during the Civil War when a totally new tax structure was introduced which proved capable, for the first time, of financing a modern state (p53). By Walpole's time 'the English state was far stronger in every respect'. It was also a state geared to different purposes.

Many of Mr Clark's revelations are the platitudes of informed 17th century historians. 'Revolution...was not planned ' (p97; cf p134). Before 1642 there was no 'conflict between a political elite which had for decades been divided into two (or more) clearly integrated parties' (p146), no 'gentry-led initiative to seize sovereignty in response to the classic Whig issues of taxation and representation' (p166). He is pushing at open doors here. Mr Clark is indeed not as well informed about 17th century history as (I have to assume) he is about 18th century history. Otherwise he could not think he was making a novel point about the 18th century when he writes 'monarchy, not democracy [*sic!*] generated society's dominant ideology' (p122). He has taken the rhetoric of 'revisionist' historians at face value. He triumphantly quotes Conrad Russell, 'the ultimate split was quite clearly a split within the governing class' (p138), as though that ended the discussion. Professor Russell is a wise historian and intended the word 'ultimate' to convey much more than Mr Clark appreciates. He does not reject 'social change theories' as cheerfully as Mr Clark (p25).

Mr Clark has his own teleology. He tells us that Hill's 'model of an urban bourgeois revolt against gentry hegemony' is 'flatly contradicted by recent work on the 18th century electorate' (p158). That is certainly no model of mine; but I don't see how any statement about 17th century history can be contradicted by work on the 18th century. Eighteenth century history shows that the 17th century revolution failed to achieve some of the objectives which some of the revolutionaries set themselves after it had begun; but that indisputable fact is rather different.

Underlying Mr Clark's approach is a conspiracy theory of history. Revolutions can happen only if planned. If we can show there was no such plan (as of course there wasn't in 1640) then there can have been no revolution. Mr Clark quotes John Cannon: 'How fragile is domestic tranquillity, how thin the veneer of civilisation, how little obedience to law can be taken for granted' (pp64-65). Approval of such remarks makes it all the odder that Mr Clark thinks real history is about the 'high politics' of kings and parliaments. What made the veneer of civilisation and obedience to the law so fragile? Is 'fuzzy and antinomian fanaticism' all that there is to be said about Milton, Overton, Walwyn, Winstanley and Hobbes? If 'in 1688 sufficient care was taken that a minimal measure of revolution followed the rebellion which overthrew James II' (p43), is it not worth asking why such care was necessary?

His exclusive emphasis on 'high political' history leads Mr Clark to equate any reference to 'underlying causes' or even 'local causes' with 'economic reductionism' (pp42, 48). His own approach seems to me to impoverish history. His methods sometimes suggest that he values victory more than truth. I was startled to find that I 'had announced in 1967 that the "Whig interpretation of history" was "the only possible historical attitude" ' (p11). What I wrote was that to look for 'those elements of the new which are emerging…is sometimes criticised as a "Whig" approach.' I suggested that it was, 'on the contrary the only possible historical attitude' if we are to avoid antiquarianism. If anyone thought it worthwhile it would be interesting to check others of Mr Clark's innumerable quotations for similar economies with the truth.

Chapter 22

Politics of discourse

These were two reviews, of Politics of Discourse: The Literature and History of 17th Century *edited by Kevin Sharpe and Steven N Zwicker, and* Dragon's Teeth: Literature in the English Revolution *by Michael Wilding, first published in the* Times Literary Supplement, *13 September 1987.*

For many years it has been necessary to say that the best history of 17th century England is written by literary critics. Historians are too busy looking at parliamentary debates, state papers, the goings on of the county gentry, and arguing with one another, to have time for literature. So they have missed one of the most illuminating sources for the ideological battles of the century. Some historians no doubt prefer it that way: they want to deny that there were any ideological battles.

But since the seminal work of Margot Heinemann and Martin Butler on politics in the theatre in the 1620s and 1630s, and the broader surveys of Jonathan Dollimore and David Norbrook, the most myopic of historians must have noticed that new ideas are about. The two books under review accept literature as a tool for historical understanding. Michael Wilding has long combined the two disciplines; some of the contributors to *Politics and Discourse* are more recent converts.

Their book begins with three high theoretical pieces by the editors, J G A Pocock and Michael McKeon. Barbara Lewalski contributes a straightforward and useful piece on Lucy, Countess of Bedford as patron of literature. David Norbrook interestingly relates *Macbeth* to political controversies arising from the writings of the very radical George Buchanan. Kevin Sharpe applies Martin Butler's insights to Thomas Carew, who, Sharpe thinks, was not just a writer of erotic lyrics: he had a political philosophy. His best known erotic poem, 'A Rapture', turns out to be 'a laboratory in which Carew creates an ideal condition so that he may the better explore an actual problem'. Carew's ideal is marriage, in which 'pleasure is reconciled to virtue'. Sharpe does not claim that 'Give me a maid about thirteen' already 'dedicated to the Queen of lust and lovers' is an epithalamion; what demographers tell us about the late age of marriage in the 17th century precludes that. But 'the imagery is religious'. The political philosophy which Sharpe claims to find in Carew is banal in the extreme. His is a suggestive if not entirely convincing essay. We shall all have to read Carew again carefully.

Annabel Patterson, who never forgets that 17th century writers had to publish under censorship, has a splendid piece on fables. Aesop was a slave, and his fables, like the stories of Uncle Remus, are a way in which the underdog can express a point of view. In 1628 in the debates on the Petition of Right, one of Aesop's fables was retold as a means of criticising Charles I's use of the prerogative—something which could not have been done directly. Annabel Patterson goes on to consider the royalist John Ogilby's use of fables to protest against what he saw as the tyranny of the Commonwealth in the 1650s.

Articles by Blair Worden, Earl Miner, Mary Ann Radzinowicz and Steven Zwieker deal with Milton and Marvell, the main authors considered by Michael Wilding. His book draws attention to political aspects of 17th century writing which traditional critics miss. Sir Thomas Browne is not a broad minded defender of religious toleration; he advocates toleration for Catholics because he is frightened of sectarian radicalism and wants to suppress it. Samuel Butler is as contemptuous of the traditional epic virtues as Milton is. Wilding compares their views on epic in fascinating detail, helping us to see both in a fresh light. A similar point is made by Earl Miner in his contribution to *Politics of Discourse*.

Close reading of Milton's early poems and of *Lycicas* enables Wilding to spot many points, obvious once made, but previously missed. He sets *Comus* against the politics of the Welsh border, the rivalry between church courts and the Council in the Marches. Comus himself represents the court and the ecclesiastical hierarchy, as well as the traditional magic of the peasantry which Puritans were trying to eradicate. Charles I's *Book of Sports* and Laud's ceremonial innovations are in the background; in the 1660s *Hudibras* was still trying to suppress a bearbaiting and a skimmington.

Wilding illustrates one persistent theme of *Paradise Lost*: the contrast between Satan's monarchical tyranny and the republican model discreetly illustrated by the ant. Milton has to make political points by casual phrases, asides and Biblical allusions: censors knew that he was politically subversive. Wilding's careful reading is wholly convincing. Mary Ann Radzinowicz's excellent piece on 'The Politics of Paradise Lost' in *Politics of Discourse* illustrates Milton's republican use of Nimrod; Steven Zwicker analyses Michael's history lesson in the last two books of *Paradise Lost* as a covert attack on monarchy ('Lines of Authority'). Wilding argues that Milton's emphasis on his blindness is countering the royalist charge that it was God's punishment on the defender of regicide. On the contrary, Milton argued, blindness brings prophetic inner vision: it was a reward for his services to God' s cause. Marvell agreed.

My one point of disagreement with Wilding is where he is most traditional. He treats *Samson Agonistes* as a poem whose moral is pacifist: Samson is 'an old style military hero', not an agent of divine retribution. But Milton thought it a religious duty to hate and punish God's enemies, who were more God's enemies than the Philistine aristocracy and priests whom Samson slaughtered? 'The vulgar only 'scaped who stood without', perhaps to take advantage of the holocaust. But Wilding's version of this interpretation is more convincing than any other I have read.

Wilding is superb on Marvell's *Horatian Ode*. He concentrates on the poet's silences. Marvell says nothing about opposition to Cromwell from Levellers and army radicals. But his image of Cromwell as the controlled falcon may be 'designed to allay suspicions about army power' and Oliver's intentions. Cromwell emerges as the force of destiny because the only alternative considered is Charles I: and he is a rival no longer. Charles II is not mentioned. Wilding sees the *Ode* as a carefully constructed call for national unity around Cromwell and his erect sword. In an equally illuminating analysis of *Upon Appleton House* Wilding insists that the ambiguities of the poem spring from ambiguities in Fairfax's position: had he really retired permanently at age 38?—and from the tact needed for Fairfax's employee in discussing them. But opposition to Levellers and other radicals, implicit in the *Horatian Ode*, is explicit here.

Blair Worden's analysis of the *Horatian Ode* in *Politics of Discourse* is more conventional. Marvell is for him 'a Cavalier poet'; the *Ode* expresses his conversion into a supporter of Cromwell. Worden has unearthed interesting evidence from newspapers of the early 1650s to illustrate matters which the poem discusses, and he rightly sees that its final thrust is forward looking, pro-Cromwellian. But he misses important points made by Judith Richards: the ode is not as sympathetic to Charles as Worden and the traditional view would have it. Charles is 'the royal actor'. It is minimal praise to say that a 17th century gentleman died in public without doing anything 'common...or mean', without making a scene out of 'vulgar spite' and having to be tied down before the axe could fall.

These two books augur well. We may yet find out what the English Revolution was about.

Chapter 23

The printing explosion 1640-1660

This is a paper which I don't think has previously been published. I have no date for it.

John Foxe attributed 'this gift of printing' to direct divine intervention. Printing greatly facilitated the spread of the Reformation in Europe, and made the fortunes of many Swiss and German towns. Lollards had circulated manuscript Bibles in English for over a century before Henry VIII's Reformation, but they were expensive—as well as dangerous. The printed vernacular text was a very different proposition. Printing stimulated learning to read; and this in return stimulated cheap printing and distribution of other books, as well as the Bible. It was a cultural revolution. Direct access to the Bible gave assurance to laymen against the clergy who hitherto had monopolised the sacred text. Henry VIII found it necessary by 1643 to abolish 'diversity of opinions', but legislation proved insufficient.

There was a minor printing explosion in Edward VI's reign. Popular Protestantism was not always popular with the ecclesiastical hierarchy: it led to social heresies. Christopher Marlowe towards the end of Elizabeth's reign was alleged to have 'read the atheist lecture' to Sir Walter Ralegh and others, discussing biblical criticism, the contradictions of scripture, comparative religion, with the scientist Thomas Hariot and others; the government's informers were scandalised. Ralegh in his *History of the World* saw Christianity as only one of many religions, and went in for a good deal of textual criticism. By that time expansion of English trade to the eastern Mediterranean and the Far East had brought Englishmen into contact with Islam and other sophisticated religions; and the Turks—suddenly a great power—were seen as possible allies against Spain and popery. The Koran was translated into English in the freedom of 1649. It worried Bunyan.

'The art of printing', said a pamphlet of 1641, 'will so spread knowledge that the common people, knowing their own rights and liberties, will not be governed by way of oppression' (Macaria). Professor Eisenstein sees the spread of printing as a great cultural turning point. Before 1640 there were no English newspapers: they were illegal. By 1645 there were 722. These figures come from the collection made by George Thomason, a bookseller friend of Milton's, who recognised the exceptional nature of the times in which he lived. He made a point of purchasing a copy of everything published in England between 1640 and 1660. In 1640 he made 22 purchases; in 1642 he made over 2,000. Production of books and pamphlets proceeded at an average rate of over 1,000 a year.

What we can never tell is how many people read these books, or had them read to them—in market places, in the New Model Army. Nor do we know how many potential authors refrained from publishing before 1640. The millenarian Joseph Mede did not risk publication of his speculations under Laud; his works were published on the insistence of Parliament after 1640. Thomas Hobbes, the greatest philosopher of his day, published his first English book in 1642, when he was 54 years of age—the age at which Shakespeare stopped writing. The early Stuart censorship was only intermittently effective; but in the two generations before 1640 there is hardly a well known poet, dramatist or historian who had not suffered from it. A great number of books by now famous authors—some by Bacon, the last three books of Hooker's *Laws of Ecclesiastical Polity*, Sir Edward Coke's *Reports and Institutes*, appeared only after the censorship had collapsed.[1] This sudden outburst of publication creates optical illusions. Bacon's ideas seem suddenly to become popular but they had probably previously circulated in manuscript, underground.

1   See my *Writing and Revolution in 17th Century England* (1985), pp39-54. Ditto plays by Beaumont and Fletcher, Massenger, Middleton, Dekker, Ford, Shirley; John Donne's sermons and other prose; Ben Jonson's prose; poems by George Herbert, Carew and Corbett. Our knowledge of the great age of Elizabethan and Jacobean literature would have been far less complete without the outburst of printing between 1540 and 1600, and the expansion of popular demand.

Perhaps even more important is the appearance after 1640 of books by persons without university education and all the conventional assumptions associated with that upbringing.

What we shall never know fully is how much continuity of underground radical use of the Bible there was from Lollards through Foxe's martyrs down to the apparently sudden appearance of biblical radicalism in the 1640s. We know that there was continuity in certain geographical areas, and in certain subjects—use of the Bible to criticise the sacraments and ceremonies of the church, denunciations of idolatry and encouragement of iconoclasm, millenarianism, the saints to judge the world, perfection in this life, the idea that all men and women may be saved, lay mechanic preaching, biblical criticism; and for recurrent heresies—mortalism, anti-Trinitarianism, scepticism about the existence of heaven, hell, the devil and sin, rejection of church marriage. Thomas Nashe speaks of a variety of sects already existing in the 1590s, with their own 'mechanic preachers'.[2]

Whether there was continuity of radical ideas or not, there can be no doubt about the wealth of unorthodox theories, some of them fairly sophisticated, which surfaced after the breakdown of censorship. This aspect of the printing explosion of the 1640s is not always sufficiently emphasised. For the first time in English history anyone could get into print who could persuade a printer that there was money in his or her idea. Significant numbers of persons (including women) who had had no university education, often no grammar school education even, found no obstacles to publication.

So reading matter was no longer supplied only by people who shared a classical education and assumed that discussion must be conducted according to established formal rules, starting from a syllogism. What became the radicals' manifesto was a sermon entitled *The Sufficiency of the Spirits Teaching without Humane-Learning*, published by Cobbler How in 1640. He argued that while learning might be useful to scholars, lawyers and gentlemen, uneducated persons were preferable to scholars in the pulpit, since the Spirit's teaching was all that mattered for understanding 'the mind of God'. All men should read the Bible and decide for themselves, not as the learned told them. How died a few months after his sermon appeared, but it attracted much attention. Of the 20,000 or so books and pamphlets published between 1640 and 1660, the majority were by authors who were 'illiterate' in the eyes

2   See my *Religion and Politics in 17th Century England*, pp89-116; T Nashe, *Pierce Penilesse, his Supplication to the Divell* (1592) (G B Harrison (ed), 1924), pp27, 57.

of academics. They knew as little Latin or Greek as Shakespeare. So in the interregnum discussions there was no longer a shared background of classical scholarship; the rules of logic which structured academic controversy were ignored. University scholars treated the newcomers with contempt, and this in its turn fuelled opposition to the universities as such. The whole classical curriculum and conventions of academic argument were called in question. Indeed, were universities of any use at all?

Self taught men like Gerrard Winstanley stressed proudly that they got their ideas not from books, or from other men, but either direct from God, or from the Bible, or from common sense. Writers of the calibre of the Leveller leaders John Lilburne, William Walwyn and John Wildman, the Ranters Clarkson, Coppin and Salmon, the Quakers Fox, Nayler, Isaac Penington and Arthur Pearson, the Muggletonians John Reeve and Lodowick Muggleton, the biblical critic Clement Writer, the opponent of witch persecution John Webster, a religious writer like William Erbery, wholly secular writers like William Blith the agricultural reformer, William Lilly the astrologer and Francis Osborne the essayist—all these could beat academics at their own games. Many of those I have named were important opinion formers. They were supported by university men like William Dell who joined in the attack on academic education. 'Antichrist chose his ministers from the universities,' remarked Dell. John Bunyan was deeply hurt by academic sneers at him for daring to preach and write without a proper education. He consoled himself with the reflection that God's own were not gentlemen, could not with Pontius Pilate speak Hebrew, Greek and Latin.[3]

In the 1640s uneducated men and women read back into the Bible themselves and their problems, and the problems of their communities, and found biblical answers there, which they could discuss with others who shared the same problems. It was a great period for public disputation. Jordan noted at least 78 recorded meetings of this type in which Baptists were involved.[4] The conclusions emerging from these biblical discussions were many and varied, not all popular with educated parliamentarians. Radicals in Chelmsford were said to think

3   The joke had been made in 1655, three years earlier, by two Quaker women, Priscilla Cotton and Mary Cole, *To the Priests and People of England*. But Bunyan, who prided himself on not taking his ideas from other people, would hardly have cribbed from Quaker women.
4   See A Hughes, 'The Meaning of Religious Polemic: Oral Debate and Pamphlet Controversies in the 1640s and 1650s'—Millersville.

that the relation of master and servant had no ground in scripture: that peerage and gentry were 'ethnical and heathenish distinctions'. They found no ground in nature or scripture why one man should have £1,000 a year, and another not £1. Universities should be abolished.[5] Baxter noted that 'the antinomian doctrine is the very same in almost every point, which I find naturally fastened in the hearts of the common profane multitude'.[6] That was a good reason for not tolerating it. Milton proudly celebrated the ferment of uncontrolled discussion in *Areopagitica* (1644).

By 1644 Edmund Calamy in a *Fast Sermon* was complaining that 'the people of the City of London have almost disputed away their repentance'; in discussing 'this opinion or that opinion' about discipline, faith and repentance were forgotten.[7] Liberty of discussion seemed to conservatives to be subverting the discipline whose establishment they saw as the only way to recover God's favour.

> What are you the better for having the Scripture in your own language? When it was locked up in the Latin tongue by the policy of Rome, you might have had a learned friar for your money at any time (to have interpreted the same); and though now you have it in your own language, you are taught not to trust your own understanding (have a care of your purses!); you must have an university man to interpret the English... Let me prevail with you to free yourselves from this bondage.[8]

The Leveller leader John Lilburne was said to have the Bible in one hand and the legal writings of Sir Edward Coke in the other. He claimed that his attack on bishops 'could neither be factious nor seditious, unless the Book of God be faction and sedition, which were blasphemy once to think'.[9] 'God has revealed the way of eternal salvation', Milton declared, 'only to the individual faith of each man, and demands of us that any man who wishes to be saved should work out his beliefs for himself.' So he justified his religious creed, for which his only authority, he said, was 'God's self revelation' in 'the Holy Scriptures'.[10] The concept of social revolution also emerged in the forties and fifties, in Biblical phrases like 'the world turned upside down' and Ezekiel's 'overturn, overturn, overturn'.[11]

5   [Anon], *Angliae Ruina* (1647), p27.
6   Quoted by W M Lamont, *Richard Baxter and the Millennium* (1979), pp128, 143.
7   F S, XIII, pp124, 145; cf P L II 556-561—'in wandering mazes lost'.
8   W Walwyn, *The Power of Love* (1643), p47, in *Writings*, pp95-96.
9   J Lilburne, *Come Out of Her My People* (1639), p25.
10   M C P W, VI, pp118-121.
11   Psalm CXLVI, 9, Isaiah, XXIV, 1-2, 20-1, Acts, XVII, 1-6, Ezekiel, XXI, 27.

The 20 years freedom of talk and publication proved a turning point in many respects. In politics, for instance, Levellers produced democratic and republican political theories of some sophistication; Winstanley and the Diggers, theories of communism; Ranters advocated free love and sexual permissiveness. Hobbes, Harrington, Milton, Marchamont Nedham were the first Englishmen to produce political theories of lasting interest (if we except More, whose *Utopia* was written in Latin). These theories look forward to Locke and the European Enlightenment.

In science England had been a backwater. James I had no use for the scientific ideas of his Lord Chancellor, Francis Bacon: his writings came into their own only after 1640, many published for the first time. In the 1650s science flourished in a purged Oxford and elsewhere, and received government support. After 1660 the scientists came together to found the Royal Society of London, of which Charles II wisely became patron. Its first secretary, John Wilkins, was symbolically both the brother-in-law of Oliver Cromwell and a future bishop. Margaret Jacob, who knows about these things, said that Isaac Newton was 'unthinkable without the English Revolution'. Professor Eisenstein thought that in the generally repressive atmosphere of the later 17th century modern science survived only because of the freedom of the press in England and the Netherlands.

In England the science of political economy was invented by William Petty, John Graunt, Gregory King, leading on to John Locke. Quakers, refusing to haggle at the market, helped to standardise prices. Simultaneously with political economy the English invented the novel—England's contribution to world literature.

Even the reaction in England after 1660 could not efface the memory of the revolutionary years. Freedom of discussion and freedom for protestant dissenters to worship in their own way were too well established. After the Licensing Act lapsed in 1695 there was no longer a government or ecclesiastical censorship. Quakers censored and often drastically amended books by their members; publishers did not accept books which they regarded as dangerously radical. Writings by Milton, Marvell and Ludlow were published, not the writings of Levellers and Diggers.

Chapter 24

'Lies about crimes'

This was the 1989 Conway Memorial Lecture, South Place Ethical Society and first published in the Guardian, *29 May 1989.*

History means two things: first the past as we believe it to have existed, and second the past as we attempt to reconstruct it in our writings. Cynics say that when historians claim to be describing the past they are really writing contemporary history—or autobiography. This is true to the extent that the new questions which each generation of historians asks inevitably reflect the interests of that generation.

This is clearly true of 17th century English history, which I know best. When Britain got manhood suffrage, historians rediscovered Leveller democracy: the rise of socialism and communism created a new interest in Gerrard Winstanley and the Diggers: the women's movement drew attention to the fact that women were not an invention of the Industrial Revolution: the student revolution of the 1960s revived interest in Ranter libertinism and scepticism. A kind reviewer even said that a book which I published in 1984—*The Experience of Defeat*, dealing with Milton and other radicals after 1660—represented my reaction to Margaret Thatcher.

It is right and proper that historians should ask new questions of the past, and such questions may well be stimulated by happenings in our own society. I can see no objection to this so long as our answers do not derive from the present. I remember having a rather unprofitable argument with a Chinese historian, who said that what went wrong in 17th century England was that the English revolutionaries lacked an organised and disciplined party with a clear ideology. He didn't say 'like the Chinese Communist Party' but that I fear is what he meant.

When I was young every bright up-and-coming historian had to discover a new revolution in the past. Even Geoffrey Elton found 'the Tudor Revolution in Government'. Others located Industrial Revolutions in 16th—and even 13th—century England. Now, quite the other way, the 'with it' thing is to abolish revolutions: to say that none of what have been called revolutions had any causes or consequences. The French and Industrial Revolutions went some time ago, the English Revolution is under attack: only the Russian Revolution has been allowed to survive, and that will no doubt go in due course.

It is possible to suspect that this change in fashion has something to do with the politics of the two periods: though in noting the swing of the pendulum as a historical fact I am not saying that we haven't all learnt a great deal from, say, Sir Geoffrey Elton's work on 16th century England and Earl Russell's on the 17th century. But finality has still not been reached.

The most fruitful change in historical attitudes in my time, I think, has been the emergence of 'history from below'—the realisation that ordinary people also have a history, perhaps that they played more part in determining the shape of the historical process, whether for change or for continuity, than we have thought. This new emphasis must, I suppose, be related to the emergence of a more self consciously democratic society. History no longer deals exclusively with kings and their mistresses, prime ministers and wars, statutes and debates in parliament.

One very general assumption in the 17th century, rarely expressed, was that the 'mysteries of state' should not be revealed to the common people. Some historians may share this assumption and so are not on the lookout for its limiting effect. All governments lie to their peoples, we know from our own recent experience; but if ministers lie today, when there is considerable chance of exposure, how much more so in the 17th century, when this possibility hardly existed. So we should be sceptical of expressions of benevolent intentions.

Over the past couple of decades, literary critics and literary historians seem to me to have been producing better history than historians strictly so called. While the latter have been busy reading parliamentary debates in which conventions of discourse insisted that no one directly attacked the king or his government but only individual ministers, literary historians have become increasingly aware of strains and tensions in the society. They are critical of Tillyard's idea that all Englishmen in the late 16th and early 17th century accepted 'the great chain of being', stretching upwards from immaterial objects through the vegetable and animal creations to man, to angels, to God. This was the world picture favoured by those who benefited by a hierarchical society: king, lords and gentlemen on top; merchants, artisans, yeomen and peasants below. But the theory of degree, Earl Russell remarked, does not go well with an inflationary spiral. Some merchants were becoming richer than many peers; many yeomen were thriving to gentility while gentlemen and even peers sank into poverty.

The old ideology was queried as social reality changed. The collapse of traditional external standards led Protestants to turn inwards, to the conscience of believers rather than the institutions of the church. It led Sir Philip Sydney's muse to tell him 'look in thy heart and write'. Sidney's intimate friend Sir Fulke Greville contrasted traditionally accepted authority with the truth of the heart when he wrote:

Yet when each of us in his own heart looks
He finds the God there far unlike his books.

The individual conscience, or intellect, is being forced to challenge accepted truisms, even when it has no alternative ideology.

So when our present government calls for a standard national historical curriculum, it all depends what sort of history. We must get away from history exclusively from on top. This might have been adequate for training a government elite, but that is not what most schools are doing now. Ministers complain that England lacks a national tradition such as France enjoys. This is true. The French tradition of popular nationalism centres on the French Revolution, the public celebration of Bastille Day, just as 4 July is celebrated in the US, 7 November in the [former] USSR—all recalling the great national revolutions of the countries concerned.

We suppressed the memory of our democratic revolution. Yet our democratic revolution was the model followed by France, the US and the USSR. In the 17th century Queen Elizabeth's Accession Day, 17 November, was a day of popular celebration. But it came to be used for demonstrations against governments which were thought to favour popery and absolutism. Pope burning became associated with Queen Elizabeth's Day, as with that other popular national festival, Guy Fawkes Day. Popular patriotism was inseparable from Protestantism. England's independence seemed to be inseparable from struggle against the great European Catholic absolutisms of Spain and France, to which the later Stuarts seemed to be more sympathetic than their peoples.

For this reason, perhaps, neither Queen Elizabeth's Day nor Guy Fawkes Day became a national festival approved by ruling persons; the former was forgotten, the latter now lacks high political seriousness. Patriotism ceased to be exclusively radical after the 18th century, when William Pitt and the radical Whigs still saw Frederick the Great as a Protestant hero in alliance against popish France. Perhaps the wars against the French Revolution and Napoleon helped to end this legend.

Patriotic history tends to be sentimentally anecdotal—Alfred and the cakes, Drake and his bowls, Nelson's 'Kiss me Hardy'. More serious patriotic history of the traditional sort was described by a former Regius Professor of Modern History at Cambridge, Sir G N Clark, as 'lies about crimes'. It would be nice if Mr Kenneth Baker recreated a more truthful patriotic history. If we just go back to national self glorification, to painting the map red, history will be in danger of becoming the plaything of party politics, to be changed with a change of government. A little self examination is in order.

We should be no less critical of some attempts to construct new historical 'models', which all too often conceal unconscious (or conscious) 20th century assumptions.

A whole ideology has been constructed around the concepts of 'modernisation', 'take off', and the assumption that modern capitalist civilisation is 'natural', that all societies strive towards it, but some are still 'pre-industrial', therefore 'backward'; they need to be encouraged by 'the West' to follow its path. We can see the consequences of this fallacious history in the plight of Third World countries today; their 'modernisation' has not been beneficial to their societies as a whole, only to small ruling cliques and outside investors. It is no more 'natural' for Asian and African countries to adopt 'Western' economic norms than to adopt parliamentary constitutions.

In my lifetime there has been a re-evaluation of English history because England has ceased to be a top nation. British freedom used to be seen as slowly broadening down from precedent to precedent until parliamentary government reached its perfection; and history, in the immortal words of Sellar and Yeatman's 1066 and All That, came to a full stop. All that we had to do was to export the English constitution to lesser nations, and we should all live happily and peacefully ever after. Alas! But the emphasis continued to lie on constitutional history: on the history of 'freedom', as it was called, as it is still called in the US. From the Angles and Saxons in the forests of Germany, there had been something specifically 'English' about liberty and constitutionalism, an idea which—against all rational probability—has recently been revived.

What I could never understand is what happened to all those free peoples who remained in the forests of Germany. Did they become Prussian Junkers? The free Anglo-Saxons brought with them to England lower classes known as boors, villeins, clowns, rascals. The meanings which those words have acquired today suggest that perhaps some free

Anglo-Saxons were less free than others. I recommend a historical study of our language to Mr Baker's consideration, too.

The idea that English history is uniquely different from that of the wicked 'continong' does not bear serious examination. To resort to national character as an explanation means that you have no explanation: national character changes with history.

In the 1920s I had a political discussion with my bank manager uncle, in which my views so shocked him that he protested, 'Surely you are patriotic enough to admit that the British Empire is the greatest force for good the world has ever known?' I replied, with teenage Whiggishness, that if it was true I hoped I should admit it whether patriotic or not; patriotism should not determine truth. There have been many worse institutions than the British Empire, but it is time we faced up to the fact that it was not an unqualified source of blessings for humanity.

Take slavery, for instance. The wealth of the first British Empire was very largely founded on slavery, of which we won a virtual world monopoly from the beginning of the 18th century. The labour of a slave in the West Indies, said the economist Charles Davenant in the late 17th century, 'is worth six times as much as the labour of an Englishman at home'. Six times: it is quite a large figure if you think about it ('worth', of course, means 'worth to his employer or owner').

No wonder the Society for the Propagation of the Gospel, which owned slaves in the West Indies, did not wish them to be instructed in the principles of Christianity lest they get ideas above their station. The churches, and English liberal opinion generally, played a great part in the 19th century in getting slavery and the slave trade abolished; and all credit to them. But by that time there were economic as well as humanitarian arguments against it. And by that time the cancer of slavery had spread all over the world.

We were not exclusively responsible for this, but we must bear primary responsibility. It was the cornerstone of our 18th century predominance.

The profits of the slave trade, and of slavery, contributed greatly to the accumulation of capital which made Britain the country of the first Industrial Revolution, and so consolidated its position as the greatest world power.

A state paper possibly drafted by Milton in 1655 proclaimed the principle that, 'since God hath made of one blood all nations of men…on earth…all great and extraordinary wrongs done to particular persons ought to be considered as in a manner done to all the rest of the human race.' A good principle, if we had lived up to it. When we teach children about the wickedness of drug-trafficking should we not remind them of the war which England fought in the mid-19th century to force the opium trade on China?

Have we come to grips with these horrors in our past, as German historians are trying to come to grips with Nazism? The presence of descendants of slaves in our country today, in large numbers, poses social problems. They come here because the economies of the West Indies have not recovered from the concentration on slave grown crops to the detriment of other forms of economic activity. For this we are mainly responsible. Is this not something that a new curriculum might encourage children in British schools to think about?

Even more obvious is England's historic responsibility for the present situation in Northern Ireland. Whether we blame the potato famine, or William III, or Oliver Cromwell—or go further back—the current war in Northern Ireland is England's historic responsibility. Oliver Cromwell proceeded in suppressing Ireland on the basis of cost effectiveness. 'If we should proceed by the rules of other states', he told his government by way of explaining his massacres of civilian populations, getting towns to surrender would cost more. He hoped, 'through the blessing of God, they will come cheaper to you.'

Other chickens are coming home to roost more slowly. Scotland was bribed and swindled into union with England in 1707, and for two centuries, on balance, Scotland did well out of it. But now? Scotland shares the depressed state of the North of England. We should clarify historically our view of and attitudes towards Scottish nationalism.

I may have seemed to have over-emphasised the dark side of English history. My intention is to redress the balance: the dangers of a nationally imposed curriculum are that it will tend to be jingoistically patriotic, to stress glorious victories like the Armada, Waterloo and the Falkland Islands. May I end with things we can be proud of—our literature, for instance? This is related interestingly to our history.

Before the 17th century England was a cultural backwater. Educated Englishmen had to be able to read Italian, Spanish and French. No English book had any reputation on the Continent except perhaps More's *Utopia*. Bacon's reputation, in Europe as in England, comes after the 17th century English Revolution. The first Englishman of letters to win European fame was John Milton. Not for his poetry, but for his propagandist *Defences Of The People Of England*, written in Latin for the intelligentsia of Europe, defending regicide and the English Republic. 'I had expected nothing of such quality from an Englishman', a startled Dutchman remarked. Foreigners coming to England wanted first to see Oliver Cromwell, then 'learned Mr Milton'.

Before 1640 England had been a scientific backwater too. In the second half of the 17th century it became the centre of world science. By the 18th century all educated Europe had to be able to read English: the ideas of the European Enlightenment were those of the Levellers, Hobbes, Milton, Harrington, Locke, and those of English scientists, Boyle and Newton.

Equally important was the English contribution to world popular literature, from Defoe onwards.

We might recall, too, the struggles against censorship that made possible this great period of our literature from Shakespeare's 'art made tongue-tied by authority' to Milton's *Areopagitica*, the classic defence of freedom to publish. Milton attacked censorship on patriotic grounds, as 'an undervaluing and vilifying of the whole nation'. 'If it come to prohibiting there is not aught more likely to be prohibited than truth itself.'

That might help schoolchildren to appreciate controversies over *Death On The Rock* and Rushdie's *The Satanic Verses*; and might lead them on to reflect about the dangers of monopoly or oligopoly in the opinion forming agencies. They should learn from 17th century history how important the jury system and the right to silence have been in preserving common liberties against intrusive governments. And they should be taught about one especially English institution—voluntary societies for reforming or abolishing this or that, such as played a big part in the abolition of slavery, and which may become increasingly important as political parties ossify.

I have left you with no big generalisations about what history is or should be, and that is perhaps a properly sceptical conclusion. Let me try one from Nietzsche. He said that 'history keeps alive…the memory of the great fighters against history—the blind power of the actual.' The past is going to have power over us anyway, but we need not be totally blind.

Chapter 25

Scepticism, values and the historian

'Scepticism, Values and the Historian'[1] was first published in a Festschrift for Hugh Stretton, former pupil and later colleague of mine at Balliol. He was a brilliant undergraduate, the only one I have ever known to be elected to a college fellowship whilst still an undergraduate. He confirmed our expectations by obtaining a first class degree. The Festschrift, entitled Markets, Morals and Public Policy, *was edited by Lionel Orchard and Robert Dare, and published by the Federation Press, Sydney, in 1989, with a foreword by John Bannon, Premier of South Australia. It celebrated Stretton's retirement from the chair of history at the University of Adelaide.*

Hugh was, I think, the cleverest of the many very clever pupils I have been privileged to have, and also perhaps the nicest.

I

There are many ways in which it behoves historians to be sceptical. As I have grown older and more short sighted, I have come, I think, to a better understanding of 17th century attitudes towards visions, signs and portents. When I walk in the country I can identify colours better than objects. If I see something white where I am expecting to see a signpost, a signpost it becomes; whereas in fact it turns out to be a piece of white paper. If I was expecting to see a ghost, it would no doubt have become a ghost. So I can understand how in the 17th century old men and women (or indeed the greater number of short sighted men and women there must have been) saw armies fighting in the sky, and other portents, at times when they were conditioned to

---

1. In writing this piece I have greatly benefited by discussions with Marcus Rediker and especially Bridget Hill.

expect them—after 1660, for instance. Respect for age being at a premium, the scepticism of the sharper eyed young would be easily laughed off. I can better appreciate Donald Pennington's remark that there is more convincing evidence for the existence of the devil in the 17th century than for many events and characters which historians describe.[2] A sceptical understanding may discourage us from talking too contemptuously of 17th century 'superstition'. When we correct the faulty vision of simple minded men and women in the past, by seeing a signpost where they saw a ghost, it is worth contemplating the possibility that it may have been only waste paper. We cannot be too sceptical of our own historical judgments.

II

Nearly 40 years ago I was one of two examiners for an Oxford University prize in Modern History. Candidates were required to answer questions in four three hour papers. It was a prestigious prize, and the entry was always good: it was fun to examine. By the time we got to the fourth paper I had spotted my potential winner, and I picked up his paper answer with eager expectation. The question to which he devoted most attention was 'Attempt a defence of Oliver Cromwell's Irish policy'. The candidate produced a carefully argued, very full essay, dealing with all the relevant points: it was not Cromwell's personal policy but that of the government of the English Commonwealth, indeed traditional English policy carried out more effectively. Ireland was a wide open backdoor to foreign invasion of England, and the regicide republic had many enemies among the European monarchies. The safety of the revolution in England depended on quickly and finally suppressing the Irish revolt, which had dragged on for eight years since 1641. Cromwell's conquest very effectively did just that. There had to be expropriations of Irish landowners in order to repay English investors who had advanced money for the conquest of Ireland. And so on, and so on. It was very competently done, but it seemed to miss the whole point of the question. Every schoolboy ought to know that the 'curse of Cromwell' had blighted Anglo-Irish relations from his day to the present. Cromwell's behaviour could be seen, on its smaller scale, as comparable with the Nazi Holocaust of the Jews, with the American atom bombing of Japan. It raised vast moral problems. So I read on with

2.   D H Pennington, *Seventeenth Century Europe*, 1970, p126.

growing concern as all the technically correct answers were meticu-
lously given. Could such an intelligent candidate really have been so
obtuse as not to grasp the implications of the question? It was almost
with despair that I turned to the last page of the answer, on which
there were two short sentences: 'So I defend Cromwell's Irish policy.
So I would defend the poisoner of my grandmother, on the grounds
that he hadn't done it messily with an axe.'

And that, of course, transformed the whole quality of the answer.
It had been a long drawn out joke at the examiners' expense. But it
was also a very economical way of dealing with the question. There
were defences to be made of the policy, once you looked at it solely
from the point of view of English interests and left out of account the
fact that the grandmother was unpleasantly dead. So awful was the
murder and its historical consequences that to give any proper consideration to them, in the 45 minutes at the candidate's disposal,
would have precluded any serious defence. So the candidate got the
prize. His name was Hugh Stretton.

I have often cited this answer as a model way of sidestepping questions which are too complicated to go into in the time available. But
the historian not pressed for time has to face them, and they are very
complicated, as Hugh Stretton very well knew. No 17th century Irish-
man could have defended Cromwell's policy. But apparently few Englishmen disapproved of his conduct in Ireland, in so far as they knew
about it: Milton and George Fox seemed perfectly happy with it. So
are we to conclude that Englishmen felt differently about such things
in the 17th century, and consequently that we must apply different
standards in assessing Cromwell's Irish policy?

There are two answers to this. First, although there was no great
vocal opposition in England to what Cromwell was doing in Ireland,
there was some: the Leveller William Walwyn, the anonymous author
of *Tyranipocrit Discovered* (1649) and others.[3] We cannot just say that
different standards applied in the 17th century. Secondly, R S Paul in
The Lord Protector (1955) compared Cromwell's Irish policy with the
dropping of the atomic bomb on Japan in 1945. Both were horrific in
themselves; both, it could be claimed, succeeded in ending a war
which might have led to even greater casualties without such drastic
action. Can we condemn the one without condemning the other?[4]

3. See my 'Seventeenth century English Radicals and Ireland', in P J Corish (ed), *Radicals,
    Rebels and Establishments, Historical Studies*, vol. XV, 1985.
4. R S Paul, *The Lord Protector*, (1955), p218. I leave aside the possibility that Japan was
    anyway on the point of surrendering in August 1945.

The long term consequences of Oliver's actions were perhaps exceptional; but the long term consequences of Hiroshima and Nagasaki may be the destruction of life on earth as we know it.

III

The historian must avoid both a patronisingly moralistic attitude towards the past and a collusive adoption of earlier standards. This may help him or her to be sceptical of the eternal validity of his or her own values.

Yet it is as tricky a business for a historian to try to apply to the past a standard different from his own as to decide not to apply it. I, and many of my contemporaries, have prejudices against burning heretics, against routine bullying of the accused in treason trials who were allowed no defending counsel, against burning women for husband murder when men were only hanged for killing their wives. But it would be indicting a whole nation if we allowed these prejudices to influence our judgement of 17th century individuals. What matters for the historian is not the rightness or wrongness of past conventions and behaviour, but why they prevailed when they did, and why they changed.

Applying 20th century standards may lead to real misunderstanding of the past. Even some good critics misinterpret Milton (I think) because they cannot accept that he really believed that it was a religious duty to hate and kill God's enemies. They argue—against all the evidence—that in *Samson Agonistes* Milton must have intended us to regard Samson as a flawed character because he pulled down the pagan temple on the Philistine aristocracy and priests—enemies of God if ever there were any—whilst 'the vulgar only 'scaped who stood without' (line 1659).

Macaulay was perhaps guilty of a comparable insensitivity to 17th century ways of thinking when he said that Puritans wished to abolish bear and bull baiting because it gave pleasure to the spectators rather than because it caused pain to the animals. When Macaulay wrote this it must have sounded like a witty knockdown argument against Puritan hypocrisy. Now it seems like a skilful piece of gentlemanly doubletalk. Those who dislike bull baiting will dislike healthy sports like fox hunting. The fact that bull and bear baiting gave pleasure to the spectators was not perhaps the primary reason for insisting on abolition, but it is a valid ancillary reason—just as many who today approve of capital punishment can rationally disapprove of public executions. There are no doubt reasons for rejecting torture or blood sports with which I should disagree, just as many who supported the abolition of slavery did so for their own selfish economic reasons. But in each case life for humanity on earth was made that much the better, however hypocritical may have been the subjective motives of some reformers.

In other cases it is easier to put our 20th century standards into cold storage. I cannot myself get very upset when I am told that John Toland bowdlerised the *Memoirs of Edmund Ludlow* when he published them for the first time in 1698. Toland's object was to benefit the Whig cause. Consequently he concealed Ludlow's millenarianism, which in the 50 years between Cromwell and William III had gone out of fashion in politics; if Ludlow had been (correctly) presented as a millenarian enthusiast it would have counteracted the effectiveness of his *Memoirs* as propaganda against absolutism and standing armies.[5]

Seventeenth century Quaker writings, including Fox's *Journal*, were severely edited and censored by later Quakers before publication or re-publication, and this was entirely comprehensible by contemporary standards. Quaker views had changed: their early bellicosity (shared by Fox before 1660) had been replaced by pacifism; Fox's claim to perform miracles was embarrassing in the Age of Reason. Such editorial behaviour, like Toland's, offends modern scholarly canons; but neither Toland nor 18th century Quakers were modern academics. Ludlow and Fox would have understood the desirability of such editing.

A more difficult clash of standards comes with the attempt to write women's history. Assumptions of male superiority were so universal in the 17th century that it is difficult to know what to do about them. It is not just the prevalence throughout the society of assumptions drawn from the Bible about the inferiority of women, which necessitated their subordination to men; it is the fact the even the most radical reformers could not escape from these assumptions. The great Leveller pronouncements, 'the poorest he that is in England hath a life to live as the greatest he; and therefore…every man that is to live under a government ought first by his own consent to put himself under that government': even Gerrard Winstanley's 'the poorest man hath as true a title and just right to the land as the richest man'[6]:

---

5. E Ludlow, *A Voyce from the Watch Tower* (B Worden (ed), Camden Fourth Series, vol 21), Introduction.
6. A S P Woodhouse (ed), *Puritanism and Liberty*, 1938, p53; G Winstanley, *The Law of Freedom and other Writings* (Cambridge, 1983), p131.

these splendid flourishes specifically if unconsciously excluded women: all the more significant if the exclusion was unconscious. Nor was it only men: Leveller women campaigned for votes for their menfolk, but never seem to have thought of asking for the vote for themselves. Votes for women are suggested only as a reductio ad absurdum by professional misogynists like the Rev Joseph Hall and the Rev Thomas Edwards.[7]

So apparently universally prevalent were these biblical assumptions about Eve and her daughters that historians are only just beginning to recognise the occasional small breakthroughs—as when the second edition of William Gouge's *Domestical Duties* (1626) contains a chapter on the duties of husbands to wives in addition to the chapter on wives' duties to husbands in the first edition (1622). The addition seems to have been a response to women's protests, possibly not without some support from Mrs Gouge. Peter Lake has discussed sensitively the ways in which Puritanism could help women to establish some independence within the limits of social conformity.[8]

The conflict of standards between 20th century historians and 17th century characters springs from the supersession of the Bible, that racist and sexist book, as the unquestionable source of all wisdom. Its tyranny had ended in intellectual circles by the 18th century—a great liberation for humanity. It was first challenged (in print, at any rate) by radicals of the English Revolution—Walwyn, Winstanley, Clement Writer, Samuel Fisher—whose biblical criticism passed via Spinoza into the European Enlightenment.[9] We can see what this meant for Protestants if we recall that Bunyan told his readers that God would regard 'with delight' the burning of most of mankind in hell to all eternity 'for the easing of his mind'; and that 'those judgements among men, as putting in the stocks, whipping or burning in the hand' were as nothing compared with the torments of hell;[10] or if we look at Northern Ireland today, or at the 'moral majority' in the USA.

So the historian must have at least two standards of judgement—that of his own age and that of the age about which he or she writes.

7.   J Hall, 'Mundus Alter et Idem' (1607), in *Works* (Oxford University Press, 1839), Xll, pp41-2; T Edwards, *Gangraena* (1646),111, Sig c 4v (after p16).
8.   See J Sears McGee's Introduction to J Bunyan, *Miscellaneous Works*, Oxford 1987, p xxix; P Lake, 'Feminine Piety and Personal Potency: The "Emancipation" of Mrs Jane Ratcliffe', *The Seventeenth Century*, vol. 11, 1987, pp143-165.
9.   R H Popkin, 'Spinoza, the Quakers and the Millenarians, 1656-1658', *Manuscrito*, vol. 6,1982, p132: 'Spinoza and the Conversion of the Jews', in C de Deugd (ed), *Spinoza's Political and Theological Thought* (Amsterdam, 1984), p174.
10.   J Bunyan, *Of the Resurrection of the Dead*, in *Miscellaneous Works*, 111, pp258, 289.

I do not myself think it right to hate God's enemies, because (among other reasons) I do not think any universally acceptable definition of 'God's enemies' can be found. Perhaps it could not be found in the 17th century, but many supposed it could, including Milton and Bunyan. 'The heroic Samson', Milton declared, 'thought it not impious but pious to kill those masters who were tyrants over his country.' Bunyan believed that persecutors had passed 'beyond the reach of God's mercy'. Milton thought the same of bishops, all of whom were destined to hell ex officio, irrespective of their private vices or virtues.[11] The fact that men disagreed about who were God's enemies shows that standards were already changing. In some ways the 20th century historian is better informed about what was happening in 17th century England than men and women who lived there.

Sometimes it is a positive help to look through the wrong end of the telescope. The fact that some would call this a Whiggish approach need not bother us too much if it helps understanding. The world of early 17th century England was changing from that which had produced the Elizabethan political consensus. Traditional gentry in the House of Commons could not understand this, and tried to solve new problems in relation to the monarchy by turning to 14th and 15th century precedents. Some 'revisionist' historians think that we should reproduce the muddles of the bewildered men of the 17th century. But the historian, with the help of far sighted individuals like Ralegh, Bacon and Fulke Greville, should be able to grasp what was happening better that most contemporaries could. We have the hindsight advantage of having read Hobbes on sovereignty, and of knowing about the post-1640 concept of mixed monarchy: we can see better than most contemporaries could that the advance of the British economy depended on the abolition of prerogative courts and of feudal tenures, on a Navigation Act and an aggressive foreign policy; and on parliamentary control of the taxation needed to pay for this.

But it is easy to fall halfway between the standards of an age written about and the standards of one's own age which are changing too. The idea that parliament represented the people of England was challenged in the 17th century but continued to be widely accepted in the 18th and early 19th centuries. It gave up the ghost when extensions of the franchise came in the later 19th and 20th centuries.

11. J Milton, *A Defence of the People of England* (1651), *Complete Prose Works* (Yale edn, 1953-1982), IV, p402; J Bunyan, *An Exposition on the Ten First chapters of Genesis, Works of John Bunyan* (G Offor (ed), 1860),11, p449; J Milton, *Of the Reformation Touching Church-Discipline in England, Complete Prose Works*, 11, pp616-617.

Many historians ignored the existence of women before the Industrial Revolution invented them with the Spinning Jenny. The Irish were ignored too until they made themselves felt in the historian's present: so were native peoples in Asia and Africa. The self evident proposition that all men were born free and equal did not lead the authors of the Constitution of the United States to think of liberating slaves. So the morality of a later age may make us aware of blind spots in earlier ages. What right have we to judge, still less to condemn? There are beams in our eyes, posterity will undoubtedly think. Our criticism of past values should help us to be sceptical of our own.

IV

One advantage of studying radicals in 17th century England is that they did in some respects (though only in some) anticipate later stances on manhood suffrage (though not votes for women), human equality, an end to veneration of authoritative texts, including the Bible, rejection of judicial torture, etc, etc. If some did anticipate these ideals, then all could have done, and we are left wondering why they did not. On the other hand, if these (to us, to me) superior standards were stated and rejected, what does that tell us about the age, about the relativity of moral standards, about their dependence on socio-economic conditions? Greek democracy was founded on slavery; has ours been founded on exploitation of three quarters of the world?

We cannot consider individual morality without taking account of its implications for society. When the saintly Richard Baxter taught that the poor should starve in time of famine, and let their families starve, rather than steal, he was putting a higher value on the sanctity of private property, and a lower value on human life, than the poor and vagabonds did in the 17th century. We are entitled to criticise him because John Donne and Thomas Hobbes earlier in the century[12] had taken the more humane view.

Our assessment of the values of the past, then, involves social issues. Public opinion in any age is formed by hegemonic groups. As society changes, so morality changes. We choose to see this as progress; and indeed the terms in which we now defend racial, sexual, national and individual liberty do seem to me an improvement on the standards of

---

12. R Baxter, *Chapters from a Christian Directory* (J. Tawney (ed), 1925), pp69-71; J Donne, *Essays in Divinity* (E M Simpson (ed), OUP, 1952), p68; T Hobbes, *Leviathan* (C B Macpherson (ed), Penguin edn), p346.

the 17th century. Have we got a better morality in these respects because we can afford it? Are the new standards luxuries enjoyed at someone else's expense?

V

My first point then is that we should be aware of conflicting standards and of problems when we try to distinguish between them. Similar problems are created by the different techniques and approaches of historians. Our attitude towards historical evidence also involves standards. Historians tend to be selective in their scepticism here, finding it easier to recognise the frailties of other historians. There are those who reject literary sources and assume that truth can be found nowhere but in the archives. William Blake on the other hand said that only a scoundrel believed public records to be true. Certainly state papers are no less subjective and in need of close reading, of interpretation, than plays and novels—in some respects more so, since they purport to be objective. Civil servants plead special cases, naturally: any state paper is written against a background of knowledge which we cannot recapture fully. Consequently its unspoken assumptions may escape us. Sir Geoffrey Elton's insistence that politico-administrative history is the only real history focuses attention on the view from on top: 'troublemakers' exist only to be ruled, to be controlled for their own good. Such history is not interested in, and can know nothing of, 'the people' whose good is being sought.

Political and administrative historians have made great contributions to 17th century history: where should we be without the great Yale editions of parliamentary debates? But political history does not tell us the whole story. Governments are not the same thing as the people. Even today, with far more representation than in the 17th century, their interests can clash: and governments[13] are not always right, as the jury taught the judge in the Clive Ponting case. Governments today lie to their peoples, with all the risks of being found out. It is hardly likely that they resisted the temptation (in the name of 'national security', of course) in the safer circumstances of earlier centuries. And even when they do not deliberately lie, there are distortions which are far more difficult for the historian to allow for, since he may share some of them—class bias, the bias of shared, one sided assumptions. If an American Secretary of State

---

13. Governments have learnt the lesson too. Cases involving the government's assessment of 'national security' are no longer allowed to go before juries.

can refuse to act against pollution today because the end of the world is coming in the near future, what are we to expect in the 17th century? It is much harder to find out what ordinary people were thinking then; but it is even more important for our assessment of the society.

In my young days English history seemed hagridden by obsolete Whig myths—the dogma of gradual progress from the forests of Germany to the perfected British constitution;[14] of the independence of constitutional from political history, of politics from society. I (among many others) thought it especially necessary to challenge the myth of unbroken continuity (or continuity broken only, uselessly, by the 'interregnum'). We also wanted to place political history in a wider context—not only economic but cultural and ideological as well. As England ceased to be top nation it became easier to see that (in the immortal words of *1066 and All That*) history had not come to a full stop with British parliamentary government.

All historians whose work is worth reading are trying to convince the reader of something. They should be watched with the care with which we watch a suspected pickpocket. Some prejudices are more self evident than others. Those historians who stress that Sir Thomas More died for the unity of Christendom sometimes fail to mention that Christian unity was maintained by burning heretics and books; More himself burnt heretics, and said he would have destroyed *Utopia* rather than see it translated into the vernacular for the vulgar to read. As long as the English Civil War remains relevant to our present discontents, there will always be historians who are temperamentally more sympathetic either to royalists, to parliamentarians or to radicals. And this will lead to nuances in interpretation for even the most conscientious of historians.

VI

There is then no value free history; no historian is without prepossessions, whether he is aware of them or not. Better for him and his readers if he is aware of them: he is more likely to control them. The Hammonds and Tawney started with prejudices against exploitation and in favour of common men and women against the propertied. This

---

14. Recently revived, remarkably, by Allan Macfarlane. As long ago as 1844 Marx was properly facetious about what was already the rather old fashioned 'freedom history of the boar'. 'The forest', Marx added drily, 'echoes back the same words that are shouted into it' (K Marx, *Early Texts*, translated and edited by D McLellan, Oxford, 1971, p117).

can lead to distortion, but need not in itself, if we watch it. The prejudices of critics of the Hammonds and Tawney are no better than the opposite prejudices, and I think more dangerous because all the evidence available to historians tends to be slanted against the poor and for the propertied, against women and for men. Men of property leave most of the written documents from which historians have to construct their stories and arguments.

Marx long ago taught us to be sceptical of 'the illusion of the epoch'—views which seemed self evident to rulers in past ages but which, on reflection, should not seem self evident to us. Examples are that the gentry in the 17th century were, as they claimed to be, 'the county community', representing the views and values of all classes in that community; that women and servants were 'virtually represented' by the male head of the household; that there was a 'white man's burden' to be shouldered in bringing civilisation to ungrateful 'natives'; that all men are free and equal in a slaveowning society. The view from below is an essential check on myopia of this kind.

It does not necessarily follow that a prejudice in favour of the status quo, or the establishment, is less likely to lead to significant new insights. In the 17th century Robert Brady's Tory prejudices helped him to pick holes in the Whig myth of the Norman Yoke and the free Anglo-Saxons.[15] Namier was accused of taking the mind out of history because he downplayed the importance of ideas. But his dislike of ideologists helped him to understand 18th century politics, where ideology had become a worked out sham. Any prejudice may lead the lucky historian to ask new questions. We should all beware of damning vices we are not inclined to.

But a prepossession in favour of the view from below is perhaps more likely to stimulate the formulation of new questions. It has long been accepted that some 20 percent of slaves died on the Atlantic crossing. We know this because it affected the profits of slave traders. But recent research, asking different questions, has shown that a similar proportion of mariners also died on this crossing. So to the net cost to the slaver and the net loss to humanity of the deaths of slaves, we have to add a further net loss of lives which did not reduce the slaver's profits, was indeed a necessary condition of those profits.[16]

15. D C Douglas, *English Scholars 1660-1730* (1939).
16. I owe this point to the important new book by M Rediker, *Between the Devil and the Deep Blue Sea: Merchant Seaman, Pirates, and the Anglo-American Maritime World, 1700-1750* (Cambridge, 1987), pp43, 47-48.

To wish to find out about the lives of ordinary people is not necessarily to suggest that they are better or wiser than their rulers. They may have been in some respects, but cannot have been in all. Yet we need to know about the ruled in order to understand the rulers. What value are we to give to their condemnation of the Many-Headed Monster? To their assumption that the bulk of the population must exist only to be ruled? That the majority are going to hell anyway? That women should be subordinated to men, servants to masters? It is easy to stand the assumptions of any earlier age on their head by applying our standards, to see the oppression of women and/or the lower orders as a reason for condemning a society. But since women and the lower orders have been oppressed throughout history we should try to be rather more nuanced than that. The civilisation of Athens? Of Elizabethan England, whose government the late Tim Curtis described as 'a beleaguered garrison'? Karl Marx on India? The hold of Paisley and his like over Northern Ireland today?

One prejudice of historians which would be avoided by greater consideration of common men and women is conspiracy theory. If you hold an MI5 view of contemporary society and believe that there can be no strikes without wicked agitators behind them, then you are likely to look for agitators in past upheavals and revolts. When 'revisionist' historians cannot find them—in 1640 and 1789 there were no people consciously and deliberately preparing for revolution—they conclude that there can have been no strike, no revolution.

Conspiracy theories tell us less about history than about the historians who adopt them. They assume that society—almost any society, apparently—is so just and acceptable that only wicked conspirators can want to introduce fundamental changes. It is analogous to 16th and 17th century beliefs in original sin: law and social order are 'necessary for preserving mankind from the outrageousness and unmeasurableness of iniquity and wickedness which would utterly ruin all human society' if natural men and women were let loose.[17] It appears from recent books that in 1944-5 many in MI5 believed that those who wanted good relations with the USSR to continue after the war must be Soviet agents: no other explanation seems to have entered their heads, and so they had to assume that Soviet agents had penetrated not only the Foreign Office but also the cabinet—some even thought MI5 itself. The 16th and 17th century witch hunters proceeded from similar assumptions to similar conclusions.

17. J Owen, *Works* (1850-1853), XII, p587.

A perhaps unconscious prejudice, or blind spot, is to ignore the existence of censorship in the past, to assume that literature produced under censorship expressed 'public opinion', that printed material necessarily stated its author's meaning. Those historians and literary critics who are guilty of such myopia would not make the same mistake in discussing Eastern Europe today. In 17th century England literary artists had to use allegory, biblical allusions, doubletalk, in order to be able to convey what they really meant rather than what they were conventionally expected to say. To ignore this is to assume that the established order is always justified because it is established. It leads to failure to consider the possibility that frequent repetition of a slogan or a truism—eg the great chain of being, the divine character of the ruler—may mean not that everybody accepts these platitudes but that they are being challenged and therefore have to be authoritatively and regularly restated.

The survival of old ideas needs less explanation than the breakthrough of new ideas. It is interesting but not surprising that Nicholas Tyacke found grass roots sympathisers with traditional Catholic ritual and ceremonies in England in the 1630s, who revealed themselves as soon as Laud made it safe for them to do so; or that John Morrill can find grassroots supporters of episcopacy and the prayer book in England in the 1650s. David Underdown describes Clubmen in the 1640s anxious to restore the status quo as they imagined it, and Austin Woolrych tells us that some New Model Army soldiers who mutinied in 1647 under the influence of Agitators then declared for a restoration of the king—not a policy the Agitators were advocating.[18] All these facts tell us something about the society which the radical revolutionaries failed to transform, and about the reasons for their failure. Although the survival of old ideas explains itself, the mechanisms by which hegemony is established and maintained are a fascinating subject for study. But I myself find it even more important to explain how new ideas broke through than to establish that old ideas could survive under challenge.

18. N Tyacke, *Anti-Calvinists: The Rise of English Arminianism, c1590-1640* (Oxford, 1987), esp ch 8; J Morrill, 'William Davenport and the "silent majority" of Early Stuart England', *Journal of the Chester Archaeological Society*, vol 58, 1975; D Underdown, *Riot, Revel and Rebellion: Politics and Culture in England, 1603-1660* (Oxford, 1985), chs 8 and 10; A Woolrych, *Soldiers and Statesmen: The General Council of the Army and its Debates, 1647-8* (Oxford, 1987), pp257-258. An earlier example of the survival of older ideas is the hope of Essex rioters in 1591 that they would be liberated by the King of Spain. See W Hunt, *The Puritan Moment: The Coming of Revolution in an English County* (Harvard, 1983), p61.

VII

History from below is more difficult to write than history from on top, and perhaps requires new techniques. You cannot find a cache of documents to form the basis of a thesis. History from below involves piecing together fragments of forgotten or neglected evidence to recover a more complete picture than political and administrative history has hitherto given us. It can hardly be done within the normal limits of a D Phil thesis [in Oxford PhDs are called D Phils]. The D Phil has much to be said for it as a means of training historians, but it is not the only way in which this can be done. I do not think Keith Thomas or Edward Thompson ever wrote a thesis: it does not seem to have made them worse historians. Anyone can drop a card index into an article, and sometimes the hard work involved in collecting facts seems to justify publication. But historical imagination must come into play in selecting and arranging so as to bring out siginificances. 'Not all facts are important', Braudel had to remind Peter Laslett; 'only those which have consequences'.[19] One danger of the thesis approach is its encouragement of the classic historian's vice of continuing to learn more and more about less and less; academic rewards go to those who know a great deal very accurately about a small subject; some never become interested in those wider aspects of society and its culture which seemed obviously relevant to historians of the pre-D Phil generation like Tawney, Trevor-Roper and Stone, L B Wright and Hexter. There may be a case for considering whether some young historians might not benefit by other methods of training.

VIII

Sir Geoffrey Elton, Conrad Russell and other historians think that state papers and parliamentary debates should be our principal sources. They are indeed important for history from on top. But they call for close reading and analysis of the same sophisticated kind as do 'literary sources'. We should always be on the lookout for censorship and evasion of censorship, for conventions of discourse which prevented men saying in public what they thought in private.[20] We should be equally sceptical about new techniques of analysis which cliometric

19 Quoted in my *People and Ideas in 17th century England* (1985), pp16-17, 131.
20. See my 'Political Discourse in Early Seventeenth Century England', in C Jones, M Newitt and S Roberts (eds), *Politics and People in Revolutionary England: Essays in Honour of Ivan Roots* (Oxford, 1986).

historians evolve in order to arrive at more 'objective' conclusions about the untidy mass and mess of historical evidence. Geoffrey Holmes rightly and usefully treated Gregory King's tables as though they were literary sources and subjected them to rigorous examination, taking into account both biographical and social factors which could have influenced his use of figures.[21] We should treat modern demographers in the same way. It is not only that the basic building blocks of most English demographers—parish registers—are fundamentally insecure. Drunken and lazy parish clerks and parsons, haphazard absence or presence of nonconformist births, marriages and deaths, clandestine and informal marriages, unsatisfactory recording of vagabonds and beggars, etc, etc.[22] It is also that demographers' estimates are often based on a tiny sample of sources, which may or may not be typical. Figures derived from these sources are adjusted by sophisticated techniques which have proved successful for later societies, but which may or may not be equally applicable to 17th and 18th century England.

One of the more ambitious of such demographers, Peter Lindert, admits that parish registers 'probably' understate nonconformist burials, but appears to regard this as of no statistical consequence.[23] Yet if (say) 41 sample parishes are to be multiplied up to 9,000 to cover the whole kingdom, it is rather important to know whether their registers include nonconformists or not, and whether they are drawn from areas in which there are many or few nonconformists. One of the most impressive tools of the demographer's trade, family reconstitution, makes assumptions about the immobility of English society in these centuries which do not appear to coincide with historical reality.[24]

Modern demographers who 'correct' Gregory King and other contemporary observers are constructing an alternative model of reality. Such models can be mistaken, and may conceal unconscious 20th century assumptions. Thus Lindert's 'reasonable hunch that one moved out of being a rural labourer as one advanced in age and experience'[25] does not correspond with anything I know about 17th and 18th century

21. G S Holmes, 'Gregory King and the Social Structure of pre-Industrial England', *Trans Royal Historical Soc*, 5th Series, 27,1977, pp41-68.
22. See my *People and Ideas in 17th century England*, ch 9, for this and the following paragraph.
23. P H Lindert, 'English Occupations, 1670-1811', *Journal of Economic History*, vol XL, 1980, pp689, 707.
24. M Chaytor, 'Household and Kinship: Ryton in the late 16th and early 17th Centuries, *Historical Workshop Journal*, vol 10, 1980, pp25-60.
25. P H Lindert, 'English Occupations', p694. Lindert's 'correction' of Gregory King by including non conformist ministers under 'clergymen' also suggests insensitivity to 17th century official usage.

wage labour. Models do not fall from heaven: they are invented by fallible scholars. If I concentrate on Lindert, it is because his speculations, about which he is usually properly cautious, have perhaps been taken unduly seriously by historians anxious to embrace the conclusions to which his statistics seem to point.[26] The evidence on which Lindert and Williamson base their models is drawn from a narrow range of samples, which have to be selected and interpreted. Their guesses at the 'corrected' figures with which they wish to replace Gregory King's vary between 1980 and 1982 by 2 percent (for labourers and paupers), 6 percent (for freeholders and farmers) and by as much as 12 percent for commerce and industry.[27] It is all still a bit fluid.

To say that Gregory King seriously underestimated English industrial and commercial development in his time may turn out to be right: Holmes has established that possibility.[28] But the extent of his underestimate and exaggerations is difficult to establish except by circular arguments. Theoretical assumptions about 'modernisation', 'take off', 'proto-industrialisation', are all hypotheses, not established facts. Some of them are rather dated hypotheses. There is much evidence to suggest that agriculture and domestic service were still in the 18th century more important than industry. The extent and dating of industrialisation remain open questions. The whole discussion is contaminated by hangovers from the debate between 'optimists' and 'pessimists' on the consequences of the Industrial Revolution. The names of the original participants in this debate suggest that their views may not have been wholly unconnected with their 20th century political opinions.[29] Similarly Mr Laslett's conception of 'the world we have lost' as a 'one class society', in which the minority 'lived for all the rest' was a political statement about the world which has certainly not been proved and should not be assumed.[30]

26. Cf P H Lindert and J G Williamson, 'Revising England's Social Tables, 1688-1812', *Explorations in Economic History*, vol 19, 1982, pp391-394, 405; P H Lindert and J G Williamson, 'English Workers' Living Standards during the Industrial Revolution', *Economic History Review*, 2nd Series, vol XXXVI, 1983, pp25-26. E A Wrigley, the greatest authority on the subject, finds that Lindert's figures, 'at least for agriculture, do not appear convincing'. See E A Wrigley, 'Urban Growth and Agricultural Change in England and on the Continent in the Early Modern Period', *Journal of Interdisciplinary History*, vol XV, 1985, p698.
27. P H Lindert and J G Williamson, op cit, p393.
28. G S Holmes, op cit.
29. I owe the argument in the preceding three paragraphs to discussions with Bridget Hill. See her *Women, Work and Sexual Politics in Eighteenth Century England* (Oxford, 1989).
30. P Laslett, *The World We Have Lost* (1965), p52. For a critique of 'statistical models and impersonal laws' and 'simplistic asssumptions about historical change', see M C Jacob, *The Cultural Meaning of the Scientific Revolution* (New York, 1987), pp217-20; cf. H G Gutman, *The Black Family in Slavery and Freedom, 1750-1925* (New York, 1977), pxx.

We should then be much more sceptical of the 'models' which social scientists and historians impose on the past. Such models do not necessarily offer more complete, or better, explanations than contemporaries were able to do; and they may obtrude 20th century assumptions into the past. Let us return to Hugh Stretton's prize winning essay. Given proper input, most of this could theoretically have been written by a well programmed computer. But the last two sentences transformed its meaning. Demographers' models of 17th and 18th century households are like Stretton's essay without the conclusion. Debates on the standard of living of the English working class in the late 18th and early 19th centuries, concentrating on wage rates for men, ignore grandmother's murder, the brutal termination of an independent mode of life which was possible so long as one retained a cottage, even a small plot of land and common rights. Higher wages for some men (if they were higher) could not compensate for the loss of independence and freedom entailed in loss of land and complete dependence on full time wage labour. In the 17th and early 18th centuries such dependence was regarded as slavery.[31] Historians too easily dismiss such phrases as rhetoric, and facile use of the phrase 'wage slavery' in the 20th century can be rhetorical. But the transition from one mode of livelihood to the other could seem like passing from freedom (on a low standard of living) to slavery (even if male wages might be higher). The family working unit, and especially the women's contribution, was disrupted. If we omit the murder of grandmother our assessment of the whole process is distorted.

The 'models' which statisticians and demographers create for their own convenience are open to the charges traditionally laid against 'naive empiricism'. Far from being 'value free', they almost inevitably assume the outlooks and values of the age in which they are invented—the standards of the market, for instance, which certainly did not prevail in the 17th century and were only just beginning to preponderate in the 18th, if then. The attempt to separate 'facts' from 'values' may preclude proper evaluation of sources, may prevent some relevant questions being asked. If Gregory King's tables are rendered suspect by his harking back to what he believed to have been true of the days of his youth, historians' models may be vitiated by drawing on assumptions from a far more distant epoch—especially dangerous if these assumptions seem 'natural' to us. The statistics and models may acquire what Donald Pennington called 'the spurious authority of a column of figures'. Lawrence

---

31. See my 'Pottage for Freeborn Englishmen: Attitudes to Wage Labour', *Change and Continuity in 17th century England*, ch 10.

Stone, scrupulously, tells us that some of his statistics are true 'plus or minus 25 percent'; Lindert admits to even wider possibilities of error. But once the statistics and models are there, the scholarly qualifications, as Pennington observes, are sometimes overlooked by later users.[32]

Statistics and models for the 17th and 18th centuries are no more infallible than the minds which thought them up. Sophisticated methods of manipulating them may multiply error unless the initial figures manipulated are 100 percent certain. So my plea is especially for historians to be sceptical of their own assumptions and standards, their own models and the intellectual bases on which they are constructed. We congratulate ourselves when we think we have discerned a signpost where contemporaries saw a ghost; but perhaps it was only rubbish after all?

IX

This leads to my conclusion, a plea for history as a cooperative discipline. There is so much still to be found out: we have not begun to write a total history of the English people. Whatever our temperamental or ideological disagreements, all historians can learn from one another. We criticise one another's hypotheses, naturally, and some will prove more useful than others; but we should welcome help from any quarter where it can be found. It is sad when victory over an opponent, or over a type of history, comes to seem more important than cooperation in the quest in which we all claim to be engaged. And it badly dissipates energy. There is no right kind of history, any more than there is a historical truth which has been or is likely to be established. The archive work of administrative historians, the technology of cliometric historians and demographers, have opened new doors, but there are no sacrosanct techniques of investigation. As Milton said in *Areopagitica*, 'truth may have more shapes than one'. He was defending conflict of ideas as the motor of intellectual progress.[33] The best that any of us can hope for is to have started up one or two hares which others may find worth pursuing, by whatever means.

---

32. D Pennington, op cit, pp17-18; P H Lindert, op cit, pp689-690; P H Lindert and J G Williamson, 1982, op cit, pp387-90, 405. (I am speaking here of the 17th and 18th centuries, for which reliable figures are rare. Things are better when we get census returns in the 19th century, though even these, we know, are liable to large margins of error. Nothing I say should be taken as relating to this later period.)
33. J Milton, *Complete Prose Works*, 11, p563.

Chapter 26

Milton, Bunyan and the literature of defeat

This was the twelfth annual Sidney Warhaft Memorial Lecture, given on 29 March 1990 at the University of Manitoba, Winnipeg, Canada, and first published in Mosaic, University of Manitoba, Vol 24, No 1, Winter 1991.

I start by pitching my claims high. Milton and Bunyan seem to me to be respectively the greatest poet and the greatest prose writer of late 17th century England, the greatest century in our literature. The author of *Areopagitica* was also no mean writer of English prose, and Bunyan's verse has, I think, been seriously underestimated, especially his satirical verse. The word 'Puritan' is notoriously hard to define, but it is difficult to think of any definition which would exclude Milton and Bunyan—though as we shall see they disagreed on theology and on much else.

I must spend a minute on my word 'defeat'. No one could be more defeated than Milton after 1660. He had defended regicide, just before and just after the execution of Charles I in 1649. He published a mocking attack on *Eikon Basilike*, 'the portraiture of His Sacred Majesty in his solitudes and sufferings', which royalists believed (wrongly) to have been written by the royal martyr himself. Milton was employed by the regicide republic and later by Oliver Cromwell as their spokesman and defender to an outraged Europe. In this role he had won unique renown—the first Englishman since Sir Thomas More whose writings were the talk of Europe. When the government of the Commonwealth collapsed in 1659-60, Milton was one of its last and most vigorous defenders. He published several pamphlets outlining his preferred alternatives to a restoration of monarchy; and in the last of these, published a month before Charles was back on the throne, Milton delivered a savage attack on monarchy in general and Charles II in particular. He was very lucky not to suffer the fate of many of his friends and colleagues who were hanged, disembowelled and quartered. Two of Milton's books were burnt by the public hangman, and he had to go into hiding. In his last pre-Restoration pamphlet he nailed his colours defiantly to the mast: 'If I be not heard or believed the event will bear me witness to have spoken truth; and I in the meanwhile have borne my witness, not out of season, to the church and to my country.' We cannot exaggerate the strength of his anti-monarchical feelings.

Add to all this that Milton was notorious for publishing a defence of divorce for incompatibility of temperament and for defending liberty of the press from pre-publication censorship—both unfashionable subjects in Restoration England. Milton was also—though this was less publicly known—a dangerous heretic, whose *De Doctrina Christiana*, the theological *summa* which Milton described as his 'dearest and best possession', could not be published in his lifetime. It has been calculated that if it had been published Milton would have been liable under the 1648 Blasphemy Ordinance to five death sentences and eight sentences of life imprisonment. We need not bother about the precise accuracy of the statistics: it is clear that Milton was not wholly orthodox.

Bunyan was 20 years younger than Milton, and a much less politically committed figure. But he had served in the parliamentarian army during the civil war, he disliked monarchy, and after the Restoration he and his co-religionists were persecuted. Bunyan had preached in a Bedford congregation, remarkably successfully. At the Restoration he was ordered to stop preaching, since he was not ordained. He refused, for he believed that preaching was his divinely appointed vocation. His judges told him that his vocation was that of a tinker, and sentenced him to indefinite imprisonment. He was in jail for 12 years—a death sentence for all but those who were exceptionally tough, morally and physically. In prison he wrote *The Pilgrim's Progress*. Released in 1672, by one of the quirks of royal policy, he at once started breaking the law again. In 1675-1676 he was imprisoned once more for six months or so. In 1685, the year of the unsuccessful rebellion of the Duke of Monmouth, Bunyan transferred all his small property to his wife, clearly expecting to be arrested again, or to have to go underground.

The vast majority of his 60 or more books were published without the licence officially required, and so were illegal. (*The Pilgrim's Progress* was exceptional in being properly licensed.) When one of Bunyan's publishers was asked why he hadn't applied for a licence for a book of Bunyan's he replied simply, 'I knew I shouldn't get a licence for Bunyan.' All of his printers were themselves radicals—jailed, fined, exiled, returning with Monmouth's rebel army in 1685. So though Bunyan was not primarily interested in politics as Milton was, the Restoration regimes forced political decisions on him. Recognising the fact of defeat will help us better to understand the writing of both Milton and Bunyan.

One vitally important point about both Milton and Bunyan which literary critics too often forget is the censorship. Both of them were marked men, whose publications were certain to be very carefully scrutinised. They never forgot it. In order to say what they wanted to say—or part of what they wanted to say—they had to resort to ambiguity, allegory and other obfuscatory evasive techniques. We must be on the lookout for these all the time if we are not to miss significances.

One or two examples. In the invocation of Book VII of *Paradise Lost* Milton writes, 'I sing...unchanged...though fallen on evil days, / On evil days though fallen, and evil tongues.' This clearly refers to Milton's post-Restoration poverty, and to the slanders upon him to which he was unable to reply. His blindness, it was repeatedly alleged, was a divine punishment for his defence of regicide. 'I sing...unchanged': we think of Milton first of all as a great poet. But in 1667 that was not his reputation: he had published one slim volume of verse twenty two years earlier. He *was* famous—or notorious—for his defence of regicide, for his ferocious attack on *Eikon Basilike*, now almost holy writ, for his impenitence in 1660, when most of his fellow republicans recanted. 'I sing...unchanged' tells his audience (fit though few) that *he* had not recanted. In *Paradise Lost* Milton could not of course attack monarchy. Instead he referred to the biblical Nimrod (without even naming him). Nimrod, founder of monarchy, Milton describes as a rebel, 'not content / With fair equality, fraternal state.' Milton could not advocate 'an equal commonwealth', so he casually mentioned the ant as 'pattern of just equality, perhaps'. There is virtue in 'perhaps'. Milton could not proclaim his heresy that the only correct form of baptism was in running water, so in *Paradise Regained* he described the baptism of Christ by John the Baptist in the river Jordan. Just to be quite safe, the description is put into the mouth of Satan. Civil marriage had been briefly established in 1653, with Milton's approval. Again, he could not mention this approval in so many words; but in *Paradise Lost* he went out of his way to make it unnecessarily clear that Adam and Eve went to bed together without any formal ceremony at all. Milton also, I regret to say, thought polygamy should be legalised. Again, he couldn't say so; but in what 19th century critics hailed as a great hymn to monogamy in *Paradise Lost*, Milton wrote, 'Hail wedded love, as saints and patriarchs used.' The *only* reason for mentioning the patriarchs was that they were holy men; and that they were polygamous.

In *Samson Agonistes* Milton normally follows the biblical narrative carefully, which makes his departures from it the more significant. Dalilah, who betrayed Samson, was put up to this treachery, the play tells us, by the priests. There is no biblical authority at all for this; but the clergy of the Church of England were anathema to Milton. In 1641 when he was free from censorship, he had expressed the view that all bishops, ex officio, would be condemned to spend all eternity in hell, regardless of their personal merits or demerits. At the end of *Samson Agonistes*, you will remember, Samson pulls the temple down on the Philistines and slaughters vast numbers. Judges XVI tells us precisely that 3,000 Philistines were sitting on the roof of the temple and were slain. But in *Samson Agonistes* the roof of the temple falls on the Philistine aristocracy and priests. The Messenger says, 'the vulgar only 'scaped who stood without.' This flatly contradicts the Bible. Why did Milton insert that line? There can be no possible explanation except that he wanted to restrict the slaughter to the aristocracy and clergy, the two groups in post-Restoration England whom he had political reasons for hating most. The vulgar were allowed to escape. Milton had been very disappointed by the failure of the English people to defend the republic in 1660, and by their apparent acceptance of monarchy. But he still knew that they were the only hope for a revival of the republic. Manoa, at the close of the play, says that Samson has left honour and freedom to Israel: 'let but them / Find courage to lay hold on this occasion.' It is impossible to pronounce these lines without heavy emphasis on '*them*', the people.

The object of *Paradise Lost*, Milton tells us, is 'to justify the ways of God to men'. In the 1660s God's ways seemed badly to need justifying—not least to Milton himself. He had devoted 20 years of his life, and believed that he had sacrificed his eyes, in the defence of the parliamentarian cause which he knew was God's. Why then had God allowed his Cause to be so utterly defeated, its advocates to be executed, imprisoned, exiled? 'God hath spit in our face', said Milton's friend Major General Fleetwood. *Paradise Lost* is, among many other things, an analysis of defeat, written by a man who, like his Samson, is 'blind, disheartened, shamed, dishonoured, quelled', and is trying to ascertain in what he could now 'be useful, wherein serve / My nation, and the work from heaven imposed.'

The reasons for defeat which he gives in *Paradise Lost* and *Samson Agonistes* are those which he thought had been the reasons for the defeat of the parliamentarians. The rebel angels, who revolted against God, were guilty of pride, ambition, self interest, greed. But, as Milton points out, they were more united among themselves than those who supported better causes. Satan himself has many heroic virtues, but he arrogantly refuses to submit to God's will, to recognise reality; and he places self above anything else. Adam and Eve fell through Eve's ambition to be wiser than Adam, through Adam's wrong decision to eat the apple and die with Eve rather than be left without her. But the poetry, the description of the earthly Paradise without Eve:

> How can I live without thee, how forgo
> Thy sweet converse and love so dearly joined,
> To live alone in these wild woods forlorn

makes it clear that at least half of Milton was on Adam's side at that moment. The feeble line telling us that Adam was 'fondly overcome with female charm' is far less convincing.

The Archangel Michael's gloomy preview of human history and Adam's discussion of it are about how we are to react to defeat. And the conclusion that Adam ultimately draws is that we should not be in too ambitious a hurry, but proceed:

> by small
> Accomplishing great things, by things deemed weak
> Subverting worldly strong, and worldly wise
> By simply meek.

Why should Adam, lord of the world, and undisputed sovereign of his kingdom of two—why should Adam want to subvert 'worldly strong'? The question answers itself. Milton is not in fact thinking of Adam, but of how the supporters of the Good Old Cause should behave in England of the 1660s.

Paradise Regained leads to a similar conclusion, though it is expressed more positively. In the poem the hero is rarely referred to as Jesus or Christ but almost always as 'the Son of God'. Why? Satan gives us the answer: 'All men are sons of God.' One of Milton's heresies was denying the divinity of Christ. *Paradise Regained* stresses Christ's humanity, shows us a man facing the sorts of temptations to which the rebel angels, Adam and the parliamentarian revolutionaries had succumbed. Satan offers the Son of God riches, luxury, power, indeed the kingdoms of this world if he will bow down and worship him. Many had been the complaints in the 1650s of army leaders having succumbed to greed, to high living, to power lust. The Son of God is offered military glory. the salvation of Israel and its people by military victory. The Son of God does not deny that his objective is to liberate Israel, 'to destroy God's enemies' as Milton put it in the *De Doctrina Christiana*. He does not reject the use of military force, any more than Milton had done. But the Son of God is wiser than those Fifth Monarchists who had desperately, courageously but hopelessly revolted in 1661. We must take cognisance of the real possibilities before embarking on precipitate action.

Remember the circumstances. Men had believed in the 1640s and 1650s that Christ's kingdom was coming in the immediate future, on what seemed good evidence. Milton spoke of Christ as 'shortly expected king' in 1641: I believe he was thinking of some date in the 1650s. Bunyan in 1658 declared that Christ's kingdom was 'at hand'. Things suddenly looked different after 1660. Bunyan tells us of the impatience which many of the godly felt. They complained that Christ 'accomplished all the first part of his priesthood in less than 40 years; but...he has been above in heaven above sixteen hundred years, and yet has not done.' Bunyan called for 'faith and patience'. Milton knew that revolution was not a political possibility until there was a great change in public opinion. He made the Son of God say that the Father 'may bring [the people] back repentant and sincere, time to himself best known.' But till then, 'to his best time and providence I leave them.'

The conclusion is the same as Adam's in *Paradise Lost*: do what small things you can when you can. All the three great poems are open-ended. Adam and Eve, reconciled, go hand-in-hand into the world to face their destiny. The Son of God, after the miracle of standing on the pinnacle of the temple, goes quietly home to his mother's house to pick up his day-to-day job of preaching. The moral of *Samson Agonistes* is the same: we must wait, refusing to be provoked by Harapha, but be prepared to act when God makes it clear that the time has come. What happens then depends on whether the people *choose* to be liberated. In *Samson Agonistes* they are offered the chance, but we do not know whether they will 'find courage to lay hold on this occasion.' Men and angels in *Paradise Lost* and *Paradise Regained* are free to stand and free to fall. History is not pre-destined. In the *De Doctrina Christiana* Milton quoted God's words in Exodus III, 8, 17: 'I have come down from that place to liberate them ...and to lead them out into a good land'—'though in fact', Milton grimly commented, 'they perished in the desert.' We are free to fall as well as to stand. As Oliver

Cromwell knew, trusting in God does not mean that we need not keep our powder dry.

I have gone on a bit about Milton. Now let us look at Bunyan. He was not a political character in the sense that Milton was. He came from a different social class. Bunyan's peasant family had been selling land for generations, sinking in the social scale. Bunyan's family, he said himself, was 'of the meanest and most despised in the land'. His father was an illiterate tinker; and a tinker was an emblem for drunkenness and immorality. Itinerants, they took their doxies with them on their rounds. Milton, in contrast, was the son of a rich London scrivener, which means among other things a money lender. Milton went to a good school, and on to Cambridge. His brother was a successful lawyer who became *Sir* Christopher. Milton originally intended to go into the church until he was so disgusted by the regime of Archbishop Laud that he described himself as 'church-outed by the prelates'. Otherwise he might have done as well in the church as Sir Christopher did at the bar: Milton—horrible thought—might have become a bishop. Milton was no democrat, and often impatient with 'the people'. But he had a social conscience. He told himself that 'ease and leisure were given thee out of the sweat of other men', and this entailed obligations to society. Milton was a sophisticated humanist intellectual, with a wide knowledge of modern European literature.

Bunyan was a self taught hell-fire preacher. So far as we know he did not even go to a grammar school. He had been brought up on chap-book romances and ballads. He got his education in the New Model Army. To have been in that army from the age of sixteen to eighteen and a half must have been an overwhelming experience for a young country yokel. Bunyan saw little active service. Parliament's victory ended the war six months after he had volunteered (or been conscripted). He remained in the garrison town of Newport Pagnell for all his two and a half years. We know from experience in 1918-1919 and 1945-1946 what happens to soldiers who have nothing to do but talk: their talk gets Bolshie. Especially in the New Model Army, where free discussion among the rank and file was positively encouraged by officers like Cromwell. Especially in Newport Pagnell, about which we have a good deal of information.

The 1640s had been a period of unprecedented ferment of discussion. Censorship and control by the church broke down in 1640, and hitherto illegal congregations were able to meet and discuss freely. All politics were discussed in religious terms in the 17th century, and the congregations became something like revolutionary cells. Before 1640 all English men and women had been legally required to attend their parish church every Sunday, where they had to listen to a parson in whose appointment they had had no say, and who had been educated (if at all) at Oxford or Cambridge, and so would not have a dangerous idea in his head. The congregations of the 1640s and 1650s were *voluntary*, not compulsory assemblies. Men and women met together in pubs, or private houses, elected their own chairmen—so called 'mechanic preachers', artisans who worked with their hands six days a week and led discussions on the Sabbath.

The Bible was believed to be the source of all wisdom on all subjects, and men and women eagerly read and discussed the Scriptures to find answers to the problems which faced them during the civil war and after victory. In the Bible they could find a wide variety of views—democracy, pacifism, communism, free love. Many believed that the millennium was imminent: orthodox scholars suggested that the 1650s was a probable date. So there was much for the troops to discuss. But it was not only the Bible. Before 1640 there had been a strict clerical censorship. When it collapsed, the number of books published rose from 22 in 1640 to about 2,000 in 1642. Newspapers were illegal before 1640; by 1645 there were 722. Previously unpublishable books proliferated—heresies from the continent, the Koran (which worried Bunyan), pornography, and political and social views of every description. So there was plenty for the troops to discuss, and they had long been starved of the opportunity.

Bunyan tells us in his autobiography, *Grace Abounding*, what sort of things they did in fact discuss. Was the Bible really the Word of God? Or was it 'a fable and cunning story', 'devised by cunning men' to hold 'poor ignorant people' in subjection? How did we know that Christianity was true and Islam false? It was no good saying Christianity was universally believed: Islam was equally widespread. 'And how if all our faith, and Christ, and Scriptures, should be but a think-so too?' Bunyan tells us he had even worse thoughts 'which at this time I may not nor dare not utter.' One wonders what they were. Bunyan met people called Ranters who believed that there was no such thing as 'sin' or a day of judgment. 'Sin' had been invented by the ruling class to keep the poor in order. We could do what we liked and not sin. Bunyan found this doctrine attractive, 'I being a young man, and my nature in its prime.'

When he was demobilised in 1647 Bunyan seems to have become a leader of the wide boys in his village of Elstow; 'a brisk talker' he called himself in retrospect. His best friend was a drunkard and swearer, and Bunyan admits to excessive swearing himself. He was chaste, he tells us, 'after his marriage' (c1649), which leaves us to guess what

happened earlier. He found the ideas of the extreme radicals attractive. But the government was beginning to clamp down. The democratic Levellers were suppressed in 1649, communist Diggers in 1650,
free thinking Ranters in 1651. Bunyan underwent a long intellectual
and religious crisis.

It ended with an emblematic scene when Bunyan, on his rounds as
a tinker, came across two or three poor women sitting in the sun outside their houses, discussing the things of God 'as though joy did make
them speak'. Bunyan was entranced by their simple faith, so different
from the clever-clever pseudo-intellectual Ranters. He sought their
company and soon joined their congregation in Bedford. Soon he was
their star preacher. But he went on arguing with Ranters for the rest
of his life. Many of the bad characters in *The Pilgrim's Progress* are
Ranters; so in some respects was Mr Badman. Bunyan was still attacking Ranter views in a commentary on Genesis on which he was
working when he died.

We must not think of 'joining a congregation' in modern terms. The
Bedford church was a political organisation. It passed resolutions on
current politics, approving the dissolution of the Barebones Parliament in 1653, disapproving when Oliver Cromwell was offered the
crown, holding a day of thanksgiving to God when he refused it. On
the eve of the restoration of Charles II, the church offered up prayers
for the nation and God's work; after the Restoration they prayed for
God to direct their governors. Then they lapsed into silence on political matters. That is one of the things the Restoration had been
about: to stop people from the lower classes discussing politics. A year
later Bunyan was in jail—no doubt with many of his co-religionists.

Bunyan was imprisoned because he would not agree to stop preaching. The books describe this as 'religious intolerance'—and so it was.
But consider it from the point of view of his judges. The sermon for
which Bunyan was best known was printed in 1658. It was on the
parable of Dives and Lazarus—the rich man who goes to hell and is
allowed a glimpse of Lazarus in heaven, 'the poor scabbed creep-hedge'
whom Dives had spurned when he begged for alms at his gate. Dives
begs that Lazarus may be allowed to dip his finger in water and moisten
Dives's lips; because it is rather hot down there. But it is too late.

Bunyan used this sermon to make a savage attack on the rich, especially the rich gentry, with many vivid personal descriptions which
I am sure must have been recognisable caricatures of Bedfordshire
gentlemen, though we cannot now identify them. And he generalised.
God's own 'are most commonly of the poorer sort'. 'More servants
than masters...more tenants than landlords, more poor than rich, will

inherit the kingdom of heaven.' 'The poor, because they are poor, are not capable of sinning against God as the rich man does.' 'They cannot, with Pontius Pilate, speak Hebrew, Greek and Latin.' 'Cain's brood' are landlords and persecutors; 'Abel's seed...have their necks under oppression.' But 'there is a time coming...that...the righteous shall wash his feet in the blood of the wicked.'

So it is not altogether surprising that the Bedfordshire gentry leapt at the first opportunity to silence the too eloquent Bunyan after the Restoration. His 'licentious and destructive principles', said a spokesman for 'moderate divines' who was soon to be a bishop, would lead to 'the subversion of all government'. 'Natural brute beasts' like Bunyan, he added cheerfully, should 'be taken and destroyed'. The gentry would have accepted Bunyan's agreement to stop preaching; otherwise jail was the only place for him—and for others like him, though Bunyan seems to have remained in prison for longer than any except notorious parliamentarian leaders. Nothing like his 1658 sermon could have been printed after 1660.

The significance of this for our purposes is that Bunyan remained passionately and theologically on the side of the poor for the rest of his life, and it is all important for his writing. In his marvellous prose he directly appeals to the uneducated. 'Words easy to be understood', he wrote, 'do often hit the mark when high and learned ones do only pierce the air'—and it is typical that he takes his metaphor from the popular sport of archery. Whether the episode of the two or three poor women in the sun discussing the things of God as though joy did make them speak actually happened, or whether Bunyan invented it, its allegorical significance is crucial: the poor and simple know the answers, the rich and educated don't. Bunyan continually had to suffer sneers because he, a tinker, who did not know one end of a syllogism from another, presumed to preach and even to publish his illiterate thoughts.

The Pilgrim's Progress is Bunyan's answer. It is the dream of an itinerant sleeping rough in a 'den'—a tinker, perhaps? The hero of the allegory is a man in rags, with a burden on his back. The rags and the burden are allegorical, of course; but there is no doubt that the hero is a poor man. He has no property. He can leave his house and family at a moment's notice; and he travels everywhere on foot. The point is made by the Pilgrim's enemies. Every one of those who oppose him on his pilgrimage is very carefully, indeed obsessively, described as a gentleman, except when he is a lord, or a lady, or a gentlewoman. They address the Pilgrim as 'Thou', and expect the deferential 'You' in reply. The Giants say to the pilgrims, 'What are you doing on my ground?' They are enclosing landlords, some of whom even enclose the King's highway. Like most 17th century enclosing landlords, they are also JPs. Giant Despair has jurisdictional rights and a lock up. We miss the political and social relevance of these carefully recorded facts; but contemporaries would not. Vanity Fair, a city of buying and selling, is very like London. The things that are sold are listed in a mad jumble. They include things sold at court and in the state church—'places, honours, preferments, titles, countries, kingdoms, wives, etc.' The Pilgrim Faithful was condemned to be burnt in Vanity Fair for 'slandering several of the nobility and most of the gentry of our town'—just like Bunyan in Bedford.

Against the griping greed of the gentry Bunyan sets the aspirations of the poor, the homeless itinerants. In the Valley of Humiliation, 'many labouring men…have got estates'. Land is 'rent free' in Emanuel's Land, 'common for all the pilgrims'—just like the Diggers' communist colonies in 1649-50. In the Celestial City all material needs are met, and the inhabitants are in continual and easy contact with the king. All this also recalls the materialist utopias which Mary Cary and many others predicted for the millennium, when the saints would rule on earth, enjoying the good things previously monopolised by their betters. But now for Bunyan the Celestial City is reached only after crossing the River of Death.

I have repeatedly stressed that Bunyan was not primarily interested in politics. But everywhere religion and politics merged. There was one group which Bunyan could never forgive—those Puritans who had sold out in 1660, compromising with the restored monarchy, reverting to the Church of England. In *The Pilgrim's Progress* we meet Mr By-ends, who is related to Lord Turnabout and Lord Time-server. By-ends is 'a gentleman of good quality', though the great grandson of a waterman, 'looking one way and rowing another'—'and I got most of my estate by the same occupation'. Faithful asks, 'Did you not know, ten years ago…one Temporary in your parts, who was a forward man in religion *then*?' (Emphasis mine; Bunyan would have been writing around 1670, so ten years would take us back to the Restoration.) Temporary, Faithful continues, 'was resolved to go on pilgrimage…but all of a sudden he grew acquainted with one Save-self, and then he became a stranger to me.' Much of Bunyan's later writing was directed against those of the godly who were tempted to compromise with the world in which so much money was to be made. 'Covetousness' was rechristened 'good husbandry' in this Thatcherite world. In Bunyan's *The Holy War*, 'the very masterpiece of hell' was to tempt the citizens of Mansoul by making them grow rich.

The Pilgrim's Progress and Grace Abounding are the two works by which Bunyan is most remembered. But The Life and Death of Mr Badman and The Holy War are also interesting from the sociological angle from which I am discussing Bunyan. The Pilgrim's Progress tells of a predestined saint, who from poverty and obscurity makes his way through terrible dangers and temptations to the Celestial City. The interesting thing is that whilst, theologically speaking, there is never any doubt about Christian's pre-destined salvation, the story does not read like that. He seems to make all his own decisions perfectly freely, and often appears to owe his escape from dangers to an accident (eg remembering in Giant Despair's dungeon that he has a key which will let the prisoners out). But of course accidents happen as part of God's overall design. This throws light on the psychology of predestinarian Puritanism. A saint may hope he is saved, but he can never be absolutely certain; he must act as a responsible free agent.

In Mr Badman we know, because the narrator tells us, that Mr. Badman, by contrast, was damned from the start—from his horrid childhood to his deceptively peaceful death. Yet he too feels a free agent. His wicked behaviour throws much light on the world of urban dissent, in which small shopkeepers feign godliness in order to win customers or hook a rich wife, in which they use false weights and measures and timely but fraudulent bankruptcies. It is a handbook to commercial morality in the new world of capitalist values in which Christian charity is too often forgotten. Mr Badman also has many Ranter characteristics, and is allowed to score telling points against the hypocritical godly from his consciously ungodly standpoint.

The literary tales of Milton and Bunyan were very different. Milton's political radicalism was covered up by his early biographer Toland and his early favourable critic Addison. They made an 18th century Whig of him—though Blake knew better. Milton came to be accepted as the orthodox Puritan poet. There are still many in the literary establishment who—against all the evidence—cling faithfully to Milton's religious orthodoxy and play down his political radicalism. Milton after all was a gentleman, a classical scholar with a university education. The tinker Bunyan on the other hand took a very long time to be accepted into the canon. In his lifetime and for a century or more after his death, he was sneered at by the intelligentsia—Addison, Young, Hume, Burke. There were exceptions—Defoe, Swift, Sterne, Cowper appreciated him, and Johnson characteristically said that any book that sold as well as The Pilgrim's Progress must have merits. From the start Bunyan's allegory sold sensationally, but mainly to the middling and lower classes—and in America, where taste was not dictated by gentlemen and Church of

England parsons. Bunyan came into his own in England only after the rise of Evangelicism and the middle class after 1832. In 1730 even a patriotic Bedfordshire historian, anxious to boast of his county's heroes, mentioned Bunyan only as the 'author of several...little books of an antinomian spirit, too frequently to be met with in the hands of the common people', who 'was, if we mistake not, a brazier of Bedford.'

Early translations of *The Pilgrim's Progress* were made into Welsh and Gaelic (so Bunyan tells us, though no Gaelic copy has survived). It was banned in Catholic countries, but there was a translation into Polish for immigrant workers in Prussia. In the 19th century it became a world best seller: missionaries had it translated into the languages of most Third World countries. There may be some significance in the early popularity of *The Pilgrim's Progress* in subordinate nations (Wales, Scotland or Ireland; Polish workers in Prussia) and in colonial or semi-colonial countries in the 19th century. One wonders what exactly its readers got out of Bunyan's book. In the mid-19th century the Taiping rebels in China came nearer to overthrowing the Emperor than any other movement before the present century. They mobilised millions of peasants. The leaders of the Taiping rebellion came from a radical Christian sect, and their favourite reading was the Bible and *The Pilgrim's Progress*. If they had won—and they came very near to conquering the whole of China—*The Pilgrim's Progress* might have become China's little red book a century earlier.

Milton was a less obvious popular best seller. But Valentine Boss of McGill tells us that the book which sold most copies in 19th century Russia, and so must have been read by more people there than any other, was *Paradise Lost* in prose translation. In 1905-6 Maurice Baring noticed that *Paradise Lost* was being avidly read by rank and file Russian soldiers in the Russo-Japanese war. What did Russian peasants get out of *Paradise Lost*? Bunyan is easier to explain: his class consciousness, his hatred of the landed ruling class (a landed class with jurisdictional rights would be familiar in most peasant countries) would have wide appeal. Perhaps the Taiping rebels understood Bunyan better than the missionaries who had him translated into Chinese?

In the case of both Milton and Bunyan the attraction must have lain in their strong emphasis on dogged resistance to prevailing evil, on determination to continue on the pilgrimage whatever the odds against. The names of Bunyan's Mr Great-heart, Mr Standfast, Mr Valiant-for-the-truth make the point. When Christian was given armour, he noticed that it protected him only against attack from the front. Even the pilgrim appropriately named Mr Fearing, who saw dangers everywhere, 'never looked back'. In the brutal persecuting world of Restoration England, where jail, financial ruin, exile, threatened dissenters, the Pilgrim's claim that he 'will constant be / Come wind, come weather' was no easy commitment. 'Therefore we dare not despair', said the Lord Mayor of besieged Mansoul in the town's darkest hour; 'but will look for, wait for and hope for deliverance still.' Emanuel's last words to his faithful were, 'Hold fast till I come.'

Here we can see links between Milton and Bunyan which identify them both as Puritans for all their theological differences. Neither advocated active resistance—partly because they were marked men and could not speak out; partly because it was politically impossible in the changed circumstances of the Restoration. But neither excluded it as an ultimate possibility. The word 'stand' is crucial for both. Adam and Eve, like Satan and his rebel angels, were free to stand and free to fall; so was the Son of God in *Paradise Regained*, who stood triumphantly on the pinnacle of the temple; and Samson, who fell and then recovered, to stand and destroy God's enemies, offering liberation to his people.

The image of the orthodox Puritan Milton, abandoning his lifetime's struggle and subsiding into a peaceful old age, can no longer be accepted. We should also get rid of the image of Bunyan as a pious 19th century non-conformist, totally non-political. We have learnt about Milton from the work which could not be published for a century and a half after he died, the *De Doctrina Christiana*. The works which Bunyan failed to publish are equally illuminating. Here is an extract from one of them. He is saying that his people must be patient under persecution, not troublemakers. But then he continues: but 'suppose they were the truly godly that made the first assault, can they be blamed? For who can endure a boar in a vineyard? [ie a persecutor in the Christian church]... Who bid the boar come here? What had he to do in God's house?'

Understanding of the historical background, I think, can help literary critics to a better understanding of the great writers of the past, just as those writings are essential evidence for historians in their attempts to understand the very different structures and standards of past societies.

Chapter 27

Democratic ideas in 17th century England

This paper was dated 19 April 1990, and does not seem to have been published. My opening paragraphs suggest a conference somewhere in Italy.

In the months since I was asked to talk on this subject the world has seen, literally seen, its first revolutions on TV. Regimes have fallen like ninepins, regimes which six months earlier seemed as secure as that of Charles I in 1639. Only ruthless use of overwhelming military force could save the Chinese regime: it failed in Romania. The impression which I suppose most of us got from TV and other reports was of the unplanned nature of the revolutions, their spontaneity. The only case where some advance planning has been claimed, the Romanian, was the last, and the one which was fairly easy to anticipate.

All historical analogies are dangerous, Joseph Stalin said; and one great difference between England in the 1640s and recent East European revolutions is that the latter had the experience to draw on of the English, American, French, Russian and Chinese revolutions, as well as unsuccessful 19th century European revolutions. The English in the 1640s had to improvise—the only republican states of any significance were Venice—an oligarchy—and the Netherlands—also an oligarchy—and our main trade rival to boot. Hence, although some use was made of Calvinist ideas from the Revolt of the Netherlands and French Huguenots, the main democratic influence was ideas from classical Greece and republican Rome: anyway, there was initially no intention of either revolution or republicanism. To win popular support, millenarian ideas—Christ's kingdom at hand—were more useful. But I want to consider not the intellectual origins of English democratic ideas, but the social background which made them possible.

If men thought about social change, they looked back to the good old days—of Anglo-Saxon freedom before the Norman Yoke was imposed in 1066, to the primitive Christian church before bishops had been invented, to Adam and Eve before the Fall of Man. Raymond Williams pointed out that the very word reformation implies a going back.

My starting point is that in mid-17th century England relatively sophisticated ideas of representative democracy suddenly appeared, of a type previously unknown. These ideas have given rise to much thought about democracy and the state from that time to the present. Why did they appear then, and why in England? To answer these questions we have to look back into previous history.

First, there were significant changes in the English state. The invention of gunpowder transformed the nature of warfare and enhanced the importance of the state. Raising an army no longer meant calling out the king's tenants in chief, who called out their tenants. Peasants were more usefully employed producing food than acting as amateur soldiers; increasingly specialists were employed who knew how to handle the new weapons. Skilled professionals had to be paid, and that meant increased taxation; the very poor or landless vagabonds were conscripted as cannon fodder.

In most European countries during the 16th century military absolute monarchies came into being, based on a bureaucracy which collected the taxes to pay the army; and the army was there to enforce payment of taxes when necessary. In England no such bureaucracy and army were established. For this there were a variety of reasons, including Henry VIII's dissipation of the plunder of the monasteries. More important perhaps was the fact that England was protected from foreign invasion by what Oliver Cromwell was to call our 'great ditch': national defence was the affair of the navy, supplemented when necessary by merchant vessels normally engaged in foreign trade in time of peace. Such taxes as were needed to pay for the navy, and for mercenaries when the government needed them (eg in 1549), were voted by parliament, the traditional representative assembly of the propertied class. Since many of the gentry had benefited from the spoliation of the church, and since foreign trade (especially cloth export) was of importance to the landed class as well as to urban merchants, parliament voted these taxes, and they were assessed and collected by the gentry, without the need for an army as on the continent. After Henry VIII's reign England was little involved in the national and religious wars which increased the necessity for absolutism on the continent. Trade flourished, colonisation of Ireland, and the exploitation, plunder and colonisation of America and the Far East were conducted by private enterprise.

But a time bomb lurked in this apparently satisfactory arrangement. What would happen when the monarchy did not, or could not, carry out policies acceptable to the taxpayers? That time came in the early 17th century, with the escalating costs of war, with inflation, and with the apparent threat to England's national independence posed by Catholic victories in the Thirty Years War. James Harrington grasped this point: power went with landed property. So long as all that was needed for warfare was to call out the feudal levy, the business of government involved merely keeping the great landowners sweet: between them the crown and the aristocracy controlled the military force. But when warfare demanded the payment of armies and manning of ships, the consent of the taxpayers was required. This was normally granted, through parliament, for the occasional emergency; but in the 17th century taxation became regular and was increasing. Since taxes could not be raised in the long run without consent of parliament and the body of taxpayers, this in effect put power to question foreign policy into the hands of parliament. It necessitated, in Harrington's phraseology, either a commonwealth or a monarchy based on a standing army, a continental type of absolutism.

These stark alternatives did not become clear for a long time. Consensus survived the 'Tudor readjustment in government', as Elton's pupils now prefer to call what used to be 'the Tudor Revolution in Government'.[1] The state took on new tasks in relation to poor relief and control of vagabonds, in regulating religion, in protecting English merchants and the English coast against pirates. All of these were welcomed by most taxpayers. But with time interests diverged. From Elizabeth's reign some were calling for a more aggressive anti-Spanish foreign policy. Private enterprise by sea dogs exerted pressure on a cautious government. Protestant solidarity led to calls for more effective support of the Dutch rebels against Spain, for English intervention on the Protestant side in the Thirty Years War. Economic considerations led to demands for government support against the Spanish monopoly

---

1. C Coleman and D Starkey (eds), *Revolution Reassessed: Revisions in the History of Tudor Government and Administration* (OUP, 1986), esp pp197-208.

in the New World, and the Dutch monopoly in the East Indies, for protection against pirates in the Mediterranean as well as in the English Channel. Export of light cloths ('the New Draperies') was seen as necessary to replace markets for heavier cloths in northern Europe lost during the Thirty Years War.

James and Charles proved increasingly incapable of satisfying these demands. For sensible financial reasons they wished to cut back on foreign commitments; for ideological reasons they were more sympathetic to Spain than to the republican Netherlands, in direct opposition to the ideological and commercial interests of many taxpayers. The execution of Sir Walter Ralegh in 1618 became a symbol of the appeasement of Spain and the rejection of the forward policy demanded by sea dogs and merchants alike. The Earl of Southampton was forbidden to lead a volunteer expeditionary force to support James I's son in law, the Elector Palatine, in the Thirty Years War.[2] James failed to protect the East India Company against the Dutch. Charles told English merchants to stay out of the Mediterranean because he could not protect them there. When Charles raised ship money without parliamentary consent in the 1630s, it was accepted at first because it raised hopes of checking piratical raids; but Charles had no intention of using his ship money fleet to forward English commercial interests or the interests of Protestantism. Instead he negotiated for an alliance with Spain.

So consensus between government and taxpayers slowly broke down. Radicals had hoped that the wealth available from the dissolution of the monasteries would be used for educational purposes and to establish a more effective system of poor relief. The monasteries' contribution to relief of the poor had not been very significant; but its loss just when economic causes were leading to an increase in eviction and vagabondage was very serious. The rapid religious changes of the 16th century were unsettling both intellectually and socially. Popular anti-papist plays and pamphlets were encouraged in the 1530s, and again under Edward VI: they were discouraged in the 1540s and under Mary Protestants were burnt. The Marian martyrs became an unforgettable symbol. Elizabeth reversed Mary's religious policy, but soon wished to discourage too much popular activity and discussion. The Book of Common Prayer, including much traditional Catholic theology and ceremonial, was imposed on all parish congregations in order to limit parsons' freedom of expression. Archbishop Grindal was dis-

2. C S P D Domestic, 1611-18, pp444, 450; 1619-23, p269; C S P Ven, 1619-21, p298.

graced and replaced by the hardline Whitgift. Queen Elizabeth was not the last English monarch to 'tune her pulpits'.

There were similar reversals in attitudes towards the Bible. Before the 1530s Bible reading had been more severely repressed in England, because of the Lollard heresy, than anywhere else in Europe. Henry VIII had realised that publication of the Bible in English could be useful to his policies. But he wanted it to be read only by men of property and gentlewomen and he wanted to abolish 'diversity of opinions'. The Great Bible (1539) was intended as an 'official' version, but after 1560 it was eclipsed in popularity by the Geneva Bible, which had what many (including James I) regarded as seditious marginal notes: hence the Authorised Version of 1611.

Archbishops Whitgift and Bancroft discouraged lecturers and popular discussions of religion: sectaries were driven underground or into exile. James and Charles forbade discussion of difficult points of predestination, and under Archbishop Laud the censorship was used against Calvinist publications. Ceremonies like bowing at the name of Jesus, placing rails round the altar, insistence on vestments, smacked of popery, and they cost the parishes money. They all represented a new role for the church in society. So did the Court of High Commission's practice of putting men on oath and then demanding that they incriminate themselves or their neighbours. Church courts had become a powerful adjunct to the prerogative courts—which also administered the oath ex officio.

Protestant orthodoxy declared the pope to be Antichrist, popish worship to be anti-Christian. So to the social tensions which we have been discussing we must add tension between the state church, its parsons and its lay officials on the one hand, and illegal nonconformist congregations and individual consciences on the other.

These reversals of policy created an appetite for religious discussion which could only occasionally be satisfied. (Remember, this was the century of the 'educational revolution': newly literate people were hungry for books.) It was the worst of all worlds for earnest men and women, who believed that their eternal salvation was at stake. Gardiner tells us that the first action of merchants on leaving the shores of England was to throw away the prayer book. Others fled to the Netherlands or New England, fearing that God was leaving England. Many returned to support the parliamentarian cause during the civil war.

Anti-clericalism had been endemic, at least from the time of the Lollards. But the Reformation gave it a new edge. The lady who was reported as saying she did not give a fart for his Grace of Canterbury (Laud) was (whether she knew it or not) picking at the irreverence of the illegal *Marprelate Tracts* of 1588-9, which referred to 'the Arch of Cant', and 'dumb dubsical John [Bishop] of good London'. Soldiers in the army sent against the Scots in 1639, who pulled down communion rails, were rejecting the special role of the priesthood as mediators of the divine mysteries. They also pulled down hedges round enclosures of common lands, and assaulted those of their officers whom they alleged to be papists. In 1640 London crowds liberated prisoners of the High Commission. Church and state seemed indistinguishable: they collapsed together.

So there were tensions not only between government and propertied class. Many of those whom contemporaries called 'the poor' as distinct from 'the people'[3] resented higher taxes, and had views on questions of foreign policy. In 1641 for instance Witney blanket makers asked the House of Lords to protect the rights and privileges of the Africa Company: this export trade was important to their livelihood.[4] The parasitism of the court, the financing of courtiers by grants of monopolies which enhanced the price of goods, impositions on imports, farming of the customs to rich merchants—all these affected rich and poor alike.

But on some issues the poor had separate grievances. They were almost exclusively liable to conscription, whether for the navy or for the army: the well to do could buy themselves off. The poor too had grasped the possibilities of using state power for change. In the 1580s and 1590s rebellious Essex labourers, and especially vagrants, hoped for a Spanish invasion to install a more egalitarian social order.[5] That was perhaps slightly fantastic; but a fundamental change of regime—not merely of the dynasty, or of religion—now seemed possible of realisation.

The new problem of vagabondage had split local communities, as the creation of a class of permanent unemployed has split our society. Parish elites—yeomen, better off artisans—shared with the gentry in administration of the poor law to maintain social order, in their readiness to limit the number of ale houses which offered a refuge and source of job information for vagabonds as well as consolation for the

3. See 'The Poor and the People' in my *People and Ideas in 17th Century England* (Brighton, 1986), Ch 12.
4. V C H Oxfordshire, II, pp247-248.
5. W Hunt, *The Puritan Moment: The Coming of Revolution in an English County* (Harvard UP, 1983), pp58-62, 147-148.

village poor. On the other hand, some at least of the poor came to regard the state, its government and its church, as enemies; and its parish elites as well.

So—to be very schematic—there seems to have been a fourfold division in society: (1) the government, the court, courtiers and their hangers-on; (2) non-court gentry and merchants, responsible tax-payers; (3) parish elites, yeomen and better off artisans and (4) the poor, including vagabonds. The literature of the time, despite the censorship, reveals tensions between 'the people' and the poor—the Fox in Spenser's *Mother Hubberds Tale*, the communist giant in *The Faerie Queene, Lear*, Jack Cade in *Henry VI, Coriolanus*.[6] After the suppression of the *Martin Marprelate Tracts* in 1589 it was dangerous to criticise the government in print; but in the 1620s Thomas Scott, in pamphlets illegally distributed from the Netherlands, was able to attack the pro-Spanish upper classes who supported the government's foreign policy, and to call on good Protestants to vote against them in parliamentary elections. Derek Hirst in *The Representative of the People? Voters and Voting in England under the Early Stuarts* (Cambridge UP, 1975) has shown an increase in conscious middling and lower class opposition to the court. The poor had little use for the state, its government, its taxes or its church. By the early 1620s foreign ambassadors in London were speculating on the possibilities of popular revolt in England, and one Puritan MP even spoke of 'a hoped for rebellion'— in his private diary, kept in cypher. Between 1628 and 1631 there were sporadic risings in the south west, anticipating the riots and disorders of 1640-1.

By 1640 there was considerable agreement among the classes who were represented in the House of Commons that government should be made more responsible to parliament. But that tells us little about 'democracy'. Here evidence is harder to come by. I will suggest several ways in which life in the society might be giving rise to such concepts.

First, the Protestant doctrine of the priesthood of all believers might suggest that all believers were equal, inferior to no man. Calvinists and other predestinarians assumed that believers were a minority, and seem to have seen no difficulty in supposing that those who ruled were roughly drawn from the elect. But others in the 17th century rejected the idea of a predestined elect; it was from the General Baptists that many of the early democrats were to emerge. Sir Thomas

6. See A Patterson, *Shakespeare and the Popular Voice* (OUP 1989).

Aston in 1641 referred to 'the old seditious argument, that we are all the sons of Adam, born free: some of them say, the Gospel hath made them free'.[7] Opponents of Laud's railing of the altar assumed that priests were not a separate caste, that laymen were their equals. In some churches the well to do got better communion wine; but the equality of all men before God was at least conceivable. Underground congregations seem from early days to have been relatively democratic organisations, rejecting the authoritarian hierarchy of the state church imposed from above. In the sects, ministers and elders were elected, all church members (sometimes including women) took part in church government. Some sects came to reject the idea of an oligarchy of the elect, and to conceive the possibility of universal salvation. If, as others believed, God was in all men and women, how could they be refused a share in government? Quakers in the 1650s believed in human equality, and the possibility of all following the divine light within them.

John Foxe's *Book of Martyrs*, widely publicised under Elizabeth, depicted the whole of human history as a struggle between Christ and Antichrist, with God's Englishmen in the forefront of those who testified for Christ. Among the Marian martyrs the overwhelming majority were men and women from the yeoman and artisan class: gentlemen and ministers were more easily able to emigrate. There were strong democratic implications here. It did not perhaps diminish the influence of Foxe's great book that Laud had (or was said to have) refused to allow it to be reprinted in the 1630s.

Some economic activities, in particular sailing ships, pointed towards greater equality. Drake's famous insistence that gentlemen must haul with the mariners is an example, as is his trial and condemnation of a gentleman on board for subversive behaviour. The egalitarian tendency of navigation is also illustrated by pirate crews, who elected their own captain, and could depose him; and whose booty, if not shared equally, was distributed on a democratically agreed scale.[8]

In 15th century armies English bowmen had laid low French knights at Agincourt and Crécy; and gunpowder was a great equaliser. Armies were of course not egalitarian organisations; but there was equality among the ranks, as was shown in Spanish armies in the 1590s which

---

7. *A Remonstrance Against Presbytery* (1641), Sig I 4v. The reference may be to the question asked in 1381, 'When Adam delved and Eve span,/ Who was then the gentleman?', which was quoted in the reigns of Edward VI and Elizabeth, and often after 1640.

8. M Rediker, *Between the Devil and the Deep Blue Sea: Merchant Seamen, Pirates, and the Anglo-American Maritime World, 1700-1750* (Cambridge UP, 1987), passim.

elected delegates when they mutinied.[9] In the New Model Army a great deal of equality was combined with promotion by merit.

An Elizabethan secretary of state assumed that the 'commonwealth consisteth only of freemen'—ie freeholders and freemen of towns. 'Day labourers, poor husbandmen…copyholders and all artificers', as well as those who own no freehold land, 'have no voice nor authority in our commonwealth, and no account is made of them but only to be ruled'.[10] On the eve of civil war a scared Lancashire baronet agreed that 'the primates, the nobiles, with the minores nobiles, the gentry, consult and dispose the rules of government; the plebeians submit to and obey them'.[11] But the plebeians were beginning to have other ideas, to think and talk among themselves about politics. It was no longer possible, after the breakdown of censorship and religious controls in 1640, to restrict political discussion to the elite. Charles I in 1628, after accepting the Petition of Right, tried hard to refuse permission for it to be printed, lest his concessions to parliament should be read and discussed by ordinary people. In 1641 the proposal to print the *Grand Remonstrance*— 'that appeal to the people'[12]— led to swords being drawn in the House. Charles professed himself 'amazed to consider by what eyes these things are seen, and by what ears they are heard'.[13] In 1642 he foreboded that 'at last the common people…[will] destroy all rights and properties', and it will all end 'in a dark equal chaos of confusion…a Jack Cade or a Wat Tyler'.[14] The lawyer Clement Walker made it an especial complaint against the army and its supporters that 'they have cast all the mysteries and secrets of government, both by kings and parliaments, before the vulgar (like pearls before swine) and have taught both the soldiery and people to look so far into them as to ravel back all governments to the first principles of nature… They have made the people thereby so curious and arrogant, that they will never find humility enough to submit to a civil rule… Ignorance, and admiration arising from ignorance, are the parents of civil devotion and obedience'.[15] The New Model Army accelerated this process, but it had started well before 1640. For a long time we have only the evidence of their enemies for what the common

9. G Parker, 'Mutiny and Discontent in the Spanish Army of Flanders, 1572-1607', *Past and Present*, 58 (1973).
10. L Alston (ed), *De Republica Anglorum, A Discourse of the Commonwealth of England* (Cambridge UP, 1960), pp20-22.
11. Sir T Aston, op cit, Sig I 4v.
12. [Bruno Ryves], *Angliae Ruina* (1647), p176.
13. J Nalson, *An Impartial Collection of the Great Affairs of State* (1687), II, pp746-747.
14. J Rushworth, *Historical Collections* (1659-1701), V, p732.
15. C Walker, *The Compleat History of Independencie* (1661), I, pp140-141, first published 1648-9.

people were thinking and doing. When we are told, for instance, that in 1643 Colchester was 'governed by a tinker, two cobblers, two tailors, two peddlars, etc', we should not take that literally. But Colchester had long had a radical reputation and there may be more substance to the 'principles they intend to rule by'. These included such ideas as that 'the relation of master and servant hath no ground or warrant in the New Testament...for there we read "In Christ Jesus is neither bond nor free".' 'The common people, heretofore kept under blindness and ignorance, have a long time yielded themselves servants, nay slaves, to the nobility and gentry; but God hath now opened their eyes, and discovered unto them their Christian liberty.' If the nobility and gentry 'will not work, they ought not to eat'. The very 'titles of dukes, marquises, earls, viscounts, lords, knights and gentlemen are but ethnical and heathenish distinctions amongst Christians'. Similar 'monstrous opinions' were frequently reported later. 'I hope within this year to see never a gentleman in England', a parliamentarian soldier told a Northamptonshire royalist gentleman; just as Oliver Cromwell hoped that the Earl of Manchester would become plain Mr Montagu again.[16]

So, long before Levellers appeared on the scene, ideas which were anti-aristocratic, anti-gentry, were familiar. They might have an economic basis—class resentment, desire for absolute property rights in their holdings, reluctance to pay tithes and church fees, hatred of urban oligarchies, of conscription—but they often acquired a religious basis. Thomas Edwards's vast *Gangraena*, three large volumes in 1646, collected evidence of views which he regarded as heretical; and though he is violently hostile, he is usually tolerably accurate in what he reports. 'Many of the sectaries of our times', he tells us, 'are not only against government in the church...but against civil government too. Monarchy and aristocracy, both kings and lords, have been cried down.' Although they seem to contend for 'democracy', yet 'their design is to have all pulled down, to have a total change made'. They claim that 'by natural birth all men are equally and alike born to like property, liberty and freedom'. This should extend to a right of recalling their elected representatives if the electors were dissatisfied with them. 'All power, places and offices...in this kingdom ought only to arise from the choice and election of the people'.[17]

It was discussion of ideas like these that Milton had celebrated two

16. [Bruno Ryves], op cit, pp26-28, 94-96. Hopes for the extinction of the gentry had been expressed in Ket's rebellion in 1549.
17. T Edwards, *Gangraena* (1646), III, pp261-262, 15-17, and passim; I, p33.

years earlier in *Areopagitica*. 'The people, or the greater part' are 'more than at other times wholly taken up with the study of highest and most important matters to be reformed...disputing, reasoning, inventing, discovering...things not before discovered or written of'. 'The immediate cause of all this free writing and free speaking', he told parliament, 'is the liberty...which your own valorous and happy counsels have purchased us... We cannot grow ignorant again, brutish, formal and slavish as ye found us', unless parliament reverts to the 'oppressive, arbitrary and tyrannous ways' of the bishops, who 'first put out the people's eyes', and then 'reproach them of their blindness'.[18] In *The Tenure of Kings and Magistrates* (1648) Milton stressed the people's right to choose their own government. Kings and magistrates were 'deputies and commissioners' who might always be called to account by 'their masters, the people'.[19] The ideas were there, then, before the Levellers.

In October 1647 the Agitators and Levellers presented to the Army Council at Putney a draft constitution, the 'Agreement of the People'. In this, in addition to points already mentioned, they called for the dissolution of the present parliament within a year, and insisted that henceforth sovereign parliaments should meet every two years. The only reservations from the power of such parliaments were religious freedom, no conscription, indemnity for actions committed during the civil war, and equality before the law.[20] (Overton in *An Appeale* had called for all laws to be translated into English, 'that so the meanest English commoner that can but read written hand in his own tongue may fully understand his own proceedings in the law'.)[21]

So who were the Levellers? As with Danton and Robespierre, Lenin and Trotsky, the social origins of the leaders were probably higher than those of the rank and file. Lilburne and Walwyn came of gentry families; Overton and Wildman were well educated, possibly at Cambridge. Thomas Prince, Edward Sexby, Maximilian Petty and William Allen had all been London apprentices. Sexby, Allen and William Thompson rose from the ranks of the New Model Army, which opened careers to the talented. Thomas Rainborough was the son of a naval officer.[21]

18. J Milton, *An Apology against a Pamphlet* (1642), *Complete Prose Works* (Yale ed), I, pp9, 2-3; *Areopagitica* (1644), II, pp535, 551-557.
19. Ibid, III, pp199-206.
20. Gardiner, *Constitutional Documents of the Puritan Revolution, 1625-1660* (third edn, Oxford UP, 1906), pp333-335. The last point was spelt out more precisely by Lt Col John Jubbes in *Several Proposals for Peace and Freedom* (December 1648).
21. See G E Aylmer, 'Gentlemen Levellers?' *Past and Present*, number 49, 1970.

The Levellers seem mainly to have originated in religious sects, especially those of London and its suburbs, especially Baptists. Their main support came from London, where their appeal was to 'clouted shoon'. The content of their policies seems likely to attract small property owners—lesser yeomen, artisans. Their ideas started, as those of parliamentarian propagandists generally did, from the rights of free-born Englishmen, harking back to the mythical days of Anglo-Saxon freedom before the imposition of the Norman Yoke in 1066. When in the civil war it was necessary to produce an authority to rival that of the king, the claim that parliament represented the people of England seemed obvious. But who are the people? Filmer and other royalists as well as Levellers, pointed out that the House of Commons represented perhaps one tenth of the people. Royalists regarded that as dismissing parliamentarian claims; Levellers saw it as an argument for extending the franchise to make the Commons represent the people.

But what people? The abandonment of historical rights in favour of natural rights called for more precise definition than the Levellers had yet undertaken. Parliament claimed to represent the people; but the Commons in 1640 had decided that only ratepayers could vote in parliamentary elections. The same was normally true of parish elections.[22] At Putney Ireton agreed with the Levellers that 'the original power of making laws...does lie in the people'. But for him 'the people' meant those 'possessed of the permanent interest in the land'—ie landed property. A nameless Bedfordshire man was determined to give 'away nothing from the people that is the people's right'.[23] So who are the people was the crucial question.

Leveller spokesmen were confused—or in disagreement among themselves—about the extent of the franchise which they wished to see established. They used the word 'people' loosely. Rainborough's famous phrase 'the poorest he that is in England hath a life to live as the greatest he; and therefore...[he] is not at all bound in a strict sense to that government that he hath not had a voice to put himself under' appears to suggest manhood suffrage.[24] So does Lilburne: 'The poorest that lives hath as true a right to give a vote...as the richest and greatest'.[25] But at Putney Petty claimed only that 'all inhabitants that have not lost their birthright should have an equal voice in elections', and suggested that

22. See my *People and Ideas*, p254 and references there cited. H Prideaux, *Directions to Churchwardens* (Norwich, 1701), p51.
23. A S P Woodhouse (ed), *Puritanism and Liberty* (1938), pp66-67, 18.
24. Ibid, pp53-56, 63.
25. J Lilburne, *The Charter of London* (1646), p4.

poor apprentices and living-in servants who were economically dependent on others were excluded.[26] Leveller spokesmen were shaken by
Ireton's point that the same arguments which justified a natural right to
the vote could justify a natural right to property: votes were normally
attached to property, and Levellers did not want to challenge property
rights.

Many Englishmen in the 17th century spoke of 'the people' without in fact intending to include 'the poor', just as they spoke of Christ
dying for all men when they meant that he died for the elect only; just
as the drafters of the American constitution considered it a self evident truth that all men were born free and equal, when in fact they
meant 'all white men'.[27] Yet when in 1649 Charles I was condemned
to death as a traitor to the people of England, the question, 'Who are
the people?' became difficult to avoid. Whether the Long Parliament
had represented the people of England depended on one's definition
of 'people'. But it was impossible to claim that the rump of that parliament which survived Pride's Purge in December 1648 represented
the people in any real sense.

This blind spot was not, however, as reprehensible as it appears to
us if we consider the society in which men and women lived. It was
composed of communities of households. The poor, and still more
vagabonds, 'masterless men', were barely part of the work community. Gregory King at the end of the century saw them as diminishing
the national wealth. Householders were responsible for their families, including their servants and apprentices: it seemed natural not to
think of servants and wage labourers as equally 'people'. 'Every pater-
familias', declared the Whig Earl of Shaftesbury around 1680, 'has...the
votes of all his family, man, woman and child, included in him'.[28] How
anyway could the illiterate vote? If by show of hands in open court,
the very poor could hardly vote freely and independently. Many argued,
with reason, that to extend the vote to all men would simply invite
corrupt landlord pressure, and bribery in boroughs.

The army had brought masterless men together in a community. It
offered the opportunity for discussion, for political education. So, to its
members at least, it seemed reasonable to demand the vote for soldiers

26. A S P Woodhouse, op cit, p53. As far as the written record goes, the Putney Debates
    were a unique occasion. One wonders how many other such discussions of the
    fundamentals of politics went unrecorded.
27. See 'The Poor and the People' in my *People and Ideas in 17th century England* (Brighton,
    1986), Ch 12.
28. Shaftesbury, 'Some Observations', in *Somer's Tracts* (1809-15), VIII, p401. Algernon
    Sidney and Locke agreed (see my *People and Ideas*, p253).

and ex-soldiers, who had contributed to the commonwealth. Many indeed argued that the army was more representative of the people of England than the House of Commons.[29]

A similar blind spot concerns women. No Leveller, and no one else, so far as I know, seriously suggested giving the vote to women. In London, and no doubt elsewhere, women petitioned, lobbied, canvassed and agitated tirelessly on behalf of the vote for their menfolk: they never seem to have thought of demanding it for themselves. They must have accepted that the head of the household 'represents' those under his jurisdiction—women and children as well as men.

Although Winstanley claimed Jesus Christ is the 'head Leveller', he preferred to use the word 'Reason' rather than 'God'. He hoped that reason would rise in sons and daughters, convincing them all of the desirability of cooperation, of equality. This rising of reason was the only Second Coming of Christ that he ever expected to see. But bitter experience taught him that a long period of education and political re-education would be needed to free people from dependence on the gentry and clergy, whose leadership they had for centuries accepted. After the crushing of his communist colony he outlined in *The Law of Freedom* (1652) what he thought the necessary institutions for this transitional period. The elected parliament and government would always be responsible to the electorate, backed by the ultimate authority of the armed people. There was to be no standing army.

Up to a dozen colonies were established during the year of the Diggers' existence. But they remained a small minority, easily suppressed in 1650. Winstanley's social analysis and political solutions, however, remain remarkable, as does the rapid development of his thinking from 1648 to 1652, after which he published no more. Winstanley insisted that the civil war had been fought not against Charles I personally, but against 'kingly power'. 'All laws...not giving a universal freedom to all but respecting persons ought to be cut off with the King's head'. There must be not just a change of rulers but a transformation in the nature of state power. If 'kingly authority be set up in your laws again, King Charles hath conquered you and your posterity...though you seemingly have cut off his head'. To an imaginary objector saying, 'This will destroy all government and all our ministry', Winstanley replied coolly, 'It is very true'. Among the few offences for which he would (temporarily at least) retain the death penalty are murder, buying and selling, taking money as a lawyer or as a preacher;

29. See my *People and Ideas*, p263, and references there cited.

and rape.[30] Winstanley attached much importance to local trial by jury, wanted jurors to be 'chosen by freemen'—ie to the exclusion of copyholders, cottagers and wage labourers.

The Levellers' main strength was in London, the army and among the middling sort in towns as well as in the separatist congregations, especially General Baptists. When in 1649 they tried to turn to the countryside in a wider propaganda campaign, it was too late to rally copyholders to their cause. They lost out both ways perhaps. The middling sort of property owners did not want rural revolt which might turn against all property. The Diggers were a constant reminder of that possibility.

The Levellers' high moment came in London and the army in 1647-9. They played successfully on the trade union self consciousness, pride and self respect of the victorious troops; they demanded the vote for soldiers and ex-soldiers. But the rank and file of the army were never fully politicised. When the Second Civil War threatened they rallied round the generals; and after the takeover of Pride Purge their wages were guaranteed.

Sixteen forty nine was the year of the great divide. The rank and file were offered service in Ireland or disbandment. Either way Army unity was shattered, and the Levellers were unable to prevent it. When Army radicals and Levellers allowed themselves to be provoked into mutinies, they isolated themselves. Their former allies among the separatist congregations and the middling sort deserted them; and it was too late to rally copyholders and the poor, even if the Levellers had been united in wanting to do so.[31] In the background is the traumatic shock of the trial and execution of Charles I, of which the Levellers disapproved, but which could appear to be the consequence of their policies.

In fact by the end of the century England—a country of no consideration, the Venetian Ambassador had said in 1641—was on the way to becoming the world's greatest imperial power.

Attaining these objectives necessitated unleashing lower class support which could turn anti-capitalist, or anti big capitalist, whether we see this as forward or backward looking. There was a threat from a real third force, though it found inadequate organisational forms. Hence the reunion of the propertied classes in 1660 and the front bench

---

30. G Sabine, p288; Winstanley, op cit, pp163, 243, 358, 366, 383, 388.
31. The mutineers at Burford in May 1649, Walker said, were 'mostly countrymen' (op cit, II, p178). It is a probable guess.

agreement of 1688—the 'revolution' which at one stroke removed any possibility of either foreign supported absolutism or any revival of radical democracy. The Levellers had to be rediscovered by historians. But their censored ideas survived to pass into 18th century radicalism, into Chartism, and into modern democratic thinking.

Here we may suspect that the theories of Thomas Hobbes are lurking. Hobbes attributed much to the psychology of man, which reflected back into the state of nature. The 'power in man that causes divisions and wars', Winstanley wrote, 'is called by some men the state of nature which every man brings into the world with him'. Winstanley rejected the Calvinist and Hobbist dogma of human sinfulness: the establishment of private property had been the Fall of Adam, not the eating of an apple. Children are born innocent but are corrupted by the competitive world in which they grow up.[32] Human nature was not something eternally fixed: it could be changed by changing society.[33] Winstanley is arguably the most intellectually consistent of all the great political theorists who emerged from the English Revolution. Freedom, democracy and true equality can be guaranteed only when 'community...called Christ or universal love' rises unimpeded in sons and daughters, and casts out 'property...called the devil or covetousness...'[34]

This leads on to a last point. Winstanley speaks continually of 'sons and daughters'. He does not give women the vote, since his community is based traditionally on the household, in which the father of the family represents his wife and children, his servants and apprentices. Some of Winstanley's ringing phrases—'the poorest man hath as true a title and just right to the land as the richest man'—seem as restricted to one sex as were the Levellers' political declarations of rights. Yet with Winstanley we cannot be quite sure. He more than once referred to 'every single man (male and female)'. 'Adam (or indeed any man or woman)'. So it is possible that he used 'man' to include women on other occasions. A Ranter tract of 1652 also speaks of 'men (male and female)'.

Lilburne in 1646 had said that 'all and every particular man and woman' are 'by nature all equal and alike in power, dignity, authority and majesty, none of them having by nature any authority, dominion or magisterial power over or above one another', except by 'mutual agreement and consent'. But I think we must assume that in practice they (and

32. L U F 268-9: p309.
33. See my 'Winstanley and Freedom' where I also suggest contrasts between the ideas of Winstanley and Filmer, Ascham, Harrington, and Locke.
34. L U F 268.

perhaps the Diggers too) took for granted that some had 'agreed and con-sented' to the exercise of their political rights by their menfolk.

Levellers wanted to establish a more democratic and more repre-sentative government. So did the Diggers, though their programme would have subverted the existing state and social order. Ranters and Fifth Monarchists seem to have rejected any government: king, par-liament and army were equally unacceptable. Fifth Monarchists wanted the rule of Christ through his saints, which presumably could only have been realised through military dictatorship. Democracy was no part of their programme.

Ranters were more anarchist in their rejection of government, in so far as we can generalise about their ideas at all. Lawrence Clarkson in his pre-Ranter days expressed a class theory of politics. 'Who are the oppressors but the nobility and gentry? And who are the oppressed, is it not the yeoman, the farmer, the tradesman and the labourer?'[35] He called, traditionally, for restoration of the long lost liberties of the freeborn people of England; but he never achieved a systematic theory of politics: by 1659 he had been converted to a pre-Quaker pacifism by John Reeve, and he surrendered politics to the ungodly. The world 'is your inheritance by birthright, and not the saints' at all'.[36]

Abiezer was a more positively political character. In 1649 he recog-nised that 'never was there such a time since the world stood, as now is'. He proclaimed that God was 'that mighty Leveller', who would 'overturn, overturn, overturn'.[37] Coppe rejected 'sword levelling': 'I only pronounce the righteous judgments of the Lord.' But he de-nounced nobles, gentlemen and property, proclaiming his belief in 'parity, equality, community' whilst expressing solidarity with 'the last Levellers that were shot to death', presumably at Burford. 'Have all things common', he adjured the rich, 'or else the plague of God will rot and consume all that you have'.[38]

Joseph Salmon, who believed that he was living in the last days, re-garded the army as 'the rod of God' to 'strike through king, gentry and nobility'; and parliament was no better than the king. But the army too was self interested.[39] Richard Coppin expressed great contempt for 'government and...dignities'. Antichrist's kingdom is 'a kingdom

35. Clarkson, A General Charge of Impeachment of High Treason in the name of Justice Equity against the Communality of England (1647), pp10-18.
36. Clarkson, The Lost Sheep Found (1660), p59.
37. A Fiery Flying Roll (1649), pp86-87, 92; George Foster also called God the 'mighty Leveller' (The Pouring forth of the Seventh and Last Viall (1650), Sig A3, p121.
38. Smith, pp88-94, 101, 112; cf pp122, 145.
39. A Rout (1649), in Smith, op cit, pp190-194.

of gain, hire and self interest'. Coppin too saw parliamentary government as no better than the king's. Cromwell's dissolution of the rump of parliament in 1653 recalled Saul's command to smite Amalek.[40] George Foster, near-Ranter, thought the rump was worse than the king had been; it was the beast that must be burned or destroyed.[41]

Captain Francis Freeman's *Light Vanquishing Darkness* (1650) echoed Winstanley's view that kingly power had survived the execution of Charles I. Only when Norman laws 'be taken away, both root and branch' will there be justice for the common people. Captain Robert Norwood too thought parliament no better than the monarch; it continued to express the interests of the Norman landed class. He advocated a Leveller programme of election of local government officers, who should be paid.[42]

The Ranters then shared many radical ideas with Levellers, Diggers, Fifth Monarchists and Quakers. But they had no political programme, and no organisation which could have given it effect if they had had a programme. Many of them were very eloquent in enunciation, Coppe especially; but it is all bluster. Most Ranters recanted under persecution, no doubt with tongue in cheek, and then lapsed into silence. Politically they were ineffective. William Sheppard the law reformer thought that Ranters—with Quakers—should be excluded from jury service because of their political unreliability.

Leveller ideas survived after their suppression in 1649. Fifth Monarchists and Quakers, like Levellers, disliked primogeniture, which had the effect of consolidating estates and leaving younger sons impoverished. Both Fifth Monarchists and Quakers wanted copyhold abolished. The Baptist Clement Writer, who wrote for 'the middle sort', declared in 1658 that 'if any divine right remain now in England, it is in the people of England'.[43] In 1647 the millenarian Baptist Thomas Collier, preaching to the New Model Army at Putney, on the text 'Behold I create a new heavens and a new earth', said that the rule of the saints would mean the end of tithes, of free quarter and of 'tyrannical and oppressing laws and courts of justice'; the laws would be in English.[44] In the mid-1640s the Fifth Monarchist Christopher Feake declared that there was 'an enmity against Christ' in aristocracy. *A Standard Set Up*, the programme

40. Coppin, *Divine Teachings* (1649), p21; *Truths Testimony* (1655), p15; *Saul Smitten for not Smiting Amalek* (1653), pp5-13.
41. Foster, *The Sounding of the Last Trumpet* (1650), pp37-39.
42. *An Additional Discourse* (1653), pp12-14, 47-51.
43. Rogers, op cit, pp121, 429, 486-487.
44. A S P Woodhouse, *Puritanism and Liberty*, pp390-396.

of the Fifth Monarchy rebels of 1657, contained many Leveller demands—decentralised law courts, abolition of tithes, copyhold and conscription. A *Door of Hope*, the manifesto of Venner's rising in 1661, insisted that thieves should not be executed, but should be put to work till they had compensated their victims; the law of debt should be reformed; town governments should be democratised.

Many contemporaries accused the Quakers of being 'downright Levellers'. Most Quakers had been staunch supporters of the good Old Cause; some approved of the execution of Charles I, and of the conquest of Ireland; Quakers wanted tithes and copyhold to be abolished. Some proposed annual parliaments, election of all state officers, unchangeable fundamental laws, economic and legal reform to benefit the poor. George Fox looked forward to the time when 'all the law books in the nation will be thrown away which are made in the will of men'. Everyone should know the law and plead his own cause. 'Away with lawyers.' 'Those who desired an earthly king' were 'traitors against Christ'. The House of Lords was no better. Views like these account for the panic fear of Quakers in 1659-60 which contributed significantly to the restoration of Charles II and the end of democracy. It looked like a revival of political radicalism. Quakers rejoined the army and offered their services to the republican government.

The fact that so many of the policies of the Levellers were shared with other groups (Ranters, Fifth Monarchists, Quakers and other sectaries) suggests that they represented the demands of a wide spectrum of society below the ranks of the political nation. This consensus in turn may throw light on the early maturity of Leveller ideas. The Diggers shared many of the negative views of this consensus; that the Levellers rejected them when they called property in question helps us to locate this consensus among yeomen and artisan householders.

Chapter 28

The duel in
European history

This review of The Duel in European History: Honour and the Reign
of Aristocracy *by V G Kiernan was first published in the* New York
Review, *14 June 1990.*

Victor Kiernan is one of the most versatile of British historians. He has
written learned monographs on *British Diplomacy in China, 1880-85,* on
Metcalfe's Mission to Lahore, 1808-9, on *The Revolution of 1854 in Spanish History,* on American imperialism in the 19th and 20th centuries, on
imperialism generally, and on state and society in Europe in the 16th and
17th centuries. He has also written about Wordsworth, 19th century
England, central Asia, Africa, India and Pakistan, and about relations between Portugal and Britain. He has translated volumes of Urdu poetry.

The story goes that he was once asked by a journal for an article on
British imperialism in China. He replied that he had rather lost interest
in that subject, but he could let them have a piece on the Jesuits in
Paraguay. The article they finally got was on English Evangelicism
and the French Revolution. What we are all waiting for is his big
book on Shakespeare.

The Duel in European History ranges through recorded history, from
Gilgamesh, Homer, and Beowulf to the present century. 'What has
been remembered of the duel', Kiernan begins, 'has been mostly of an
anecdotal kind'; and at first sight his seems an anecdotal book. It is
stuffed with excellent anecdotes, but there is a steady and consistent
theme running through it, implicit rather than explicit. In trying to draw
this theme from the material I have quoted freely, since I cannot match
Kiernan's incisive prose. The duel for Kiernan is a conflict between
two men, usually accompanied by an 'elaborate etiquette...upheld by
"seconds".' It was, he writes:

amidst the chronic warfare of the 16th and 17th centuries that the modern duel took shape. During that time of transition from medieval to modern, state power and the reign of law were being established by absolutist monarchy; but aristocracy, its half-brother, survived in altered guise, a permanent anachronism, and often canker, in the life of Europe. Private warfare between baronial families or factions was suppressed with difficulty; in France in the second half of the 16th century, with religious combustibles added, it flared up into civil war. Madrid in the next century was still disturbed by brawling among noblemen and their retinues... Compared with these manifestations of the unruly aristocratic temper, the duel can be viewed as an advance towards a more limited trespass on law and order. It can be viewed too as a more decent reprisal than assassination, the poisoning of opponents for instance so much a matter of use and wont in the Italy of the Borgias.

By comparison with the blood feud and gang warfare, or with judicial trial by combat, 'a well-conducted duel might be deemed part of a civilising process'. But the emphasis here is on 'well conducted': a certain level of political organisation and enforcement of order is an essential preliminary.

So for Kiernan the duel assumed the ascendancy of aristocratic classes, military by vocation or 'at least never forgetful of a sword-bearing ancestry'. Liability to the ordeal of the duel was 'a burden imposed on itself by the elite and the gage of its right to be considered a higher order'. Duelling and its code of honour 'came to form a powerful link between all noble ranks, and "strengthen their sense of belonging to a single privileged class".' For the man of noble birth it was all the more natural to put himself above the law because 'he, as seigneur, had been in command of justice in his own domain. On a reduced scale he was so still in France down to 1789, in England as a JP [Justice of the Peace] far longer.'

> Members of an elite class claim respectful treatment from one another; as their class matures and learns to cultivate the art of living, its manners—within its own ranks—become more polished... The duel itself grew into a ritual, as formal as a church service. [It could] uplift and ennoble the most banal dispute, the most blockish combatant, somewhat as the royal uniform transformed its commonplace wearer... Gentlemen must be ready to fight, but with decorum and dignity, not like the noisy plebeians they had too often resembled. Everything in the ceremonies of the duel was of a kind to stamp it as the affair of an elite.

Swift paid tribute to the duel as the gentleman's means of upholding his right to be treated civilly.

Hence the importance of seconds in preparing for a duel. They were not merely assistants to the main combatants: they were also 'delegates of the class to which all concerned belonged and whose standards of conduct all of them were taking the field to vindicate'. They were at once partisans and neutral umpires; it was an accepted part of their duty 'to examine the facts of the case, and cooperate in seeking a peaceful solution if this could comport with the self respect of both disputants'.

Kiernan insists on the social exclusivity of the duel. In matters concerning honour,

> the gentleman stood outside any social contract binding on the common man; he belonged to a superior social order which made its own rules. Absolute monarchs compelled their nobles in early modern Europe to submit to many restraints, but noblemen obstinately insisted on keeping one area of freedom, symbolically vital to them if practically meaningless...

Kings and governments might feel safer if they left their nobles 'free to work off discontents by fighting one another'. The ultimate hallmark of gentility was 'the right of gentlemen to kill each other'.

So the duel had to be regulated by accepted codes of conduct, of 'honour', whose acceptance was the test of a gentleman. Hence government reactions to the duel were ambiguous. From time to time there would be a feeble attempt to suppress duelling—by James I in England, by Louis XIV more successfully in France; but normally the monarchy's bark was worse than its bite. All but the very lowly or the very unlucky could expect to be pardoned for infringing laws against duelling.

As the wealth of intermediate sections of society increased, laws regulating extravagance on religious or moral grounds became ineffective. Class distinctions in apparel were impossible to enforce, and 'formal manners have been more and more important as a supplement to fine dress' As newly rich parvenus aspired to gentility, the obligation to fight duels in order to defend their 'honour' became an acid test. 'One may wonder', Kiernan comments ironically, 'how many impoverished scions of old families relieved their feelings by picking a quarrel with bourgeois gentilhommes.'

So as Kiernan sees it, the duel 'cannot be made to look rational in terms of the individual, but only as an institution from which a class, a social order, benefited'. In the army two officers who quarrelled had to fight, whether they wanted to or not, because otherwise the regiment was dishonoured. The 'penalty for rejecting a challenge was far more severe than any condemnation by the elite of its members' lapses from the morality of parsons.' Justice was unattainable in this imperfect and unequal world; all that a gentleman could hope to win, at a high price, was the respect of his equals. 'Any failure of nerve on the part of a member of the elite', Kiernan concludes:

> reflected on the whole body, and if often repeated would undermine it. There can be detected here the instinct of a garrison, such as any dominant class in a sense is, encamped in the midst of a population always passively or actively hostile, a lurking premonition of a day of wrath.

In time the elaborate punctilios of the duel became increasingly out of place in modern society. Kiernan puts it harshly:

> the willingness of so many men, young men in particular, to risk death, maiming, or exile, on the spur of the moment, suggests an infantile mentality, minds incapable of serious thought, and reacting to any stimulus like automata. Such minds belonged to a class bereft of any social function, or any healthier one than war, that could not be better performed by others, and drying up mentally or morally well in advance or its material decline.

The irrationality of the duel came to be rejected by 'middle class elements, urban and rural, feeling their growing strength and resentful of the ascendancy of those above them: their creed, in the years before they were strong enough to compel blue blood to accept them as a partner, was Puritanism.'

Duelling and standing armies arose together, Kiernan thinks, with the army regiment as a main forcing house for the duel. We sometimes forget how socially important armies were—not only in continental absolute monarchies but also in Great Britain.

Armies were of crucial importance for purposes of order—or repression—at home and of chronic warfare abroad; rulers could not afford to fall out with the men who led them. Since their wars were as foolish or immoral as any duels could be, in fact very much like duels on an international scale, they were in a poor position to preach.

Most heads of state also commanded the army, nominally or in fact.

War and the duel thus fulfilled analogous functions.

Chinese Boxers, fanatic Mahdists, Zulus, brought to bay by more advanced military forces, made up for what they lacked by priding themselves on spirit and endurance, and threw themselves against Europe's machine guns. In no very different way the military section of Europe's upper classes, falling behind in education and intelligence, pinned their faith to 'character', most easily defined as ability to face shot and shell, or the duelling sabre or pistol, undaunted. It was a philosophy not without practical returns, over a long period. Small European forces conquered a great part of the world; what mattered much more was that almost all attempts at revolution inside Europe were crushed.

The duel 'helped to build up the morale which made these achievements possible.'

The decline of the duel is thus for Kiernan inextricably linked with the rise of a capitalist economy. Holland, 'the most middle class country of Europe' after its successful war of independence against Spain, was the one least inclined to duelling. In the Dutch East Indies there was a death penalty for duelling—and it was enforced. France was the country of the duel par excellence, despite literary opinion opposed to it (Rabelais, Montaigne, Corneille, Pascal) and occasional attempts to curb it. In Spain and Italy duels were less punctilious: Spaniards preferred assassination, a French lady was told in the late 17th century. But Cervantes in *Don Quixote* was one of the earliest to mock duelling. The Catholic church, to its credit, always opposed duelling, though bishops and parish priests were as responsive as Protestant clergy to the pressure of aristocratic patrons, and Pascal made much of Jesuit casuistry's softness on the subject. In Sweden the Protestant hero Gustavus Adolphus made duelling a capital crime. He is said to have notified two senior officers preparing to fight that the survivor would be executed. That worked. Duelling in Sweden 'dropped out curiously quickly' after the brief 17th century age of Swedish military glory had passed.

In England, which followed the Netherlands on the capitalist road, the number of recorded duels declines after around 1620, and then more swiftly after the civil war of the 1640s. Puritans opposed duelling. After the restoration of the monarchy in 1660 the practice revived: a demoralised aristocracy, Kiernan says, 'was bent on reasserting itself'. Charles II issued a proclamation against duelling, but went on pardoning offenders. It was 'a cheap way of rewarding loyalits and humouring the Cavalier faction at large.' That good bourgeois Pepys disapproved. The short-sighted scientist William Petty, when challenged to a duel, exercised his right to choose weapons by opting for axes in a dark cellar. That worked too. When in the 18th century the British Empire demanded larger and larger armies and navies, duelling revived. Kiernan attributes this to middle class youths, now able to obtain commissions, aspiring to gentility.

In post-Restoration Ireland duelling became 'an everyday occurrence [among] the landowning class created by what in all its stages was a very brutal colonial conquest'. Even in the 18th century if a magistrate tried to enforce the law against duelling, he was liable to be challenged himself. Lawyers were known to quit the courtroom 'to take a shot at one another'.

In the slave plantations of the West Indies 'Europe's worst instincts found a natural habitat [since] ideas of the superiority of class or of race have much in common... In societies based on violence and inhumanity men might well be readier to hazard their lives in the heat of the moment. It was an atmosphere not unlike Ireland's, only far worse.' Early British India also reminds Kiernan of Anglo-Ireland 'in many bad ways'. In India a duel 'enabled middle class Britons to see themselves as part of a nobility of race, a *Sahib-log* or — a later term with the same meaning—*Herrenvolk*.' (In the 20th century, Kiernan observes, fascism 'resurrected duelling, along with so much other debris from the past.' It was legalised in Hitler's Germany, and 'smiled on' in Mussolini's Italy.)

In England, as in France, men of letters were divided, but more often in opposition to duelling. Shakespeare, Kiernan suggests, thought courage was better shown on behalf of one's country than of oneself, and foreshadowed the enlargement of 'honour' from personal to public or patriotic. (Here I cannot help wondering why in one of Shakespeare's last plays, *Cymbeline*, the most urgently matriotic speeches are given to the two nastiest characters—the Queen and Cloten.) The fact that Swift was a dean did not affect his approval of duelling. Richardson was critical; Defoe, Smollett, and Sheridan thought duelling ridiculous; Fielding and Goldsmith were more ambiguous. Johnson was predictably pertinacious in favour, though worried sometimes about squaring it with Christianity. Adam Smith, less predictably, regretted the inevitable decline of warlike spirit in civilised societies: 'A coward', he wrote, 'a man incapable either of defending or of revenging himself, evidently wants one of the most essential parts of the character of a man.'

Jeremy Bentham brings us into the modern world. He saw reputation as 'a kind of fictitious object of property', as Hobbes had seen it as 'an argument and sign of power'. Characteristic of the transition is Walter Scott, to whose influential ambiguity on the subject Kiernan devotes a chapter. Byron saw the ludicrous side of duelling, though he was capable of threatening a challenge in a moment of anger. The duel was fair game for Dickens, who revelled in 'ridicule of a foppish, effete aristocracy'. Gilbert and Sullivan, and Lewis Carroll, finally laughed the duel off the stage it had held for so long.

'Abandonment of the duel', Kiernan concludes, was 'a not insignificant symptom of the approaching demise of the long-drawn aristocratic ascendancy in England...the sharp decline of land rents, from the 1870s, completed its supersession by a very mixed tutti-frutti plutocracy':

> Fine points of 'honour' wilted in the climate of cotton-mill and Stock Exchange, and pecuniary satisfaction was preferred to that of the pistol: damages were obtainable from the courts for libel, or wife-enticement, or breach of promise.

By the end of the century 'it may well be that a good many duels really were fought for no better motive than to get into the news, to cut a dash.' The death rate was not alarming. A mid-19th century authority calculated from a sample of 200 British duels that there was one death in every 14 cases, and one man wounded in every six.

It was perhaps easier for Englishmen to give up the duel, Kiernan reflects, because of their country's 'unique accumulation of other aristocratic institutions or symbols or ceremonies, presided over by the monarchy and ensuring the desired continuity.' But the duel died hard even in England. In 1804 occurred the only recorded encounter between two dukes: fortunately bloodless. Six prime ministers fought in the late 18th and early 19th centuries, including Pitt and Wellington (both while prime minister), Fox, and Canning; Peel was twice a challenger.

The duel was far less deeply rooted in southern than in northern Europe; and this was reflected in its greater prevalence in Anglo-Saxon America than in the Latin countries. Racial mixing, as in Mexico or Brazil, made the practice 'less congenial'. In the US, Kiernan suggests, 'desire to impress the black man' led to 'a hypertrophied version of the desire in Europe to impress the lower orders.' In Russian 19th century literature duelling looms large, from Pushkin and Lermontov onwards. Kiernan has some fascinating remarks about them, and about Dostoevsky, Herzen, Tolstoy, Turgenev and Chekhov.

Duelling, Kiernan points out, was predominantly (though not absolutely exclusively) a male institution. It emphasised 'the gulf between the sexes, as well as the classes'. It made man appear as 'woman's natural guardian, protector, possessor'. And he wonders, apropos Goldsmith's *Vicar of Wakefield*, 'how many "shotgun weddings" took place under threat of a challenge from truculent brothers or fathers.'

Gentlemen normally wore swords to show that they were gentlemen. Pistols were a product of advancing European technology. They came to replace the sword—'earliest in unmartial England'—because fencing had become 'so skilled an art that a tiro had little chance'. Smollett noted that the pistol was an equaliser. There were other consequences. 'Unlike modern Americans', Kiernan suggests, 'gentlemen were not likely to have pistols in their pockets all the time.' Pistols rendered impromptu duels less likely: some preparatory formalities were required that allowed time for reflection.

The unexpected aperçus which the author throws off from time to time are part of the charm of his book. Pursuing the analogy between war and the duel he suggests that 'the calamitous faith in the offensive, accepted by the army planners before 1914, may be...seen as cognate expressions of the aristocratic spirit,' which steeled men to fight duels. Or again: 'The "phoney war" on the western front in 1939-1940...was not without some resemblance to a duel preceded by an agreement to fire in the air.'

More speculatively, Kiernan remarks that 'the formative period of the duel, and of the classes which practised it, also inaugurated the modern theatre... This was the great age of modern tragic drama,' especially in England and in France. This can hardly be mere coincidence. In tragedy the purgation by ritual violence of morbid social emotions, more than usually tempestuous in that age of change and dislocation, was apotheosised:

> Aristocracy...like monarchy...grew more and more into an actor, playing an elaborate part. Its mannered style of living, not without elements of permanent human value, could dazzle the aspiring bourgeois, as could its bravery in war...

Certainly a man schooled to behave politely to someone about to try and shoot him might well be capable of civility in any circumstances.

Reverting to the analogy with war, Kiernan notes that 'a good part of the vocabulary of war and diplomacy was coming to be French; a remoter parallel may be detected in the French passion for imposing fixed rules on the drama, with which also the duel had so much in common.'

This is an ambitious and daring book, with whose main thesis not everyone will necessarily agree, though I find it convincing myself. It is packed with intriguing and often amusing detail, and it is well argued. Kiernan's main achievement is to relate the duel consistently to the societies in which it flourished and declined. The book is full of ideas, and it is spiced with sardonic wit: 'If the chief ordinary occupation of members of the duelling class was killing animals, it might be felt as no great departure if they occasionally tried to kill each other, by way of a change.' And, 'at the end of a day competing in the chase, men spent the night trying to drink one another under the table. A gentleman could no more flinch from the bottle than from the bullet.' The book contains a formidable number of obscure pieces of useful information. How many of us knew that in 1985 a successful appeal was made in a Scottish law court for the right to have a case decided by battle, a right never formally abolished in that country?

Kiernan is no sentimental devotee of the duel—far from it. Yet his deep sense of social history enables him to make a case of sorts for it in its time. It was:

> a remarkable manifestation of the refusal to compromise... This un-yielding temper could feed the self-admiration of a class, but it could soar higher. It had its roots in a physical courage which was for Shakespeare, if not the supreme virtue, the ark of the covenant of all virtues, and which a sympathetic philosopher might think of as the crude adoles-cence of moral courage. With the coming of the bourgeois era of util-itarianism, cash nexus, and scramble for money, there was value in anything that could remind men of higher motives, stemming from concern for the social whole... The concept of honour lay open to all Falstaff's gibes, but it derived from a very old emotion of obligation to community or country, like that of Shakespeare's republican Romans.

That is a thought for Mrs Thatcher's England, and possibly for other countries. Kiernan is not only a very good historical techni-cian, as well as poet and literary critic: he is also a moralist who tries to understand men and women of the past in their own terms, with-out allowing moral disapprobation to colour his judgement, in the hope that history may teach us something.

Chapter 29

Toleration in 17th century England: theory and practice

This was a lecture given at York University on 9 November 1990, and not previously published.

Historians of toleration usually talk about theories of toleration, and depict a gradual victory of reason and common sense over irrational prejudice. This movement, slowly broadening down, is sometimes interrupted by thinkers who 'fail to see the logic of their own arguments', as when the very tolerant Milton and Locke refuse to extend religious toleration to Roman Catholics. I shall return to them later, only saying here that whether we agree with them or not in refusing toleration to Roman Catholics, it was *not* because they failed to understand their own arguments. It is 20th century commentators who fail to understand what Milton and Locke were talking about.

I want to suggest that the evolution of toleration was not a smooth intellectual process, proceeding from argument to argument till all were convinced. If we look at the struggle for toleration on the ground, so to speak, taking account of the attitudes of heretics demanding freedom of worship and of those who resisted those demands, the picture looks rather different. Historically, toleration is a practice rather than a theory.

But I don't want to suggest that what the books say about progress is not absolutely right. We cannot too often remind ourselves that English men and women were being burnt alive for their religious beliefs as late as 1612, and that Archbishop Neile of York, who participated in sentencing the last victims, said in 1639 that he thought it would be a good thing to revive the practice. (Burning heretics had done the church a great deal of good, he said nostalgically—as he no doubt thought of the flogging, ear-slitting and branding which Archbishop Laud favoured.) But Neile was too late: the revolution of the 1640s prevented any revival of burning for heresy (though women continued to be burnt for husband murder well into the 18th century: men were only hanged for killing their wives). But when bishops came back with the king in 1660, Thomas Hobbes was afraid they would try to burn him. I am sure Hobbes was right in thinking that some bishops would have liked to burn him. But it really was too late, though men continued to be hanged for blasphemy and rejecting the Trinity as late as the 1690s. 17th century England has its similarities with the Iran of Ayatollah Khomeini.

From time immemorial there had been a national church in England, which until the Reformation had been part of a greater international church. But since the Reformation the monarchy had been more closely identified with the church. The king was head of the Church of England. All English men and women were members of this church. After 1660 many dissenters—though not Quakers—resisted expulsion from this church. They believed they were still loyal to the Church of England as established in the 16th century. Occasional conformity was not merely a discreditable trick by which some dissenters qualified themselves to hold office in local government; it was also evidence of a strongly held wish to remain part of the national church. Both Milton and Bunyan quoted the 39 Articles to show their loyalty to this idea of the Church of England (TSFP 147). William Walwyn was one of the very few Leveller leaders who did not join a separatist congregation in the 1640s: he made it his duty to swing first his parish, then his ward, to support the cause of parliament. Gerrard Winstanley the Digger must have returned to the Anglican church in the 1660s because he held local government offices: perhaps that is why he conformed. Replacement of the local unit of the parish by the voluntary churches of dissent is one of the signs of the growing mobility of the society.

I shall talk about 17th century people whom I know best—Bunyan, the early Quakers—though I am sure my points could be made on the basis of any number of other examples.

After the tumultuous decades of the 40s and 50s dissent was too strong to be driven underground or into exile. Bunyan first had to face intolerance in 1660, when he was 32 years old. He had been only

12 years old when in 1640 the traditional Church of England collapsed, and with it the censorship which the Church had controlled. For the next 20 years men and women were no longer legally obliged to attend their parish church every Sunday and listen to the ministrations of a clergyman in whose selection they had had no say, and whose theology and personality they might detest. During these decades frustrated sectaries heckled parsons, seized pulpits from their legal occupants and preached themselves. No one could stop laymen— and indeed women—from preaching. All over the country congregations sprang up which ran their own affairs democratically just as they wished. Many elected a so called 'mechanic preacher', an artisan (unordained, of course) who worked with his hands six days a week and took the chair at a discussion group on the seventh day. The tinker Bunyan was a mechanic preacher. Men and women were free to choose between several places of worship, even to choose none at all. It was a quite unique experience for them. But as radicals came to believe that Parliament and its propertied supporters would never agree to genuine religious freedom, many began to talk of replacing Parliament by the rule of the saints.

The press was free after 1640, and open to people who could not possibly have got into print earlier. Bunyan in the late 50s enjoyed— the right word, I think—a fierce and scurrilous theological controversy with early Quakers. But in 1660 all that changed. Bishops came back with Charles II. Once more all were deemed to be members of the Church of England, liable to be fined if they did not attend its services every Sunday. They had to pay tithes and to accept the discipline of church courts. Religious meetings other than those of the national church were again illegal. Laymen were of course forbidden to preach— not to mention women. JPs from the gentry who had been panic stricken by the upheavals of the 40s and 50s could now take savage revenge against those whom they regarded as their enemies.

At the Restoration Bunyan was arrested, charged with illegal preaching to illegal conventicles. He was told he must either give an undertaking never to preach again, or go to jail indefinitely. Bunyan believed he had been called by God to preach, and that he could not give it up. His judges replied that his vocation was that of a tinker, not a preacher. He was a layman, unordained, and uneducated in the sense that he had not been to a university or even (so far as we know) to a grammar school. A tinker indeed was socially the lowest of the low. So they sent Bunyan to prison, where he remained for 12 years. In most cases this would have been a death sentence in view of the horribly insanitary condition of English prisons; but Bunyan, like George Fox, was exceptionally tough, morally and physically. He survived.

An example of religious persecution, the books say; and so it was. But let us look at it on the ground. Bunyan's spell in prison was longer than that meted out to anyone at the Restoration who was not a regicide or an active revolutionary leader. Bunyan was no political leader; politics were by no means his main concern. Why was he singled out for such severe treatment by the Bedfordshire justices?

One sermon by Bunyan which was printed in 1658 may give us a clue. It was on the parable of Dives and Lazarus, the rich man who goes to hell whilst the 'poor scabbed hedge-creep' Lazarus, whom Dives used to spurn as he lay at his gate begging for alms, went to heaven. Dives, you will remember, was permitted to see Lazarus in heaven; he begged that Lazarus might be allowed to dip his finger in cold water and moisten Dives's lips, because he was getting rather hot down there. But it was too late. Bunyan, a regular hell fire preacher, used this parable to put the fear of hell into rich men, Diveses. Throughout his writings Bunyan was always passionately on the side of the poor, fiercely hostile to the rich. In *The Pilgrim's Progress* every one of the bad characters is invariably—obsessively—described as a lady or a gentleman except when they are lords. 'The poor', Bunyan wrote (later), 'because they are poor, are not capable of sinning against God as the rich man does'. 'More servants than masters...more tenants than landlords, will inherit the kingdom of heaven.' Christ rejects 'the great ones that were the grandees of the world' preferring 'hedge-creepers and highwaymen'. 'God's little ones...are not gentlemen...cannot, with Pontius Pilate, speak Hebrew, Greek and Latin.'

In his sermon on Dives and Lazarus Bunyan seems almost to have some individuals in mind when he describes how 'the great ones of the world will go strutting up and down the streets', 'hunting and whoring...dancing and playing'. 'They will build houses for their dogs, when the saints must be glad to wander and lodge in dens and cabes of the earth'—like the dreamer of *The Pilgrim's Progress*, you will remember. The phrases I have just quoted come from the one sermon of Bunyan's that had so far been printed. What did he say in all the other sensationally popular sermons? Were they even more offensive? Were the characters denounced in them even more recognisable?

The Bedfordshire gentry described Bunyan as 'a pestilential fellow', the worst in the county. A pamphleteer described him as 'a turbulent spirit', whose 'licentious and destructive principles' would lead to the 'subversion of all government'. 'Natural brute beasts' like Bunyan, said the reverend writer of these remarks, 'should be taken and destroyed.' He described himself as a spokesman of 'the moderate divines', and he was soon to become a bishop. One wonders about the less moderate.

The Bedfordshire gentry knew a lot about Bunyan, just as a godly nonconformist preacher. He had been a soldier in the army which had defeated Charles I. The congregation of which he was a leading member had been active in politics in the 1650s—as most of the separatist congregations were. It applauded the army's expulsion of the Rump of the Long Parliament in 1653, and recommended suitable persons to sit in the 'Barebones Parliament' which the army leaders then set up. The congregation urged Oliver Cromwell not to accept the crown when Parliament offered it to him in 1657; when he refused it they set aside a day of thanks to God. They opposed the Restoration of Charles II, after which they never again recorded any discussions on politics. That was what the Restoration had been about.

The Bedfordshire gentry wanted to silence Bunyan. If he had agreed to silence himself, he would have gone free. Instead he spent 12 years in jail, at the cost of who knows what suffering to his wife and five children, one of them blind. His second wife's first child died when she was 'dismayed at the news of her husband's arrest'. When he was ultimately released, Bunyan at once started breaking the law again. Most of the 40-odd books which he published between his arrest and his death in 1688 were printed illegally, without licence. His printers were almost invariably seditious radicals, who spent most of their time in and out of prison, who were pilloried, suffered heavy fines, fees and damages; one of them fought for Monmouth in his rebellion of 1685; others went into exile. When a printer was asked why he had not licensed one of Bunyan's books before publication, as the law required, he replied simply, 'I knew I shouldn't get a licence for Bunyan'. His reputation had spread from Bedford to London. So though Bunyan was certainly not a political figure, he had politics forced upon him by the policies of post-Restoration governments and JPs.

The authorities were right to be worried about the dangers of unrest after 1660. There were many plots for armed revolt in the years 1660-63, in some of which Bunyan's friends were involved. They culminated in the Yorkshire rising of 1663.[1] The government tended to regard any illegal meeting as potentially seditious. How could they distinguish?

So when Bunyan faced the Bedfordshire justices in 1661 he thought he was refusing to give up his God given vocation of preaching; they

---

1. R L Greaves, *Deliver us from Evil: The Radical Underground in Britain, 1660-1663* (OUP 1986), passim.

thought he was a dangerous agitator who was stirring up class hostility in the very delicate situation of post-Restoration England, just recovering from a revolution in which the revolutionaries had spoken on behalf of the poor as Bunyan did. The issues are not clear cut, not pure.

Two quite different politico-religious systems of values were in conflict. The Bedfordshire gentry believed it to be their duty to prevent disorder, and in particular to prevent any revival of the revolutionary activities of the 40s and 50s. Bunyan's motives were religious, not political, not revolutionary; but they led him to take actions which the Bedfordshire justices could not but regard as seditious. They were enforcing the laws of the land. Bunyan's example raises sharply the question—still relevant today—of whether resistance to the law is ever legitimate when it seems to be dictated by sincere conscientious beliefs (though 17th century laws were not passed by democratically elected parliaments). Bunyan, so far as we know, took no part in seditious conspiracy, but many of his close associates did. For Bunyan and his like their congregations were defensive units of freedom and solidarity in which they could continue the sort of unhampered worship and discussions to which they had become accustomed in the 40s and 50s.

Quakers faced similar problems. We think of Quakers as pacifists, people who take no part in politics. That is true of 18th century Quakers. But it was not true of Quakers in the 1650s and early 1660s. Many Quakers had fought in the parliamentarian armies against Charles I, and did not resign from the army when they were convinced. They protested when they were dismissed because of their refusal to take oaths and because their egalitarian principles, as one general put it, were 'inconsistent with the discipline of an army'. Many rejoined the army in 1659-60 in the hope of preventing a restoration of monarchy.

Most of the leading Quakers in the 50s (and not only Quakers) expected the Second Coming of Jesus Christ and the millennium in the immediate future. Quakers inherited many of the radical principles of Levellers, Diggers and Ranters, the radical wing of the parliamentarians, all of whom had been suppressed between 1649 and 1651. (The first appearance of Quakers dates from 1652-3). Like Bunyan, Quakers attacked the rich and spoke up for the poor. 'O ye great men and rich men of the earth', Fox cried in 1653, 'weep and howl, for your misery is coming.' Quakers refused to remove their hats in the presence of social superiors or magistrates, and they used the familiar 'thou' rather than the deferential 'you' when speaking to their betters. These were old radical habits. Quakers attacked lawyers, and wished to abolish them: they wanted drastic reformation of the law on behalf of the poor. Most upsetting was their habit of making public symbolic demonstrations. It was odd when Fox walked through Lichfield, naked except for a loincloth round his middle for decency's sake, shouting, 'Woe to the bloody city of Lichfield!' It was rather more odd when Mary Todd 'pulled up all her clothes above her middle, exposing her nakedness to all', crying 'welcome the resurrection'. Similarly with public burnings of the Bible, by others as well as Quakers, because it was not the word of God, because it deceived the people.

Quakers refused to pay tithes, and incited others to refuse. Tithes went to support a clergyman in every parish in the country: Milton and many others thought that religious freedom was impossible without their abolition, which would have amounted to disestablishment of the state church. But conservatives saw such a church as essential to thought control. No television, no radio, no press, no media: that left indoctrination to university trained official interpreters of the Bible, appointed, not elected by parishioners. They could be relied on not to have a dangerous idea in their heads.

In the sudden and unaccustomed freedom of these decades, discussion and speculation ran riot on all sorts of subjects hitherto taboo. Democracy, communism, free love, the desirability of church marriage, comparative religion, the truth and reliability of the Bible—all these had been the subject of eager argument. The Quaker Samuel Fisher published a large and scholarly tome showing that the Bible was so internally inconsistent and self contradictory that it could not be the word of God. Ranters argued that 'sin' had been invented by the ruling class to keep the lower orders down; and that you could sleep with anyone your conscience told you that you might. The young Bunyan liked that, 'I being a young man and my nature at its prime.' One Ranter claimed that God had told him to break all the Ten Commandments at one time or another except 'Thou shalt do no murder'. He wondered whether that was still to come. Quakers participated actively in all these discussions, normally on the radical side. They were often confused with Ranters, and indeed many Ranters after their suppression in 1650-1 became Quakers.

Quakers used extremely bellicose (biblical) language, which may have been intended allegorically; but what would nervous contemporaries have thought? Edward Burrough, political spokesman for the Quakers, cried in 1655, 'Let not your eye pity nor your hand spare, but wound the lofty and tread underfoot the honourable of the earth.'

Audland in the same year said, 'The sword of the Lord is in the hands of the saints and this sword divides, hews and cuts down deceit.' No wonder contemporaries were worried by the fact that Quakers were rejoining the army in the 1650s. Howgil, another leading Quaker, said a year later, 'Spare none, neither old nor young; kill, cut off, destroy, bathe your sword in the blood of Amalek.' When Christ comes, Burrough declared in 1657, 'all that would not that Christ should reign, slay them before him.' Fox stated that 'the saints of the most high God are coming to break [his enemies] in pieces.' 'The saints shall judge the world...whereof I am one.' 'A day of slaughter is coming to you who have made war against the Lamb and against the saints... The sword you cannot escape, and it shall be upon you before long.'

Fox wrote a tract specially for members of the army, urging them to 'see that you know a soldier's place...and that ye be soldiers qualified.' Fox frequently urged Cromwell and the army to pursue an aggressive European crusade against popery. 'Let thy soldiers go forth', he told the Protector in January 1658, 'that thou may rock nations as a cradle.' 'Had you been faithful to the power of the Lord', he complained to the army in the following year, 'you had gone into the midst of Spain...gone over them as the wind, and knocked at Rome's gates before now, and trampled deceit and tyrants under.' In 1659 he told 'soldiers and true officers...if ever you...come again into the power of God which hath been lost, never set up your standard till you come to Rome.'

The Quakers had enjoyed the protection of the radical New Model Army against conservative JPs and town magistrates. Colonel Scroope, commander of the garrison of Bristol, declared in 1654 of Quakers that 'if the magistrates did put them in prison one day, he would put them out the next.' When the garrison was moved from Bristol, Quakers had a much tougher time. In 1659-60, the restoration of monarchy appeared to be looming, Quakers offered their support to the republican government and the army in order to keep out Charles II. 'Those who desired an earthly king', Fox snorted, were 'traitors against Christ.' 'True Christians will have no king but Christ.' Quakers rejoined the army, raised troops, accepted office as JPs. Some think that panic fear of Quakers and their subversive intentions did much to expedite the restoration of monarchy. There was much talk of 'arming the Quakers'. Some thought 'the whole army would be reduced to follow' the Quakers.

Only after the Restoration, and after a revolt in London by desperate Fifth Monarchists which terrorised London for days, was the Quaker peace principle announced, in January 1661. Their proclamation of pacifism was an attempt to distinguish Quakers from Fifth Monarchists and other still belligerent sectaries. In the long run the peace principle established the Quakers as a community who abjured 'the carnal sword' and withdrew from political activity. It was a recognition that the millennium was not coming in England in the near future, that the saints were not going to rule, and ultimately that Christ's kingdom was not of this world. This was a great reversal. But it took time for the fact to be accepted.

Many Quakers in 1661 regarded the peace principle and the discipline which was necessary to enforce it as a betrayal of Quaker principles. There were many splits—John Perrot and his followers, the Story-Wilkinson separation. Many Quakers took part in the Yorkshire rising of 1663; as late as 1685 at least 12 Quakers joined Monmouth's rebellion, of whom three were executed. For these reasons conservatives were slow to accept the genuineness of Quaker pacifism and so the possibility of extending toleration to them. Quakers continued to refuse payment of tithes with greater courage and determination than other sects. Their rejection of oaths was another sticking point: refusal to take the oath of loyalty to the restored monarchy entailed a jail sentence and was presumptive evidence of disloyalty. Not till 1696 was the genuineness of Quaker principled objection to oaths recognised, and they were allowed to affirm.

I am not suggesting it was right to persecute Quakers or Bunyan—far from it—but that it was not a simple straightforward issue of 'religious freedom', in which all the reasons are on one side. Extreme language and provocative gestures were natural reactions to frustration: Quakers (and others) felt that they had to make a scene in order to get a hearing. What I am suggesting is that in the 17th century, when state and church were one—perhaps in other societies where party and state are one—toleration is a political issue, inseparable from politico-social questions which historians of toleration sometimes overlook.

It is not easy for us to understand why many sincere defenders of religious toleration like Milton drew the line at toleration for Roman Catholics. They were prepared to grant freedom to way-out Ranters, to Quakers who disrupted other people's church services, to Fifth Monarchists who believed in establishing the rule of the saints, by force if necessary. Historians of toleration often say that Milton and Locke failed to understand the logic of their own arguments. That is, frankly, just silly. They were very intelligent men: they had what they (and many others) believed to be good reasons for refusing toleration to papists. We may not accept these arguments; but we must try to understand them. Men felt that they were involved in a life and death struggle between Protestantism and the forces of Antichrist, that England's national independence and the future of humanity were at stake. It was not possible, such men thought, to extend freedom of organisation to Catholics, to the adherents of Antichrist—the pope and his followers. There could be no compromise with papists who had tried to subordinate England to Spain in Bloody Mary's reign, had organised the Spanish Armada, Guy Fawkes's Plot, and what was believed to have been Queen Henrietta Maria's popish plot in the 1630s, at which Charles I and Archbishop Laud were held to have connived.[2] It was widely believed that Catholics could obtain papal authorisation for taking oaths of loyalty which they had no intention of keeping. All this did not prevent Protestant and Catholic gentlemen getting on amicably in their counties, nor Milton enjoying the hospitality of cardinals when he visited Rome. But the institution of the Roman church could not be tolerated. Catholicism, Milton said, was not a religion but a political conspiracy. Bunyan and many others associated all persecution with Antichrist.

The beleaguered Irish were seen as participants in the international popish plot against England. In the 1590s there were Spanish armies in Ireland supporting an Irish rebellion; in the 1640s Irish rebels were commanded by an archbishop sent from Rome for that purpose. In the 1690s, again, James II, in alliance with Louis XIV, aimed to recover his throne in England via Ireland. Even the 1715 and the 1745 rebellions, unsuccessful though they were, contained a potential threat of restoration of Catholic absolutism with French support. Rivalry with France and Spain continued to be seen in religious terms well into the 18th century, when Frederick the Great was (to us rather implausibly) hailed as a Protestant hero. Catholic emancipation was facilitated by the French Revolution, after which Anglo-French colonial rivalry looked even less like a religious conflict. Earlier Catholic emancipation in England would have seemed like the emancipation of Antichrist.

Neither Bunyan nor George Fox made grand statements on the principle of toleration. Both would have rejected the idea of their 'sect' being 'tolerated'.[3] They believed that theirs was the church of Christ,

---

2. C Hibbard, *Charles I and the Popish Plot* (North Carolina UP, 1983), passim.
3. I owe this point to Elizabeth Tuttle, *Religion et Idéologie dans la Révolution Anglaise, 1647-1649* (Paris, 1989), pp45-46.

and demanded freedom to proclaim it. 'The laws of man can but settle a sect', declared the Quaker Edward Burrough; 'true religion can never be settled by that means' (*Works* 590-13: EoD 145). Intolerance, he argued, led necessarily to hypocrisy. Hence, like Milton, he insisted on the widest freedom for all Protestants. Enforced unity was anti-Christian. The word 'toleration' means acceptance of something on a temporary basis, something not in itself desirable. The Edict of Nantes granted toleration to Huguenots in France, but it was always a grudging toleration, and the edict was revoked in 1685. English radicals wanted 'liberty of conscience' rather than 'toleration', freedom to believe and to organise as they wished. They rejected the idea of a compulsory national church in favour of voluntary congregations which might (or might not) be part of a loosely organised national church. Conservatives thought this would lead to confusion and anarchy. The parish was inextricably associated with local government—and in fact dissenters had—in defeat—to accept exclusion from local and central government after 1660 as well as exclusion from the universities which trained the clergy for the national church.

I am trying to argue that toleration came not because men became wiser and nicer but because circumstances had changed. One way out is to say that toleration comes only when men become indifferent to the issues involved. If those issues were serious, this is to say that the virtue of toleration is the result of the vice of indifference. But what the historian has to explain is why men and women became indifferent to what had once seemed—literally—life and death issues.

Indifference at the government level came when rulers no longer feared that heretics wished to/were able to subvert the existing state of society—eg by a rule of the saints, by turning the world upside down; or by undermining the existing social order (eg by abolishing tithes) and existing ideology (eg by undermining the authority of the Bible).

Indifference from below came when heretics were no longer ordered (under threat of violence) to believe what they could not believe. Belief is not totally voluntary: standards of faith change with social conditions—eg the ending of the use of torture in treason trials—not because it was now felt to be wrong, but because it was seen to be unnecessary and unreliable as, for instance, better rules of evidence were elaborated. Burning heretics was discontinued (among other reasons) because it roused too much sympathy for the victims, and so no longer discouraged others. Some martyrs in Mary's reign were themselves in favour of burning heretics. The wide extension of printed material and the possibility of discussion among the inarticulate led to rethinking here. John Owen and Oliver Cromwell both advocated toleration even when their own party was in power.

So what were the changes in conditions? I have nothing very original to suggest here, but it may help to bring together familar facts and to suggest interconnections.

1. Expansion of world trade led to closer contacts with Islam and Jews in the Middle East, and with the ancient civilisations of India, China and Japan, as well as with Africa and America. It had to be recognised that Christianity was not unique: vast areas of the world existed in which its truths were unknown, but which nevertheless had attained a level of civilisation at least comparable with that of Europe. Men also learnt that Turks were more tolerant than Christians. Sir Henry Blount's *Voyage into the Levant* (1636) compared Islam favourably with Christianity: cf F Osborn. When Turks invaded Germany in 1663, the Reverend Ralph Josselin was only mildly shocked by some saying that they hoped the Turks would overrun Christianity, because then they would gain their liberty. That was going a bit far, Josselin thought: nevertheless he believed that 'God may do good' by the Turks.[4] Conservatives used the tolerance of the Turks as an argument against allowing toleration in a Christian country.[5]

2. Toleration was a practical necessity if money was to be made through international trade—as the Turks had learnt, as freebooters operating in the West Indies soon learnt too. The Navigation Act of 1651, confirmed after the Restoration, set England's sights on becoming master of the trade of the world: the economic argument for toleration was a powerful one in 17th century England. Archbishop Laud's intolerance of Dutch and Walloon refugees had ruined the clothing industry of Kent: it was reversed when a parliament met. The Act of Uniformity of 1662 was observed to benefit our trade rival the Netherlands by driving skilled artisans into emigration: and by then articulate MPs were there to draw attention to the fact. Dissenters came mostly from the trading sector of the population, which strengthened the argument for toleration.

3. Recognition of the existence of other civilisations and other religions led in the freedom of the 40s and 50s to thoughts about comparative religion. The Koran was published in English translation in 1649;

---

4. *Diary of Ralph Josselin, 1616-1683* (A Macfarlane (ed), 1976), p502.
5. Nathaniel Hardy, 'The Arraignment of Licentious Libertie, and Oppressing Tyrannie', First sermon preached to the House of Lords on 24 February 1646, p10.

it worried Bunyan greatly. All sorts of new mental horizons were opened up. In the mid-50s Jews were readmitted to England after 350 years of absence. Economic arguments were mainly responsible. The uniqueness of the Bible, and its authority and reliability, were all open for discussion. By the second half of the century this was a subject of jokes in Restoration comedy. When Lady Brute in Vanbrugh's *The Provoked Wife* was faced with the biblical injunction to love our enemies, her answer came pat: 'That may be a mistake in the translation'. By the end of the century Mary Astell could respond to the old argument in favour of the inferiority of women—that God created Adam before he created Eve—by the simple observation that God created the animals before Adam: what should we conclude from that? Personal experience in colonial Surinam led the novelist Aphra Behn to create the noble savage, and to allow him to laugh at the Trinity.

4. The new astronomy also cast doubts on the uniqueness of this earth, and consequently on the uniqueness of Christianity. The new science came into its own after 1640, when the writings of Bacon and others were popularised. Charles Webster has emphasised the encouragement of science by interregnum governments,[6] an encouragement which Charles II was wise enough to continue.

So the ferment of discussion of the revolutionary decades compounded the effects of the expansion of knowledge of the world and the universe. A single state church of which all English men and women were members simply broke down: so did its censorship. Twenty years of consumers' choice in religion, based on free discussion, could not be obliterated. Theorists of toleration like Lord Brooke, Walwyn and Milton were reacting to these circumstances—a society in which mobility was suddenly accelerated by the civil war, armies carrying the culture of the metropolis to the 'dark corners of the land', and finding sometimes unexpected allies waiting for them. The Quakers started in the dark north. It was impossible ever to return to the intellectual world of pre-1640. The country yokel John Bunyan unlearned and learned everything during his two and a half years of garrison service in the town of Newport Pagnell, where the radical discussions of the rank and file caused the gravest alarm to its commanding officer.

5. The years 1640-60 made dissent too strong to be crushed or harried out of the land, as had been serious intentions before 1640. On the other hand dissenters realised that they were not strong enough to

6. C Webster, *The Great Instauration: Science, Medicine and Reform, 1626-1660* (1975), passim.

control the state without perpetual fighting, ruin and disruption of the families of the small shopkeeper class. They were themselves, they found by bitter experience, hopelessly divided: the dissidence of dissent. All came ultimately to accept partial freedom, religious rather than political. The English nation ceased to be co-terminous with the Church of England. After 1689 it was discovered that the existence of two nations did not mean anarchy, or loss of government control. Once dissenters had accepted their position as a subordinate part of the nation, with freedom of religious worship at the expense of exclusion from central and local government and from the universities, a modus vivendi could be worked out. Exclusion from local and national government meant that dissenters lost the support of the gentry which had been such a feature of earlier puritanism. A gentleman had to be able to represent his county on the bench and in Parliament. The two nations were socially divided. Recognition that Christ's kingdom was not of this world, the failure of revolutionary millenarianism, of the rule of the saints, was a great turning point, the consequence of the trial and failure of the radical revolution. The dissenting interest became the trading interest. Exclusion from the universities proved a blessing in disguise: dissenters got a far better education at their own dissenting academies than they would ever have done at Oxford or Cambridge, though the social cachet was lacking. Degrees could be obtained from Scottish universities or Leiden.

6. The Church of England after 1640 never recovered the position of economic and political dominance to which the Laudians had aspired. Bishops came back in 1660, but they had no High Commission Court or Star Chamber to enforce unpopular policies by branding and ear slicing. Excommunication ceased to be an effective sentence because it was unenforceable against the vast dissenting population. 'It was only their not going to church', one employer reassured his employees: who would mind that, now that fines for non-attendance were ineffective, and jobs were easily available elsewhere in the increasingly mobile society?

The solidarity of dissent had long been demonstrated. Dissenters had learnt to take full economic advantage of family and church connections in their business transactions. Even before 1640 Nehemiah Wallington was able to find support and protection among the godly of East Anglia when forced to leave London. Town corporations had shown their ability to put group solidarity above political considerations in their resistance to the Major-Generals' rule in 1655-6; they showed the same solidarity in response to the purges initiated after 1660, and again in the 1680s. Charles II, who wanted to tolerate dissenters and so win their support for the crown, was a better analyst of the situation than the bishops and those MPs who wanted to take a hard line against dissenters. Most dissenters asked only to be left alone: erratic and spasmodic persecution was for them the worst of all possible fates. The wisdom of the king's policy was recognised by the Toleration Act of 1689.

7. Abandonment of the millenarian hope, of the rule of the saints, combined with a declining belief in hell—these intellectual changes achieved what Hobbes had thought essential for civil peace: an end to effective belief in rewards and punishments in the after life—the greatest stimulus, in his view, to determined revolutionary activity. Soon after the Restoration Henry More spoke of talk of Antichrist not as dangerous but as vulgar. The name of Antichrist had slipped out of polite conversation. When John Mason announced that the end of the world was to begin in Water Stratford in 1694, and drew large crowds there, he was not prosecuted: he was advised to take physic.

8. By the end of the 17th century it had come to be appreciated that market forces were more effective in controlling dissent than erratic state terror. As with the press: totally effective censorship was beyond the capacities of the government. A printing press was a cheap and portable piece of equipment; it was impossible to prevent the smuggling into the country from abroad of illegal literature. The would be police state was woefully inefficient by modern standards. The Licensing Act was allowed to lapse in 1695 because publishers could now be relied on in their own interests not to publish seditious material. Ludlow's and Milton's prose were reprinted from the revolutionary era, not the writings of Levellers, Diggers and Ranters. When Quakers reprinted the works of their founding fathers, they omitted most of the pamphlets from which I have quoted. Quakers themselves restrained their rank and file from indulging in the wilder gestures—disrupting services, going naked for a sign—that had seemed necessary in face of the imminent millennium. The Toleration Act, by repeating Charles II's arrangements for licensing nonconformist congregations, gave some government control; it was exercised through the congregations themselves, and so was more efficient. Toleration proved a more effective way of controlling dissent than persecution.

Locke supplied a satisfactory theory, drawing on way-out radical writings of half a century earlier; but the main impetus may have come from practical expediency rather than from philosophy.

So my suggestion is not just that toleration results from indifference, but rather that the breakdown of one type of authoritarianism tends to lead to the temporary victory of another authoritarianism. Only when both sides have exhausted themselves can the possibility of neither winning outright be grasped, and the small voice of reason make itself heard. One hopes that this will happen ultimately in Eastern Europe today.

Chapter 30

Quakers and the English Revolution

This was a lecture delivered at Friends' House, London, on 1 March 1991, and was first published in The Journal of the Friends' Historical Society, *Vol 56, No 3, 1993.*

The early history of the Quakers has been transformed during the past generation. The new discoveries started from non-Quakers—Alan Cole and Barry Reay; but they have now been accepted for publication by the *Journal of the Friends' Historical Society.* Most of what I shall say derives from the work of Barry Reay. Early Quakers were not pacifists, nor did they abstain on principle from political activity. Fox and others advocated an international millenarian crusade. The Peace Principle was first published in January 1661. It took time and a good deal of organisation before it was adopted by all who called themselves Friends: there were many splits in the process. The society which emerged was very different from the Quakers of the 1650s—so much so that perhaps we need a different word for the period 1651 to 1661, with which I shall deal.

Our first problem is that of sources. Quakers rewrote their own history. They edited earlier texts, including Fox's *Journal.* Many tracts of the 1650s either were not reprinted or were reprinted only in a modified form. There is nothing wrong with this, of course: Lodowick Muggleton drastically edited writings of the chief prophet, John Reeve, when he republished them after Reeve's death. When John Toland edited the republican Edmund Ludlow's *Memoirs* for publication in 1698 he omitted much of Ludlow's millenarianism so as to make his anti-militarism more acceptable to late 17th century Whig opinion. His object was to make Ludlow useful to the Good Old Cause in changed circumstances: Ludlow I am sure would have agreed. What was important for later Quakers was the message of salvation: bellicose millenarianism would have given the wrong impression after 1661. But the practice created problems for historians, who until very recently relied on later reprints of pamphlets of the 1650s.

Who were the first Quakers? It is not an easy question to answer with certainty. Early Quaker historians relied, necessarily, on George Fox's *Journal* for the early years of what became the Society of Friends. Naturally Fox's *Journal* is about the groups which owed their convincement to him. But Fox and other early leaders were bringing together pre-existent groups such as Fox found waiting for his message when he journeyed north in 1651—Grindletonians, Seekers, Ranters, Muggletonians, what Fox called 'shattered Baptists'. There was in this decade very little Quaker organisation, though possibly rather more than in other 'sects' to which we give labels. The word 'Quaker', like the words 'Puritan', 'Anabaptist', 'Leveller', was a label applied by enemies, rather like 'red' today: it has no more precise meaning than that. The Quakers originated in the north, and such organisation as they had was for long centred on Swarthmoor Hall, where Margaret Fell lived. In 1652 the only groups regarding themselves as followers of Fox were in the northern and north western counties. But then they undertook a campaign to the south, and by 1656 they are to be found over most of England. It was a rapid and most impressive spread—to enemies rather frightening.

Sectarian names are largely applied by historians after the event, names which would not have meant much to contemporaries. We still argue about whether Bunyan was a Baptist or a Congregationalist. We do not know what label, if any, to apply to Oliver Cromwell or John Milton—fairly well documented characters. Sectarian labels are a product of the period after 1660, when persecuted communities had to organise and discipline themselves in order to survive, and when governments wanted them to be labelled in the interests of keeping them under control. But Quakers in fact even in the 1650s kept up by correspondence perhaps better organisation than any other group which we later recognise as a sect.

Quakers are a product of the revolutionary decades of the 1640s and 1650s, the greatest upheaval in English history. Before 1640 all English men and women were deemed to belong to the national church, and had a legal obligation to attend worship in their parish church every Sunday, to listen to a clergyman in whose selection they had had no say, and whose theology and/or personality they might detest. Before 1640 there was a strict censorship, which prevented the printing of 'unorthodox' books. The bookseller George Thomason, a friend of Milton's, realising that he was living in momentous times, started in 1640 to buy and keep a copy of every book or newspaper published, and he continued until 1660. In 1640 he bought 22 books; by 1642 the number was 1,966, and it continued to average over 1,000 a year until 1660. In 1640 he bought no newspapers: they were illegal. By 1641 there were four, and by 1645 there were 722. We can only guess at what this meant for a reading public which had clearly been starved of material under a censorship which prevented the publication of legal works by Sir Edward Coke, of works on the millennium by scholars like Thomas Brightman and Joseph Mede. Thomas Hobbes chose not to publish at all before 1640, when he was 52 years old—the age at which Shakespeare died.

There was a similar liberation of religious discussion. Hitherto illegal groups were now free to meet where they could—in private houses, in ale houses, in the open air—to discuss what they wanted to discuss, not what the university educated parson of their parish decided they should listen to, without discussion. In an age with no daily press, no TV, no radio, the clergy were the opinion formers. The government's object had been to have an approved interpreter of the scriptures—the source of all wisdom and truth—in every parish in the country. But now men and women were free to form their own groups, under an elected chairman—so called mechanic preachers—and to discuss what interested them, as they wished. Women took part in these discussions: some women preached, to the horror of traditionalists.

The parochial system was financed by tithes. Every man was supposed to pay 10 percent of this income to the parson. Tithes fell especially heavily on the peasantry who had to pay in kind—one tenth of their crops or animals. Radicals had long opposed tithes, and Quakers took over this opposition, though the campaign preceded them and was not limited to them. Milton thought that religious freedom was impossible without abolishing tithes. The Quaker Anthony Pearson said that tithes should have been cut off with the king's head. But abolishing tithes would have undermined the national church and substituted a voluntary system. Tithes were also a form of property: many gentlemen had inherited tithes which before the Reformation had gone to monasteries and since then had been collected by the lay successors to monastic property. In any case refusal of a long established customary payment like tithes would set a bad precedent: 'No tithes, no rent' was a frequent cry of alarm from the gentry. Some churches actually closed down for lack of maintenance. This was a real problem for conservatives as they tried to consolidate their revolution in the 1650s. Cromwell is alleged to have said that no temporal government could survive without a national church that adhered to it. But tithes were naturally unpopular.

Before 1640 it was assumed that politics were the exclusive concern of the upper classes. An Elizabethan secretary of state declared that 'day labourers, poor husbandmen, yea merchants or retailers that have no free land, copyholders and all artificers...have no voice or authority in our commonwealth, and no account is taken of them, but only to be ruled.' This applied in practice. When in 1628 Charles I ultimately and grudgingly accepted the Petition of Right, embodying the first concessions made by the monarchy to parliamentary claims, the Commons asked that it should be printed. Charles refused, furious at the idea of the vulgar seeing such a document and perhaps even discussing the extent of the royal prerogative. In 1641, a year before civil war, the House of Commons drafted the 'Grand Remonstrance', a catalogue of all the ways in which they thought the king's ministers had been at fault. A very critical document, it passed in the House by a narrow majority. It was then suggested that the 'Remonstrance' should be printed. This caused outrage among the minority, that criticisms of the king should be exposed to the lower classes. Swords were actually drawn in the House—for, I believe, the only time in history so far, so outrageous did the proposal seem.

Yet with the breakdown of censorship, with freedom of assembly and with no limits on what might be discussed, there were no longer any secrets of state. In the free-for-all discussions which followed, every subject under the sun was canvassed. Levellers called for a democratic republic, and proclaimed human equality. Diggers advocated a communist society, others equality of women and men, civil marriage and free love. The authority of the Bible and the existence of heaven and hell were questioned. Ranters asserted the eternity of matter (which at one time interested George Fox)—all these were freely discussed. Milton's *Areopagitica* proudly hailed this new world of liberty. Ministers and bishops were mocked. In London and especially in the army there was a free thinking milieu from which Levellers, Ranters, Muggletonians, Quakers and Bunyan emerged. Quakers were later said to have 'reclaimed such as neither magistrate nor minister ever speaks to'—which suggests that the first Quakers appealed to a lower social class than they did later.

Let us forget for a moment that the Quakers after 1661 were a peaceful, pacifist religious society. Let us look at them, as contemporaries did, in sociological terms. Quakers reproduced many traditional lower class social heresies looking back to the Lollards. They refused to pay tithes, and were persecuted for that. They proclaimed human equality by refusing to doff their hats in the presence of social superiors or magistrates. This seemed to Quakers a religious principle. They refused oaths, which were regarded as essential to 17th century judicial processes. Again they saw this as a matter of religious principle; 17th century authorities saw it as subversive of law, property and society. Quakers were prepared to make solemn affirmations, but would not take an oath on the Bible. They perpetuated hand fast marriages and other traditional ceremonies when the authorities insisted that only church marriages were valid. Quaker rejection of tithes implied rejection of a state church.

Most separatist congregations which came into the open after 1640 were grouped around a charismatic preacher; and, as Congregationalists, Presbyterians, Baptists emerged, they established a priesthood. Quakers carried the Protestant principle of the priesthood of all believers to a rejection of any salaried ministers. The 'sense of the meeting' was their democratic alternative.

Quakers had exceptionally liberal attitudes towards women. Christ could speak in either sex at Quaker meetings. There were many Quaker women missionaries. Quakers rejected the haggling of the market. Their yea was yea, their nay was nay. Amazingly, they nevertheless prospered in business. They had come out of the middle ages into the modern world. Quakers had a modern attitude towards time too. Their watches summoned them to meetings, not church bells. Some early Quakers indeed thought it wrong to have stated times and places for meetings. This was a matter of controversy among Friends after 1660.

After parliament's victory, in 1647 the radical New Model Army of the career open to the talents took over effective power. Two years later it purged parliament and brought the king to trial as a traitor to the people of England. The House of Lords was abolished, the republic proclaimed. Bishops had been abolished in 1646. Anything might happen.

Many expected King Charles to be succeeded by King Jesus. Millenarian hopes were rife, founded on the best scholarly interpretations of the biblical prophecies, which seemed to point to the 1650s as the period when the millennium was likely to begin. George Fox thought he was living in 'the last times'; 'the mighty day of the Lord is coming' when the saints will reign—'of whom I am one', Fox added. Such remarks were not reprinted in later collected editions of Fox's works.

Among the few specific things Fox tells us about his early preaching—which in the *Journal* sounds orthodox enough—is that he had 'great openings concerning the things written in the Revelation', which was for him the most relevant book in the Bible. It may well be that millenarianism played a far greater part in his preaching and in the interests of his audiences than he was later to record. After the Restoration the millenarian moment had passed, and Quakers played it down; but that was not true of the 50s. The only movement which enjoyed a comparable popular success was that of the Fifth Monarchists, also millenarians. Gerrard Winstanley, who founded a communist colony in Surrey three months after the execution of the king, held that the Second Coming meant the rising of Christ in all 'sons and daughters'. He believed that Christ was reason, and that his rising would lead all to see the rationality of cooperation rather than competition, and would lead to the peaceful establishment of a communist society. And, he said, he expected to see no other Second Coming. Many were later to attribute the origins of the Quakers to Winstanley—wrongly, I think.

The free-for-all of the 40s released long held but suppressed radical traditions which Quakers inherited—refusal of hat honour, use of 'thou' to social superiors, demands for law reform, for better treatment of the poor, for 'handfast' marriages rather than a church ceremony. Burrough at least among the early Quaker leaders was aware of the heretical tradition which the Quakers inherited.

In the civil war most of those who were later to become Quakers had been staunch parliamentarians, 'they stood by [parliament] in time of greatest dangers in all the late wars', said Howgill. Many Quakers had been in the army, 'many precious men ventured their lives and lost their blood' to win liberty 'as men and Christians.' James Nayler agreed; Quakers 'generally did venture their lives and estates with those that are in present government [1658], purchasing their freedom as men with great loss.' The army, Margaret Fell said, had been 'a battle axe in the hand of the Lord.' George Bishop told Oliver Cromwell in 1656 that the original Parliamentary Cause was 'the highest on which men were ever engaged in the field'. Bishop rebuked Cromwell for betraying this cause.

Quakers did not resign from the army on pacifist grounds when they were convinced: they were expelled for refusing oaths, Fox and Burrough complained. Henry Cromwell thought 'their principles and practices...not very consistent with civil government, much less with the discipline of an army'. But Byllynge claimed to be 'an owner of the sword in its place'. Fox thought that one Quaker soldier was worth seven non-Quakers. Far from disapproving of military service he wrote a tract for members of the army, urging them to 'see that you know a soldier's place...and that ye be soldiers qualified.' The New Model Army was a uniquely democratic force, which for a time played a very

radical role. Without it there would have been no religious toleration, no abolition of monarchy or House of Lords, no protection for
Quakers against JPs—and no conquest of Ireland, of which Quakers
showed no disapproval. But the Levellers failed to win control of the
army in 1647-9; the Fifth Monarchists in 1653-5. Quakers went on
hoping that the army might resume its radical role right down to 1660.

Fox often urged Oliver Cromwell and the army to undertake a crusade against popery in Europe. In January 1658 he told the Protector
that if he had 'minded the work of the Lord as he began with thee at
first...the King of France should have bowed his neck under thee.'
'Let thy soldiers go forth...that thou may rock nations as a cradle.'
Later, addressing 'inferior officers and soldiers' as against the generals,
Fox said, 'Never set up your standard till you come to Rome.'

Quakers frequently used disturbing military metaphors. 'Gird on
your sword,' Burrough urged 'the Camp of the Lord in England', 'and
prepare yourselves for battle.' 'Let not your eye pity not your hand
spare, but wound the lofty and tread underfoot the honourable of the
earth.' Howgill cried, 'Spare none, neither old or young; kill, cut off,
destroy, bathe your sword in the blood of Amalek.' Audland repeated
the message: 'The sword of the Lord is in the hands of the saints, and
this sword divides, hews and cuts down deceit.' Burrough, envisaging
the imminent Second Coming, insisted, 'All that would not that
Christ should reign, slay them before him.' And Fox warned, 'A day
of slaughter is coming to you that have made war against the Lamb and
against the saints. The sword you cannot escape, and it shall be upon
you before long.'

How seriously are we to take this alarming language? When Margaret Fell asked in 1656, 'How is our war prospering in England?' she
presumably referred to the successful propaganda campaign which
Quakers had undertaken. But were the reiterated public threats of
Quaker leaders all metaphorical? Conservatives may perhaps be forgiven for not being quite sure: they did not know, as we know, that the
Quakers were to proclaim pacifism as a principle after 1661. In the
1650s they knew only that Quakers were a radical group, reproducing
many of the ideas of Levellers, Diggers and Ranters, all of whom had
been suppressed between 1649 and 1651, immediately before the appearance of Quakers on the national scene. In the mid-50s Quakers
were recruiting rapidly. Alarm was not entirely unreasonable. Quakers were 'turners of the world upside down'—to cite words used by
William Penn in his Introduction to Fox's *Journal* in 1694.

Some Quakers defended regicide. George Bishop expressed approval of the army's purge of parliament in December 1648, and

thought that Charles's execution had been 'for the preservation of the public interest'. It was God, Burrough belived, who 'overthrew that oppressing power of kings, lords...and bishops, and brought some tyrants and oppressors to just execution.' 'Some tyrants' could hardly have excluded Charles I, Strafford and Laud. Bishop defended Cromwell's brutal conquest of Ireland: no Quaker seems to have opposed it on principle. The Irish were Antichristians.

Quakers, as Levellers had done, cried out against the oppression of the poor. A rich man, Fox said, is 'the greatest thief', since he got 'his goods by cozening and cheating, by lying and defrauding'—another tract not reprinted in Fox's *Works*. Here was strong biblical language again. 'Weep and howl, for your misery is coming', Nayler told 'great men and rich men'. Fox strongly supported law reform, and opposed hanging for theft. 'Throw away all law books', he recommended; law should be made known to the people. 'Away with lawyers'—recalling Winstanley this time. 'If a lord or an earl come into your courts', Fox said, 'you will hardly fine him for not putting off his hat... It is the poor that suffer, and the rich bears with the rich.' With reference to the Quaker refusal of oaths he added, 'Some you have made to swear, some you have made to pay for swearing.' (Neither of these tracts was reprinted in his works.) Quakers came to believe that the cause had been betrayed.

Slow disillusionment set in as Cromwell tried to come to terms with the 'natural rulers', as generals got rich and the army was deliberately depoliticised. It came to exist only to collect the taxes to pay for the army to collect the taxes... Burrough warned Cromwell that he and his government had neglected 'to take off oppression, and to ease the oppressed', ignoring 'the grievious cry of the poor'. Like Winstanley, he insisted that 'the same laws stand still in force by which tyranny and oppression is acted.' 'You have promised many fair promises to the nation,' said Fox, 'but little have you performed.'

In May 1659 the army restored the Rump of the Long Parliament to power, and with it hope for the radicals. Fox announced euphorically that 'the Lord Jesus Christ is come to reign... Now shall the Lamb and the saints have victory.' 'The way of the coming of his kingdom hath seemed to be prepared,' Burrough told MPs, by the 'mighty things' done in England. But this hope depended on the survival of the republic. Fox laid a programme of reform before parliament—toleration, abolition of tithes, law reform, a large programme of expropriation—of church, crown and royalists' lands, and of monastic lands which had been in the possession of gentry families for over a century. The proceeds would go to pay for the army and to the poor, who should also have all manorial fines and profits, 'for lords have enough'. This was a larger programme of expropriation than even the communist Winstanley enivisaged. Howgill in 1660 pointed out that confiscated estates would maintain 'an army in the nation for many years'—a double cause of alarm to landed gentry.

Burrough asked parliament 'to establish the [Leveller] Agreement of the People'. He emphasised Englishmen's birthright freedom in Leveller language, describing himself as 'a friend to England's commonwealth', as 'a freeborn Englishman'. 'We look for a new earth as well as a new heaven', he announced ominously. But the hope was short lived. As the threat of a restoration of monarchy loomed, Quakers (and other radicals) became more desperate. 'Is there no hope of your return to the Good Old Cause?' Burrough asked the army—four months before Charles II returned to the throne. 'Whoever are against the Good Old Cause and perfect freedom,' he declared, 'we are against them and will engage our lives against them.'

Quakers were opposed on principle to the restoration of monarchy. 'Those who desired an earthly king,' said Fox, were 'traitors against Christ.' 'Talk of [restoring] the House of Lords' was 'a dirty, nasty thing.' Burrough assured the army that 'we will engage our very lives against the enemies of the Good Old Cause.' A royalist feared that 'the whole army should be reduced to follow the Quakers.' The consequence was panic fear of Quakers, which Barry Reay, the best informed historian on this subject, thinks contributed significantly to the speed with which Charles II was—to his own surprise—recalled to the throne.

The fear seemed well founded. Quakers' numbers were uncertain, but they had rapidly increased in the decade of their existence. They repeated many Leveller, Digger and Ranter claims. They rejected oaths, believed to be the cement of society, and tithes, the foundation of a national church. They taught that the Bible was so internally contradictory and inconsistent that it could not be the word of God. The Quaker Samuel Fisher argued this case in a weighty scholarly tome published in 1660. It influenced Spinoza, and through him enlightened European opinion generally. For the Baptist Thomas Collier Quaker doctrine meant, 'No Christ but within, no scripture to be a rule, no ordinances, no law but their lusts, no heaven nor glory but here, no sin but what men fancied to be so.' Fox claimed to be freed from sin on earth; renewed 'to the state of Adam...before he fell.' Burrough taught that the saints 'may be perfectly freed from sin in this life so as no more to commit it.' Fox and many others denounced preachers who 'roar up for sin in their pulpits.' 'We have given our money and spent our labours in following them,' Fox exploded, 'and now they have gotten our money, they hope we will not look for perfection...on this side of the grave, for we must carry a body of sin about us... Oh deceivers!' Not to believe in the existence of sin had disturbing social implications.

As far as the Quakers were concerned, by 1659-60 the army offered the only hope for reform—if it could be radicalised again. Bishop, Burrough, Howgill, Isaac Penington, all defended the army's intervention in politics in 1659. Burrough acted as political leader of the Quakers in this period: Fox withdrew into the background. Burrough, Byllynge and other Quaker leaders negotiated seriously with the republican government for cooperation to prevent a restoration of monarchy, and for social reforms. In 1659-60 Quakers were rejoining the army, and there was much talk of 'arming the Quakers'. Quakers acted as commissioners of the militia, as JPs. They were the last defenders of military dictatorship in England. But the defeat of the radicals, when it came, was so overwhelmingly decisive that it had to be accepted as the work of divine providence. How were Quakers to react to the collapse of their political hopes?

Here I want to speculate briefly, asking questions which go beyond the evidence. Had the Quakers a political programme? In the light of what we know of post-Restoration Quakers it seems a silly question: in the light of what we now know of Quakerism in the 1650s it forces itself upon us. Quakers expected the rule of the saints (of whom Fox was one), and expected that rule to bring about a better society. I have cited the programme which Fox put before the restored Rump in 1659; it would necessitate legislation. But had Quakers an agreed political programme?

The Nayler case in 1656-7 must have caused serious rethinking among Quakers. Nayler's entry into Bristol, re-enacting Christ's entry into Jerusalem, led to what must have been a totally unexpected political storm. Parliament spent months fiercely debating whether or not Nayler should be condemned to death. Conservatives seized on Nayler's alleged blasphemy to call for stricter laws preventing free discussion, controlling itinerant ministers appealing to the lower order. Nayler's main defenders were army officers. Cromwell used the occasion to negotiate a new, more conservative constitution, which would both limit toleration and perhaps ultimately get rid of army rule and replace it by the rule of traditional law.

How did the Quakers react? Their tactics of demonstration and confrontation had been useful advertisements in local politics, winning support for Quakers who were roughly handled by magistrates. But the Nayler case had brought the whole power of the state to bear against Quakers, something beyond their ability to resist. They virtually disavowed Nayler. The attempted alliance with army and republican governments in 1659-60 against a restoration of monarchy seems to have been a last desperate attempt at winning some share in policy making. When that failed there had to be a total rethink.

From about August 1659 to the beginning of 1660 George Fox withdrew from all activity, and seems to have undergone some sort of a spiritual crisis, if not a nervous breakdown. He took no part in the negotiations with republican politicians and army leaders which Burrough and others undertook at this time, and seems to have been increasingly sceptical of them. He was unenthusiastic about Quakers taking up arms, but did not come out against it, even when asked. When he emerged from his 'time of darkness', by which time the Restoration was clearly looming, he seems to have decided that political action must be renounced. 'Nothing but hypocrisy and falsehood and fair pretences were seen among you', he told 'those that have been formerly in authority'. 'When you pretended to set up the Old Cause, it was but your silliness; so that you long stunk to sober people.' Fox must have realised during his period of abdication that the restoration of monarchy was inevitable, and that the millennium was not coming just yet. Perhaps indeed his withdrawal had been due to his recognition of the 'silliness' and irrelevance of the frenzied activities of the republicans, and to his inability to prevent Quaker participation in them. So Charles II came back in May 1660.

Eight months later, on 9-10 January 1661, there was a violent revolt by Fifth Monarchists which for a short time terrorised London. Many Quakers were arrested on suspicion of connection with this revolt. Twelve days later the 'peace principle', henceforth characteristic of Quakerism, was declared. 'The spirit of Christ', Fox declared, 'will never move us to fight a war against any man with carnal weapons.' This was a new principle. There had been Quaker pacifists in the 50s, including John Lilburne and the sailor Thomas Lurting. But there was no official endorsement of pacifism. As late as December 1659 Hubberthorne had publicly rebuked Baptists for declaring that they would be obedient in civil matters to any government established in England. Hubberthorne thought that this sold the pass to Charles Stuart. If he should 'come…and establish popery and govern by tyranny,' he told the Baptists, 'you have begged pardon by promising willingly to submit… Some did judge ye had been of another spirit.' But as the cause of the republic crumbled, Fox's new found pacifism won rapid acceptance. Burrough came to see the Restoration as a judgement of God upon England for the betrayal of the 1650s. 'They once had a good cause,' he told Charles II, 'and the Lord blessed them in it.' This was intended as a warning to the restored monarch. But within a week of the King's arrival in London Margaret Fell had drafted a declaration renouncing 'carnal weapons', which was signed by Fox, Richard Hubberthorne, Samuel Fisher and four others. The Peace Principle seven months later was also signed by Fox, Hubberthorne and ten others. The Restoration came because the parliamentarian radicals were hopelessly divided. Quakers themselves were not united. Support for the peace principle was by no means unanimous. Some thought that the new discipline which accompanied it amounted to apostasy—a breach with the absolute individualism of the inner light in all believers.

Sixteen sixty was a defeat for all radical social policies. It marked the end of millenarian hopes. The peace principle recognised these unpleasant facts, and differentiated Quakers from irreconcilable Fifth Monarchist insurrectionists who advocated inaugurating Christ's kingdom by immediate military violence.

So acceptance of the peace principle marked the end of an epoch—recognition that Christ's kingdom was not of this world, at least not yet. Abandonment of the rule of the saints, possibly through the army, ended the perceived Quaker political threat, though it took some time for non-saints to appreciate this. It marked the end of the doctrine of perfectibility of earth as a political principle. It was a great turning point, shared by most other dissenters—as they now reluctantly became.

Early Quakers had attacked the very idea of a state church: some disliked any form of organisation. They insisted that they were not a sect, not a church. But after 1660 some form of discipline ('good order') became increasingly necessary, if only to withstand persecution, to agree on appropriate forms of presentation of their message, to define who was and who was not a Quaker. The sense of the meeting was the compromise which gave a minimum of organisation: but above it a traditional hierarchical structure had to be erected—quarterly meetings, national meetings.

Financial questions were involved. Who paid for itinerant ministers? Fox had money in his pocket when he started on his mission, but he was dependent on sympathisers for hospitality en route. There were dangers here, as for more conventional sects—of becoming dependent on the rich and respectable, and so giving them privileged treatment. Some have seen a takeover of Quakerism by the well-to-do Margaret Fell and William Penn, the friend of James II, and Margaret Fell's husband from 1669, George Fox. The first suggestion of a peace principle in 1660 seems to have come from Margaret Fell. There was of course no conspiracy here: any leader would have had to take similar action if the Society of Friends was to survive. Ranters who remained disorganised disappeared; Muggletonians who were almost equally without organisation were subjected to the discipline imposed by the infallible Lodowick Muggleton, and anyway were not interested in proselytisation.

The peace principle distinguished Quakers from the irreconcilable Fifth Monarchists who had risen in hopeless revolt in January 1661. The Quaker leadership tried hard to live down their image as 'fanatics'. They ceased to perform miracles: George Fox's *Book of Miracles* was not published. Public gestures like 'going naked for a sign' were discouraged. Itinerant ministers were restricted, not least by the Act of Settlement of 1662. (This had been a wonderful liberation, especially for women Quakers, wandering unchaperoned all over Great Britain, rebuking Oxford and Cambridge undergraduates, journeying to the pope, the Great Turk and to New England—least tolerant of all.)

Some Quakers thought the peace principle and accompanying discipline amounted to apostasy, betraying the absolute individualism of the inner light. Many were the splits—Perrot, whom Fox admonished for wearing a sword, and who rather endearingly objected to holding meetings at stated times and places. (Dewsbery in 1659 had pleaded with Friends 'to meet as near as may be at the time appointed'). The Story-Wilkinson separation was more specifically on issues of discipline. Many Quakers continued to plot against the government: 400 pairs of pistols were said to have been imported for 'the Quakers' in August 1661. In 1663 many Friends had a 'deep hand' in the Northern Plot; 1,000 were expected to rise, and many did. As late as 1685 at least a dozen Quakers joined in Monmouth's rebellion, of whom three were executed. A Quaker commissioned by Monmouth to recruit Clubmen enlisted some 160 by appeals to the danger of popery. Quakers held state office in the New England colonies, and lobbied in parliamentary elections in England in 1678-80, when the radical cause seemed to be reviving. Penn was election agent for the republican Algernon Sydney.

This brings me to a question on which I hardly dare to touch: how far was Fox the undisputed leader of the Quakers before 1661? Was there such a leader? Nayler was described as 'the head Quaker' in parliament in 1656-7, and the savagery of his punishment suggests that he was seen as a symbolic target. Nayler was eight years older than Fox. He wrote the first Quaker book, in 1653; between 1655 and 1656 he published no less than 13 pamphlets answering attacks on Quakers.

Edward Burrough—a much younger man—seems to have been the political spokesman for Quakers from the mid-50s; he took the lead in negotiations with the Commonwealth government in 1659-60, when Fox withdrew from activity. Margaret Fell at Swarthmoor seems to have been in charge of correspondence and had much organisational responsibility. I imagine that such leadership as there was before 1660 must have been collective rather than individual. Fox's mysterious withdrawal after August 1659 may have been the result of the defeat of his preferred policies, which were finally vindicated in the acceptance of the peace principle.

Were there divisions? Francis Howgill continued to use bellicose language after January 1661. 'The godly', Howgill still proclaimed, would 'trample down the powers of darkness and the seat of violence, for ever.' Ames, also after the peace principle, said, 'The battle is the Lord's and strength and power is from the Lord manifest in you... The might of the noble of the earth shall vanish as the smoke, and the strength of kings shall be as stubble before the fire; not by the arm of flesh or carnal weapons to destroy the creatures, but by the spirit of the living God.' Who exactly of the leadership supported the original peace principle in 1661? Did Howgill? Did Ames? But all this is mere speculation.

Fox's takeover of leadership was facilitated by the premature deaths of most of the other leading figures. Parnell had died in 1656 at the age of 19, Camm and Lilburne in 1657, Nayler in 1660. George Fox the Younger followed in 1661, Burrough, Hubberthorne and Ames in 1662, Audland in 1664, Fisher in 1665, Farnsworth in 1666, Howgill in 1669. It is a remarkable tribute to the killing power of 17th century gaols, a long sentence in which only the toughest, morally and physically, could survive—as Fox did, as Bunyan did. There were resignations—Perrot, Pearson, Bishop, Byllynge—and emigration. Whitehead and Dewsbury were virtually the only surviving leaders from the 50s. The way was clear for Margaret and George Fox who were married in 1669 to take over and for Robert Barclay to rewrite Quaker theology in his *Apology for the True Christian Divinity* of 1676. It was published in the same year as his *Anarchy of the Ranters*, disavowing unseemly 'enthusiasm'.

Another consequence of the Peace Principle and the discipline necessary to enforce it was that the Society of Friends became in fact a sect like other sects—something which had seemed impossible for earlier Quakers expecting the rule of the saints. 'The laws of man can but settle a sect,' Edward Burrough had said; 'true religion can never be settled by that measure' (*Works*, pp509-513), but true religion in Burrough's sense has not yet been settled in England.

After 1661 the publications of Quakers were subjected to de facto censorship—first informally by Fox, after 1672 more formally. In consequence the writings of Nayler disappear from sight, and his name is rarely mentioned. Even in 1716 his *Collection of Sundry Books* was published only after much debate and with many misgivings; and many of his writings were omitted. Writings by Burrough, Howgill and George Fox the Younger were reprinted, but again with significant omissions, notably of Burrough's writings around 1660. Isaac Penington's works from his pre-Quaker period were not reprinted, and there were omissions from those of his political tracts of 1660 which were reprinted. George Fox, in editing his *Journal* for publication from the so-called *Short Journal* (1663-4), omitted many passages referring to his millenarian expectations, to his Cromwellian sympathies, his claims to be the Son of God or Moses, to his miracles, to the fact that he lent a meeting house to soldiers. Thomas Ellwood further edited it for publication in 1694 so that 'nothing may be omitted fit to be inserted, nor anything inserted fit to be left out.' What was fit in 1694 was very different from the revolutionary 50s.

So the world was left with the 18th century image of pacifist Quakers, wearing quaint, old fashioned, homespun clothes, using quaint, old-fashioned speech forms like 'thou' and 'thee', refusing to swear or to remove their hats in court in a quaint, old fashioned way. This image was easily read back into the 17th century, not without some help from the Quakers. So it was surprising to rediscover what Quakers had been like in the 1650s.

But that must not be the last word. Quakers have given the world more than any other 17th century group. And the essential Quaker message was not lost. Margaret Fell recalled Fox saying, on the second day of her acquaintance: 'You will say that Christ saith this, and the apostles say this; but what canst thou say?' 'I saw clearly we were all wrong,' Margaret Fell commented; he 'opened us a book that we had never read in, nor indeed had never heard it was our duty to read in it, to wit the light of Christ in our consciences'—the consciences of ordinary men and women.

Chapter 31

Premature
obsequies

This was first published in History Today, *Vol 41, April 1991.*

Events in Eastern Europe in 1989-90 witnessed to the death not of
Marxism but of the political practice of Communist parties there.
Any ideology which cannot be freely discussed gets corrupted. But
ideas do not necessarily die because horrors were committed in their
name. Hardy's

> After two thousand years of mass
> We've got as far as poison gas

is no more and no less relevant to the Gulf War than Ceausescu to
Marxism. Christianity survived the tortures of the Inquisition, the
burning of heretics and witches, the wars of religion and massacres of
American Indians. What happened in the countries of Eastern Europe
owed more to their previous history than to the ideology which rulers
professed.

'The death of Marxism', like 'the end of ideology' and 'the end of
history', derives from the wishful thinking of academics who believe
their own society must be eternal because it is comfortable for them.
Inhabitants of the Third World may be less sure that history is over,
leaving them permanently subordinate. As Saul Bellow put it, 'Russia's
oriental despotism comes from the past—little to do with this present world of ours.' We may compare Mao Tse Tung's remark: 'It is too
early to see the French Revolution clearly yet.'

When I am asked whether I am a Marxist I have learnt to reply,
'What do you mean by Marxism?' There are many Marxisms about
these days—Maoism, Trotskyism, Stalinism, structural Marxism. But
usually what the questioner means is, do I accept a body of dogma to

which I want to make history conform? In that sense I am not and never have been a 'Marxist'. I prefer to describe myself as Marxist influenced. But if what we are talking about is the influence of the events of 1989-1991 on countries which professed Marxism as an ideology. I think it is irrelevant to general questions about history. I refuse to answer when an American asks whether I am a 'new historicist'. I have strong surviving hangovers of English empiricism. I am not a political philosopher, just a historian interested in 17th century England: I am chary of philosophical generalisations.

During the past century many Marxist ideas have been incorporated into the thinking of historians, including those who regard themselves as anti-Marxists. That society must be seen as a whole; that politics, the constitution, religion and literature are in some way (often indirectly) related to the economic structure and development of that society; that there are ruling classes; all these are now historians' commonplaces. Jack Hexter is the doyen of anti-Marxists: but when he tells us that Shakespeare's Richard II is about property—hence its appeal to London apprentices and merchants—his approach is manifestly Marxist. The connections between Protestantism and the rise of capitalism, between the Puritan ethic and labour discipline, were developed by Weber and Tawney (neither a Marxist, though Tawney might be described as 'Marxist-influenced') and are now common historical currency.

Some Marxists oversimplified by postulating an economic 'base' controlling a political and ideological 'superstructure'. It is far more mixed up than that, as a glance at very recent work by David Harris Sacks on Bristol, David Rollison on Gloucestershire, and David Underdown on Dorchester will confirm. (Sacks, *The Widening Gate: Bristol and the Atlantic Economy, 1450-1700* (California UP, 1991); Rollison, *The Local Origins of Modern Society: Gloucestershire, 1500-1800* (1992); Underdown, *Fire from Heaven* (1992).) None of these is a Marxist, so far as I know. But that is my point: Marxism has been so incorporated into historical thinking that one doesn't know.

If we go back to what men in the 17th century thought, Philip IV, Mazarin and their ambassadors in London were agreed that a republic would be a more formidable rival for economic reasons. This was because taxpayers would pay to finance a great navy, whereas they would never willingly consent to pay taxes to give the government—any government not controlled by parliament—a standing army.

Marx's categorisation of feudal, as followed by capitalist, society is reproduced in a bowdlerised form by modern American theories of 'pre-modern' ('pre-industrial') and 'modern' ('industrial') societies, which avoid the rude word 'capitalist' but mean the same thing. They take over Stalin's additional thesis that capitalism inevitably succeeds 'feudalism', and so the theory justifies enforced 'modernisation' of 'backward' Third World economies. Those who use this jargon are no more consciously Marxist than those who employ a loosely Freudian terminology to describe historical characters are committed 'Freudians'.

Marxists apply the word 'revolution' to changes which have far-reaching consequences in many areas of society—the French Revolution, the Russian Revolution, the scientific revolution, the Industrial Revolution. Some historians argue that such concepts are misleading. They wish to abolish the English and French revolutions, the Industrial Revolution. Long term changes in society, they insist, are determined by other causes (price movements, demographic changes); the fact that they sometimes seem to have been accompanied by political changes is accidental.

This assumes a stereotype of 'revolution' as something caused by wicked agitators (like strikes). Subversives plan revolutions: if there is no plan, there is no revolution. My main interest is in the 17th century English Revolution. Here very special pleading is needed to claim that what happened was not a revolution, had no long term causes or consequences. It is argued, correctly, that no one willed it. There were only one or two republican MPs in the Long Parliament when it met in November 1640; eight years later parliament had Charles I executed and proclaimed the republic.

But nobody planned the French Revolution either, and though by 1917 the Bolsheviks had a theory of revolution (based on the experience of the English and French revolutions) they did not make the Russian Revolution: they took advantage of the collapse of the Tsarist state under pressure of military defeat and financial inviability. The English Revolution started under similar circumstances, though with no preceding revolutionary model to follow, only the Biblical concept of the millennium, a concept which was as seductively misleading as TV images of Western capitalism for Eastern Europe today. In 17th century England, republican theories had to be worked out from scratch in the practical experience of fighting two bloody civil wars. England has had no revolution since the 1640s. But in 1989 we saw on TV what revolutions are like—the solidly massive crowds motivated irresistibly by determination to overthrow a regime which had become intolerable; the impossibility of resorting to force for a regime which had lost confidence in its ability to rule. Before the Long Parliament met in 1640, London crowds released political prisoners; in May 1641, at the decisive moment of the revolution, the fate of Charles I's minister, the Earl of Strafford, lay—in the words of Brian Manning—not with king or parliament, 'but with the mass of the ordinary people of London'.

Communist parties in Eastern Europe had ceased to be able to control popular thinking. The illegal religious congregations which sprang up all over southern and eastern England in 1640-1 correspond to the illegal political groupings of Eastern Europe—united only in an opposition which sprang from many different causes. The breakdown of authority in 1640 made possible unprecedented freedom of discussion and of the press, out of which theories of Leveller democracy, Digger Communism, as well as the novel political ideas of Hobbes, Milton and Harrington, were to emerge. The English people educated one another in these years, celebrated by Milton's *Areopagitica*. What they did not achieve was unity in rival theories of government and of the church.

Most of Eastern Europe never had a Protestant reformation, nor the English tradition of competing religious sects. But its people too are likely to have difficulty in agreeing on what shall replace the discredited ideas of the Communist parties. 'I can tell you, Sirs, what I would not have,' said Oliver Cromwell in 1641, 'though I cannot what I would.'

When I started writing about English history I was anxious to establish that a revolutionary transformation occurred in the mid-17th century; I went out of my way to use Marxist jargon which I should now think wholly inappropriate. I brandished the words 'feudal' and 'bourgeoisie' like weapons. Many English historians think 'bourgeoisie' must be restricted to town dwellers. Since most of those who sat in the House of Commons were country gentlemen, it was unproductively provocative to call them 'bourgeois'—although their actions looked forward to the 18th century when (in Edward Thompson's words) agriculture was 'England's greatest capitalist industry'. After the mid-1950s I was, I hope, more careful and less strident.

So I have changed my vocabulary, but I do not think I have shifted very far on my main 'Marxist' point about 17th century England. I still think that the events between 1640 and 1660 are aptly described as a revolution, since they led to vast changes in the history of England and of the world. England in the early 17th century was a third rate power. Governments of the old regime were both financially unable, and politically unwilling, to support the expansion of English trade, in the Far East, the Mediterranean, or in America. Charles I told merchants to keep out of the Mediterranean because he could not protect them against pirates there. (Nor indeed could he protect English vessels in the Channel or south coast dwellers against pirates.) He could not even repulse an invading Scottish army. England, said the Venetian Ambassador, was 'useless to all the rest of the world', 'of no consideration'. Yet, as many Englishmen had long recognised, the possibilities for English commercial and colonial expansion were great.

In the 1650s Blake's fleet swept the Mediterranean clear of pirates, and Cromwell sent the first state sponsored expedition to the West Indies. By the end of the century England possessed the most powerful navy in the world, which it used for aggressive imperial expansion. It was soon to win a virtual monopoly of the immensely profitable slave trade. Ireland had been brutally conquered and had become a colony, exploited to England's advantage (Marx's pregnant remark that the English Revolution shipwrecked on Ireland still offers food for thought). England at the beginning of the 17th century imported corn; many people starved when harvests were bad. By the end of the century England exported corn, and its population did not know starvation even in the 1690s when Frenchmen and Scots did. England was already on the way to becoming the country of the first Industrial Revolution.

This transformation would have been impossible without the legislation of the revolution, confirmed at the Restoration. The Church of England was subordinated to parliamentary control, as was taxation (and therefore foreign policy). This paid for a vast navy to be used for imperial purposes—three Dutch wars, colonial wars against Spain and France. The freedom of the press and of discussion during the revolution allowed new political, religious and scientific ideas to flourish: 'Newton would have been impossible without the English Revolution', wrote Margaret Jacob. The whole tone of post-Restoration intellectual life was different from that before 1640. Charles II very sensibly became patron of the Royal Society, something inconceivable before 1640. Dissent established itself as a second nation, strongest among merchants and artisans. The ideas of the European Enlightenment are those of the English Revolution—of Harrington, Hobbes, Levellers, Milton and Samuel Fisher. These ideas profoundly influenced the American and French revolutions.

It is absurd to say, as some historians do, that this transformation could have happened without revolution. The new policy necessitated heavy taxation; before 1640 crown and parliament had failed to agree on reorganisation of finance because they could not agree on foreign policy. If parliament voted money for its sort of war, the king spent it on another. After 1660 parliament voted limitless supplies for the navy, none for a standing army, which might threaten a restoration of absolutism.

The influence of Marxism has been visible in relating literature to society. Many literary critics who do not regard themselves as Marxists now recognise that we cannot understand our literature in its greatest century if we do not understand the history, any more than we can understand the history if we ignore the literature. The pioneers were Robert Weimann, Margot Heinemann (see her excellent chapter on 'Political Dawn' in *The Cambridge Companion to English Renaissance Drama*, Cambridge UP, 1990) and A L Morton, but very many others have contributed, few of them Marxists (David Norbrook, Jonathan Dollimore, Martin Butler, Jackie Di-Salvo, Susan Staves, Michael Greenblatt, Michael Wilding). Looking at society as a whole has led to a great flowering of history from below, in which Edward Thompson, Keith Thomas, Peter Burke, Raphael Samuel and Barry Reay have been prominent, again mostly non-Marxists.

Marxism ignored the separate importance of women's history. This failure goes back to Marx himself, who was unable to escape from Victorian values. Much good work has been done by feminists and other women historians, some of them Marxist or Marxist influenced. In the English Revolution women played a prominent part—in the religious sects, as prophetesses, in the Leveller democratic movement; but they made no demands for political rights or equality for themselves. Marxism must incorporate feminist insights before we begin to understand the role of the other 50 percent of the population in the English Revolution.

Marxism has helped to pose useful questions which traditional historiography, concerned with kings and parliaments, state papers and the correspondence of the gentry, had missed. Political events in Eastern Europe seem to me irrelevant to the value of the Marxist interpretation of history, whose dialectic can help historians to escape from economic or demographic determinism. Better understanding of the history of the English people will help us to understand our present society and its problems. There are still barriers of misunderstanding between Marxists and non-Marxists, but Clio has many mansions. Truth, Milton said, may have more shapes than one.

The Soviet historian M A Barg has just published in Moscow a book entitled *The English Revolution of the Seventeenth Century: Three Portraits of its Leading Figures*. It is, most unusually, in English translation. The book's vocabulary is severely Marxist, and it is clumsily translated; but it has illuminating insights into the relationship between historical personalities—Cromwell, Lilburne, Winstanley—and the world in which they lived. Those who do not already know Barg's work might expect Marxism to be deader in the USSR than anywhere; but this book is new, provocative and stimulating. I recommend it to premature mourners for Marxism.

Chapter 32

Protestantism, pamphleteering, patriotism and public opinion

This was a paper given at a conference in Germany, published in Nationale und Kulturelle Identität: Studien zur Entwicklung des Kollektiven Bewusstseins in der Neuzeit *edited by B Gieren.*

My brief for this paper was to consider how the escalation of political and religious pamphleteering during the 16th and 17th centuries fostered the development of 'public opinion' in England and thus contributed to the development of a new kind of cultural and national identity. I find this a difficult subject on which to generalise; I can only offer some thoughts about different aspects of politics and religion during these centuries as they relate to cultural and national identity. I think I see rather complicated connections between the facts and processes which I shall emphasise: I am less sure that I can express them with any clarity.

Politics and religion are of course inseparable in the 16th and 17th centuries; and I do not need in speaking to a German audience to emphasise the importance of the vernacular Bible in forming cultural and national identity: the English are the people of the Book. But I want to look at an earlier strain in the formation of English cultural and national identity.

The Norman Conquest established a French ruling elite in England;

for at least a quarter of a millennium after 1066 the rulers and the ruling class were Frenchmen, speaking French, often owning properties in what we now call France. Kings of England were still trying in the 15th century to become kings of France too.

Our present English language is a fusion of (among other things) French and Anglo-Saxon. These languages were originally spoken by two different classes. The beasts of the field, cows, calves, sheep, pigs, are denominated by teutonic words; those animals when served up for the aristocracy to eat became beef, veal, mutton, pork—delicacies which the lower orders rarely ate. The names by which the Anglo-Saxons called their lower orders—boors, churls, rascals, villains, clowns—are now terms not so much of social as of moral opprobrium in the English language. Base and boorish are contrasted with free, noble and gentle.[1]

From Anglo-Saxon times there has been a continuous literature in 'English', but courtly culture was French. English was legally recognised in 1362, and a newly sophisticated English literature began to appear, with Gower, Chaucer and Langland. The Wycliffite translation of the Bible came a year or two later. Something had happened to English society. What was it?

Among other contributions to the emergence of English as the national language we must include the military necessities of the Hundred Years War against France. Even before the widespread use of gunpowder, the power of the long bow was unhorsing the aristocratic knights whose dominance had hitherto been secure. At Crécy and Agincourt plebeian English archers shot down the chivalry of France: bowmen became the core of the army, in whose language the officers of that army had of necessity to be fluent.

There were economic pressures too. Towns, especially London, were growing in economic importance: merchants spoke English, towns were represented in parliament. The market demanded increasing lay literacy: well before the impact of printing, that meant literacy in English. Language therefore was a class issue. Norman-French survived longer than anywhere else in the law—that bastion protecting the property of the ruling class—of whose mysteries it was undesirable that the plebs should be too well informed.

Down to the 17th century English Revolution—and beyond—the principal popular radical myth was that of the Norman Yoke—that all the woes of England dated from the Norman Conquest, when an alien

---

1. Cf R Williams, *The Long Revolution* (1961), p217.

king and aristocracy overthrew the rights of freeborn Englishmen. But the Normans, wrote Richard Verstegan in 1605, 'could not conquer the English language as they did the land'.[2] The political struggles of the English Revolution turned on restoring these rights, and giving Englishmen laws in a language which they could understand.

The classic exposition is John Hare's *St Edward's Ghost, or Anti-Normanism* (1647). Hare insisted that the language should be purified of Gallicisms. But he also proposed the abolition of 'all laws and usages introduced from Normandy', which would have necessitated major legal and social reforms; and he referred to 'that general and inbred hatred which still dwells in our common people against both our laws and lawyers'.[3] Linguistic patriotism involved class politics. For Gerrard Winstanley in the mid-17th century the enemy was the Norman aristocracy, supported by lawyers and priests. Lawyers had their mumbo-jumbo in law-French; the secret language of priests and universities was Latin.

So we come to religion. Lollardy, the first great English popular heresy, dates from the late 14th century. It centred on reading the Bible, newly translated into English. The strength of the movement was to be found among middle class lay men and women, with support from some gentry and some priests. By definition a movement of English speakers, its leaders emphasised above all preaching, education and discussion in the vernacular, as against the Latin mass and ceremonial. The church was more severe in suppressing vernacular versions in England than anywhere else in Europe (except possibly Bohemia), because in England there was a widely circulating manuscript vernacular translation a century and a half before the Reformation, as there was not, for instance, in France.

Lollardy survived throughout the 15th century, and even expanded; it was subsumed as a radical wing of Protestantism after the Reformation. By that time the spread of literacy and of printing were vital to popular Protestantism.

The Reformation therefore replaced the division between French and English speakers by a division between a gentry ruling class, whether Catholic or Anglican, and lower class popular heresy emphasising preaching and discussion, calling for social reform. There was still no single 'public opinion'. In the liberty of Edward VI's reign grabbers of monastic lands found it expedient to give freer rein to radical Protestantism.

---

2. R Verstegan, *Restitution of Decayed Intelligence* (1605), p22.
3. For Hare see my *Puritanism and Revolution in 17th Century England* (1958), pp79-80.

There were innumerable local presses at work: the later concentration of printing in London and the two universities was a means of conservative control. Pamphlets were illustrated and cheaply produced; the Bible was issued in parts so as to be cheaper and so more accessible to the lower classes. A poet and pamphleteer like the economic and social reformer Robert Crowley deliberately published in cheap editions.[4] The appeal to the people was accompanied by an emphasis on simple prose. Archbishop Cranmer claimed that 'my words be so plain, that the least child...in the town may understand them'.[5] The supreme exponent of the popular style, Hugh Latimer, bishop and martyr, urged in a sermon preached before Edward VI: 'Therefore, you preachers...speak against covetousness and cry out upon it. Stand not ticking and toying at the branches nor at the boughs, for then there will new boughs and branches spring again of them; but strike at the root and fear not these giants of England, these great men and men of power, these men that are oppressors of the poor'.[6] In verse too the popular translators of the Psalms (Sternhold and Hopkins, Crowley) eschewed the Italianate forms of court poetry and adopted ballad metres.

The origins of Henry VIII's Reformation of the 1530s bore little relation to popular Protestantism: the king had earned the title of Defender of the Faith from the pope by attacking Luther. His objects in supporting Reformation were to free himself from dependence on the papacy (so that he could divorce Katharine of Aragon and marry Anne Boleyn) and to plunder the wealth of the church. He intended his Reformation to be an act of state, deriving from parliamentary legislation and the gentry's complicity in looting the monasteries. But to ensure some popular support, and to win intellectual legitimation, he found it necessary to sanction the publication of printed Bibles in English. Once that was done, Protestant doctrines were there for all to discuss. The floodgates had been opened. It was no good trying, as Henry later tried, to abolish 'diversity of opinions'. Statutory prohibition of discussion of the Bible by anyone below the rank of yeoman, or any woman who was not a lady, proved simply unenforceable.

Henry VIII's chief minister, the wily Thomas Cromwell, realised the importance of popular propaganda. He positively encouraged use of ballads, plays and pamphlets against popery. John Bale, future bishop, was one of many who wrote popular plays characterised by plebeian

---

4. J N King, op cit, pp101-102, 129, 152, 327, 345.
5. Ibid, pp139-140, 210, 469-470.
6. *Sermons* (Parker Society, 1844), p247.

scurrility. Most of these plays have been lost, no doubt because later Anglican censors disapproved of them. But Protestant theories of comedy, from Bale to Sir Philip Sidney, helped to elevate the status of the genre.[7]

From the start there was also a spontaneous protest literature—Simon Fish's *Supplication for Beggars* (1529), Henry Brinkelow's *Complaint of Roderick Mors* and *Lamentacion of a Christian against the Citie of London* (1542 and 1545) all called for the church's wealth to be used for the benefit of the poor. Thomas Lever, in a sermon of 1550, made the political point: 'Papistry is not banished out of England by pure religion, but overrun, suppressed and kept under within this realm by covetous ambition... If ye will have a godly Reformation...trust not the servants of Mammon...spoilers of the people, with the setting forth of your godly laws'.[8]

In Edward VI's reign Protestants highjacked the great pioneers of English literature for their cause: Chaucer and Langland were reprinted in many popular editions as proto-Protestants. This was made possible by the presence of a good deal of anti-clericalism in their writings: Bale initially attributed *Piers Plowman* to Wyclif. But it also owed much to attributions to them of anonymous works, some possibly of Lollard origin, which were more clearly heretical. Piers Plowman became a spokesman for the common people against enclosure, and against the misappropriation of monastic lands by the aristocracy and gentry—a demand that was repeated by Gerrard Winstanley during the English Revolution. Spenser self consciously wrote in the tradition of *Piers Plowman*. More important still, John Foxe incorporated Chaucer among the precursors of Protestantism in his best selling *Book of Martyrs*, one of the most influential works of the century. The fact that most of the martyrs burnt in Queen Mary's reign were men and women from the artisan class reinforced Foxe's view that it was simple people from the lower orders who most ardently supported God's cause against the papal Antichrist.[9]

The more enterprising English printers in the mid-16th century seem to have been Protestant by inclination. Printing made it possible for laymen to publicise their views in Edward VI's reign: book production

7.   J N King, *English Reformation Literature: The Tudor Origins of the Protestant Tradition* (Princeton UP, 1982), pp49-50, 93-94, 264-273, 305, and passim; D Norbrook, *Poetry and Politics in the English Renaissance* (1984), esp ch 2.
8.   T Lever, *Sermons* (E Arber (ed), 1901), p95.
9.   J N King, op cit, pp71, 100-101, 322-325, 446-447; J Foxe, *Acts and Monuments of the Christian Church* (J Pratt (ed), no date), II, pp257-263, IV, pp248-250, and passim.

in 1548 was far more than double the average for the last five years of Henry VIII, and went higher in 1550.[10] This explosion anticipates that of the 1640s. Under Mary (1553-8) all these developments were reversed: Protestantism had to go underground. But by then Catholic laymen, including artisans, were also taking part in theological discussions. The Catholic church itself was forced to produce its own English version, first of the New Testament (1582), then of the Old Testament (1609-10). A discussion was ensured from which a public opinion or public opinions were forming. Things would never be quite the same again.

I turn now to a different subject—foreign policy. England, or rather Britain, became an island again. Until the middle of the 16th century English foreign policy had for four centuries been focused almost exclusively on France. But by then the attempt of English kings to conquer France had fizzled out: the loss of Calais in 1558, England's last French possession, merely confirmed the obvious. English policy was reorientated towards the British Isles, turned inwards. Wales was incorporated into England in Henry VIII's reign, and Henry was proclaimed King of Ireland in 1541. Serious colonisation of Ireland by Englishmen and Scots dates from the later 16th century. Comic Welshmen are a stock stage asset in Elizabethan and Jacobean drama: English nationalism is asserting itself against lesser breeds who came to England seeking employment. England's traditional enemy, Scotland, the auld ally of France, became England's ally after Scotland accepted Protestantism; and this was confirmed by the union of the crowns when James VI of Scotland became James I of England in 1603.

But long before that William Cecil had been pursuing a 'British' foreign policy, concentrating on the unity of the British Isles and on sea power.[11] Crowley, editor of *Langland*, was one of the first to propagandise on behalf of 'the island of Great Britain'.[12] Britain became 'the beleaguered isle', an enclave of Protestantism surrounded by Catholic monarchies, supposedly anxious to suppress England's Protestant independence. Patriotism and Protestantism fused. There were allies

10. J W Martin, *Religious Radicals in Tudor England* (1989), citing the unpublished London University PhD thesis of Patricia Took, 'The Publishing Career of Robert Crowley: A Sidelight on the Tudor Book Trade', in *Publishing History*, 14 (1983), pp87-88, and references there cited.
11. J E A Dawson, 'William Cecil and the British Dimension of Early Elizabethan Foreign Policy', *History*, 241 (1989), *passim*; cf H Kearney, *The British Isles: A History of Four Nations* (Cambridge UP, 1989), ch 7.
12. J N King, ' "Phylargie of Greate Bretayne" by Robert Crowley', *English Literary Renaissance*, 10 (1980), pp53-55; C Z Wiener, 'The Beleaguered Isle: A Study of Elizabethan and early Jacobean Anti-Catholicism', *Past and Present*, 51 (1971), *passim*.

among Protestants on the Continent—Dutch rebels fighting against Spain, Huguenot rebels in France—but Elizabeth had no intention of forming such alliances. Her government found itself respectable but increasingly isolated.

The 16th century saw absolute monarchies consolidated on the Continent. England was, in Oliver Cromwell's words, 'happy in being environed with a great ditch',[13] with no land frontiers to defend once Scotland became an ally. It needed neither a standing army nor the bureacracy which went with it. After Henry VIII had dissipated the wealth of the monasteries, no English government could afford such luxuries. So sons of the English gentry lacked the job opportunities open to their Continental equivalents. They became mercenaries in foreign armies, or they took to the sea—as pirates, as colonisers (including colonising Ireland), even as traders. There is a marked shift in English policy—from France to the Atlantic. Richard Hakluyt's *Principal Navigations, Voyages, Traffiques and Discoveries of the English Nation* is as much a document of English patriotic literature as Foxe's *Book of Martyrs*, John Leland's *Itinerary*, John Stow's *Survey of London* and William Camden's *Britannia*. English literature is becoming nationally self conscious; and nationalism now means trade and colonial expansion.

The 1580s mark something of a turning of the ways, an attempt by English conservatives to call a halt to the Reformation. Returned Marian exiles had been incorporated in an episcopal church which was now becoming more confident. From 1572 the Bishops' Bible was striving, not very successfully, to displace the popular Geneva Bible of 1560, which had followed Tyndale in having 'seditious' marginal notes. In 1577 the 'Puritan' Edmund Grindal was sequestrated from his Archbishopric of Canterbury: he was succeeded by the much more conservative John Whitgift in 1583. The invasion of England from the mid-1570s by Jesuit missionaries scared the government into discouraging popular discussion of all sorts. Under Whitgift nonconforming Puritans were steadily extruded from the church, and driven either into exile or underground. The censorship became more severe.

The year 1588-9 saw publication of the illegal *Marprelate Tracts*—witty, irreverent, scurrilous. Their author reverted to the propaganda techniques of Edward VI's reign, but his public saw links reaching even further back: Piers Plowman was called 'grandsire of Martin

---

13. W C Abbott (ed), *Writings and Speeches of Oliver Cromwell* (Harvard UP, 1937-47), IV, p715.

Marprelate'.[14] Discussion was continued by exiled radicals like Thomas Scott in James I's reign and others down to 1640, despite harsh penalties on those who were caught—or their distributing agents.

The lines were being drawn more sharply between traditional radical Protestantism and the state church, the embattled bastion of conservative Protestant nationalism. Thomas Scott's illegal pamphlets argued urgently for international Protestant solidarity, especially in defence of beleaguered Protestants in Thirty Years War Germany. Criticism of the governments of James and Charles I was intensified by their appeasement of Spain when that great power looked like becoming dominant over Europe. Opponents of the court were spoken of as 'the patriots'. Radical Protestantism, deriving from native Lollards, German Anabaptists and Familists, passed ultimately into nonconformity. Meanwhile the popular style, Protestant ballads and plays, fell out of fashion.[15]

The call for an anti-Spanish policy on religious grounds chimed in with commercial designs on the wealth of the New World, still monopolised by Spain. This too was the subject of a propaganda campaign in print. 'Can you do God better service', asked the author of a pamphlet dedicated in 1615 to the Virginia Company, 'than in promoting his kingdom and demolishing daily the power of Satan' in America?[16] A pamphlet of 1650 was more direct in linking religion with commercial aggression. 'Look westward then, ye men of war, thence you may behold a rising sun of glory with riches and much honour, and not only for yourselves but for Christ'.[17] Five years later Oliver Cromwell launched the first state sponsored English invasion of the West Indies, of which he declared 'enlarging the bounds of Christ's kingdom...to be the chief end'.[18]

Confirmation of Charles I's Popish Plot seemed to come in the mid-40s, when Ireland was in full revolt against England. Its armies were commanded by a papal nuncio, sent from Rome for that purpose. One horrible outcome was the brutal Cromwellian conquest of Ireland, with its massacres and transportations. The Irish people found themselves at the receiving end of English Protestant nationalism, with consequences that are still with us.

14. L H Carlson, *Martin Marprelate, Gentleman: Master Job Throckmorton in his Colors* (San Marino, 1981), pp340, 376.
15. J W Martin, *Religious Radicals in Tudor England*, pp10, 30, 35.
16. T Cooper, *The Blessing of Japheth, Proving The Gathering in of the Gentiles and Finall Conversion of the Jewes*, Sig A 2-3.
17. T Thorowgood, *Jewes in America*, Sig c 3v.
18. *Writings and Speeches of Oliver Cromwell*, IV, p713.

Finally, I still have problems about the concept of public opinion. No doubt you have clear definitions: I am sure sociologists have. If there was anything that could be called public opinion before the invention of printing, it is unknowable. But how are we to assess public opinion in censored societies? It is unlikely that everybody accepts the official line, whether of established church or ruling party: but contrary evidence is obtainable only when the censorship is inefficient or when publication abroad is possible—both applied in early Stuart England—or in times of political crisis, when by definition consensus breaks down and there is no single public opinion. Even what seemed to be accepted formulations disintegrated in the melting pot of the 40s and 50s. For a time it seemed to be agreed that parliament's enemy was the Norman Yoke—royal tyranny established in 1066 over the free Anglo-Saxon people. Kings had broken the law and must be subordinated to it. But Levellers said, 'Our very laws were made by our conquerors'; for them the Norman Yoke included the House of Lords. Winstanley thought it included Norman gentry and freeholders. Similarly with the concept of Antichrist. First it was the pope in Rome, then Laud and the bishops, then the king who was believed to be in collusion with Rome; in the civil war royalists were 'the Antichristian party'. For Winstanley the gentry were Antichristian. Some saw Oliver Cromwell as Antichrist. There was no agreement among the king's enemies even on the meaning of the words in which their pamphlets described his misdeeds. Even more difficult: what is public opinion in a post-revolutionary society, like England after 1660, or Russia after Stalin? Does the agreed consensus of the ruling class speak for the whole public? The self made Duke of Albermarle in 1671 assumed that 'the poorer and meaner people have no interest in the commonweal but the use of breath'[19]—the pre-revolutionary view.

---

19. *Observations upon Military and Political Affairs* (1671), p146. Written much earlier, in prison, and published posthumously.

Chapter 33

Freethinking and libertinism: the legacy of the English Revolution

This was a paper delivered at a conference held in Le Moyne University in October 1991. It has not been previously published.

Eighteenth century infidelity—sceptical libertinism—goes back to what used to be called 'the Puritan Revolution'. Whether the one caused the other is a matter for discussion, but that 18th century heterodoxy was anticipated during the English Revolution is easily demonstrated.[1]

First we must recall the circumstances of that revolution. England before 1640 was a society that had never known freedom of discussion. There had been censorship ever since the coincidence in time of the invention of printing with the Protestant Reformation and the translation of the Bible into English. Censorship was not always effective, but it was there as a deterrent, and it was tightened up as revolution approached in the 1630s. All English men and women were deemed to be members of the state church, legally bound to attend services in their parish church every Sunday; it was a legal offence to attend 'conventicles', discussion groups not authorised by the national church.

---

1   See also my *The English Bible and the 17th Century Revolution* (1993) for further evidence of the many statements made here.

Yet the Protestant Reformation and the availability of the Bible in English for an increasingly literate laity had intensified discussions over a whole range of subjects extending well beyond the narrowly theological. How should the church be governed? Should local congregations be subordinated to a national church? Was the English hierarchy of bishops, deans and chapters, and parish clergy authorised in the Bible? Why should all English men and women be legally compelled to pay tithes to a minister whom they had not chosen and whose personality or theology they might detest? Why might not congregations choose their own minister? Was the royal supremacy over the Church of England sanctioned in the Bible?

There was a third coincidence in time—the combination of the Copernican revolution in astronomy with the geographical opening up of America, Africa, and Asia. The world and the universe suddenly seemed very different places. Men became aware of other world religions that could not be dismissed as mere 'heathenism'; and of the possibility that the earth was not the centre of the universe, with all the questions which that raised.

These and related problems had been discussed long before the English government collapsed in 1640. The Protestant state church had always faced a dilemma. The basis of its rejection of Romish traditions had been the appeal to the Bible, the sacred repository of all truth that had at last been made available in print for all to read. But, discussion of the Bible, by the uneducated as well as their betters, led to unorthodoxies that it was impossible to control. Illegal congregations sprang up which rejected the state church; significant numbers of persons emigrated to the Netherlands or to America, often because of dissatisfaction with the Anglican church. Many genuinely felt that 'God was leaving England', his favoured nation since the days of Wyclif and the Reformation of Edward VI and Elizabeth. Charles I and his chief minister, Archbishop Laud, were believed by many to be betraying the Reformation, backsliding to Catholicism. The Thirty Years War (1618-1648) was a catalyst here. There seemed a real danger in the 1620s and 1630s that Protestantism on the continent might be destroyed, and England would not be safe if that happened. Catholic victories were accompanied by a resumption of church lands confiscated at the Reformation. So there were many reasons for opposing the pro-Catholic foreign policy of Charles I and Laud.

There was then much to discuss when censorship and ecclesiastical controls broke down in 1640. Illegal congregations came up from underground, and new ones formed themselves in the unprecedented freedom. In some areas parish churches were deserted. Discussion groups assembled under 'mechanic preachers', artisans who worked six days a week and preached to voluntary congregations on the Sabbath. Discussion, both verbal and in print, was suddenly liberated. Ideas that had long been muttered in alehouses could now be freely aired; and as they were aired they were modified and refined by discussion, and other novelties suggested themselves. It must have been a very exciting time.

Initially discussion started from the Bible, which was agreed by nearly everyone to be the source of all wisdom. But once free discussion prevailed, men and women found that they disagreed in its interpretation. Inevitably the authority of the Bible itself came into question. Milton decided that 'the entire Mosaic Law is abolished'; 'the law is now inscribed on believers' hearts by the spirit'. This licensed all individuals to interpret the Bible for themselves. 'Attention to the requirements of charity is given precedence over any written law'.[2]

Towards the end of Elizabeth's reign inquiring explorers and colonisers like Sir Walter Ralegh and Thomas Hariot were questioning the Bible's status because of its internal contradictions. Christopher Marlowe, with the widest historical and geographical imagination of any Elizabethan dramatist, was associated with their 'school of night', whose members were accused of 'atheism'. ('Atheism' is used during this period to describe any deviation from 'orthodoxy', or any readiness to tolerate.) Hariot said that belief in heaven and hell 'worketh so much in many of the common and simple sort of people that it maketh them to have great respect to their governors'.[3]

How could Cain say, 'every one that finds me shall slay me' when the only other man in the world was his father, Adam? Why should 'the Lord set a mark upon Cain, lest any finding him should kill him'? Verses circulated suggesting that God, the afterlife, heaven and hell, were all 'only bugbears', invented to 'keep the baser sort in fear' and to defend the social order, especially the property of the well to do. Such ideas were not limited to intellectuals. A shoemaker of Sherborne said men in his area (which was also that of Ralegh) thought that hell was poverty in this world. Similar ideas were to surface after 1640; Ranters and others followed Marlowe in arguing from the Bible that

2   J Milton, 'Of Christian Doctrine', in *Complete Prose Works* (New Haven and London, 1953-82), VI: pp368, 521, 526, 537-541, 639-640; cf 'A Treatise of Civil Power', VII: p248; and *Paradise Lost*, XII: pp300-306, 523-524.
3   Simon Shepherd, *Marlowe and the Politics of the Elizabethan Theatre* (Brighton, 1986), p155.

there had been men before Adam.[4]

There was much serious biblical criticism from the early 1640s. John Wilkins, future bishop, decided that the 'penmen of Scripture' might have been grossly ignorant. He thought the biblical miracles could be explained by natural causes.[5] Lord Brooke in his *Discourse of the Nature of...Episcopacie* (1642) asked difficult questions about the authorship of books of the Bible.[6] There were also scholars who had not enjoyed a university education. Thomas Edwards in 1646 described how the radical minister William Erbery, en route for Wales, spoke at an informal meeting in Marlborough. He denied the divinity of Christ, and was taken up by a member of his audience who cited John I.5[7] and other texts against him. Erbery replied: 'Those words were not in the Greek, but put in by some who were against the Arians.' What is remarkable about this story is not that such a conversation arose spontaneously in a pub, where at least one other person had some theological knowledge, but that Erbery could trump his text so effectively. How many such discussions went on unrecorded, all over the country, as men found themselves newly liberated to discuss fundamentals without inhibitions? The Leveller John Wildman in the Putney Debates of 1647 argued that 'it is not easy by the light of nature to determine there is a God. The sun may be that God. The moon may be that God'.[8] The Arminian minister John Goodwin denied the literal authority of the Bible.[9] Before the poet Thomas Traherne went up to Oxford in 1653 he was a conscious sceptic, whose doubts extended to the authority of the Bible.[10]

Others went much further. The communist Gerrard Winstanley anticipated the idea that religion was the opium of the people. 'While men are gazing up to heaven imagining after a happiness or fearing a hell after they are dead, their eyes are put out, that they see not what is their birthrights, and what is to be done by them here on earth while they are living'—as 'indeed the subtle clergy do know.' The Fall of Man, the Incarnation, Crucifixion, Resurrection and Ascension

---

4   See my *The World Turned Upside Down* (Penguin edn) pp144, 163, 174, 201, 205-207, and passim.

5   J Wilkins, *A Discourse Concerning a New World and Another Planet* (1641), pp10-14.

6   Lord Brooke, *A Discourse opening the Nature of that Episcopacie which is exercised in England* (1642), in William Haller (ed), *Tracts on Liberty in the Puritan Revolution*, 3 vols (1934), II, pp119-120.

7   T Edwards, *Gangraena*, 3 vols (1646), I, p78.

8   A S P Woodhouse (ed), *Puritanism and Liberty* (1938), p161.

9   J Goodwin, *Divine Authority of the Scriptures Asserted* (1648), quoted in W Haller (ed), *Tracts on Liberty*, I, pp83-84.

10 G Wade, *Thomas Traherne* (Princeton UP, 1944), pp43-44.

were all allegories for events that take place in the hearts and consciences of men and women. 'The Scriptures were not appointed for a rule to the world to walk by without the spirit...for this is to walk by the eyes of other men.' Of the biblical narrative Winstanley coolly observed: 'whether there were such outward things or no it matters not much.' For Winstanley, as for Marlowe, heaven, hell and the devil have no existence outside human beings.[11]

The London merchant William Walwyn and the Wiltshire clothier Clement Writer used the internal contradictions and inconsistencies of the Bible to argue that it could not be the Word of God. 'The Scripture reports the miracles', wrote Writer. 'Can the miracles reported by Scripture confirm that report?' Writer claimed to write for 'the middle sort and plain hearted people'.[12] The radical John Webster wrote an influential book against belief in witchcraft in which he challenged Fellows of the Royal Society who thought scepticism about witches would lead to scepticism about the existence of God. Webster believed that the Bible had been deliberately mistranslated in order to support belief in witches.[13] Milton insisted that the Bible must be interpreted in accord with 'the duties of human society'. Divine ordinance, he said, 'can bind against the good of man,...yea his temporal good not excluded'.[14]

This sceptical discussion was summed up by the ex-Baptist Quaker Samuel Fisher in a massive tome published in 1660, *The Rusticks Alarm to the Rabbies*, whose title indicates that it represents a lower class response to established religion. But it was also a serious scholarly work, though written in a rollicking, alliterative style. Fisher applied Renaissance standards of textual criticism to the Bible. He concluded that the Bible was 'a bulk of heterogeneous writings, compiled together by men taking what they could find of the several sorts of writings that are therein, and crowding them into a canon or standard for the trial of all spirits, doctrines, truths; and by them alone'.[15] Fisher treated the Bible as a book like any other. He thought it was read too much and quoted too often. That, after a century of Protestant bibliolatry!

Fisher was important because he wrote in the vernacular, in a racy

---

11   See my *The World turned Upside Down*, pp144-145, 177-179, 262.
12   C Writer, *Fides Divina*, quoted in *The World turned Upside Down*, pp265-266.
13   See my, *Religion and Politics in 17th Century England* (Brighton, 1986) pp333-334.
14   J Milton, *Animadversions upon The Remonstrants Defence Against Smectymnuus* (1641), *Complete Prose Works*, I, p699.
15   S Fisher, *The Rusticks Alarm to the Rabbies* (1660), pp296-435; my *The World Turned Upside Down*, p267.

popular style; and no one could accuse him of being an infidel. Only the shutdown of the censorship in the year in which his book was published prevented it from being widely discussed, but we know that it was widely read. Fisher's work became known to Spinoza, as Popkin has shown, and played no insignificant part in stimulating his critique of the Bible.[16] So through him the biblical criticism of the English Revolution found its way into the European Enlightenment. Others who played a part in disseminating Fisher's ideas include Benjamin Furley, whose library at Rotterdam was at the disposal of scholars, and Anthony Collins, whose *Priestcraft in Perfection* (1710) and still more his *Discourse of Free-Thinking* (1713) incorporated Interregnum work on the contradictions and inconsistencies of the Bible.[17]

That religion was politics is very clearly recognised in the 17th century. Francis Osborn pointed out in 1656 that 'the exploding of...belief [in heaven and hell] would be of no less diminution to the reverence of the civil magistrate than the profit of the priesthood'.[18] By May 1661 Samuel Pepys was listening to a mathematician who did not so much 'prove the Scripture false as that the time therein is not well computed or understood'. Robert Boyle in 1663 said that anti-Scripturism 'grows...rife, and spreads...fast'.[19] Six years later John Owen thought that 'no age can parallel that wherein we live' for atheism, unknown in 'these parts of the world...until these latter ages'.[20] That is the sort of thing old men say in every age; but an Italian traveller in England in the same year agreed that 'atheism has many followers in England'.[21] A few years later the author of *The Whole Duty of Man* recognised that atheism was fashionable, and called urgently for defence of the Bible against criticism.[22] The Boyle Lectures were founded for just such a purpose. Swift no doubt exaggerated in 1708 when he said that the body of the people were freethinkers; but many

16 R H Popkin, 'Spinoza, the Quakers and the Millenarians, 1656-1658', in *Manuscrito VI* (Brazil, 1982), p132; 'Spinoza and the Conversion of theJews', in C De Deugd (ed), *Spinoza: Political and Theological Thought* (Amsterdam, 1984), p174.

17 A Collins, *A Discourse of Free-Thinking* (1713), especially pp47-99; cf A Collins, *A Discourse of the Grounds and Reasons of the Christian Religion* (1724). See also T. Ballard (ed),*A Complete Catalogue of the Library of Anthony Collins Esq* (1731), parts 1 and 2, passim; *Biblioteca Furleiana* (Rotterdam, 1714).

18 F Osborn, 'Advice to a Son', in *Miscellaneous Works*, 11th edn, 2 vols (1722), I, pp86, 99.

19 R Boyle, 'Some Considerations Touching the Style of the Holy Scriptures', in T Birch (ed),*The Works of the Honourable Robert Boyle*, 6 vols (1773), II, p295.

20 J Owen, *The Works of John Owen*, (1850-1853), XIII, p364, cf IX, p345 (1672); VIII, pp612-616 (1685).

21 *The Travels of Cosimo III, Grand Duke of Tuscany, through England* (1821).

22 'The Ladies Calling' in *The Works of the Author of* The Whole Duty of Man (1704), pp109-110, 251-269.

similar remarks could be cited.[23]

So widespread was the radical idea that religion had been invented to keep the lower orders in place that defenders of Christianity took it over. Robert South, Bishops Samuel Parker and Gilbert Burnet, and Jeremy Collier all insisted that, irrespective of its truth or falsehood, belief in religion and in rewards and punishments in the afterlife was essential to the maintenance of social subordination. In 1664 Joseph Glanvill dedicated his *Scepsis Scientifica* to the Royal Society, stressing the Society's role in 'securing the foundations of religion against all attempts of mechanical atheism'.[24] In 1681 Bishop Parker, Andrew Marvell's butt, agreed that 'plebeians and mechanics have philosophised themselves into principles of impiety, and read their lectures of atheism in the streets and heighways'.[25] Craftsmen and labourers were 'able to demonstrate...that all things come to pass by an eternal chain of natural causes': human nature was a mere machine.[26] Bishop Burnet convinced the libertine peer Rochester on his death bed that it was wrong to attack Christianity *publicly*.[27]

All this was part of a much wider movement of thought. D P Walker has analysed the decline of belief in hell in this period, and Keith Thomas the decline of casuistry.[28] Many other changes suggest a greater sensitivity to the pain and suffering in others. Torture ceased to be used in judicial proceedings; executions for witchcraft declined gradually as men and women ceased to believe in the direct intervention of the devil in human affairs. Providential history, in which God directly determined events, became old fashioned even for a royalist like Clarendon; Winstanley and Harrington related political to economic change. Calvinism, the dominant trend in English thinking for the previous century, lost its hold over intellectuals; with it declined the belief that the majority of the human race is condemned to spend all eternity in hell, and that there is nothing they can do about it.

The period also saw the end of many once powerful religio-political

---

23   J Swift, 'An Argument to Prove, That the Abolishing of Christianity...may... be attended with some Inconveniences...' in *The Prose Works of Jonathan Swift* (1939-1974), p26 and passim.

24   Quoted in *Change and Continuity in 17th Century England*, rev edn (1991), p259.

25   S Parker, *A Demonstration of the Divine Authority of the Law of Nature, and of the Christian Religion* (1681), ppiii-iv.

26   E N Hooker, 'Dryden and the Atoms of Epicurus', in H T Swedenborg Jr (ed), *Essential Articles for the Study of John Dryden* (Hamden CT, 1966), p241.

27   G Burnet, 'The Life and Death of...John Earl of Rochester', in *The Lives of Sir Matthew Hale,...Wilmot, Earl of Rochester; and Queen Mary* (1774), pp58, 76-79.

28   K V Thomas, 'Cases of Conscience in 17th Century Europe', in J Morrill, P Slack and D Woold (eds), *Public Duty and Private Conscience in 17th Century England: Essays Presented to G E Aylmer* (OUP, 1993).

myths. A scholarly consensus had expected the millennium to come in or around the 1650s; Milton's 'shortly expected king' of 1641 assumed this. George Fox had called on Oliver Cromwell to overthrow Antichrist—one of the necessary preludes to the end of the world—by invading France and Spain and going on to sack Rome, Antichrist's headquarters. Marvell urged the Protector to extend the British Empire in order to expedite the millennium. But later in the century, though Dryden and many other poets advocated imperialist expansion, the millenarian motive had disappeared. Antichrist had been a symbolic hate figure under which radicals subsumed everything which they detested in English society. By 1664 Henry More sneered at 'the rude and ignorant vulgar' who 'have so fouled' the words Antichrist and Antichristian that they are now 'unfit to pass the lips of any civil person'.[29] The rude and ignorant went on talking about Antichrist at least until the time of William Blake.

In 1660 bishops and church courts came back; parsons were restored to their parochial livings, and tithes were maintained to pay them. 'If there was not a minister in every parish', Robert South told the lawyers of Lincoln's Inn in 1660, 'you would quickly find cause to increase the number of constables'.[30] But it proved impossible to root out dissent and maintain a single national church. Excommunication ceased to be a serious punishment when men and women could simply transfer to another congregation. Nottinghamshire employers told their workers in 1675 that the worst penalty that church courts could impose on them if they refused to pay tithes on their wages was excommunication, 'which was only their not going to church'.[31] Roger L'Estrange, the great harrier of Dissenters, had to admit by 1668 that juries would not convict the authors of what he regarded as gross libels on the bishops and clergy of the Church of England.[32] 'The most effectual (not to say the most fashionable) argument for liberty of conscience', Henry Stubbe suggested in 1673, was lack of religious belief.[33] The Toleration Act of 1689 was the reluctant recognition of this fact. Dissenters won freedom of worship, though not political equality.

A different trend leading to sceptical libertinism was antinomianism.

---

29 H More, A Modest Enquiry into the Mystery of Iniquity (1664), Sig A3v.
30 R South, Sermons Preached upon Several Occasions (1737), I, p131. South had previously written panegyrics upon Cromwell.
31 Economic Problems of the Church (1968), p86.
32 Quoted by R L Greaves, Enemies under his Feet: Radicals and Nonconformists in Britain, 1664-1677 (Stanford, 1990), pp176-178.
33 H Stubbe, A Further Justification of the Present War Against the United Netherlands (1673), pp70-71.

The Protestant emphasis on the priesthood of all believers established a direct connection between the faithful and God. During the Interregnum this was extended to mean that whatever one's own conscience told one to do must be God's will. In Milton's summary, 'the practice of the saints interprets the commandments.' And, he added, 'we are released from the decalogue', which he did not believe to be a faultless code. We ought 'to believe what in our own consciences we apprehend the Scripture to say, though the visible church with all her doctors gainsay'.[34] The Ranter Laurence Clarkson extended this argument slightly but very significantly when he said, 'No matter what Scripture, saints or churches say, if that within thee do not condemn thee, thou shalt not be condemned.' Unlike Milton, Clarkson suggests that the Bible does not matter. Other Ranters denounced the Bible as the cause of all quarrels and bloodshed in the world. Thomas Tany thought that there would never be peace till all Bibles were burned. He burnt one in a public demonstration.

Clarkson used the supremacy of the individual conscience to legitimise sexual libertinism. 'There is no such act as drunkenness, adultery and theft in God... Sin hath its conception only in the imagination... What act soever is done by thee in light and love, is light and lovely, though it be that act called adultery.' 'Till you can lie with all women as one woman, and not judge it sin, you can do nothing but sin... No man could attain to perfection but this way'.[35] Clarkson revealed that at one time or another God had told him to break all the commandments except 'Thou shalt do no murder'; and he wondered whether and when that would be added to the list. Clarkson practised what he preached, sleeping with any 'maid of pretty knowledge' who was willing.[36]

The Ranter Abiezer Coppe agreed that 'sin is finished'. 'Wanton kisses', he claimed, 'have been made the fiery chariot to mount me into the bosom of...the King of Glory... I can...kiss and hug ladies, and love my neighbour's wife as myself, without sin'.[37] God's service, Coppe said, is 'perfect freedom and pure libertinism'. He was not using 'libertinism' as a mere synonym for 'freedom'. He knew very well the specifically sexual sense that it could have. Coppe indeed went out of his way to shock the prudish. Being 'dead drunk every day of the week' and lying 'with whores i' th' market place' were no worse sins than the

---

34   J Milton, *Complete Prose Works*, VI, pp525-526.
35   L Clarkson, *A Single Eye* (np, 1650), pp6-16.
36   My *The World Turned Upside Down*, pp214-216, 315.
37   Ibid, pp210-213, 315.

clergy's grinding the faces of the poor by forcing them to pay tithes.[38] Coppe was not original: there had been 'libertines' in Essex in 1551, and later men there who denied the existence of 'sin'.[39]

The legend of gloomy Puritans who hated pleasure dies hard. But nothing could be less true of the radical revolutionaries, whose maxim might have been, 'Life, liberty, and the pursuit of happiness'. Milton and the Leveller Richard Overton, like Thomas Hobbes and many others, believed that the soul was mortal; happiness was to be sought on earth—a doctrine that contemporaries associated with libertinism. The Diggers expected 'Glory here!'—heaven on earth and only on earth. Mortalism removed the fear of eternal torment in hell, which was one reason why it appealed to Lodowick Muggleton.[40] Milton believed that matter was good, since it had been created out of the substance of God; it and the pleasures of the senses were to be enjoyed. In *Paradise Lost* the angels eat, digest and excrete their food, and interpenetrate sexually, though in an appropriately angelic manner. Adam and Eve made physical love before the Fall—'whatever hypocrites austerely talk', Milton added, to show that he knew how unorthodox he was being. 'The happier Eden' was Adam and Eve 'emparadised in one another's arms'. It was Voltaire who noted that Milton was the first to speak in favour of romantic love; Adam chose to fall because he could not conceive of living without Eve, even in Paradise. Hobbes believed that human actions were motivated by the pursuit of pleasure and avoidance of pain. Ranters thought sin was finished and ended, and Coppe conducted a campaign against sexual repression.[41] So radicals came to use the appeal to the individual conscience to justify what conservatives thought socially intolerable sexual conduct.

Ranters thought the Scripture a tale, a history, a dead letter. The Christ who died at Jerusalem was nothing to them: Christ is in all believers. Ranters were not isolated extremists. They won some sympathy by making themselves spokesmen for the poor. John Bunyan, always a passionate defender of the rights of the poor, was for a time under Ranter influence. They brought him to wonder 'whether the holy Scriptures were not rather a fable and cunning story than the holy and

---

38 A Coppe, A *Fiery Flying Roll* (1650), in A Hopton (ed), *Selected Writings* (1987), pp16, 22.
39 R H Hilton, *The English Peasantry in the Later Middle Ages* (Oxford 1975), p24; J B Horst, *The Radical Brethren* (Nieuwkoop, 1972), p134.
40 *Milton and the English Revolution* (Penguin edn), pp317-323.
41 Ibid, pp456, 468.

pure Word of God...' How could we know that the Bible was true and the Koran false? (The Koran had been translated into English in 1649.) The Bible might have been 'written by some politicians, on purpose to make poor ignorant people to submit to some religion and government.' 'Paul...being a subtle and cunning man, might give himself up to deceive others with strong delusions.' 'How if all our faith, and Christ, and Scriptures, should be but a think-so?' And Bunyan had worse thoughts which even many years later he dared not utter.[42]

His Ranter friends condemned Bunyan as 'legal and dark; pretending that they only had attained to perfection that could do what they would and not sin'. (That, as we have seen, was Clarkson's doctrine; and Bunyan found it 'suitable to my flesh...I being but a young man, and my nature in its prime.')[43] Although Bunyan came to reject Ranter libertinism, it continued to haunt him. Many of the characters in *The Pilgrim's Progress*, *The Holy War* and *Mr Badman* have recognisable Ranter characteristics. Bunyan was still arguing against the Ranter view that God had not created the world in a treatise on which he was working at the time of his death.

It is not surprising that the Blasphemy Act of 1650 was directed mainly against Ranters, as Coppe himself recognised. They advocated behaviour that was disruptive of existing social norms and standards; even Milton, himself often described as a libertine, approved of the Blasphemy Act. Ranters were suppressed, and Coppe was compelled to recant. Clarkson became a Muggletonian.

By 1660 the radical revolutionaries were hopelessly split among themselves, and exhausted by their failure to agree. In *Areopagitica* Milton had optimistically anticipated that free discussion would lead to agreement, consensus, on what the Word of God said. Alas. For Winstanley the Bible demonstrated the natural rights and natural equality of all men; recognition of that would—he thought—lead all to accept a communist society. Levellers agreed about natural rights, but thought that private property was sacred. Then the question arose whether the very poor could be trusted with the vote. Some radicals wanted the godly to rule; others addressed themselves to copyholders and artisans, regardless of their godliness. Bishops came back with the king in 1660 to restore order and discipline.

---

42 J Bunyan, *Grace Abounding* (OUP, 1977), pp16-17, 31-32; My *A Turbulent, Seditious and Factious People: John Bunyan and his Church* (Oxford, 1988), pp75-77.
43 J Bunyan, *Grace Abounding*, p17.

So after 1660 the Bible lost its overriding political authority as a book whose texts could solve all problems. God himself was on trial after the Restoration: Milton's task of justifying the ways of God to men was highly topical. An empiricist pragmatism fitted the state of affairs: the events of 1649 and 1660 seemed to have happened of their own accord. Harrington's political theory made better sense than that of the Levellers: the crude fact was that property ownership had been decisive over the wishes both of the majority and of the godly minority. Harrington's emphasis on the balance of property and Hobbes's emphasis on the brutal facts of power undermined radical democratic theories.

The Restoration of 1660 had been a compromise between royalists and parliamentarians in which many of the revolution's achievements acceptable to conservatives had been preserved—parliamentary control of taxation and the church, abolition of feudal tenures, confirmation of the Navigation Act and of the aggressive colonial foreign policy which it envisaged, continuity of the huge navy now financed by taxes voted by parliament. Charles II and James II tried to set back the clock to 1640 to destabilise the settlement of 1660; 1688 confirmed that settlement, whilst establishing the legend that it merely restored the old English constitution.

As I have tried to show, the crucial significance of the events of the 1640s and 1650s in establishing the post-1688 constitution was hushed up. Much literature was published in the 1690s and later dealing with party politics, political manoeuvring, corruption, etc; but those who mattered in politics after 1688 had no desire to revive the wider issues discussed in the 1640s and 1650s. Protagonists of the 18th century Enlightenment quoted the English constitution as interpreted by Locke rather than the ideas of the English Revolution. It was conservatives like Swift, Atterbury, and the Lower House of Convocation who kept insisting that 1688 was a pale reflection of 1641, and that the atheism and licentiousness of the Augustan age derived from the radicals of the Interregnum.[44] Those contemporaries who stressed connections between the 1640s and 1690s were those who wished to denigrate radical ideas. When I use the phrase 'hush up', I mean that whilst conservatives exaggerated and generalised wildly in smearing all republicans with 'enthusiasm' (irrational) or 'extremism' (dangerous), radicals were too

44 See, for example, Swift's 'Sermon upon the Martyrdom of Charles I', *The Prose Works*, vol IX; and *The Representation of the Present State of Religion Among Us, With Regard to the Late Excessive Growth of Infidelity and Heresy and Profaneness* (1711).

prudent to stress the origin of their ideas in the regicide republic. It would have been bad form and counterproductive.

Yet the ideas survived verbally. In 1709 Edward Ward's *History of the London Clubs* suggested that 'the wicked seeds of sedition and dissension are speedily disseminated among the weaker brethren' in these clubs. 'Nor...have there been any plots or conspiracies in any reign but what have been first hatched and nourished in these sorts of societies.' According to Ward, 'the Atheistical Club', whose members regarded themselves as 'generous restorers of the people's liberty', urged 'all men' to 'set up to be their own master, and cast off the yokes of lawful authority'.[45]

After 1660 slowly and reluctantly the religious sects abandoned the quest for political power and accepted the position of second class citizens in return for religious toleration—intermittent until 1689. Quakers proclaimed the peace principle in 1661 and withdrew from direct political action. This had important consequences from our point of view. Henceforth Quaker writings were self censored: the fierce demands of Fox and other Quaker leaders that Oliver Cromwell should lead his armies to conquer Rome disappeared. There is nothing about them in Fox's *Journal*: in the many reprints of Quaker writings in the late 17th and early 18th century their earlier bellicosity was suppressed. It has had to be rediscovered by modern scholars.

It was not only Quakers. When in 1698-9 John Toland printed Edmund Ludlow's *Memoirs* he carefully omitted the old republican's revolutionary millenarianism and hankering after a dictatorship of the godly, whilst retaining his critique of standing armies, so relevant to the politics of the 1690s. In Toland's version Ludlow seemed to be a Williamite Whig. Toland may well have similarly bowdlerised Algernon Sidney's *Discourses Concerning Government* when he published them in 1698. Middle of the road parliamentarians, whose works had hitherto been suppressed, were printed or reprinted. But even the lapse of the Licensing Act in 1695 did not lead to republication of the writings of Levellers, Diggers, Ranters, or Fifth Monarchists. Publishers with an eye on the market censored themselves here: this was more effective than government censorship had ever been. In Toland's *Life of Milton*, for example, there is barely a hint of his very dangerous religious heresies; and his defence of regicide and his republicanism are played down. Together with Addison's deliberate sanitising of Milton, this helped to create the image of Milton as the orthodox

---

45   E Ward, *The History of the London Clubs* (1709).

Puritan and radical Whig that confused critical views of him until relatively recently.[46]

Radical traditions survived but did not get into print. Benjamin Furley, free thinking Quaker heretic, friend of Sydney, Locke, and the Third Earl of Shaftesbury, who died in 1714, played a big part in Toland's intellectual development in the Netherlands in 1693. In Rotterdam Furley had a famous library of heretical books by most of the great English republicans and democrats, including two works by Gerrard Winstanley, and others by Lilburne, Clement Writer, Coppe and other Ranters, John Webster, Roger Williams, Sir Henry Vane, early Quakers, and Muggletonians.[47] Biblical criticism from the revolutionary decades survived through Fisher mediated by Spinoza, and was summed up by Toland's *Christianity not Mysterious* (1696) for which Toland was twice unsuccessfully prosecuted by the clergy.[48] In his last book Edward Thompson has established the survival into the 18th century of political antinomianism: he lists many books by Ranters and Muggletonians which were reprinted in the mid and later 17th century: 18th century antinomianism, he argues, was 'an artisan or tradesman stance', nourishing a 'robust anti-Court and sometimes republican consciousness'.[49]

By the end of the century the Bible had lost its uniquely authoritative position as a guide to action in all spheres of life. Hobbes's sceptical attitude towards the Bible and religion in general contributed to the unbelief fashionable at the court of Charles II. 'To say [God] hath spoken to him in a dream', Hobbes remarked, 'is no more than to say he dreamed that God spake to him... So that, though God Almighty *can* [my italics] speak to a man by dreams, visions, voice and inspiration, yet he obliges no man to believe that he hath so done to him that pretends it, who (being a man) may err, and (which is more) lie.' Hobbes's wit was no less lethal, his use of brackets no less telling, when they were turned against the clergy's claim that they had a divine right to collect tithes from their flock: 'Of the maintenance of our Saviour and his Apostles, we read only that they had a purse (which was carried by Judas Iscariot).' 'The Apostleship of Judas is

46 My *The Experience of Defeat: Milton and Some Contemporaries*, ch 10.
47 *Biblioteca Furliana* (Rotterdam, 1714), and my *The World turned Upside Down*, ch 11.
48 M Jacob, *The Newtonians and the English Revolution, 1689-1720* (Cornell UP, 1976), p216. Professor Jacob describes Toland as a Protestant for political reasons though not a Christian.
49 E P Thompson, *Witness Against the Beast: William Blake and the Moral Law* (Cambridge, 1993). Thompson associated Blake with the antinomian tradition.

called (Acts I.20) his bishopric'.[50] Hobbes's conviction that belief in rewards and punishments in the afterlife destabilised society and the state perhaps contributed to the decline of this belief as a motive for political action towards the end of our period.

Restoration comedy took over, less seriously, much of the sceptical libertinism that had been so earnestly discussed in the 1640s and 1650s. When Lady Brute in Vanbrugh's *The Provoked Wife* (1697) was told that the Bible said man must return good for evil, her reply came pat: 'That may be a mistake in the translation.' The former royalist Samuel Butler denied the Scriptures to be the Word of God and used Hobbesian arguments against miracles.[51] Rochester attacked the contradictions of the Bible even on his deathbed; he still thought that all came by nature. The stories of the creation and fall were parables. He had doubts about rewards and punishments after death and rejected monogamy.[52] We may also include Aphra Behn as a sceptical freethinker. Her *Oroonoko*, published in 1688 but written earlier, is one of the earliest noble savage stories, and perhaps the first significant English novel, if we except *The Pilgrim's Progress*. Oroonoko's honour and truthfulness are contrasted with the deceit and treachery of Christians (except for a Frenchman who was 'a man of little religion, yet he had admirable morals and a brave soul'). The Trinity made Oroonoko laugh. To introduce Christianity into the West Indies, Aphra Behn wrote (and she had lived there), would 'but destroy that tranquillity they possess by ignorance; and laws would but teach 'em to know offences of which now they have no notion'.[53]

In 1695 an Oxford Master of Arts published a letter to a nobleman in London in which he solemnly discussed 'some errors about the creation, general flood and the peopling of the world'. 'The most rational way to examine these problems', he insisted, 'is by the laws of gravity, or by the hydrostatics.' The biblical accounts are unacceptable: 'the present age will not endure empty notions and vague speculations... We presently call for clear proof or ocular demonstration.' 'The universal disposition of this age is bent upon a rational religion'.[54] A century earlier the surreptitious discussion of such matters in Ralegh's circle was denounced as 'a school of atheism'.

50 T Hobbes, *Leviathan* (Everyman edn), pp411, 475, 564, 557.
51 S Butler, *Prose Observations*, (Hugh de Quehen(ed), OUP, 1979); pp85, 124.
52 G Burnet, *Life of Rochester*, pp18-58.
53 L P, 'Two Essays', in *Somer's Tracts* (1748-1751), XI, pp291-308.
54 A Behn, 'Oroonoko, or the Royal Slave', in Montague Summers (ed), *Works of Aphra Behn* (1915), V, pp157-166, 175, 196 and passim.

Now the Master of Arts did not even think them worth arguing about.

There was no English Enlightenment in the 18th century because the job had been done in the 17th century: the ideas of the European (and Scottish) Enlightenment derive from the biblically inspired discussions of the English Revolution, though by the end of the century its more extreme ideas had been purged from printed memory. I stress printed. For what got into print depended on what publishers thought would sell. Unprintable, 'extreme' ideas from the legacy of the revolution were no doubt discussed in clubs like Toland's secret society, which 'designedly shunned the multitude' and respected the laws that protected property. It was a select dining club as well as a conspiratorial society, whose credo and programme were published in Latin in 1720, and in English translation only in 1751.[55] A more plebeian club was the Robin Hood Society, where tailors, bakers, butchers, and shoemakers met to air (among other things) their doubts about the Bible.[56] The radical Whigs, Thomas Hollis and Richard Baron, who in the mid-18th century were accused of religious heterodoxy, were men steeped in the writings of the 17th century English radicals. It was Catharine Macaulay's republican *History of England in the 17th Century* (8 vols, 1763-83) that taught radicals that history did not begin in 1688.[57] But even at that late date there was irrational opposition to her case. Every opportunity was taken to insinuate either that a woman could not have written the *History*, or alternatively that she shouldn't have. Every opportunity was taken to stress the eccentricities of her private life rather than her very relevant message.

---

55 Toland, *Pantheisticon* (English translation, 1751), pp9-6, 57-59, 70, 95-107 and passim; cf E Ward, *The History of the London Clubs*, quoted above.

56 R Lewis, *The Robin Hood Society: a Satire by Peter Pounce* (1756), pp v-vi, 19, 79.

57 B Hill, 'The Republican Virago', *the Life and Times of Catharine Macaulay, Historian* (1992), chs 3 and 8.

Chapter 34

Popular religion in 17th century England

This article was first published in Early Modern History, *Vol 1, No 2, January 1992.*

Some of the most exciting work on English history recently has been written about 'history from below'—the history of ordinary men and women, not of kings and queens, prime ministers and parliaments, or of 'the county community' of the gentry to the exclusion of the majority of occupants of counties. In the history of 17th century England 'history from below' has necessarily included a reconsideration of popular religion. In the 17th century it was impossible to separate religion from politics: church and state were one. Before 1640 all Englishmen and women were members of the state church, legally bound to attend their parish church every Sunday, to listen to the preaching of a minister in whose appointment they had no say and whose theology or personality they might detest. They had to pay 10 percent of their earnings to maintain him, whether they liked it or not. Proposals to abolish tithes, often made by radicals, would have meant abolishing a state church, since if ministers were left to depend on the voluntary contributions of their parishioners few would have been likely to survive. Milton thought the abolition of tithes was essential if religious freedom was to be established in England. The Quaker Anthony Pearson said that tithes should have been chopped off with the king's head. The censorship—strict in theory if not always efficient in practice—was run by the church. Church courts punished 'sin', which then, as now, usually meant sex. Anyone who wished to worship in ways different from those of the state church had to break the law—to join underground conventicles, or else to emigrate if he or she could afford it.

All this changed in the 1640s. Censorship collapsed. Control by church and government collapsed. We can now hear ordinary people talking in their own words for the first time—not as their betters described them with fear and contempt. One of the few things we have learnt to avoid is talking patronisingly of religious radicals as 'the lunatic fringe' in the revolutionary decades. This phrase tended to be used in the past about any ideas which were outside the normal experience of Oxbridge common rooms: the communism of the Diggers, the sceptical libertinism of the Ranters, the social protest of Anabaptists and Quakers, the class awareness of John Bunyan. Such protests were often expressed in biblical language, but that does not necessarily make it lunatic. What we should look for is the social content of the religious ideas expressed in the years before the censorship closed down again in 1660.

In the 1640s there was a fantastic printing explosion. The London bookseller, George Thomason, who realised he was living in a remarkable age, collected a copy of every book, pamplet and newspaper published. In 1640 he collected 22 books or pamphlets, in 1642 nearly 100 times as many, and he averaged over 1,000 titles a year until 1660. In 1640 it was illegal to publish a newspaper; by 1645 there were over 700 in existence. Books on every subject were published, because people wanted to buy and read them: they had long been starved of reading matter.

Before the Long Parliament met in November 1640, a London crowd had released prisoners from Archbishop Laud's jail; in May 1641 Londoners clamoured for the execution of the hated Earl of Strafford, and frightened the king into agreeing to it. Like the East European crowds seen on TV in 1989, these Londoners knew what they were determined to get rid of rather than what they should put in its place; and they were certainly not manipulated by ideologically motivated agitators.

What we call religious congregations—discussion groups would be the modern equivalent—sprang up everywhere in the new liberty of assembly. They met in pubs or private houses for want of better places. They selected their own 'mechanic preacher' as chairman, and discussed whatever interested them. Historians anachronistically apply sectarian labels like 'Congregationalist' or 'Baptist' to these groups, but such labels had little meaning before 1660. We don't know how to label even such well documented figures as Oliver Cromwell, Milton and Bunyan. The groups were fluid; individuals moved from one group to another, sermon tasting, discussing, arguing, as Milton described them with pride in *Areopagitica*.

A recent historian thought he had proved that the 'Ranters' to whom contemporaries referred in the years 1649-51 did not exist, because he could find no Ranter organisation, no agreed Ranter theology, no accepted Ranter leaders. By the same arguments we could prove that Baptists, Congregationalists and Quakers did not exist, nor indeed Levellers. Only after 1660 was organisation forced on what we may then begin to call sects. In England after 1640 secret groups came up from the semi-underground, like the Yorkshire Grindletonians, and others in what had once been Lollard areas. Many popular heretical traditions must have survived. George Fox's mother descended from Marian martyrs; so, it was believed, did the family of Margaret Fell, who was to become Fox's wife. When the New Model Army entered the former royalist territory of the north of England at the end of the civil war, such groups welcomed it; and the army offered the strongest support for toleration down to the Restoration of 1660.

In this world of excitement and free speculation opened up by the revolution, many people—especially after the execution of King Charles I in 1649—expected the coming of King Jesus, to inaugurate the millennium. This was not the idea of a 'lunatic fringe', as it would be today: the greatest scholars of the century, from John Napier (inventor of logarithms) to Isaac Newton, applied themselves to interpreting the prophetic books of the Bible, in which the course of human history was believed to be laid out. By the early 17th century a consensus had been reached that the 1650s seemed a likely date for the 'last times'. This idea was popularised by parliamentarian propagandists, who had to persuade men to fight against the king. What higher cause than to fight against those whose religious policies were delaying the Second Coming? 'Who would not be glad to see Jesus Christ?' asked John Cook, later to be Charles I's prosecutor at his trial for treason against the English people. When Milton in 1641 called Christ the 'shortly expected King', he was probably thinking in terms of a dozen or so years.

Milton—a sober intellectual, no irrational enthusiast—thought that the coming millennium would mean 'an end to all earthly tyrannies', a decent society in which the saints would rule rather than the ungodly. George Fox looked forward to the imminent rule of the saints, 'whereof I am one', he declared ominously. John Cook thought the king's trial was a foretaste of the last judgement, in which the saints would sit in judgement on God's enemies. Milton agreed. If the millennium was approaching in the near future, there was no need for sectarian organisation. The saints must prepare for the coming good society. But congregations of the radical godly remained disunited, and divided amongst themselves. 'Mechanic preachers' had their own little congregations, only occasionally and loosely linked with other groups. Countless itinerant preachers toured the countryside, establishing new links but no settled organisation. After 1649 the republican government (effectively dominated by the army grandees) allowed religious toleration but suppressed secular radicals like the democratic republican Levellers (suppressed 1649), the libertarian communist Diggers (suppressed 1650), and the sceptical libertine Ranters (suppressed 1651).

There was much disillusionment in the 1650s, when the high hopes raised in the 1640s had been dashed. Bishops and church courts had indeed been abolished, and a degree of religious toleration established. But the millennium had not come. The programmes of the millenarian groups of the 1650s—Fifth Monarchists, Quakers, Muggletonians —had much in common with the programmes of the suppressed secular radicals: defence of the interests of the poor, criticism of the law and demands for its reform, refusal of respect to social superiors and magistrates by doffing the hat and referring to them as 'you' rather than 'thou'. Quakers and other radicals had concentrated on trying to alert English citizens to the imminence of the millennium—by gestures like interrupting church services, 'going naked for a sign' (except for a loin cloth for decency's sake), or like James Nayler's symbolic entry into Bristol in imitation of Christ's entry into Jerusalem. Thomas Tany and others publicly burnt Bibles because the text was idolised rather then the spirit of Christ within believers. Quakers spoke of 'steeplehouses' because only the congregations of believers deserved the name of church. When Nayler was savagely attacked in the 1656 parliament, army officers were his stoutest defenders. In return, Quakers proved to be the last supporters of military dictatorship in 1659-60. In the years after 1654 Quaker numbers increased rapidly. Their intentions were unknown, but their radical politics and close association with the army led to panic reactions amongst conservatives. Fear of Quakers had a great deal to do with the rapid restoration of Charles II to the throne of his fathers in 1660—much to his astonishment.

Revolutionary millenarianism did not long survive the Restoration. The expected dates in the 1650s and 1666 came and went. In December 1659 the Baptists announced that they would be obedient in civil matters to whatever government was established in England. They were rebuked by the Quaker Richard Hubberthorne for betraying the Lord's cause and giving Charles II a blank cheque. But the Quakers too were rethinking—13 months and one unsuccessful Fifth Monarchist revolt later they announced the peace principle, by which they bound themselves not to resort to 'the carnal sword' for political ends.

The overwhelming wave of public opinion on whose crest Charles II was wafted home in 1660 seemed to Quakers and other radicals a demonstration that historical events were determined by God, not by the efforts of men. It was some time before pacifism was accepted by the whole Society of Friends: there were splits, resignations and backslidings, and some Quakers even fought for Monmouth in 1685. But ultimately pacifism and abstention from active politics were established as norms, and internal organisation made it possible to determine who was and who was not a Quaker.

Some preachers who were to be dissenters after 1660 had accepted livings in the tolerant Cromwellian state church. Among them was the pastor of what was to become Bunyan's congregation in Bedford. Quakers—most determinedly not a sect—were perhaps the first to get organised nationally. But their emphasis on the inner light in all believers was inherently anarchistic: some of them objected to fixed times and places for meetings. Only after Charles II sat on the throne which King Jesus had been expected to occupy did Quakers decide that the millennium was not imminent, and adopt the peace principle.

This evolution was shared by other sects. There were some dissenter plots against the government, which R L Greaves has traced in detail (*Deliver Us from Evil: the Radical Underground in Britain, 1660-1663* (OUP, 1986); *Enemies under his Feet: Radicals and Nonconformists in Britain, 1664-1677* (Stanford University Press, 1990)). But although such plotting alarmed governments, the results were minimal until Monmouth's rebellion in 1685, which had much support from dissenters. In 1688 William of Orange prudently brought a large army with him which was at least as important in discouraging radical republican revolt as in disposing of James II.

After 1660 popular religion could not be driven back underground or into exile, though many dissenters voluntarily left the country. Intermittent persecution forced organisation upon dissenters. Refugees moved from one county to another, where friends or religious associates gave them financial support; so experience was pooled. The government unintentionally helped to organise dissent by its declarations of indulgence, which licensed congregations through their ministers, who could be held responsible for their good behaviour. The day of mechanic preachers was over. The government's erratic religious policies sometimes brought groups of ministers together in jail, where they had opportunity to overcome their disagreements and plan the organisation of their sect for the future, as Bunyan and some of his co-religionists did in the 1660s. Before his imprisonment in 1661 Bunyan had fiercely attacked Quakers; after the shared experience of jail it was a Quaker who helped to get Bunyan released. The Restoration government's Act of Settlement put an end to the wanderings of itinerant preachers (including women) as well as of vagabonds looking for work.

The same retreat from millenarianism affected all those whom we must now call dissenters. Independents and especially Presbyterians bitterly resented their exclusion from the Church of England, of which they claimed to be the true representatives; but the Declarations of Indulgence of Charles II and James II were open only to congregations licensed by the government, and the licence allotted a sectarian label to each congregation. Bunyan's congregation had great difficulty in deciding whether it was 'Baptist' or 'Congregationalist'.

The price which dissenters had to pay for worshipping as they thought God wished was exclusion from central and local government, and from the universities. This meant that they lost the gentry supporters who had been extremely influential in pre-1640 Puritanism. No gentleman could afford not to play his part in governing his county as a JP, or to be deprived of the possibility of standing for election to the House of Commons. Dissenters probably got a better education at their dissenting academies than they would have done at Oxford or Cambridge; the academies were more modern, more scientific, less classics bound. But they lacked the social cachet which only Oxford and Cambridge could give. The sons of gentry non-conformists reverted to the Church of England. Some dissenters went to Scottish universities, or to Leiden or Padua for medicine.

So there were two nations—Anglicans, and dissenters. Dissenters were second class citizens, forced to turn their energies to industry and money making. The wealth of London dissenters made them financially useful to governments; the economic argument for religious toleration was at least as effective as any other in ultimately bringing about the Toleration Act of 1689. Bunyan, and many Baptists and Quakers, had always been passionately on the side of the poor against the rich. But dissenting ministers, lacking the tithes which maintained clergy of the state church, had to be paid by the voluntary contributions of their flocks; so ministers could not afford to offend their richer members. All this contributed to a passive acceptance of an increasingly prosperous society.

Many dissenters emigrated—conservatives to New England, radicals to the West Indies. In England some Leveller and Ranter ideas survived, but have left little trace in the censored literature of the later 17th century. We obtain glimpses—in Blake's writings, for instance, especially his *Milton*. Goldsmith praised the Levellers. The radical Whig Thomas Hollis gave a copy of Gerrard Winstanley's *The Law of Freedom* to Henry Fielding. But in the course of the 17th century the intellectual climate changed, secularised. Milton wrote his *De Doctrina Christiana* in Latin because he hoped it would reunite European Protestantism on a new radical basis. After his death his executors, knowing it was too hot to publish in England, tried to get it into print in the Netherlands, in Latin. The whole power of British diplomacy was brought to bear, and the dangerous text was safely hidden away among the state papers. When it was rediscovered it was published in 1825, on the orders of the king, translated by a bishop. The dynamite of the 1670s was now a damp squib. For by then the French Revolution had popularised new, secular ideologies of revolt; and English dissent had become respectable, had forgotten its revolutionary past. Some historians forget it too. But it is as wrong to look at 17th century Baptists and Congregationalists through 19th century spectacles as it is to impute their later pacifism back to the belligerent Quakers of the 1650s.

For the roots of the secularisation we must also look back to the religious radicals of the mid-17th century. The all-importance of the Bible for politics led to a new popular interest in Biblical criticism, in order to ascertain what the good book really said. Many came to believe that it had been adapted or mistranslated to suit the purposes of the ruling class. People like Gerrard Winstanley, William Walwyn, Clement Writer, and many Ranters, produced reasoned arguments to show that the Bible was inconsistent and sometimes self contradictory; so it could not be the infallible word of God, but was a historical document to be interpreted like any other. This critical movement culminated in the work of Samuel Fisher, an ex-Baptist turned Quaker. He published a large tome in 1660 which summed up radical biblical scholarship. This was rather late for it to have much influence on English radicalism, but his book came to the notice of Spinoza, and through him Fisher's conclusion passed into the mainstream of the 18th century European Enlightenment. Fisher's book is very learned and scholarly. But it is written in a rumbustious popular style, full of alliterations like 'that papistical posture of parish churches and pastoral relation to such as are not sheep', and 'the rabble of the ruder sort of Ranters'. Fisher called his book *The Rustics Alarm to the Rabbies*, thus emphasising that it was ordinary peasants who were threatening the clergy, the universities, and the biblical text which was used to buttress the hierarchical order of society.

So the heritage of the radicals of the English Revolution passed into the mainstream of the Enlightenment even when it was forgotten in

England—if it ever was forgotten. In the revival of radicalism in the later 18th century Catherine Macaulay's *Republican History of England in the 17th Century* played a big part; American revolutionaries looked back to the experience of the English Revolution, and their staunchest supporters in England were dissenters. The dissenting interest remained the bulwark of English radicalism down to and after the foundation of the Liberal Party.

Chapter 35

Edgehill and beyond

This was a review of The People's War in the South Midlands 1642-5, *by Philip Tennant. It was first published in* Cake and Cockhorse *(Banbury Historical Society, Vol 12, No 4, 1992).*

Anyone who is led by Dr Tennant's sub-title to expect glorification of a popular struggle, whether against king or parliament, will be disappointed. The author's subject is the sufferings of the ordinary people of the South Midlands as they endured the depredations of both sides in the civil war of 1642-5. Troops hastily scrambled together had to be paid, fed and housed, arrangements for these purposes being devised ad hoc. In theory both king and parliament levied taxes to pay for their forces; but actual hard cash was always in short supply. Both sides had to live at the expense of the countryside, moving around to seek fresh pastures as one area had been squeezed dry. Both sides demanded free quarter, sometimes promising repayment at a later date. Local commanders imposed their own demands for cash, labour, services and equipment. The bewildering marches and counter-marches of the two armies, for which military historians have struggled to find strategic reasons, were as often as not, Dr Tennant hints, caused by the search for unexploited territory to live off.

There is little here about battles, of the great constitutional issues at stake. Dr Tennant is concerned with the effects of the armies on the remainder of the population. The more one examines a specific area, he sums up, the more it becomes clear that for a few short years at least, the lives of ordinary villagers, with their age old preoccupations of field and market, weather and harvest, labour and rest, were profoundly disrupted' (pxii). This is to ask novel and salutory questions. The author has made very thorough use of parish records, sources hitherto neglected for such purposes, and—more cautiously—of pamphlets in the Thomason collection. The picture presented is gloomy.

Household belongings as well as food and horses were requisitioned. Just before the battle of Edgehill, for instance, Widow Wootton of Tysoe lost 'twelve Cheeses worth eight shillings, half a pigge worth six shillings, foure yards of new Cloath worth 13 shillings, a flaggon and foure sawcers worth three shillings' (p56). Ralph Ellis of Butlers Marston had to provide quarter for 20 men and their horses for two days; they consumed 30 loads of hay, and 72 sheep were stolen (p57). Whole herds of livestock were distrained from some villages; horses seized supposedly for army use were sold for individual profit: there was no redress (p153). Horses were essential to rural labour and rural mobility; but horses were in permanent demand by both armies, and were seized ruthlessly. In time of harvest this might be devastating.

Trade was disrupted by destruction of bridges for military reasons. Travel permits were increasingly required, even for short distances, and could be withheld by any local commander. In October 1643 the king forbade any trade to London and other cities under parliamentary control (p154). Parliament similarly forebade trade from London to Worcestershire and Herefordshire in 1645, disrupting the cloth trade (pp154-155). The risks of travel were increased by deserters or other highwaymen: the latter word derives from this period (p150).

King and parliament each regarded themselves as the only legitimate rulers of England. In June 1643 two royalist officers were authorised to seize from the counties of Gloucester, Worcester, Warwick and Oxford 'as many Horses, Carts and Carters as shall be required' to cart ordnance from Worcester to Oxford (p156). The parliamentarian besiegers of Banbury in September 1644 were ordered to seize from villages within ten miles of the town 'such number of workmen for pioneers as they shall think fit' (pp193-194). Forced labour might last for weeks on end—without pay (p167).

In April 1645, as the king's army approached Worcestershire, 'great store of biscuit bread' was required, plus 3,000 bushels of wheat, 500 shovels, spades, pickaxes and other implements, and huge quantities of hay, straw, oats and beans, together with 28 teams of at least five horses, 'a strong and able cart and two carters with each team', all supplied with food for three days. Parliament threatened reprisals against any constable who complied with these orders (p247). What a life! Later in the year Prince Maurice ordered all Worcester's able bodied males between the ages of 16 and 60 to report for work on the city's fortifications, on pain of death (p266). In the summer of 1644

Major Pont's troop, numbering 42 men with 45 horses, was quartered upon the village of Hanwell for nine weeks, 'promising to pay' but not performing (p187).

The battle of Edgehill, Dr Tennant reminds us, was fought over 'rich farmland, partly ploughed', partly pasturing sheep. After the battle stragglers from both armies, 'cold and hungry and therefore plundering', took what they wanted from the neighbouring villages (p67). Carts were requisitioned to carry 3,000 to 4,000 wounded soldiers to Warwick (p67). In January 1643 royalists were stealing horses by the hundred, loading carts with looted goods which were promptly sold at local fairs for the profit of the plunderers. In Northamptonshire and Warwickshire many villages were left with 'neither beds to lie on, nor bread to eat, not horse, cow nor sheep' (p82).

Billeting meant nothing so simple as one household putting up a single soldier. Well over 100 parliamentarian troops, many with horses, received free quarter for two days and nights at Bishops Itchington in 1644, six named householders putting up 53 of them (p177). Houses and fences were pulled down, fruit trees destroyed, wherever it suited military convenience (p96). In Tredington '40 of our best houses' were plundered by royalist cavalry, 'which had already impoverished largely royalist Worcestershire' (pp106-107). Schools were especially vulnerable, many being seized for military purposes (p148). Vagrants abounded. When quarter sessions were resumed in Warwickshire at the end of hostilities, they had to deal with almost three times as many cases of poor relief as before the war (p141).

Most aristocratic houses had been built to stand a siege. The destruction of such houses in the war, which Dr Tennant deplores (pp214-222), and 'slighting castles' after it, had the advantage of demilitarising the society. Aristocratic revolt was less likely; mobility was freer. The church, usually the most defensible building in any village, was often fortified as well as being used to house troops or prisoners. King Charles ordered Boarstall Church to be demolished in the interests of the security of the Oxford royalist garrison (pp229-230). Another perhaps fortunate consequence of the war was the reduction in size of many forests (refuges for outlaws) as trees were cut down to build fortifications or to use as fuel (p255).

As Dr Tennant recognises, there were reasons for 'the indiscriminate pillage'. For both sides, 'food was often non-existent for days on end', pay was 'meagre and almost invariably long in arrears'. 'Sickness and death were common, outbreaks of plague prevalent' (p118). A soldier whose leg was 'broke to pieces' in the siege of Banbury Castle had to pay 13s for a horse litter to bring him home and 41s for medical treatment (p144). Prisoners of rank were ransomed, the money normally going into the pockets of their captors.

Refreshingly the stereotypes of godly parliamentarians and chivalrous cavaliers has no place in Dr Tennant's book. A parliamentarian veteran of Adderbury tore the Bible to pieces to show his disapproval of his vicar (p161). The royalist commander of Lark Stoke was accused of inciting his men to follow his example in raping local women (p207). One plundering parliamentarian officer, Major George Purefoy, Governor of Compton Wynyates, had as his chaplain the Ranter Abiezer Coppe, who believed that 'sin was abolished'. After having had a profitable war, Purefoy was knighted at the Restoration (p170). Colonel John Bridges was another who had a good war. In 1645 he told the constable of Twyning, near Tewkesbury, that unless he immediately paid in six months of contribution money allegedly due, 'you are to expect an unsanctified troop of horse among you...they shall fire your houses without mercy', and 'hang up your bodies wherever they find them' (p207). He did fire the Catholic fortified house at Lark Stoke (p208).

Atrocities were not peculiar to either side. Lord Byron celebrated Christmas Day 1643 by massacring 20 parliamentarians—'which I find the best way to proceed with these kind of people'. After the capture of Beoley House, Worcestershire, the parliamentarian soldiers 'put all the Irish there to the sword', as well as burning the house to the ground. In October 1644 a parliamentary ordinance ordered that no quarter should be given to any Irish or papist born in Ireland. Royalist women camp followers were killed after Naseby (pp211-212).

Dr Tennant's book is a valuable corrective to most works on the civil war. He shows us an England which recalls Yugoslavia today: the breakdown of government left crude military violence unchecked. His worm's eye view does not tell the whole story; but it is one that we had forgotten. It is hardly surprising that the last year of the war saw the emergence of 'Clubmen' in many counties—neutrals whose one objective was to keep the combatants out of their area. Their slogan, 'If you take our cattle / We will give you battle', sums up the frustration and anger to which parliament ultimately responded by creating the New Model Army, regularly paid and disciplined. 'The counties of Stafford, Warwick, Leicester and Northampton', said one parliamentarian, 'have suffered more within six weeks than would pay our new army in six months' (p258). Once the greater resources of London and the parliamentarian south east were mobilised, the war was soon finished off, the Clubmen rallying to the New Model Army. For a short time in the late 1640s it was a popular army. Its other ranks called for wider representation for ordinary people in parliament. But that is another story.

The author and the Banbury Historical Society are to be congratulated on producing this thoughtful and thought provoking work.

Chapter 36

Professor William B Hunter, Bishop Burgess and John Milton

This article was first published in Studies in English Literature, 1500-1900 (SEL), Vol 34, No 1, winter 1994. It responds to two separate articles in the same periodical by Hunter, 'The Provenance of the Christian Doctrine: Addenda from the Bishop of Salisbury', SEL 33:1 (winter 1993).

Hunter argued that Milton was not the author of the De Doctrina Christiana *(DDC), a very heretical treatise first published in 1825 and usually (and I think rightly) attributed to Milton. The interested reader is referred to other contributions to this discussion in SEL, numbers 32 to 35.*

Milton's spelling has been modernised, as in the Complete Prose Works of John Milton, *Don Wolfe and others (eds), 8 volumes (Yale UP 1953-82)—henceforth Yale Prose. The DDC is printed in Yale Prose, Vol VI.*

I

Ever since Milton was accepted in his own century as one of the greatest of English poets, there have been people who would feel more comfortable if—notwithstanding his contemporary reputation—Milton could be shown to be an orthodox Christian. The task has become more difficult, and a solution more anxiously desired, since publication of the very heretical *De Doctrina Christiana* in 1825.[1]

---

1. All references to Milton's prose are modernised and are to the *Complete Prose Works of John Milton*, D Wolfe et al (eds), 8 vols (New Haven, Yale UP, 1953-1982), henceforth *Yale Prose*. Subsequent references will generally appear parenthetically in the text. *DDC* appears in vol 6.

Should it be ignored, or can it somehow be explained away? Professor Hunter has long asserted Milton's orthodoxy. Now he has discovered a new ally—Bishop Burgess.[2]

Like everybody else, I imagine, I was totally ignorant of this 'distinguished intellectual and religious leader whose opinions it is wrong to ignore'. I turned eagerly to the *Dictionary of National Biography* for enlightenment. Lives in the *DNB* vary from excellent to poor according to the contributor; so it was reassuring to find Burgess's entry over the initials TFT. In my young days T F Tout was the model of scholarly accuracy, a man of immense erudition, a generous critic but severe when he thought severity was called for. Tout's account of Burgess (1756-1837) is mostly favourable: his industry in the diocese of Salisbury 'was quite remarkable at that time'. He wrote an anti-slavery pamphlet and more than a hundred other works. He was the first president of the Royal Society of Literature. Only on one point, the bishop's views on the *DDC*, is Tout critical. Here his generosity gives way to irony. When Burgess 'had some cherished principle or opinion to defend...he threw away discretion and impartiality.' Burgess, Tout implies, was in his dotage when he published *Milton Not the Author of the Lately Discovered Work 'De Doctrina Christiana', Three Discourses Delivered at the Anniversary Meetings of the Royal Society of Literature in the Years 1826, 1827, and 1828* (1829). Burgess 'exhausted the patience' even of his own Society. Tout may be a safer critic here than Professor Hunter, since he had no 'cherished principle or opinion to defend'.

In 1815 Burgess had defended the orthodox doctrine of the Trinity. Even more important, he was a passionate opponent of Catholic Emancipation: part of his case against Milton's authorship of the *DDC* was that it was insufficiently anti-Catholic. This was not a charge brought against Milton by many 19th century critics. On the contrary, in the changed historical circumstances, Milton's refusal to grant toleration to Roman Catholics was embarrassing. Here Burgess was no impartial scholar but a partisan defending a losing cause.

The *DDC* does not attack the papal Antichrist as frequently and as fiercely as the good bishop would have wished. Indeed the word 'Antichrist' occurs only once directly and once indirectly in the

2. This article responds to two separate earlier *SEL* articles by William B Hunter: 'The Provenance of the *Christian Doctrine*,' *SEL* 32,1 (winter 1992): pp129-142; and 'The Provenance of the *Christian Doctrine*: Addenda from the Bishop of Salisbury', *SEL* 33, 1 (winter 1993): pp191-207.

treatise (pp604, 798). Why? Milton is writing for convinced opponents of popery. But the word Antichrist had been overused as a term of abuse during the English Revolution. First Antichrist was the pope; then he was the Anglican bishops, and the king who protected them. Royalists during the civil war were denounced as 'the Antichristian army'. Oliver Cromwell became Antichrist; Gerrard Winstanley applied the term to all landowners and gentry. It had lost any precise meaning. And its use was associated with millenarians like those Fifth Monarchists who rose in bloody but hopeless revolt in 1657 and 1661. The words 'Antichrist' and 'Antichristian', wrote Henry More in 1664, have been so fouled by 'the rude ignorant vulgar' that they have become 'unfit to pass the lips of any civil person'.[3] In the *DDC* Milton accepted that reformed religion was 'adequately fortified against the Papists' (p120), and directed his appeal to all rational Protestants, including Anglicans. To labour the equation of the Pope with Antichrist would only alienate moderate men.

Bishop Burgess was not one to appreciate literary tact. His anti-Catholicism was pure odium theologicum. In his day there was no Catholic threat to England's national independence such as Milton and other Protestants had feared from the church which he described as 'a Roman principality', 'a priestly despotism under the cloak of religion', which 'extirpates all religions and civil supremacies'.[4] Burgess wrote as a partisan in the full fury of the campaign against Catholic Emancipation, which he would have regarded as the emancipation of Antichrist. So he thought the *DDC* half hearted in its anti-Catholicism. In fact he could have found plenty of anti-Catholicism in the treatise if he had read it more carefully—attacks on Catholic sacramental doctrines and the mass, on works of supererogation, on papal flagellators, and on the pope's claim to be head of the church. The *DDC* identified Catholicism with idolatry (pp37, 39-40, 43, 48, 51-53, 56, 69-70, 117, 120, 203, 423-424, 451-452, 536, 541, 553-568, 584-585, 611-613, 642-643, 670, and 693-695). Many of these passages are late additions to the *DDC*, testifying to 'a continued and increasing anti-Catholicism'.[5]

Hunter takes another point from Burgess, probably unwisely. 'Our recent translation' of the Bible cited in the *DDC* (6:242) could, Burgess

---

3. H More, *A Modest Enquiry into the Mystery of Iniquity*, Sig A 3v, pp185-187. I owe this reference to the kindness of Dr W R Owens of the Open University.
4. *Yale Prose*, 4:321-322 (*First Defence*) and 2:565 (*Areopagitica*); 7:254.
5. M Kelley, *This Great Argument: A Study of Milton's 'De Doctrina Christiana' as a Gloss upon 'Paradise Lost'* (Princeton UP, 1941), p70; henceforth GA. Subsequent references will be given parenthetically in the text.

thought, refer only to 'the Arian version of the New Testament by Fel-binger, published at Amsterdam' in 1660—thus suggesting a Dutch author for the DDC (SEL 33, p196). Burgess dismissed the more obvi-ous Polyglot Bible of 1657 produced by Brian Walton. Walton, as it happens, was well known to Milton. He had been curate at All Hallows, Bread Street, Milton's parish, in 1623-26. They remained on friendly terms, and Milton may have used his influence with the government to obtain authorisation for Walton to import 7,000 reams of paper duty free. The poet is much more likely to have thought of the Polyglot Bible as 'our recent translation' than an Arian New Testament published in Amsterdam of which there is no reason to suppose he had ever heard.[6]

The bishop, we must recall, had to deal with the text of the DDC immediately after it had been published; he cannot be blamed for fail-ing to notice the many parallels between it and Milton's published works. But thanks to the labours of Maurice Kelley, Barbara Lewalski, Anthony Low, Mary Ann Radzinowicz, and many others, and publi-cation of the Yale edition of Milton's prose, scholars now have less excuse. They need only a little empathy with Milton the subversive. Professor Hunter suggested that John Carey deliberately translated the Latin text into words which Milton had used elsewhere, in order to stress resemblances. This is not a generous suggestion, nor a very plausible one: most of us know from experience that, if we repeat a thought which we have already expressed in print, the same or simi-lar words are likely to occur to us.

Burgess's thesis on the DDC was well publicised. He was a man of some standing in his profession, but—as Tout indicated—after three attempts he totally failed to convince his scholarly contemporaries. His views were 'dismissed by everyone concerned with the authenticity of the ascription to Milton', as Hunter himself admits (SEL 33, p191). Later scholars were no more appreciative. 'Masson and Parker fail even to mention Burgess' (SEL 33, p205). Tout brushed aside Burgess's thesis as the maunderings of a senile scholar whose pet theories had been upset by publication of the DDC. "The absence of copies [of Burgess's Three Discourses from any library] needs to be accounted for', writes Hunter. 'Arguments from silence' (to which Hunter often re-sorts) 'are inconclusive but can be suggestive' (SEL 32, p131). I fear that Tout has explained this silence.

---

6.   J M French, *Life Records of John Milton*, 5 vols (Rutgers UP, 1949-58), 4:14-15, 3:231-232, 335; cf W A Turner, 'Milton's Aid to the Polyglot Bible', *MLN* 44, 5 (May 1949), 345.

Yet there must have been many among Burgess's contemporaries who would have been delighted, for their own ideological reasons, to welcome an effective demonstration of Burgess's case. The fact that they (and their successors) allowed his arguments to fall into oblivion suggests that they concluded that it would be more effective to pretend the *DDC* did not exist than that it was not Milton's work. Those who wish to claim the poet for 'orthodoxy' will no doubt continue trying to explain away the by now well established congruence between the *DDC* and Milton's other writings. But Milton's authorship cannot be disproved by reviving arguments about handwriting on the title page or the unreliability of Daniel Skinner, well known to Masson and Parker. The overwhelming case for Milton's authorship can be challenged only by confuting the arguments of Kelley, Lewalski, Low and Radzinowicz.

II

If not Milton, who did write the *DDC*? In his 'Addenda' Professor Hunter—abandoning his first guess of John Goodwin—has plumped for the bishop's theory that it was an unknown Dutchman, since many of the sources used in the *DDC* derive from the continent. But since the treatise's declared objective was to reunite European Protestants around a more radical theology, the emphasis on Swiss, French, and Dutch treatises was to be expected. Where else but in The Netherlands was the free ranging anti-Trinitarianism which Milton favoured published? Hardly in Geneva: French liberal Calvinists published in The Netherlands. Nor in England.

Professor Hunter must find a Dutchman (or other European Protestant) who had the vast biblical learning, the knowledge of Hebrew, the leisure and the dedicated industry to write such a vast treatise, apparently without anyone knowing anything about it. He was on such intimate terms with Milton that he entrusted him with his dangerous 'dearest and best possession', but he has left no trace in Milton's correspondence or in the recollections of his friends. Hunter's second guess was Isaac Vossius, who was in London after the Restoration, when 'direct association with Milton became distinctly possible, though no early biographer mentions it' (*SEL* 33, p200). Since Vossius was a protegé of Charles II and frequented his court, the biographers' silence is easily explained. Nor is it likely that the man who the king said would believe anything so long as it was not in the Bible would have devoted years of labour to a treatise based on 8000 biblical proof texts (6:106). Hunter's latest desperate guess is John Buxtorf (1599-1664), professor of Hebrew at Basel University (*SEL* 33, p203). Hunter offers no evidence of any link between Buxtorf and Milton—another significant silence—and the date of Buxtorf's death is inconvenient.

If someone else wrote the *DDC*, how did the manuscript come into Milton's possession? Did the author keep a copy? Why did it not survive? How did the manuscript come to be copied by Milton's amanuenses, who were amending it while it was in Milton's possession—emendations which relate significantly to *Samson Agonistes*? Was the Dutchman's copy being amended to keep pace with these alterations? Why did the Dutchman make no effort to reclaim his 'dearest and best possession' after Milton's death? If he had a copy of his own why did he not publish it in The Netherlands? The questions are endless.

The unknown author should be fairly easy to identify. He had published treatises on divorce. Milton has a very idiosyncratic definition of 'fornication' as grounds for divorce: 'any notable disobedience or intolerable carriage in a wife' (*Tetrachordon, Yale Prose*, 2:672). Selden, whom Milton regarded as an authority on such matters (*Commonplace Book, Yale Prose*, 1:403; *Doctrine and Discipline, Yale Prose*, 2:350), 'still more fully explained this point' in his *Uxor Hebraica*, two years later than Milton (*Second Defence, Yale Prose*, 4:625). The author of the *DDC* also saw 'fornication' as a reason for divorce, and also had an unusual definition of the word: 'continual headstrong behaviour', 'the lack of some quality which might reasonably be required in a wife' (*Yale Prose*, 6:378). He too attributed his view to Selden's *Uxor Hebraica* (*Yale Prose*, 6:378). Interesting coincidences.

The author of the *DDC* shares Milton's tastes in Greek literature, quoting Homer to illustrate predestination (*Yale Prose*, 6:202), exactly as Milton does in *The Doctrine and Discipline* (*Yale Prose*, 2:294). He quotes Greek drama less frequently than the poet, but when he does he chooses favourites of Milton's. (Three plays of Euripides are cited in the *DDC*. There are 19 references to him in the whole of Milton's oeuvre, excluding the *DDC*, as against five to Aeschylus.) The *DDC* quotes the Scottish theologian John Cameron, whom Milton cites five times in *Tetrachordon* (*DDC, Yale Prose* 6:534). Like Milton, the author of the *DDC* approves of civil marriage (*Yale Prose*, 6:561; *Colasterion*, 2:750; *Hirelings*, 7:297-300). Both held the rather unusual view that congregations should assess their pastors (*Of True Religion, Yale Prose*, 8:435; 6:600).

But many problems remain. For instance, the reference to 'our countryman, Ames' in the *DDC* (6:706). Hunter endorses Bishop Burgess's brash statement that 'Ames had no significant English connections'.[7] But this will not do. Ames was born into an old Norfolk family in 1576 and established his reputation as an English scholar. He was a Fellow of Christ's College, Cambridge, until he was 'by the Urgency of the Master...driven both from the College and University'.[8] Ames became City Lecturer at Colchester, but the bishop forbade him to preach. So Ames joined the brain drain to The Netherlands, where he became chaplain to the English Governor of Brill, until pressure from the home government got him dismissed. Ames became Professor of Theology at Franeker University, and in 1626 its Rector. In the late 1620s he thought of emigrating to New England, and the Governor of Bermuda tried to lure him thither. Ultimately Hugh Peter persuaded Ames to become pastor to the English emigré congregation in Rotterdam. He died there in 1633. Only a very ill informed Dutchman could claim him as 'our countryman'.

But Ames was much more than a countryman for Milton. A fellow of Milton's college, he failed to become its Master because he held the wrong theological views—which Milton would no doubt have thought the right ones. Otherwise Ames might have been Master when Milton was an undergraduate. Ames must have been a legendary figure for Milton, who was proud to hail him as 'our countryman'.[9]

Here we may consider Hunter's claim that Milton wrote 'from the perspective of the Church of England' (*SEL* 33, p195). I find this surprising. Even Burgess recognized that Milton departed from 'our English theologians' (pp6, 12). Whether or not the 'fatal and perfidious bark' in *Lycidas* was the Anglican church, the ensuing attack on 'such as for their bellies sake/Creep and intrude and climb into the fold' must refer to the clergy of that church. Writing under censorship, Milton could hardly have expressed himself more clearly. The tracts in which Milton demolished episcopacy in the early 1640s are remarkable for their sustained venom. Anyone who has tried to persuade himself that Milton wrote 'from the perspective of the Church' whose prelates had 'church-outed' him should reread *Of Reformation, Of Prelatical Episcopacy, Animadversions, and Reason of Church-Government*. Prelates were

---

7. *SEL* 33, p197. We begin to see why the bishop was not appreciated as a Milton scholar.
8. T Goodwin, quoted by W Haller, *The Rise of Puritanism* (Columbia UP, 1938), p75.
9. Milton's image of the 'wayfaring' or 'warfaring Christian' in *Areopagitica* may derive from Ames's *An Analytical Exposition of Both Epistles of the Apostle Peter* (1641; Latin original 1635) (K L Sprunger, *The Learned Doctor William Ames* (University of Illinois Press, 1972), p147). Ames's works were printed in England only after censorship collapsed in 1640 (p259).

responsible for the censorship (*Animadversions, Yale Prose*, 1:667-676; *Areopagitica, Yale Prose*, 2:539-542). The 'inquisitorious and tyrannical duncery' of 'this impertinent yoke of prelacy' was 'a schism itself from the most reformed and most flourishing churches abroad', and 'a sore scandal to them' (*Reason of Church-Government, Yale Prose*, 1:820-823; Book 2, chapter ii passim; and p791; *Of Reformation, Yale Prose*, 1:526). England's 'pretended episcopacy cannot be deduced from the apostolical times' (*Of Prelatical Episcopacy, Yale Prose*, 1:647-652). It alienates us from 'all Protestant princes and commonwealths', and should be abolished so that we may 'come from schism to unity with our neighbour reformed sister churches' (*Of Reformation, Yale Prose*, 1:541-551, 556-617; *Animadversions*, 1:726-728, *Reason of Church-Government*, 1:825-861; *Defence*, 4:498-499).[10] Church endowments are a bribe to God for absolution from murder, adultery, and other crimes (*Hirelings, Yale Prose*, 1:307). Prelacy indeed is more Antichristian than Antichrist himself; and Milton predicted that bishops would be 'thrown down eternally into the darkest and deepest gulf of hell' (*Of Reformation, Yale Prose*, 1:616-617)—a violence of expression present nowhere else in his writings. Milton favoured election of ministers by the congregation (*Of Reformation, Yale Prose*, 1:541-549 and passim; *DDC, Yale Prose*, 6:594-805); the Anglican Church did not. Milton rejected the ceremonies of 'church-masquers' (*Yale Prose*, 1:526, 547-548, 589-590, 600, 828, 840, and 931-935).[11] England alone of Protestant countries has no divorce for adultery or desertion.

Milton also insisted that of 'jurisdictive power in the Church there ought to be none at all', particularly objecting to 'the bar of a proud judicial court where fees and clamours keep shop and drive a trade, where bribery and corruption solicits' (*Yale Prose*, 1:831-838, 849). In the *Second Defence of the People of England* he urged Oliver Cromwell to 'remove all power from the church', but warned that 'power will never be absent so long as money...extorted by force even from those who are unwilling, remains the price of preaching the Gospel' (*Yale Prose*, 4:678). Milton believed that abolition of tithes was necessary

10. Milton was not original here. Martin Marprelate had pointed out in 1588 that the Swiss, Scottish, French, Bohemian, and Dutch churches, among others, regarded episcopal authority as Antichristian (M Marprelate, *Oh Read Over D John Bridges (An Epitome)*, p6).

11. In an interesting article T C Miller has argued, on the basis of Michael's speech in *Paradise Lost* 12.505-551, that Milton came to believe that all earthly churches compromise or pervert the truth. This, Miller suggests, is confirmed by the *DDC, Yale Prose*, 6:589-590 ('Milton's Religion of the Spirit and "the state of the Church" in Book XII of *Paradise Lost*', *Restoration: Studies in English Literary Culture, 1660-1700*, 13, 1 (Spring 1989): pp7-16). Milton appears to have joined no church.

to religious liberty (*Yale Prose*, 7:275-276). In 1652 in his *Sonnet to Cromwell* he had begged him to 'Help us to save free Conscience from the paw/Of hireling wolves, whose gospel is their maw'; and in another sonnet he praised Vane because he knew 'Both spiritual power and civil, what each means,/What severs each'. All this contradicts Burgess's extraordinary claim (which Hunter endorses) that 'litigation for tithes was emphatically not an English practice', and so 'no English writer would think to attack it' as the author of the *DDC* does. Argal (the gravedigger's Latin seems appropriate)—argal Milton cannot have written *Of Reformation* with its reference to 'the ignoble Hucksterage of piddling Tithes' (*Yale Prose*, 1:613), nor *Reason of Church-Government* (*Yale Prose*, 1:848-849), still less *Hirelings* (edited by Hunter as Milton's work) which speaks of tithes as 'wrung out of men's purses to maintain a disapproved ministry against their conscience' (echoing the *Second Defence* quoted above), 'by law to be recovered', 'by worldly force and constraint'. Hireling tithe gatherers eat 'the bread of violence and exaction', in 'a kingdom of force and rapine' (*Yale Prose*, 7:281, 292, 297, and 309-313). Milton and the author of the *DDC* agreed that enforced payment of tithes was as bad as anything in Islam (*Yale Prose*, 7:318; 6:598).

How does Hunter explain such phrases if ministers never 'went to court over the issue' (*SEL* 33, p198)? When the author of the *DDC* denounces clerical litigants for tithes as 'wolves' (*Yale Prose*, 6:598), he is reverting to the language of Lycidas and the sonnet to Cromwell. There is much confirmatory evidence from 17th century sources for legal compulsion to pay tithes—including Leveller pamphlets, Quaker accounts of their sufferings, and Anthony Pearson's classic *The Great Case of Tithes* of 1657.

The *DDC*'s 'the church has no need of a liturgy' (*Yale Prose*, 6:670) picks up earlier remarks by Milton. The Anglican liturgy is 'the Skeleton of a Mass-Book' (*Of Reformation*, *Yale Prose*, 1:597; cf 1:522). Antichrist's liturgy, 'conceived and infanted by an idolatrous Mother' (*An Apology*, *Yale Prose*, 1:940; cf *Animadversions*, *Yale Prose*, 1:662, 677-695), was 'a perpetual cause of disunion', which 'hinders piety rather than sets it forward'. It is 'a provocation to God' (*An Apology*, *Yale Prose*, 1:937-943; cf *Animadversions*, 1:684-685). The undesirability of set forms is confirmed by *Paradise Lost* 5.144-149. 'Neither can any true Christian find a reason why a liturgy should be at all admitted', Milton summed up in *Eikonoklastes* (*Yale Prose*, 3:503-505; 'constancy in the cuckoo', pp551-553).

Hunter echoes Burgess in saying that 'Milton disagreed with the

Church of England not on its doctrines but on its form of government' (SEL 33, p192); but not much is left of that Church when one rejects episcopacy, ecclesiastical jurisdiction and censorship, tithes and the liturgy. The 39 Articles remain, whose absence from the DDC Hunter uses, remarkably, as an argument against Milton's authorship (SEL 33, p205, n14). Milton quoted the 39 Articles only in *Of True Religion*, where he is trying to appeal to English Protestants. The Articles, indeed, themselves a compromise document, say nothing about marriage, divorce, or mortalism, and refer only indirectly to bishops. But they specifically defend the Trinity, for Milton's opposition to which there is evidence from outside the DDC. His tongue was well in his cheek in 1673. Hunter's wish to depict Milton as 'closer to the great traditions of Christianity, no longer associated with a merely eccentric fringe' (p166),[12] may, I fear, contain an element of eccentric wishful thinking.

Enough, I think.

Before we start looking for a Dutch author, let us consider how many direct or indirect references to England and English affairs there are in the DDC. First, and decisive in itself, is page 599: litigation about tithes 'does not go on in any reformed church except ours'. Could that have been written by a Dutchman? Milton in *Hirelings* had already said, 'Our English divines, and they only of all protestants' claim tithes as legally due to them (*Yale Prose*, 7:281). 'When anyone of ours [ie our divines] hath attempted in Latin to maintain this argument of tithes...they forbear not to oppose him, as in a doctrine not fit to pass unopposed under the gospel' (*Yale Prose*, 7:289; cf 7:297).[13]

Why should the unknown Dutchman repeatedly discuss the permissibility of running away or compromising when confronted with political danger, and of lying and deceiving on behalf of God's cause? (DDC, *Yale Prose*, 7:605, 762-765, and 801.) If Milton is the author there is no problem in these instances; if not, here are more remarkable coincidences for Hunter to explain away. Attacking idol worship is common Protestant form; but the DDC asks specifically whether 'someone who professes the true religion' may 'take part in idol worship if and when the performance of some civil duty makes it necessary' (p694). The question assumes the existence of compulsory church attendance—revived in post-Restoration England. It is also very relevant to *Samson Agonistes*.

---

12. W B Hunter, 'Forum: Milton's Christian Doctrine', *SEL* 32, 1 (winter 1992), 163-166; 166.
13. This is one of the parallels with the DDC to which Hunter did not draw attention when editing *Hirelings*.

Other suggestive parallels appear. The *DDC*'s 'vindication of God's justice' and of divine providence (p397) recalls not only the opening of *Paradise Lost*, but also the consternation of all those who had regarded themselves as God's servants in the English Revolution. Texts recalling *The Tenure of Kings and Magistrates* are cited to justify the election of kings (*Yale Prose*, 7:795-796). The *DDC*'s lengthy discussion of Sabbath observance (pp504, 704-715) suggests England rather than The Netherlands, and appears to echo *Hirelings* (*Yale Prose*, 7:709; cf 3:295). Saturday Sabbatarianism (*DDC*, *Yale Prose*, 6:709-711) relates even more narrowly to English experience. The same is true of civil marriage, introduced by the Barebones Parliament in 1653 (pp561, 573; *Hirelings*, *Yale Prose*, 7:298-300). Adam as a representative person (*DDC*, *Yale Prose*, 6:384) is typical of English covenant theology. Discussion of public and private fasting (pp678-680) probably relates to controversies caused by the regular monthly fasts ordered by the Long Parliament. Reference to the calling of the Jews (pp617-618) recalls discussions arising from Manasseh ben Israel's attempt in the 1650s to obtain permission for Jews to return to England. Concern with Islam (p598 etc) picks up English discussions following the translation of the Koran in 1649; Francis Osborn, Henry Stubbe, John Bunyan and many others participated in them. Discussion of astrology ('there is some astrology which is neither useless nor unlawful'—p696) recalls the popularity of astrology in England in the 1650s and 1660s. It was a Dutchman who said, 'You are great astrologers in England now'.[14] There are possible references to Ranters in the *DDC* (pp144, 151 and 166) and to other extremists from whom Milton differentiated himself (pp541, 700; cf *Of True Religion*, *Yale Prose*, 8:423-426). 'The Samaritans believed Christ first for the woman's word', wrote Milton in *A Treatise of Civil Power* (*Yale Prose*, 7:248); 'The Samaritans believed in Christ first of all because of the words of the woman', echoed the author of the *DDC* (*Yale Prose*, 6:590). Both may derive from Wollebius.

III

Various passages in Milton's writings indicate that he had had in mind something like the *DDC* for many years. I have suggested elsewhere that the poet's close study of the Bible in connection with his divorce

---

14. *Mercurius Politicus*, 33, 16-23 January 1651, p545.

pamphlets may have given him the idea of converting his theological index into a full dress treatise.[15]

(a) The last words of Milton's *Defence of the People of England* (1651) are (for the sake of) 'men of every land, and, particularly, all Christian men…I am at this time hoping and planning still greater things, if these be possible for me, as with God's help they will' (*Yale Prose*, 4:537). The opening sentence of the *DDC* is addressed to 'All the Churches of Christ and to All in any part of the world who profess the Christian Faith'. It is the only 'still greater' Latin work which Milton wrote.

(b) The concluding sentence of *A Treatise of Civil Power* (February 1659), after attacking control of religion by the magistrate, said, 'Of these things perhaps more some other time.' Hunter's note to *Yale Prose*, 7:271, rightly refers this to the *DDC*, Book I, ch xxvii.

(c) In *Hirelings* (May 1659) Milton wrote, 'somewhere or other, I trust, may be found some wholesome body of divinity, as they call it, without school terms and metaphysical notions, which have obscured rather than explained our religion.' Hunter's note to *Yale Prose*, 7:304, refers plausibly to the *DDC*; cf especially p580.

(d) *Of True Religion* (1673) deals with the 'groundless fear' that discussion of Scripture 'would unsettle the weaker sort'. 'At least', Milton urges, 'let them have leave to write in Latin, which the common people understand not; that what they hold may be discussed among the learned only': and he quoted his *Logic*. The note to *Yale Prose*, 8:437, rightly suggests that hope for toleration of Protestant dissenters in that year of relative freedom might lead Milton to envisage the possibility of publishing the *DDC* (in Latin).

IV

Professor Hunter inexplicably overlooks the political situation in England after the restoration of monarchy and episcopacy. In May 1659 Milton had looked back wistfully on 'this liberty of writing which I have used these 18 years on all occasions to assert the just rights and freedoms both of church and state' (*Hirelings, Yale Prose*, 7:275). He continued to use this liberty, attacking monarchy in general and Charles Stuart in particular in *The Ready and Easy Way to Establish a Free Commonwealth*, a week or two before the king returned to England.

The Restoration shattered the hopes of a better society for which

---

15. C Hill, *Milton and the English Revolution* (London, 1977), pp125, 133. Cf *DDC*, *Yale Prose*, 1:533-534, and references there cited.

Milton had laboured for the best 20 years of his life. He came close to sharing the fate of many of his friends and colleagues—hanging, disembowelling, and quartering. Henceforth he had to be extremely cautious in anything that he published. The facile syllogism, 'Milton could have written an Arian poem in *Paradise Lost*: he did not; therefore we can ignore the evidence for anti-Trinitarianism in the *DDC*',[16] forgets that if he had published such a poem he would have been risking his liberty, possibly his life. Martin A Larson's calculation that under the 1648 Blasphemy Ordinance the author of the *DDC* would have been liable to seven capital charges and 11 involving life imprisonment may have exaggerated statistically;[17] but there can be no doubt that anti-Trinitarianism was savagely punished even before 1660. In 1648 the Westminster Assembly of Divines recommended that the anti-Trinitarian John Bidle should be put to death. Under the Commonwealth Bidle was imprisoned, banished and sentenced to life imprisonment. After the Restoration he was jailed again, and died in prison. Hobbes thought the post-Restoration bishops would like to burn him; a man was hanged for denying the Trinity as late as 1699. Newton and Locke kept their doubts about the Trinity to themselves. Milton had reason for caution.

Yet he had to publish *Paradise Lost*, which he knew was a great poem, and which he believed contained important lessons for his audience.[18] Publishing under censorship, and himself a marked man, Milton naturally did not emphasise his heresies: as Hunter says, *Paradise Lost* 'can be read as orthodox'.[19] But other careful readers as well as the theologically trained Defoe spotted anti-Trinitarianism in the epic. It seems amusing to us that the censor raised difficulties about Milton's reference to an eclipse which 'with fear of change perplexes monarchs' (*PL*, 1.597-599). But a perceived threat to monarchy was exactly the point at which a censor would be most alert.[20] Always Milton had to try to anticipate and circumvent his likely objections.

Professor Radzinowicz, who appreciates Milton's difficulties in the 1660s, quotes Samson, who admitted that he served the Philistines:

16. Cf A C Dobbins, *Milton and the Book of Revelation* (University of Alabama Press, 1975), p133. Cf W B Hunter: publishing the *DDC* would have been 'an easy feat before the Restoration' (*SEL* 32, p130). So would suicide.
17. M A Larson, 'Milton's Essential Relationship to Puritanism and Stoicism', *PQ*, 6, 2 (April 1927), 201-220; 208.
18. J T Shawcross, 'Forum: Milton's Christian Doctrine', *SEL* 32, 1 (winter 1992), 155-62; 156 and 159.
19. W B Hunter, 'Forum', p132; my emphasis.
20. *Yale Prose*, 1:585. For the political importance of astrology in these years see M McKeon's excellent book, *Politics and Poetry in Restoration England* (Harvard UP, 1975).

by labour
Honest and lawful to deserve my food
Of those who have me in their civil power.
(lines 1365-1367)

He too was an alien in his own country.[21] This consideration may cast light on the bewildering number of Milton's amanuenses. Who would take on such a dangerous job? Only someone devoted either to Milton's person or his politics, or someone badly in need of money. The story of Milton's forcing his daughters to read to him in unknown languages may refer to occasions when no amanuensis was available and Milton needed to check a reference.

In 1659-60 Milton published A *Treatise of Civil Power*, *Hirelings*, and *The Ready and Easy Way*, in an attempt to reunite supporters of the Good Old Cause. He failed. In 1673, when the government for its own reasons had shifted its balance away from bishops and the royalist gentry to an alliance with Protestant dissenters, *Of True Religion, Heresy, Schism, and Toleration* (1673) aimed at uniting enemies of Catholicism by minimising the seriousness of theological questions which divided them. For this purpose 'dieser sehr schlau Politicus', as Milton was called by a man who knew him well, had reason to introduce deliberate ambiguities, hurrying over matters which separated Arians and Socinians from those who regarded themselves as orthodox Protestants.[22]

In the *DDC*, as Lewalski rightly emphasizes,[23] Milton's hope was to reunite European Protestantism against Catholicism. Hence the difficulty which scholars have found in defining the precise nature of Milton's anti-Trinitarianism. He was never guilty of writing abstract scholarly treatises for their own sake. Nor was he inclined to line up under someone else's banner. He was a Miltonist anti-Trinitarian. Once we take into account the world in which Milton had to live and write, there are very strong reasons for anonymity and for delaying publication if it was he who composed the *DDC*.

Apart for 1659-1660 and the brief flurry in 1673, from around 1655 till his death in 1674 Milton took virtually no part in public life. He concentrated on his three last great poems and on the *DDC*. The careful wording of the Anonymous Biographer, 'finished after the

---

21. M A Radzinowicz, *Toward* Samson Agonistes:: *The Growth of Milton's Mind* (Princeton UP, 1978), pp159, 169-70.
22. H L Benthem, *Engländischer Kirch und Schulen-Staat* (Luneburg, 1694), p58. Benthem is quoting Theodore Haak.
23. B K Lewalski, 'Forum: Milton's Christian Doctrine', *SEL* 32, 1 (winter 1992), 143-154.

Restoration', leaves open the possibility that other treatises—for instance the *Logic* and the *History of Britain*—may also have been recast then for publication.[24]

Maurice Kelley demonstrated the close parallels between *The Art of Logic* and the *DDC*. Milton is unusual among theologians in attempting to apply principles of logic to the mysteries of the Trinity. So, as it happens, is the author of the *DDC* (Part 1, chapters v, vii-viii). Also to be found in the *Logic* are rejection of transubstantiation, defense of polygamy, the conditionality of divine decrees, creation ex nihilo, the eternity of matter, and refusal of toleration to papists. The *Logic* was published in 1672, when the press was relatively free. Milton may have intended it to prepare his public for the heretical *DDC*.

The History of Britain (believed to have been written around 1648-9) had been published in 1670. It starts by 'imploring divine assistance, that it may redound to his glory and to good of the British nation' (*Yale Prose*, 5:4). This is almost echoed in the *DDC*: 'Now, relying on God's help, let us come to grips with the subject itself' (p204). I do not think any others of Milton's works have a similar exordium. In the *History* Milton mentions 'the liberty, not unnatural, for one man to have many wives' which 'other nations used' (*Yale Prose*, 5:103).[25] Children pay for 'the sins of their fathers' in the *History* as in the *DDC* (*Yale Prose*, 5:403; *DDC*, pp385-387). The clergy in Anglo-Saxon England were 'pastors in name but indeed wolves' (5:175)—as they had been in *Lycidas*, in the sonnet to Cromwell, as they were to be in *Hirelings*, in *PL* 12.507-510, and in the *DDC* (p598).

V

Hunter rightly says that the writings of Barbara Lewalski, Mary Ann Radzinowicz, and myself would be quite different but for Kelley's work (*SEL* 32, p129). Yet he himself writes almost as if *This Great Argument* had never been written. The Yale edition of the *DDC* gives, on a rough count, some 428 instances of parallels or analogies between *Paradise Lost* and the *DDC*. Volume 8 of the *Yale Prose* reprints the arguments at the head of each book of *Paradise Lost*. In 19 pages there are 35 references to parallels with the *DDC*.

Some of these deal with the fundamentals of Milton's theology,

---

24. B K Lewalski, 'Forum', pp147-148.
25. Cf *Commonplace Book, Yale Prose* 1:411-413 on Anglo-Saxon polygamy, and *DDC*, pp356-381. See also L Miller, *John Milton among the Polygamophiles* (Loewenthal Press, 1974), pp3-12, 40, 118-120, and 325-327.

starting from the creation of the world, of man and the Fall (GA, pp126-128, 143-155). 'The basic determinant of setting and temporal order' in *Paradise Lost*, Kelley tells us, 'is to be found in the views stated in the systematic theology. In both works, hell is located beyond the limits of the visible universe; and the creation and apostasy of the evil angels, for whom hell was created, took place before the formation of the world... Much of Book VII is a rapid blank verse summary of the doctrines enumerated in Book I of the *De Doctrina*' (GA, pp192-199). Adam and Eve—like the rebel angels—were free to stand or to fall (*DDC, Yale Prose*, 6:160-167, 351-352, and 384). Their temptation was a 'good temptation', sent to strengthen and purify, in the sense of *DDC*, page 338. The process of redemption is the same in both works (and in *Samson Agonistes*)—calling, regeneration, repentance, faith, and justification (GA, pp157-170). We know good only by knowing evil, as in *Areopagitica* (GA, pp51, 141). The 'one just man' of *Paradise Lost* 11.818 echoes *DDC* pages 483 and 493. Justifying the ways of God to men, the theme of *Paradise Lost*, runs through the whole of the *DDC*.

Minor points noted by Kelley include the Archangel Michael as leader of the angels, Satan's names, his despair, and even his wandering over the earth (GA, pp138-189). He needed divine permission to leave hell (*DDC*, pp347-350; *PL* 1.493-496). That the name of Joshua corresponded to Jesus is noted in both; each led the children of Israel through the wilderness to the land of Canaan. The *DDC*'s heresies are present in *Paradise Lost*, though expressed with an ambiguity too skilful to be accidental. Anti-Trinitarianism, for instance.[26] 'Of all creation first/Begotten Son'—and many other references to the Son as a 'creature' ('First of created things'—*DDC*, p206). In Book 10 of *Paradise Lost* the picture of ultimate glorification and the renovation of all things versifies *DDC*, page 632. For the role of the Son see *DDC*, pages 434-435, and Kelley, pages 34-52, and chapter 4 passim, especially pages 84-106. Kelley is especially good on the parallel use of proof texts in the two works.

Polygamy too: 'Hail wedded love.../ By saints and patriarchs used' (*PL* 4.750-762; *DDC*, pp356-358). Milton would have enjoyed mocking critics who think these lines refer to monogamous wedlock, without asking themselves why the patriarchs are dragged in—as they always were

---

26. I agree strongly with Professor Lewalski that 'Milton cannot be classified in terms of any of the common christological positions' (*Milton's Brief Epic* (Brown UP; 1966), p157. Subsequent references will be to *MBE* and will appear in the text). Why indeed should he be except to suit academic convenience?

in the frequent 17th century discussions of polygamy (cf *DDC*, Book I, ch x). Milton's defence of polygamy was notorious even in his lifetime.[27] Mortalism, the doctrine that the soul dies with the body, also had to be expressed cautiously. But it too is in *Paradise Lost* as well as in the *DDC* (GA, pp32, 154-155). Milton's materialism derives from creation ex deo; matter is good and can never be destroyed (GA, pp122, 125). Since all matter derives from God, the differences between angels and men, soul and body, spirit and matter, are of degree, not of kind. Angels eat and digest food, as Milton goes out of his way to tell us in *Paradise Lost* (5.434). Heaven may be more like earth than we think (5.576).

Marriage is an affair of mutual love and help, though the husband has the greater authority (*DDC*, pp355-356). Since the Fall divorce is permissible where love does not exist, or has ceased to exist (*DDC*, pp369-381; *PL* 12.596-605). Marriage is a civil contract, not a religious ceremony (*DDC*, pp. 561, 573). Once we have the clue, it is clear that Milton in describing the union of Adam and Eve before the Fall makes exactly this point: 'other rites/Observing none' (4.736-737). The inferiority of women in principle, I regret to say, is stressed in both works. 'This...is the opinion of God' (*DDC*, p782).

Milton's views on predestination and free will, on reprobation, on God's foreknowledge of what men freely decide, are alike in both works (GA, pp15-19, 73-83). That God's decrees are contingent is repeatedly emphasised in both (*DDC*, Book 1, ch iii, pp163-165, 173, 177-178, 236, 343-344, 506, *PL* 3.95-134, 4.66-67, 5.501, 535-538, 6.911-912, 9.151-152). Only the elect are predestined. But Christ died not for the elect alone, but for all mankind. The spirit of God is given to all men/all believers (GA, pp42-43, 83). God permits evil, though good can come out of evil as light out of darkness. Milton was not altogether happy with the phrase 'original sin' (*DDC*, pp389-390). Nevertheless he used it at least once in *Paradise Lost* (9.1003-1004), and the concept is omnipresent. Hell is an internal state (*DDC*, pp628-630), vividly expressed in Satan's 'Myself am hell' (*PL* 4.75). Signs of the coming end of the world are similar in the *DDC* (pp615-617) and *Paradise Lost* (12.535-42). With the Last Judgment in *DDC*, pages 621-622, compare *Paradise Lost* 3.323-31; 10.55-62; and 12.458-465, 545-561. Both look forward to the ultimate period when 'regal sceptre then no more shall need, / God shall be all in all' (3.339-341; *DDC*, pp437, 626-627).

---

27. L Miller, Appendix II, 'Milton's Reputation as a Polygamophile, 1644-1717'. Hunter notes triumphantly that polygamy finds no place in *Paradise Lost* 11 and 12, but does not mention Book 4 (*SEL* 32, p192).

For Milton, Christian liberty extends to political liberty (*DDC*, pp537-538). Abdiel's patience under suffering and refusal to surrender to superior force make him the personification of zeal as defined in the *DDC* (Book II, chs i and vi), linking him with Samson and of course with Milton himself. Bad kings proliferate in *Paradise Lost*, together with the immorality of royal courts (1.490-502, 3.190-192; *DDC*, pp796-977). Kings should be elected (*DDC*, p796)—not a Dutch problem, we may note. Denunciation of 'lewd hirelings' in *Paradise Lost* 4.193 recalls *DDC* 1, chapter xxxi, as well as *Lycidas* and *Hirelings*. Advice repeated in *Paradise Lost* and the *DDC* includes the desirability of showing respect for superiors (*DDC*, p758; *PL* 2.477-479, 3.349-352, 5.289, 358-360, and 6.746). The devils observe due subordination. 'Elegance' is described as a virtue in both works. The Bible should be available for all to read. 'Be wisely ignorant', says the *DDC* (p424); 'be lowly wise', says *Paradise Lost* 8.173. Private prayers may be silent. Any place or posture is suitable for prayer (*DDC*, 670-673; cf *PL* 5.144-149, 6.832-834). The virtue of temperance is recommended by Michael in *Paradise Lost* 11.530-534 and in the *DDC*, Book II, chapter ix. *Paradise Lost* 3.648-655 is 'little more than a mosaic of the proof texts of a single paragraph of the *DDC*' (*Yale Prose*, 6:346; GA, p198).

On the first page of the *DDC* its author proclaims that for 1,300 years before the Reformation there had been universal apostasy. This was a very radical idea shared by men like William Walwyn, William Erbery, John Saltmarch, Sir Henry Vane, Roger Williams, John Reeve (founder of the Muggletonians), William Sedgwick, Henry Stubbe, Isaac Penington and other early Quakers, and some Ranters.[28] In *Of Reformation* (1641) Milton dates the apostasy from Constantine (*Yale Prose*, 1.551-560, 576-579); later he suggested that 'apostasy crept in by degrees' from apostolical times (*Of Prelatical Episcopacy*, *Yale Prose*, 1:647-52; *Reason of Church-Government* (1642), *Yale Prose*, 1:827; cf *PL* 12.507-540). Subsequent references to the apostasy varied between these dates (*Tetrachordon* (1643), *Yale Prose*, 2:700-701; *Eikonoklastes* (1649), *Yale Prose*, 3.514-515; *Hirelings* (1659), *Yale Prose*, 7:290-293). The *DDC*'s date, from the end of the second century AD, splits the difference. Whatever the date the idea was constant.

---

28. I discuss the apostasy more fully in my *The Experience of Defeat: Milton and Some Contemporaries* (Viking, 1984), pp297-304.

VI

Barbara Lewalski and the Yale editors noted many parallels between the *DDC* and *Paradise Regained*. Among the most important is covert anti-Trinitarianism (*MBE*, pp134-139, 143-148, 150-155, 157-163; *DDC*, pp414-452). The humanity of the Son of God is stressed throughout *Paradise Regained*, as is the concept that 'all men are sons of God' (*MBE*, pp133-139). The Son's humanity regained lost Paradise. The Son is described as a prophet, defined in the *DDC* as 'anyone endowed with exceptional piety and wisdom for the purpose of teaching' (p572; cf *MBE*, p185). Moses, Joshua (= Jesus), and Job are all forerunners of Christ (*MBE*, pp168-172, 205, 212-213; cf *DDC*, p740 with *PR* 3.92-95).

Milton's materialism originates in a 'refusal to distinguish fundamentally between angels and men, matter and spirit'. It is 'a foundation stone of Milton's thought and perhaps his most significant and daring departure from orthodoxy' (*MBE*, p140). The *DDC*'s distinction between two stages of Christ's kingdom, of which the second will be the millennium, is crucial to *Paradise Regained*. Christ's kingdom is not to be gained by force, though the ultimate object is 'to crush his enemies' (*DDC*, pp435-437, 762). Bad kings are repeatedly denounced. Milton's favourite concepts of avarice and ambition, temperance and magnanimity, are in *Paradise Regained*. So is his idea of liberty as something negative, passivity (*MBE*, p162). The Son of God's words in *Paradise Regained* 2.473-477:

> to guide nations in the way of truth
> By saving doctrine...
> Is yet more kingly, this attracts the soul,
> Governs the inner man, the nobler part,

are almost a versification of *DDC*, page 12, as the editor points out. The *DDC* says 'Obedience to God's commandments makes nations prosperous,...fortunate, wealthy and victorious, and lords over other nations' (p804). The Son of God agrees:

> What makes a nation happy, and keeps it so,
> What ruins kingdoms, and lays cities flat,
> These only with our law best form a king.
> (*PR* 4.362-364)

In *Paradise Regained* 1.210-13 the Son of God exemplifies the right of individuals to speak in church (cf *DDC*, p608).

Nowhere else but in the *DDC* (pp544-552), I think, does Milton insist that the only proper baptism of adults is in running water, though the 'profluent stream' of *Paradise Lost* 12.442-445 (echoing the *DDC*, pp544-552) hints at it pretty clearly. But in *Paradise Regained* Milton uses similar phrases, going out of his way to describe the immersion of the Son of God by John the Baptist. It is another instance of Milton's necessary caution that the description is first attributed to Satan (*PR* 1.72-81, 273-280).[29] When Hunter says flatly that 'nowhere in the canonical works does Milton support adult against infant baptism' (*SEL*, 33, p205), contrasting the *DDC* (pp544-552), his statement, strictly interpreted, is defensible. But it takes no account of *Hirelings*, which assumes that adult baptism is the norm ('Either they [ministers] themselves call men to baptism, or men of themselves come,' *Yale Prose*, 7:248). Elsewhere there is much mention of adult baptism, with no suggestion of disapproval (*Of Reformation*, *Yale Prose*, 1:555-556; *The Doctrine and Discipline of Divorce*, *Yale Prose*, 2:231-222, 302; *History of Britain*, *Yale Prose*, 5 passim; *History of Moscovia*, *Yale Prose*, 8:512, 514; *PL* 12.439-445). I find only one mention of infant baptism—perhaps a significant silence—and this is in *Of True Religion*, where Milton is consistently ambiguous about unorthodox beliefs which he shares. 'The Arian and Socinian are charged to dispute against the Trinity: they affirm to believe...according to Scripture.' 'The Anabaptist is accused of denying infants their right to baptism; again they say, they deny nothing but what the Scripture denies them' (*Yale Prose*, 8:424). Milton was being careful not to align himself openly with the much maligned Arians and Anabaptists whose views he shared.

Anthony Low in *The Blaze of Noon* provides 'evidence of close compatibility between *Samson Agonistes*' and the *DDC*.[30] The temptations which Samson had to face and overcome, from Manoa, Dalila, and Harapha, were 'good temptations', leading to true repentance (unlike Dalila's), following the *DDC*'s pattern. Reprobation is rescinded by true repentance. Samson's 'sense of heaven's desertion' echoes *DDC*, pp631-632. Samson was saved by faith in God alone. His revenge on the Philistine aristocracy and priests was not personal but directed against God's enemies, whom it is a religious duty to crush

(Low, pp187-188, 192-193, and 224). He was acting 'not as a private person, but as a magistrate and deputy of God' (Low, pp198-199, 204).

Milton's mortalism is implicit in *Samson Agonistes*. 'The play, in its imagery and the very texture of its language, posits an indissoluble connection between soul and body—just as in *Paradise Lost*' (Low, p225, cf *DDC*, pp318, 400). As in *Paradise Regained*, the negative aspect of Samson's liberty is stressed (Low, 71, 86, 89). The *DDC's* insistence that 'we are undoubtedly to speak the truth, but...not to an enemy...not to an oppressor' (*DDC*, pp762-765), justifies Samson's deception of the Philistine authorities (Low, pp75-76). 'Those who persevere, not those who are elect, are said to attain salvation' (*DDC*, p529) fits *Samson Agonistes* perfectly, and solves the artificial problem of whether Samson was a saint or a damned soul.[31] Samson is given the 'decent Christian burial' on which the *DDC* insists (pp744-745; Low, pp131-132).

Professor Radzinowicz published *Toward Samson Agonistes: The Growth of Milton's Mind* four years after Low's *The Blaze of Noon*. She too recognises the close relationship between the poem and the *DDC*. 'Many of the most crucial concerns of the drama—vengeance and anger, chastisement and repentance, atheism and idolatry, good conscience and sincerity, liberty of interpretation and the primacy of Scripture—are subjects which post-Restoration amanuenses revised' in the *DDC*, and so were nearly contemporaneous with the composition of *Samson Agonistes*.[32] Professor Radzinowicz is especially perceptive on anti-Trinitarianism in *Samson Agonistes* as well as in *Paradise Lost* and *Paradise Regained* (pp315-339).

'Revisions [to the *DDC*] demonstrate Milton's constancy after the Restoration to the very lines of argument to which he had pointed in the political tracts advocating the Good Old Cause' (Radzinowicz, p159). Late revisions include the abrogation of the Mosaic law for Christians. Samson comes to his fullest sense of personal identity when he speaks from awareness of 'my self? my conscience and internal peace'. He now 'enjoys Christian liberty', and decides to go to the pagan temple (Radzinowicz, pp156-157). Many revisions in the *DDC* show Milton conscious of the 'need to affirm the virtue of independent action upon the basis of personal conviction', whether in the case of Samson or that of Milton's contemporaries (Radzinowicz, pp158-159).

31. Joseph Wittreich's *Interpreting 'Samson Agonistes'* (Princeton UP, 1986) attempts to make out a case for the latter fate.
32. M A Radzinowicz, p401, quoting George N Muldrow, *Milton and the Drama of the Soul: The Theme of Restoration of Men in Milton's Later Poetry* (Mouton, 1970), pp254-262. Subsequent references to Radzinowicz will appear in the text.

Samson Agonistes recognizes that God's justice is on trial: it has been called in question by the Restoration when, in Major General Fleetwood's words, 'God had spit in the face' of those who believed themselves to be his faithful servants. 'Patience', said the *DDC*, 'is the virtue which shows when we peacefully accept God's promises, supported by confidence in the divine providence, power and goodness; also when we bear any evils that we have to bear calmly, as things which our supreme Father has sent for our good... Opposed to this is impatience towards God, a sin which even the saints are sometimes tempted to commit' (p662; cf p424; Radzinowicz, pp236-237). Samson's grinding at the mill with slaves picks up a metaphor familiar in Milton's writings; cf 'the slavish pounding-mill of an unhappy marriage' (*DDC*, p379) with *The Doctrine and Discipline of Divorce* (*Yale Prose*, 2:258).

The contingency of divine justice is made clear at the end of *Samson Agonistes*. Samson's destruction of the Philistines gave his people the opportunity to win freedom, 'let but them/Find courage to lay hold on this occasion' (lines 1,715-1,716).[33] As Milton knew, they did not win their freedom then. But the memory of Samson, and the retelling of his story, could still lead others to be their own deliverers. 'Conformity not with the written but with the unwritten law...the law of the spirit...must be considered as the form of good works' (*DDC*, pp192-199, 532, and 639-640). Hence the importance of 'rousing motions' such as those which Samson obeyed. His decision, on second thoughts, to go to Dagon's temple witnesses to Christian liberty as opposed to literal acceptance of the Mosaic law. As in *Paradise Lost*, good is always contingent: virtue is shown in action (Radzinowicz, pp153-158, 186, and 349).

More than a century ago that great scholar David Masson, without benefit of Kelley and his successors, described the *DDC* as 'an indispensable commentary to some obscure parts' of *Paradise Lost*: 'The Miltonic philosophy...is here exhibited coolly and connectedly'.[34] The case for Milton's authorship of the *DDC* is established by this close congruence between it and works published over Milton's name in his lifetime. Even if—per impossibile—the *DDC* was removed from the canon, Milton would not be left any 'closer to the great tradition of Christianity'. Evidence for his major heresies would remain in other

---

33. This repeats *DDC*, p508.
34. David Masson, *The Life of John Milton and the History of his Time*, 7 vols. (1859-94), 6:817-840. It is to Masson's research that we owe most of our knowledge of Daniel Skinner (6:790-808).

works—anti-Trinitarianism, mortalism, materialism, polygamy, divorce, adult baptism in running water. The DDC did not reveal Milton's unorthodoxy; it opened our eyes to heresies ambiguously presented in works published under censorship.[35]

VII

Finally, a word about Hunter's dismissal of the DDC as 'one of the dullest religious tracts to be found anywhere'.[36] He must, fortunately for him, have read very few 17th century theological treatises. Many readers today do find 17th century theology tedious, since it has lost its urgent political relevance. But how many other theological treatises are relieved with flashes of Miltonic eloquence, worthy of *Areopagitica*? I have given many examples of Milton's trenchant one liners. Here are one or two more. His opening statement, 'It is disgraceful and disgusting that the Christian religion should be supported by violence', sets the tone (p123); we may compare his proof of the existence of God: 'it is intolerable and incredible that evil should be stronger than good, and should prove the true supreme power: therefore God exists' (p131). He illustrates the contingent nature of God's decrees by quoting Exodus 3:8,17: 'I have come down from that place to liberate them...and to lead them out into a good land'; and concludes drily 'in fact they perished in the desert' (p155).

He delights in writing irreverently on subjects which his opponents took more seriously than he did: 'Turning the Lord's supper into a cannibal feast' (p554). Zanchius expounds the Incarnation 'as confidently as if he had been present in Mary's womb and witnessed the mystery himself' (p422). 'I am not one of those who consider the decalogue a faultless moral code'; it can 'contain nothing relevant to gospel worship' (p711). 'God either is or is not really like he says he is. If he really is like this, why should we think otherwise? If he is not really like this, on what authority do we contradict God?' (p136). 'The pre-eminent and supreme authority...is the authority of the

35. When Professor Hunter edited *Of Civil Power* for volume 7 of Milton's *Complete Prose Works* in 1980 he noted 11 parallels with the DDC. In editing *Hirelings* for the same volume he spotted only two parallels (notes 48 and 71). No doubt he thought that the thesis of the tract recurs so frequently in the DDC (esp Book 1, chapter xxxi) that the parallels were not worth noting. But he might have picked up several others— Melchizedec and tithes (*Yale Prose*, 7:284-287, 300: DDC, 6:517); Milton's dislike of margins overloaded with notes (7:293-94; DDC, 6:122, etc); his approval of civil marriage (7:297-300; DDC, p561); and repetition of this favourite phrase 'avarice and ambition' (7:318; DDC, p 598).
36. W B Hunter 'Forum', p166.

Spirit, which is internal and the individual possession of each man' (p587). 'One man, and he with motives of gain, should not be stuck up in a pulpit and have the sole right of addressing the congregation' (p608). 'Strictly speaking, no work or thing is obscene' (p770).

He can startle us with paradox and irony. 'The practice of the saints interprets the commandments' (p368). 'There is some hatred...which is a religious duty, as when we hate the enemies of God or of the church' (p793). 'The laity, as priests call them' (p571). He enjoys controversy. 'It is amazing what nauseating subtlety, not to say trickery, some people have employed in their attempts to evade the plain meaning of these Scripture texts [about the Trinity]... They have followed every red herring they could find... To save their paradox from utter collapse they have availed themselves of the specious assistance of certain strange terms and sophistries borrowed from the stupidity of the schools' (p218). 'There are some people...who...do not hesitate to assert that God is, in himself, the cause and author of sin... If I should attempt to refute them, it would be like a long argument to prove that God is not the devil' (p166). 'Attention to the requirements of charity is given precedence over any [biblical] written law' (p532). 'Anyone with any sense interprets the precepts of Christ in the sermon on the mount not in a literal way but in a way that is in keeping with the spirit of charity' (p553). 'It is not the universities...but God who gives us pastors and teachers' (pp571-572).[37] His verbal wit anticipates Marx: 'Christ...redeemed us...from the works of the law, or from the whole law of works' (p531).[38] I can only conclude by quoting Barbara Lewalski, in a different context: 'As I encounter this persona, with or without name and initial, and date attached, I can only call him—John Milton' ('Forum', p153).[39]

---

37. Cf W Dell, *Several Sermons and Discourses* (1709): 'Antichrist...chose his ministers only out of the universities' (p246).
38. The trick is common in Milton's other works: 'Lust is the friendship of ignorance, or rather the ignorance of friendship' (*Prolusions*, Yale Prose, 1:295): 'Circumstances which are Judaical rather than judicial' (*Doctrine and Discipline of Divorce*, Yale Prose, 2:332); 'To suppress the suppressors' (*Areopagitica*, Yale Prose, 2:568): 'Defending the defenders' (*Second Defence*, Yale Prose, 4:534); 'Still watching to oppress Israel's oppressors' (*Samson Agonistes*, lines 232-233). Cf Marx's 'to expropriate the expropriators'.
39. I am much indebted to Barbara Lewalski and Maurice Kelley for generous help and advice in writing this article.

APPENDIX

The following is a brief and schematic list of parallels between the *DDC* and Milton's other works. I have mostly omitted *Paradise Lost (PL)*, *Paradise Regained (PR)*, *Samson Agonistes*, and *The Art of Logic*, since these have been amply covered by Kelley, Lewalski, Low and Radzinowicz.

1. Commonplace Book
It is lawful to use classical authorities. *Yale Prose*, 1:376-377; cf 6:387.

Lying is in some circumstances permissible. 1:384-386, cf 6:762-765.

Polygamy. 1:397, 400-405, 411-413; cf 6, Book I, ch viii, 335-381, 651, and *PL* 4:750-762.

Divorce. 1:406-410, 414; *Doctrine and Discipline of Divorce*, 2, passim; *Tetrachordon*, 2, passim, *Judgement of Martin Bucer*, 2:432; cf 6:371-381, 651.

Against indiscriminate charity. 1:417-418; *Of Reformation*, 1:589-591; cf 6:746, 790.

Usury. 1:418-419; *Doctrine and Discipline*, 2:289, 320, 322; *Tetrachordon*, 2:656, 661; cf 6:651, 775-778.

Kings are not the Lord's Anointed. 1:474; *Eikonoklastes*, 3:586-587; *Defence*, 4:403, 499; *Brief Notes on a Sermon*, 7:475-476; cf 6:797-798.

Compulsion not to be used in religion. 1:476-477; *Reason of Church-Government*, 1:332-333; *Treatise of Civil Power*, 7:245-246; cf 6:123, 436, 536-541, 566, 584, 589-590, 612-613, 797-799.

2. Of Reformation
There should be freedom to 'sift and winnow' any Christian doctrine. 1:519; cf 6:122.

Popery is idolatry. 1:520-523, 590, 602. Idolatry a ground for divorce comparable with adultery (*Doctrine and Discipline*, 2, chs viii-ix); cf 6:386, 690-696.

Against liturgies. 1:522; *Animadversions*, 1:662, 677-693; *An Apology*, 1:937-939; *Eikonoklastes*, 3:503-505, 551-553; cf 6:670, and *PL*, 4:144-152.

'The unresistible might of weakness.' 1:525; *Reason of Church-Government*, 1:825-833; *An Apology*, 1:951; *Defence*, 4:338; cf 6:436 and *PL*, 12:566-569.

Against ceremonies. 1:526-527, 547-548, 589-590, 600; *Reason of Church-Government*, 1:828, 840-844; An Apology, 1:931-935; cf 6, Book II, ch iv.

Disinterested search for truth. 1:535; cf 6:121.

Egypt as a place of bondage. 1:545, 793; *Defence*, 4:353, 532; A *Letter to a Friend*, 7:325; cf 6:706-707, 711.

Sons of God. 1:547; *Reason of Church-Government*, 1:837, 842; cf 6:178, 197, 206-213, 495-497, 511-513, 547.

No distinction clergy/laity. 1:547-548, 824-845; *Hirelings*, 7:320; cf 6:558 (priesthood of head of household), 570-573, 594.

Christians took over pagan rites. 1:556, 688-689; cf 6:667.

Against the Fathers, Councils, antiquity and scholasticism. 1:565-570, 602-603, 624-652; *Of Prelatical Episcopacy*, 1:624-652; cf 6:127, 177, 180, 827.

'Shortly expected King'. 1:616; *Animadversions*, 1:706-707; cf 6:615, 623-627, though here the imminence of Christ's kingdom is less confidently asserted.

3. Of Prelatical Episcopacy

All-sufficiency of the Bible. 1:624-625; *Reason of Church-Government*, 1:746-749, 826-830; cf 6:125 and passim.

Against human traditions. 1:626, 650-652; *Of True Religion*, 8:421; cf 6:576-591, and PL, 12:511-512.

Avarice and Ambition. 1:646; *Eikonoklastes*, 3:542; *Second Defence*, 4:680, *Character of the Long Parliament*, 5:443; *Ready and Easy Way*, 7:422; cf *Of Reformation*, 1:613, 6:598 and PL, 12:511.

Bishops = Presbyters. 1:647-52; cf 6:593.

4. Animadversions

Ministers should have a trade. 1:676-677; *Hirelings*, 7:306; cf 6:599-603.

Against tautological prayers. 1:682; cf 6:672.

God not the author of laws destructive of human society. 1:699, *Doctrine and Discipline*, 2:342; *Tetrachordon*, 2:588, 604-605, 623-624, 638-639; *Colasterion*, 2:750; cf 6:379-380.

For Scripture against authority. 1:699-700; cf 6:591.

Pastors not feeding sheep. 1:726; *Second Defence*, 4:650; *Hirelings*, 7:279-280; cf 6:595-599 and *Lycidas*.

Mocking popish 'Mother Church'. 1:727-728; An Apology, 1:940-941; cf 6:592.

5. Reason of Church-Government

Natural law engraved on hearts. 1:764; cf 6:382.

Mosaic Law = beggarly rudiments. 1:765; *Hirelings*, 7:281-282; cf 6:517-531.

God gave the Jews a king in wrath. 1:781; *Tenure of Kings and Magistrates*, 3:213-216, 234; *Defence*, 4:347, 377-378; cf 6:677. Bad kings—6:796-797, *PL*, 1:490-502.

Acts 9, 13-15, and other texts to justify self government of congregations. 1:789, 842-849; cf 6:594, 603, 609, 797-798, 805.

Punishment. 1:835; cf 6:396.

God hardening sinners' hearts. 1:836; cf 6:198-199, 331, 336-337, and *PL*, 3:185-202.

Pious self regard. 1:842; cf 6:719-720.

Divine image in man. 1:842; *Tetrachordon*, 2:591; cf 6:185-396.

6. An Apology for a Pamphlet

We should hate the enemies of the Church. 1:901, cf 6:743, 762.

No word or thing is obscene. 1:901-904; *Defence of Himself*, 4:744-745, 771-772; cf 6:770.

Dislike of marginal annotation. 1:822, 910, 921-922, 945; *Colasterion*, 2:724; *Hirelings*, 7:294; cf 6:122.

Law as schoolmaster. 1:949-950; cf 6:548.

7. Doctrine and Discipline of Divorce

Superstition of scarecrow sins: things indifferent. 2:221, 228, 342; *Areopagitica*, 2:563; *Tetrachordon*, 2:588, 613-614, 638-639; *Colasterion*, 2:750; cf 6:525-541 and *PL*, 12:295-306.

Daily increase of truth. 2:224; *Areopagitica*, 2:554, 566; cf 6:121-123, 585-589.

Appeal to learned, not simple and illiterate. 2:233; *Of True Religion*, 8:437; cf *DDC* in Latin.

Deviate from the law for charity's sake. 2:236-238, 340; *Tetrachordon*, 2:637; cf 6:640, 707-708.

Scripture and Reason, 2:242, 342; *Tenure*, 3:206; cf 6:222, 239.

Grinding in the mill. 2:258; cf 6:379 and *Samson Agonistes*.

Quoting Homer on predestination. 2:294; cf 6:202.

Against transubstantiation and consubstantiation. 2:325; *Of True Religion*, 8:424; cf 6:552-554.

Adultery—easily forgiven. 2:331-333; *Tetrachordon*, 2:591, 674; cf 6:381.

8. Of Education
Fortitude and patience. 2:409; cf 6:738-739.

9. Judgement of Martin Bucer
Sole authority of the Bible. 2:433; cf 6:123-124.

10. Areopagitica
Censorship = popish. 2:493, 505-507, 537-540, 548-49, 569; *Of True Religion*, 8:434; cf 6:577-578.
Know evil to know good. 2:514-515, 527, cf 6:352-353 and *PL*, 4:220-222, 9:1070-1080.
Fortunate Fall. 2:527-528. Cf 6:394-398; Book I, ch xviii; and *PL* 12:473-476.
Heretic in the truth. 2:543; *Treatise of Civil Power*, 7:248; cf 6:510-513.
For free discussion. 2:550; cf 6:121-123 and passim.
Truth = discussion, though called sects. 2:550-556; cf 6:123.
Believers = stones of the temple. 2:555-556; cf 6:499-500.
Popery not to be tolerated. 2:565; *Of Civil Power*, 7:254-255; *Of True Religion*, 8:429-432; cf 6:690-695.

11. Tetrachordon
Knowledge of Hebrew. 2:596-597, 671; cf 6:182, 234-235, 251, 362-363, 671.
Naming animals in Paradise. 2:602; cf 6:324 and *PL*, 8.
Marriage and the Church's union with Christ. 2:606-607, 739; cf 6:500.
What God did before the Creation. 2:663; cf 6:299.
Women subordinated. 2:589; *Second Defence*, 4:625; cf 6:609, 782.
Vertumnuus as expert in shifts and evasions, 2:675; cf 6:260.

12. Colasterion
Charity overrules law. 2:750; cf 6:532.
Marriage = a civil affair. 2:750; *Hirelings*, 7:297-300; cf 6:561.

13. Tenure of Kings and Magistrates
Kings = deputies and commissioners. 3:199, 213-216, 233-234; *Defence*, 4:347-348, 370-371, 403-408, 432-435, 466-467, etc. Cf 6:795-796.
Resistance to the magistrate may be a duty. 3:199-200; cf 6:800-801.
Quotes Euripides. 3:205; *Defence*, 4:440; cf 6:407.

14. Eikonoklastes

Men of truest religion accounted sectaries. 3:348; *Areopagitica*, 2:566; cf 6:123.

Actions more important than words. 3:360; cf 6:622-623; *PL*, 12:581-582.

Against uxoriousness. 3:421, 538; *Second Defence*, 4:625; cf 6:609, 782.

Immorality of royal courts. 3:569-570; cf 6:796-797.

15. Defence of the People of England

Tyranny and superstition. 4:535; *Eikonoklastes*, 3:509; *Ready and Easy Way*, 7:421; cf 6:118.

16. Second Defence

Truth defended by reason as well as by arms. 4:553; cf 6:122-123, 583-592.

Protestantism = orthodoxy. 4:619; cf 6:574.

Selden and Divorce. 4:625; cf 6:378.

17. Treatise of Civil Power

For individual interpretation of Scripture. 7:241-244; cf 6:120-121, 583-592.

Whatever churches and doctors say. 7:243, 248-249; cf 6:592, 639-640, 711, and passim.

No church may impose its own interpretation of Scripture. 7:243-244; cf 6:584, 590.

Discipline = voluntary by churches. 7:245; cf 6:607-614.

Concept of blasphemy. 7:246-247; cf 6:698-700.

Definition of heresy. 7:247-253; *Of True Religion*, 8:421-426; cf *Areopagitica*, 2:543 and 6:123-124, 603-604, etc.

Samaritans believed Christ on the woman's word. 7:248, cf 6:590.

Conscience against churches. 7:248; cf 6, passim.

Against persecution, but no toleration for papists. 7:254-255; *Of Reformation*, 1:531; *Of True Religion*, 8:429-432; cf 6:797-798.

Justification by faith, not works. 7:255-256; cf 6:457-460, 539.

Against imposition of time or place on worshippers. 7:262-265; *Hirelings*, 7:295; cf 6:708-715.

Magistrates to protect religion, not enforce it. 7:262-273; cf 6:708-715, 797-798.

Church and excommunication. 7:268-270; cf 6:611.

18. Hirelings
Remuneration of ministers. 7:281-319; *Letter to a Friend*, 7:330; cf 6:595-603.

Presbyters and deacons. 7:283; cf 6:593.

Melchizedec and tithes. 7:284-287; cf 6:517.

Laymen may be priests. 7:286, 298, 319-320; cf 6:558, 570-573.

Each particular church absolute in itself. 7:292; cf 6:602-603, 609.

Freed from Sabbath observance. 7:295; cf 6:351-355, 704-715.

Adult baptism. 7:298; cf 6:544-552.

Scripture to be available for all. 7:302-303; *Of True Religion*, 8:434-435; cf 6:577-579, 600.

Against university as source of pastors. 7:315-317; cf 6:572-573, 594.

Enforced tithe payments make Christianity no better than Mohammedanism. 7:318; cf 6:598.

19. Proposals of Certain Expedients
Just division of commons will make the nation rich and populous. 7:338-339; cf 6:367: polygamy will prevent fields going to waste for want of labour.

20. Of True Religion
Against Catholicism. 8:417, 421-424, 429, 434; cf 6:577-584.

Word of God vs implicit faith. 8:419-421; *Of Civil Power*, 7:243; cf 6:132.

For Protestant unity and toleration. 8:424, 434-437; cf 6:120-124.

God not responsible for sin. 8:424; cf 6:153-202.

Arianism and Socinianism—Milton's ambiguity. 8:424-425; cf 6:280.

Trinity not in the Bible—Milton's ambiguity. 8:424-425; cf 6:214, 218, 278-79, 420.

Christ's satisfaction: free will vs free grace. 8:425; cf 6:189-190, 444.

Idols are laymen's books. 8:433; cf 6:693.

Congregation to examine teachers. 8:435; cf 6:600.

Write in Latin for the learned only. 8:437; cf *DDC* in Latin.

21. Sonnets
15—'Piedmont'. Commanded to curse God's enemies. Cf 6:675.

16—'On His Blindness'. God does not need good works. Cf 6:186-187, 645, and *PL*, 4:412-419.

17—(to Henry Laurence) and 18—(to Cyriack Skinner). Temperance versus luxury. Cf 6:733.

174 P. Laslett